Fodo

ROCK & ROLL TRAVELER
GREAT BRITAIN & IRELAND

THE ULTIMATE GUIDE TO FAMOUS

ROCK HANGOUTS PAST AND PRESENT

BY ED GLINERT & TIM PERRY

Fodor's Travel Publications, Inc.

New York • Toronto • London • Sydney • Auckland

Visit us on the Web at www.fodors.com/

Copyright © 1997 by Ed Glinert and Tim Perry
Map copyright © 1997 by Fodor's Travel Publications, Inc.
Fodor's is a registered trademark of Fodor's Travel Publications, Inc.
All rights reserved under International and Pan-American Copyright Conventions. Published in
the United States by Fodor's Travel Publications, Inc., a subsidiary of Random House, Inc., New
York, and simultaneously in Canada by Random House of Canada, Limited, Toronto. Dis-
tributed by Random House, Inc., New York.
*No maps, illustrations, or other portions of this book may be reproduced in any form without
written permission from the publisher.*

First Edition

ISBN 0–679–03118–9

Library of Congress Cataloging-in-Publication Data
Perry, Tim.
    Rock & roll traveler Great Britain and Ireland : the ultimate guide to famous rock hangouts past
and present / by Tim Perry and Ed Glinert. – 1st ed.
        p.   cm.
    Includes bibliographical references (p.   ) and index.
    ISBN 0-679-03118-9
    1. Rock music—Great Britain—Guidebooks.   2. Rock music—Ireland—Guidebooks.
3. Musical landmarks—Great Britain—Guidebooks.   4. Musical landmarks—Ireland—Guidebooks.
5. Great Britain—Guidebooks.   6. Ireland—Guidebooks.   I. Glinert, Ed.   II. Title.
    ML3534.P456   1997
    781.66'0941—dc21   97-29402
                                                                                                                            CIP
                                                                                                                            MN

The Authors

By the same authors: Fodor's *Rock & Roll Traveler USA.*

Ed Glinert is a staff writer for *Private Eye* and has contributed to many newspapers and
magazines, including London's *Sunday Times* and *Mojo*. He is currently working on an architectural and historical gazetteer of Manchester.

Tim Perry has written for the Rough Guides and the Eyewitness travel series and does the
nightlife section for Fodor's *UpClose London*. He also contributes to the music pages of
The Independent and other music and entertainment journals.

Photo Editor: Sara Rumens
Text and Cover Design: Guido Caroti
Production Editor: Janet Foley
Copy Editor: Deborah Carroll
Map Editor: Robert P. Blake
Production/Manufacturing: Robert B. Shields

Special Sales

Fodor's Travel Publications are available at special discounts for bulk purchases for sales promotions or premiums. Special editions, including personalized covers, excerpts of existing
guides, and corporate imprints, can be created in large quantities for special needs. For more
information, contact your local bookseller or write to Special Markets, Fodor's Travel Publications, 201 E. 50th St., New York, NY 10022; Random House of Canada, Ltd., Marketing Dept.,
1265 Aerowood Dr., Mississauga, Ontario L4W 1B9; or Fodor's Travel Publications, 20 Vauxhall Bridge Rd., London SW1V 2SA, England.

PRINTED IN THE UNITED STATES OF AMERICA
10 9 8 7 6 5 4 3 2 1

CONTENTS

A NOTE FROM THE AUTHORS

We all know people who go on vacation and come back with stories not of the major tourist sights, but of some obscure neighborhood or town that was mentioned in a song or of a great spot where their favorite band used to hang. Yet when it comes to travel guides and brochures, rock and other popular music is largely ignored—which is why it seemed obvious that we should write this book (along with the companion volume Fodor's *Rock & Roll Traveler USA*). So if going to London means sifting through the record stores of Soho and catching a gig in Camden Town in preference to seeing the Changing of the Guard, then we hope this book is on your wavelength.

Our aim was to provide a good read; something that's as enjoyable while you're kicking back on the sofa as it is useful in your day pack while wandering around the cities. We also set out to provide more than something that just reels through the famous rock landmarks like Abbey Road, the Hacienda, or the Cavern. The stories in here will also take you to the set of railings outside a Manchester police station to which Jimi Hendrix was once handcuffed; the five-star Belfast hotel where the Clash stayed while fans rioted in the street below, and the Scottish airfield that not only witnessed Elvis's only appearance on British soil but was also where Keith Moon had a drunken altercation with a ticket turnstile. We tried to give a nod to the cream of the local bands and high-light the current scene in major cities. While London has undoubtedly a richer rock his-tory and scene than any other place in the world, we also go to the likes of Ian Curtis's Macclesfield, the remote Welsh farmland where Led Zeppelin holed up to write some of their most famous songs, and the stunning County Down coastline where Van Morrison went on a feeding frenzy. We've included many former homes of the stars and other pri-vately owned places (please don't give us a bad name by hanging around too much or inviting yourself in for afternoon tea).

Inevitably we had conflicts of space trying to combine practical information and histori-cal facts about where the great songs were written and where those who wrote them were born, got married, got out of their heads, or even died. There's no way everything can go in (and there are several megabytes of info still lurking in our Macs). Fans of par-ticular genres or artists might complain there's not enough of this or too much of that. Bear in mind that the book is focused on locations. If a band hasn't written about a par-ticular place, or done something of note at specific locations, then they're not going to get as much attention as the Smiths, the Beatles, or Led Zeppelin.

We hope you grab a friend, compile some tapes, do the travel bit, and let us know how you get on. We'd be more than happy to get letters care of Fodor's Travel Publications, 201 East 50th Street, New York, New York 10022 (www.fodors.com), or e-mail us (tim@tperry.demon.co.uk).

Tim Perry and Ed Glinert

London, May 1997

ACKNOWLEDGMENTS

The list of names below is as comprehensive as our memories could make it, but if you helped out and you're not here…sorry, we couldn't have done it without you.

TIM WOULD LIKE TO THANK: John Breslin, Oliver Bennett, and Daniel Jerome for recalling memories from their distant past; Sarah Champion for her knowledge of techno, drum & bass, and everything dance. Just a fraction of those who fielded queries in the London area are Slim, Tim Pan Alley, Nigel Frieda, Ginny at Bad Moon, Mark and Donna at Mean Fiddler, Roger Armstrong, all at Helter Skelter, and Lisa at Church Studios.

Neil Anderson made an excellent host in Sheffield, and Tim Strickland, Sean Mullarkey, Graham Renshaw, Bob Worm, Bob Mirfin, Richard Kirk, and Martin Lilliker all came up with top nuggets of information.

Others throughout Britain who have helped include Amos Anderson, Eddie Blower, Dave Brayley, Ken Brown, Wayne Coleman, Jeff Cripps, Paul Davies, Kevin Fitzgerald, Lisa Hoftijzer, Alistair McKay, Neil at Flying Fish in Brighton, the elusive Simon Phillips, Ronan at Nightshift (Oxford), John Sicolo, Jim Simpson, Cris Warren (*Venue* magazine, Bristol), Bryan Wilkinson, Jonathan Wing, and all the dozens of library information officers throughout the country who helped identify addresses and phone numbers.

In Northern Ireland, I'd like to say thanks and hello again to Paddy Calvert, Colin Crooks, Dougie Knight, Albert the cab driver, Gary McCausland, Jackie Flavell, Rosalind Wheeler, Joris Minne, Tony Talbot, Billy and Madge Perry, and not forgetting Terri Hooley: Put him in the Hall of Fame. In Dublin, Siubhan Daly from Dublin Tourism, Niall Stokes, Niamh O'Reilly and Mette Borgstrom (*Hot Press*), Tim Gleeson, Smiley Bolger, and David Allen all did their bit and more.

ED WOULD LIKE TO THANK: Marian Walsh for driving around London, Liverpool, and Manchester and for so much encouragement; also, Fiona Sheppard (The List), Betty Glinert, Rowan Pelling, Angus McKinnon, John Nicholson, Denise Harrop, Lucy Richmond, Dave Pegg, Francis Wheen, Chris Silvester, Paul Herrmann, Barry Fantoni, Michael Horovitz, and Martin Morris.

Both authors would like to say a big thanks also to the people at Fodor's who were up for this all the way. Particular thanks to editor Nancy van Itallie, who also picked up on the Rock & Roll Traveler idea all those years ago; to Guido Caroti for the excellent design; and to Sara Rumens for getting the brilliant array of pics together.

London calling to the faraway towns—The Clash, "London Calling"

Three things really set London apart from any other city in Europe: the number of major music-industry offices and publications; the preponderance of live venues; and the ever-changing nature of the scene. London completely dominates the British music industry. No other cities have branch offices of all the major record labels. Most of the most successful indie labels of the past—Island, Stiff, Rough Trade—and present—Mute, One Little Indian, Creation—have started in London. Though some of the major studios in Britain today are tucked away in the countryside, it is London where much of the recording is still done at places like Sarm and Matrix. The country's—make that the world's—most famous studio, Abbey Road in northwest London, is still going strong. All the leading weekly and monthly music magazines are based here, and sooner or later all the bands that make it—from the Beatles to Oasis—leave their provincial homes to move down here.

Probably the only major artist who never played London was Elvis Presley. Apart from that, anyone who is hellbent on world domination plays the capital: Jimi Hendrix in the '60s coming over to play the major venues or a little indie band of today that has worked extra shifts to fly over from the United States to get a gig. The place is blessed with some great venues, from small pubs in Camden Town through small clubs like the Garage and Underworld to bigger places such as the Forum (formerly the Town and Country) and the Brixton Academy. Unfortunately, some have disappeared—the Marquee, the UFO Club, and the Roundhouse, whose future as a live music venue looks bleak.

The story of London rock & roll is the tale of one tribe replacing another. One musical style has replaced another with alarming regularity. The earliest rock & roll scene started, as many other genres have since, in the heart of the West End in Soho. Most musicologists pinpoint the birthplace as the long-gone 2i's coffee bar. The alternative was the jazz cellars playing what they called New Orleans jazz (a misleading term that jazz clubs still use) to describe the fact that they had no noisy saxophones, though Dixieland jazz is a more fitting description.

The list of people who made it out of the 2i's—Cliff Richard, Tommy Steele, and Marty Wilde are at the head—may not seem that magnificent in retrospect, but the place was a magnet for kids from all over the southeast and pushed U.K. rock & roll acts into the pop charts. At best, Richard and company were deodorized copies of already squeaky-clean figures like Buddy Holly, but meanwhile, others were getting together in skiffle bands playing R&B. With a little help from blues purists, headed by Alexis Korner's Blues Incorporated ensemble, they started playing the Marquee and other London clubs and pubs starting around 1962. The best bands to emerge from this scene were the Rolling Stones, the Who, the Yardbirds, the Pretty Things, and the Kinks, followed closely by the Small Faces, who, with a keen ear to the street fashion grapevine, unashamedly billed themselves as Mods. The phenomenal commercial success of these bands, coupled with that of the Beatles, now firmly ensconced in the capital, spurred the Swinging '60s into top gear in clubs like Scotch of St. James and Ad-Lib, where the got-rich-quick young stars could misbehave in comfort before retiring to their new pads around Chelsea's King's Road.

Meanwhile, in jovial little Soho coffee bars and Bunjies on Litchfield Street in Covent Garden (the last remaining example), the folk scene that was rooted in the '50s was galvanized by Bob Dylan's visits to London in the early '60s. Paul Simon hung around the city for a couple of years writing some of his most famous songs. He played these joints alongside Brit folkies like the Scottish Al Stewart and Bert Jansch and other visiting Americans like Phil Ochs and Tom Paxton, who were in turn acquainting themselves with Celtic folk heritage.

By 1966, bands were looking elsewhere for inspiration. Hot on the heels of the San Francisco experience, musicians were making new sounds, experimenting with slowed-down R&B jams using feedback, pedals, and other weird noises, plus strobing lights. This was the British version of psychedelia, with Pink Floyd doing the innovating in underground clubs like the UFO and Middle Earth. Soon the Beatles and the Stones chipped in with tracks like "Strawberry Fields Forever" and "She's a Rainbow," and the Jimi Hendrix Experience, now under the management of ex-Animals bassist Chas Chandler, was writing and recording innovative psychedelic sounds in London.

The scene soon segued into progressive rock. Like its predecessor, it was London-centered, catching on here well before the rest of the country. Floyd was again to the fore, along with King Crimson and Yes, followed by Genesis and Emerson, Lake and Palmer. Diversionary input was provided by among others David Bowie, Fleetwood Mac, Tyrannosaurus Rex, and Jethro Tull.

By the mid-'70s progressive bands were playing the Roundhouse in Camden Town, Soho's Marquee, and other larger venues, quickly moving out of the gig circuit into arenas. When a call for plain, back-to-basics goodtime R&B sounds came, the so-called pub rock bands revitalized live music in the capital. The music was mainly unimaginative, but the groups—Dr. Feelgood, Ducks Deluxe, Brinsley Schwartz, and later, Eddie and the Hot Rods and Graham Parker and the Rumor—had enthusiasm and energy. Dr. Feelgood in particular gathered a huge following at Islington's Hope and Anchor; other key venues were the Nashville Rooms in West Kensington and Putney's Half Moon.

By opening up such venues, the pub rockers did much to pave the way for punk. London, of course, didn't invent the screw-the-system attitude of punk (Detroit and New York can argue that one out), but it, and Malcolm McLaren in particular, did put the ideas into a package that sold and shocked. The Sex Pistols were manufactured from a bunch of hangers-on at McLaren's Sex boutique in Chelsea. They (plus the other four main movers of the first wave of punk: the Clash, the Damned, the Stranglers, and the Jam) used London's landmarks and social issues—apartment tower blocks, welfare offices, the royal family—to express their views.

The first punk festival at the 100 Club inspired the second or new wave of punk bands. A group of suburban Pistols fans called the Bromley contingent spawned Siouxsie and the Banshees and Generation X. Other prominent new bands that came out of London, playing dives like the long-gone Vortex and Roxy, were Squeeze, the Police, the Ruts, Elvis Costello, X-Ray Spex, the Cure, and Wire.

Most of the new-wavers were dressed-up pop bands. Just as in the '60s, people wanted to experiment, and in came labels such as Rough Trade and Mute with challenging new sounds from bands like the Raincoats and Depeche Mode. Ironically, the indie label ethos was pre-punk; it was started in 1975 by Chiswick, which put out discs by the Count Bishops and the 101ers (featuring a pre-Clash Joe Strummer). They were joined by Stiff, who made the successful switch to punkier sounds, introducing Elvis Costello and the Damned (who would later swap over to Chiswick). Another London-based pre-punk indie was Step Forward (Chelsea, the Cortinas, Wayne County), set up by Miles Copeland, brother of the Police's Stewart Copeland.

The rise of extreme right-wing parties saw the formation of Rock Against Racism (RAR), which had its first major festival in Hackney's Victoria Park, with the Clash headlining. RAR's work had both social and musical advantages. Their gigs introduced many young punks to black music, particularly reggae and ska, for the first time. The late '70s and '00s saw these types of music gain a toothold in the clubs (the poppy Madness was the only capital band to be loosely tied in with the live ska scene).

This time also saw a new rebellion, but one done in smarter clothes and makeup, with no political issues involved. The New Romantics, headed by Spandau Ballet, Visage, and other Roxy rehashes, created a vibrant club scene that started out in small West End joints like the Blitz and Le Beate Route and moved on to the plush Camden Palace. For the rest of the '80s no one sect or fad lasted for long. The clubs were playing everything from hip hop and rare groove to goth punk and new-wave remnants. The bands on the live circuit were harder to categorize, and London for once didn't dominate the numbers. Locals during this period, like the House of Love and Carter the Unstoppable Sex Machine, were generally dubbed indie (a term that stuck even after they signed to major labels) and proved popular on the gigging front but offered little in innovation.

The '90s started with London very much in the shade of the Manchester baggy (a.k.a. "Madchester") scene; by the time London-based bands like Blur jumped the bandwagon it had already broken down. London's next musical cue came not from the bands spouting sensitive lyrics and Bowie-leanings like the much-touted (London) Suede, but from an undercurrent of laddishness—a celebration of soccer, drinking, and copping off with women—that was in a way an uncoordinated reaction to the political correctness of the '80s. For many bands, there was no better way of expressing laddishness than delving back into history, taking a leaf out the Small Faces lyric book, and adopting mockney (fake cockney) accents. It was a time to be proud of little England once again. At the forefront of what the press labeled the Britpop boom was the repackaged Blur. To promote this laddish image they drank in some pretty dire pubs in Camden Town, a low-rent area that always appealed to rock types. However, spurred on by the media looking for something new to write about, all wanna-be indie bands in the area did likewise, as did lots of pubescent fans. Blur's comeback success opened the door for others like Elastica, the legendary liggers of Menswear, and even formerly serious 4AD types Lush, to have chart hits. Even out-of-towners such as Oasis and Pulp started hanging around Camden.

The American grunge invasion was over and the patriotic elements of the music press were thinking back to the days when the Beatles and the Stones (and dare we forget, the Dave Clark Five) conquered America. Someone invented the term "Britpop"; those who wanted to be taken more seriously as musicians tried to apply the term "Britrock." Whatever it was called, the poppy rock music that came out of London in the mid-'90s was retro. The bands were happy to pay homage to acts from the past, and many even took the former lead singer of the Jam as a sort of "modfather" and allowed him to inflict '60s retreads on the nation.

Of possibly more lasting importance is the dance-rock crossover sound of the Prodigy, Orbital, and Underworld, the ambient sounds of the Aphex Twin, and the drum & bass craze headed by Goldie and LTJ Bukem, all of whom have come out of the general London area. Meanwhile, back on the live scene, the beauty of London is that it has always been big enough to support several different fads and scenes at any one time, and the venues, if not the pop charts and media, still provide plenty of choice.

A London 40

The Pretty Things, "London Town" (1965)
David Bowie, "London Boys" (1966)
John Martyn, "London Conversation" (1968)
Canned Heat, "London Blues" (1970)
Chuck Berry, "London Berry Blues" (1972)
Procol Harum, "A Souvenir of London" (1973)
Ralph McTell, "Streets of London" (1974)
Darryl Hall and John Oates, "London Luck and Love" (1976)
T Rex, "London Boy" (1976)
The Clash, "London's Burning" (1977)
The Jam, "London Traffic" (1977)
The Jam, "London Girl" (1977)
Sham 69, "Red London" (1977)
Stranglers, "London Lady" (1977)
Vibrators, "London Girls" (1977)
Wings, "London Town" (1978)
Warren Zevon, "Werewolves of London" (1978)
The Clash, "London Calling" (1979)
Electric Light Orchestra, "Last Train to London" (1979)
Charlie Harper, "Barmy London Army" (1980)
Light of the World, "London Town" (1980)
XTC, "Towers of London" (1980)
The Pogues, "Dark Streets of London" (1984)
ABC, "Tower of London" (1985)
The Pogues, "London Girl" (1986)
The Smiths, "London" (1987)
The Pogues, "Lullaby of London" (1988)
Big Audio Dynamite, "London Bridge" (1989)
Joe Jackson, "Down to London" (1989)
Jean Michel Jarre, "London Kid" (1989)
The Pogues, "London You're a Lady" (1989)
Saint Etienne, "London Belongs to Me" (1991)
Kingmaker, "Everything's Changed Since You Been to London" (1992)
Black Crowes, "P.25 London" (1994)

Blur, "London Loves" (1994)
Elvis Costello, "London's Brilliant Parade" (1994)
Gene, "London Can You Wait?" (1994)
Archive, "Londinium" (1996)
Collapsed Lung, "London Tonight" (1996)
Divine Comedy, "In and Out in Paris and London" (1996)

A GEOGRAPHICAL NOTE

London's neighborhoods can be identified by postal codes, which appear on the nameplates of virtually every street. "BR" in an address indicates that it can be reached from British Rail stop named. "Tube" indicates the underground (subway) stop closest to the sight.

CENTRAL LONDON

Bloomsbury, WC1

Students and tourists dominate the streets of leafy Bloomsbury, a short stroll from the heart of Soho. Bloomsbury is home to the British Museum and the main campus of the University of London, plus several pleasant Georgian squares whose parks are great for hanging out in summer.

EATINGDRINKINGDANCINGSHOPPINGPLAYINGSLEEPING

The best place for gigs in this area is **UNIVERSITY OF LONDON STUDENT UNION** (*see below*). **THE RAW CLUB** (112a Great Russell St., tel. 0171/637–3375), under the YMCA, hosts acts such as (London) Suede and offers indie, soul, house, and reggae nights. The 650-seat **BLOOMSBURY THEATRE** (15 Gordon St., tel. 0171/383–5976) puts on some good showcase gigs by the likes of Ray Davies, Mark Eitzel, and Tasmin Archer; Tindersticks chose it as the setting for their live album, *Tindersticks—The Bloomsbury Theater 12.3.95.* **THE END** (16a W. Central St., tel. 0171/379–4770) was set up in fall 1995 by Mr. C of the Shamen, who DJs on Fridays when he's in town. Decked out with lots of wood, metal, and Philippe Starck furniture, it's one of the capital's most stylish clubs. The music concentrates on drum & bass, techno, and house. Farther along toward the City of London, **TURN-MILLS** (63 Clerkenwell Rd., EC1, tel. 0171/250–3409) is the venue for the Heavenly Social, with resident DJs the Chemical Brothers, Richard Fearless, and Jon Carter.

Courtesy of Turnmills

DJ Sister Bliss spins at Turnmills

BRITISH MUSEUM

During a 1977 visit to the museum, Wire's Bruce Gilbert saw porters clear a room of exhibits, install a long table with a white cloth, place a vase of flowers on the table, and then leave the arrangement in an otherwise empty room. The spectacle inspired the title and cover of the group's 1978 album, *Chairs Missing.* Tucked away from the Elgin Marbles, Egyptian mummies, and other spoils of the colonial years is a small popular arts section where you can see Paul McCartney's handwritten lyrics to "I Want To Hold Your Hand." *Great Russell St., tel. 0171/636–1555. Russell Square tube.*

CENTRAL LONDON SCHOOL OF ART AND DESIGN STUDENT UNION

The Sex Pistols played their second gig here on November 7, 1975, a show booked by Sebastian Conran, son of style baron Terence Conran, college chum of Glen Matlock, and future Clash hanger-on. Coincidentally, Joe Strummer had been a student here. Other former students include the Bonzo Dog Band's Viv Stanshall and Neil Innes. *Southampton Row at Theobalds Rd., tel. 0171/405–3898. Holborn tube.*

INTERNATIONAL TIMES HQ

Along with *Oz*, International Times (*IT*), based in this Georgian terrace and run by Barry Miles (now Paul McCartney's biographer), was London's leading late-'60s counterculture mag, propagating an alternative lifestyle and underground scene then in its infancy. Some of the most avid readers were the cops, who regularly raided the place, busting one of the editors, John "Hoppy" Hopkins (who also helped run the nearby UFO club) in 1967 for possessing pot, and returning three years later on moral grounds after *IT* had made the mistake of printing homosexual personal ads some 20 years before everybody else. In a trial at the Old Bailey, the editors were convicted of conspiring to corrupt public morals, fined £100 each, and given a suspended sentence that would have sent them to jail for 18 months if they repeated the misdemeanor at any time within the following two years. *102 Southampton Row. Russell Square tube.*

MATRIX STUDIOS

This three-studio complex is one of the very few recording houses not to abandon London for its western suburbs. Matrix, started in the late '70s, had several key clients in new-wave days: The Police cut several tracks of *Outlandos D'Amour,* Marianne Faithfull did *Broken English,* and the Stray Cats cut their debut album. A few years later the Smiths worked on their first two albums; fellow Mancunians the Fall have been regular visitors throughout their career. In the '90s the studios have been used by Blur (*The Great Escape*) as well as the Lemonheads, Massive Attack, the Rentals, and P.J. Proby on a comeback venture. *35 Little Russell St., tel. 0171/500–9950. Tottenham Court Rd. tube.*

MOULIN ROUGE (CAT STEVENS'S FATHER'S RESTAURANT)

In a flat over a restaurant owned by his Greek father, Cat Stevens (now Yusef Islam) was raised as Steven Georgiou. The restaurant is now known as Alfred. *49 New Oxford St. Tottenham Court Rd. tube.*

ULU—THE UNIVERSITY OF LONDON STUDENT UNION

Since the late '70s, when they put on shows by punk bands as diverse as Joy Division and Killing Joke, the ULU has occasionally grabbed the best up-and-coming bands that arrive in the city. In the mid-'80s they had another purple patch, as Primal Scream and All About Eve played for free in the bar area while Sonic Youth, Einstürzende Neubaten, and many of the bands that came out of *NME*'s (*New Musical Express*'s) influential *C86* compilation tape played cover-price gigs in the main hall. Another rich crop of gigs came along at the start of the '90s, when the top American bands of the day, including Pearl Jam, Nirvana, the Spin Doctors (then No. 1 in the United States), and Superchunk (who filmed a long-form video release here), made appearances. Radiohead also played here then.

In 1994 the Union had to make substantial renovations to satisfy fire requirements, but by the end of 1995 it was back to booking some of the best new bands, including Ash and the Bluetones as well as Bis, Luna, Drugstore, and the Longpigs, who came here to do a live Radio 1FM broadcast. *Malet St. at Torrington Pl., tel. 0171/580–9551. Euston Square tube.*

Covent Garden and Holborn, WC2

Although it lacks the personality of neighboring Soho to the west, Covent Garden is packed with tourists. The centerpiece is the wrought-iron-and-glass Piazza building, which was until 1974 the city's main wholesale produce market. After the market traders moved out, the district became deserted by day; at night the well-heeled came for the theaters and opera houses. In 1980, when developers threatened to modernize the area, the authorities stuck huge preservation orders on everything. Buildings were spruced up, the old market space was renamed the Piazza, and outlets selling trinkets, overpriced T-shirts, and pricey gift items moved in.

The '90s have seen cappuccino joints aplenty and too many performing artists taking up too much space. Covent Garden has also attracted mainstream publishing and graphic design houses, many (mostly overpriced) restaurants and brasseries, and several character-free pubs that always seem to be crowded with people in suits.

North of the irritatingly busy Covent Garden tube station is Neal Street, which leads to Neal's Yard, a miniature New Age version of the market in converted warehouses. It's a celebration of vegetarianism (but the meat-free cafés are no good), though there are some decent clothing stores in the surrounding streets. The streets east of the Piazza around Drury Lane and its theaters have remained refreshingly free of gentrification. To the south, en route to the Thames, is the Strand, home of the Savoy Hotel and now one of the city's most poignant interfaces of homeless people and the well-heeled.

Up toward Tottenham Court Road tube station, on the edge of Soho, is the city's most famous rock and roll strip, Denmark Street, once the center of the nation's song writing business and now packed with musical instrument stores.

Covent Garden has long had a rock history. Even back in market days, there were a number of dives, like the psychedelic Middle Earth in the late '60s and the Roxy, the city's first punk-only venue, 10 years later. The district has also been popular with video makers: To shoot their video for "Vienna," Ultravox chose the cutesy, cobbled streets around the Piazza rather than the Austrian capital.

Jane Hancer

Denmark Street, 1997

EATINGDRINKINGDANCINGSHOPPINGPLAYINGSLEEPING

The main tourist rock venue is the **ROCK GARDEN** (*see* Around Central Covent Garden, *below*). The **12 BAR CLUB** (*see* Covent Garden—Denmark Street, *below*), specializing in rootsy and acoustic music, is one of London's best small venues. The long-running **BUNJIES** (*see* Around Central Covent Garden, *below*) puts on low-key acoustic and spoken word seven nights a week. **KINGS COLLEGE STUDENT UNION** (MacAdam Bldg., Surrey St., tel. 0171/836–7132) puts on only a few gigs each year, but they tend to be quite prestigious affairs: In June and September 1995 it presented the U.K. debuts of the Foo Fighters and the Amps, respectively. **THE AFRICA CENTRE** (38 King St., tel. 0171/836–1973) mostly has music from that continent but occasionally brings in rock acts: The The made their debut here in 1979, and when the guest list for a 1992 gig by (London) Suede exceeded the club's capacity, scuffles broke out on the street after the doors were closed.

Generally, it doesn't matter which pub you choose to drink in—it's bound to be crammed full of media types after work.

For indie and alternative records, the place to go is the tiny **ROUGH TRADE** branch (*see* Around Central Covent Garden, *below*). **RAY'S JAZZ SHOP** (*see* Around Central Covent Garden, *below*) stocks records from early 20th century to futuristic freeform. **FAT CAT RECORDS** (19 Earlham St., tel. 0171/209–1071) is a basement store with a reputation for stocking all the latest underground dance sounds. Don't miss the book selection at **HELTER SKELTER** on Denmark Street (*see* Covent Garden—Denmark Street, *below*).

Around Central Covent Garden

BUNJIES FOLK CELLAR

During the '50s this area and Soho to the west were dotted with coffee bars that catered to the emerging youth trends by opening in the evening and providing skiffle and other transatlantic sounds. One of the few still remaining is Bunjies, which opened in 1954 and was named for the original owner's hamster. During the '60s Rod Stewart, David Bowie, Paul Simon, and Donovan made appearances, and in 1965 Al Stewart had a Friday night residency here; on finishing his set, he'd nip over to Les Cousins Club in Old Compton Street to watch the all-nighters with Paul Simon or Phil Ochs.

More recently, the mainstays of the British folk scene, including Martin Carthy, Bert Jansch, and Ralph McTell have played. Club regular Peter Cadle wrote the full story in *Bunjies: Nights in the Cellar*, published in 1995. The place, still with a very '60s feel, puts on acoustic evenings and comedy. During the day, it's a good licensed vegetarian café with very low-priced drinks. *27 Litchfield St., tel. 0171/240–1796. Leicester Square tube.*

LONDON COLISEUM

Built in 1904 and the home of the English National Opera since 1968, this was where the Who performed *Tommy* in 1969 after the more prudish Opera House had turned them down. Past employees include Joe Strummer, who worked here as a cleaner in 1974. *34 St. Martin's La., tel. 0171/632–8200. Leicester Square tube.*

RAY'S JAZZ SHOP

Rolling Stones drummer Charlie Watts has been a regular customer of this store almost since the day it opened in June 1956. In the basement is a battered old kit he borrowed from the owners during the Stones' earliest days. The place holds a diverse stock, covering everything from trad to freeform and worldbeat. *180 Shaftsbury Ave., tel. 0171/240–3969. Tottenham Court Rd. tube.*

ROCK GARDEN

Eyeing the success of the Hard Rock Cafe, a group of young entrepreneurs decided to go one step further and open a rock-themed restaurant with a prime gigging space attached. They got their way in 1976 when Georgie Fame opened this club in a former banana warehouse. Since then, the Rock Garden has tended to put on bands at the early stages of their careers. The Stranglers played that year and were showered with spaghetti thrown by unimpressed diners. The following year Talking Heads supported the Ramones, while in 1978 some of the up-and-coming groups included Dire Straits, the Police, and U2. Iron Maiden and UB40 made appearances in 1979, while the Smiths played what was only their fifth gig, on March 23, 1983.

The list has tailed off in recent years, although the early '90s saw (London) Suede and the Auteurs. Admission ranges from £5 to £8, which is expensive for unknown bands, though if you eat in their (Covent Garden-priced) restaurant, admission is free weekdays. *6–7 The Piazza, tel. 0171/836–4052; http://www.rockgarden.co.uk. Covent Garden tube.*

ROUGH TRADE RECORDS

Rough Trade opened this branch, just about the best place to find new and alternative sounds in central London, at the end of the '80s. Upstairs is Slam City Skates, full of skateboard and snowboard gear plus the trendiest names in U.S. streetwear. Downstairs, via a spiral iron staircase, are the records. The stock is pretty similar to that of the

Notting Hill branch (*see* West London *in* Outer London). The place generates a fair number of prestigious in-store events, with people squeezing in to see the Beastie Boys, Pavement, Hole, Sonic Youth, PJ Harvey, and the like. *16 Neal's Yard, tel. 0171/240–0105. Covent Garden tube.*

[THE ROXY]

Chaguarama's, an unsalubrious gay club, officially reopened as the Roxy, the first customized punk venue in the capital, on January 1, 1977, with a gig by the Clash. Even though the general feeling was that the venue was not the best for listening to live bands, this two-level dump became the center of punk culture—*the* place to pose in safety pins and bondage trousers. It quickly began to attract the second wave of punk bands, who had formed in the wake of the publicity surrounding the Pistols, such as Wire, X-Ray Spex, and the Slits, as well as bandwagon-jumpers like the Cortinas, the Lurkers, Johnny Moped (with whom Chrissie Hynde made her U.K. stage debut here in February 1977), and the Nipple Erectors.

Live at the Roxy, London WC2

At that time there weren't enough good live punk bands to sustain a "scene," and those that did show promise, like Wire and the Buzzcocks, quickly wanted to move on. The club lasted only a matter of months, closing in April. Nevertheless, it spawned two live albums. The first, *Live at the Roxy, London WC2,* which came out a few days after the venue closed, included the Adverts, Wire, X-Ray Spex, the Buzzcocks, and Eater. The second, *Farewell to the Roxy,* had the less substantial Blitz, Acme Sewage Company, U.K. Subs, and Billy Karloff and the Goats.

Resident Rastafarian DJ Don Letts used his spare moments to shoot footage for his documentary *The Punk Rock Movie,* which captured the full sleaze, including punks shooting up heroin in the toilets and self-mutilation by members of the audience. There is no longer any sign of the club; a clothes store stands in its place. *41–43 Neal St. Covent Garden tube.*

STRINGFELLOW'S

Peter Stringfellow, who started out promoting bands in his native Sheffield, is never far from the gossip sections of the media thanks to this flash club that attracts celebrities from all over the world. Sometimes the clientele makes the news, such as when Stephanie La Motta (daughter of boxer Jake), who had had an affair with Ringo, presented Julian Lennon with a white horse here at his 19th birthday party in March 1982. At other times Stringfellow himself makes the news, not least for refusing fat people entry to his club. *16–19 Upper St. Martin's La., tel. 0171/240–5534. Leicester Square tube.*

STUDIO 51

Invariably referred to also as Ken Colyer's Jazz Club, this basement venue opened in 1951 offering live trad (traditional) jazz music. By the early '60s it was putting on bands like the Rolling Stones, who had an early residency here, and the Yardbirds, who started experimenting with feedback here. Toward the end of the club's run, the Boomtown Rats did their first gig in England here, at a showcase for Phonogram records. The space is now occupied by a stationery store; a plaque on the wall outside reads: "Ken Colyer 1928–88 played New Orleans jazz here in the basement 'Studio 51' 1950–73." *10–11 Great Newport St. Leicester Square tube.*

Covent Garden and Holborn—Around Kingsway

BLITZ

A contemporary of late-'70s–early-'80s clubs like Le Beate Route and Billy's (Le Kilt), Blitz was one of the earliest centers of the New Romantic movement. Spandau Ballet played their first public gig—promoted by Steve Strange—here in December '79. Chris Blackwell of Island Records was in the audience and offered them a contract after the show. They turned him down and set up their own Reformation label. Spandau was one of the bands filmed for a TV documentary called *Blitz Kids* shot not here but at the Scala Cinema (*see* King's Cross, *below*), and by the end of the year they had a Top 5 U.K. hit. It's now Brown's "members only" nightclub. *4 Great Queen St, tel. 0171/831–0802. Holborn tube.*

DE LANE LEA MUSIC/KINGSWAY RECORDING STUDIO

Just over a month after arriving in London, in October 1966, Jimi Hendrix dropped into this studio on busy Kingsway to record "Hey Joe," produced by his new manager, Chas Chandler. Things didn't go well; Hendrix got into a bum mood because the recording level wasn't as loud as he wanted, and Decca, who four years previously had turned down the Beatles, rejected the single, telling Chandler: "He hasn't got anything"; Polydor issued it instead. Hendrix returned a number of times over the next few months, cutting "Stone Free" ("Hey Joe"'s B-side), "Can You See Me?," "Love or Confusion?," and "The Wind Cries Mary." Other De Lane Lea/Kingsway recordings include part of the Who's *Sell Out*, the score for George Harrison's *Wonderwall* movie, and Syd Barrett's final studio work with Pink Floyd—the schizophrenic "Jugband Blues."

In 1973, soon after the still-operating De Lane Lea concern left for bigger premises, Ian Gillan, who had just quit Deep Purple, bought the place cheaply. He soon found out why he'd gotten a bargain. The studio was in the basement, and the new tenants upstairs, the Civil Aviation Authority, had installed their computer room directly above the studio. They complained about the bass resonance and obtained an order prohibiting amplified recording during office hours. The place soon closed; the aviation people have moved out as well. *129 Kingsway. Holborn tube.*

LEGASTAT DOCUMENT COPIERS

David Bowie had a part-time job in this office copying documents for law firms (Britain's major courts are nearby). While working here, he wrote most of "Space Oddity," bringing in a Stylophone to work out his ideas on company time. *57 Carey St. Holborn tube.*

LONDON SCHOOL OF ECONOMICS

Mick Jagger studied at this university college but left in 1963 when the Rolling Stones were signed up. His attendance was noted in Bowie's much-requested masterpiece, "The Laughing Gnome," with the line about a Rolling Gnome at the London School of Eco-gnomics. A Sham 69 gig at the LSE in 1978 attracted hardcore *sieg-heiling* Nazis, who wrecked the joint; the band later distanced themselves from this kind of following by doing some Rock Against Racism benefits. *Houghton St, tel. 0171/405–7686. Temple tube.*

THEATRE ROYAL DRURY LANE

Although it puts on mainly big-hitting musicals, this theater, first established here in 1663—the present building dates from 1812—has presented some rock. Caravan recorded their live album, *Caravan and the New Symphonia,* here in October 1973; Tim Hardin joined Can onstage for a rendering of the "Man From Baltimore" in November 1975; and Adam and the Ants cut "Plastic Surgery" for the *Jubilee* movie three years later. At a Christmas 1994 Pulp gig, theater management feared that the foot-stomping crowd would literally bring the balcony down and called an early end to the night. *Catherine St. at Russell St., tel. 0171/836-3352. Covent Garden tube.*

Covent Garden and
Holborn—Around the Strand

CHARING CROSS PIER

To promote their "God Save the Queen" single, issued in spring 1977 during the Queen's Silver Jubilee hype, the Sex Pistols organized a Thames riverboat party, held on Jubilee day itself, June 7. Two hundred-odd noisy punks and record executives from the Pistols' label, Virgin, sailed off down the Thames aboard the suitably named Queen Elizabeth in the early evening, under the ever-watchful eye of the river cops. The vessel steamed east to Beckton and turned back to the city. As it passed the Houses of Parliament, the Pistols launched into a super-loud version of "Anarchy in the U.K." The by-now increased police flotilla demanded that the Pistols dock at the nearest pier. The Pistols' response as the river police jumped onto the boat was to perform a version of Iggy's "No Fun." When those aboard the Queen Elizabeth disembarked at Charing Cross Pier, cops from the Met who had been waiting on shore weighed into the crowd. Amid scuffles, 11 were arrested, including the band's manager, Malcolm McLaren, who acted as decoy by shouting "fascist bastards" at the police while the band sneaked away up the Embankment. *The Embankment, just east of Hungerford Bridge. Embankment tube.*

HEAVEN

Before Richard Branson's Virgin concern bought this huge, mainly gay club in 1980, it had been the Global Village, a disco where Freddie Mercury was a regular visitor on Saturday nights. Over the years, various bands have made personal appearances here: Spandau Ballet (December 1980, just after the release of their first single), New Order (London debut, February 1981), Southern Death Cult, who made their debut here in 1982, and the Orb in 1988. For the most part it is house and techno, though Thursday nights are devoted to Megatripolis, a Glastonbury-ish vibe. *The Arches, off Villiers St., tel. 0171/930-2020. Charing Cross tube.*

[LYCEUM]

This former opera house, a top mod hangout and disco in the mid-'60s, commanded some of the best shows in the city through to the early '80s. In October 1969 Led Zeppelin played (unintentionally) on the 54th anniversary of the dropping of a Zeppelin bomb on the theater. On December 15, 1969, the Plastic Ono Band—John Lennon, Eric Clapton, George Harrison, and Keith Moon—made their debut at a "Peace for Christmas" show, with proceeds going to the U.N. Children's Fund. It was the first time that two Beatles had appeared together onstage since the group's final concert in San Francisco's Candlestick Park in August 1966. On June 14, 1970, at another benefit here—this time for Dr. Spock's Civil Liberties Legal Defense Fund—the headliners, billed as Eric Clapton and Friends, came onstage as Derek and the Dominos, a name coined at the last moment by manager Tony Ashton; it was their world debut.

The most momentous Lyceum gig of the '70s was Bob Marley and the Wailers' July 18, 1975, show, historic for *Live!* (a.k.a. *Live at the Lyceum*), the resulting album that featured "No Woman No Cry." It was Marley's breakthrough album in the United Kingdom. In July 1976, the Lyceum was the scene of the Sex Pistols' first gig at a major venue, though they weren't the headliners. Two years later, Cabaret Voltaire were booed off the stage here, but their set emerged as a live album in 1981. In 1981 also Prince made his U.K. debut here. The venue shut down soon after and remained closed until fall 1996, when it reopened for the *Jesus Christ Superstar* musical. *Wellington St. at the Strand, tel. 0171/656–1803. Covent Garden tube.*

SAVOY HOTEL

Scenes from D. A. Pennebaker's Bob Dylan documentary, *Don't Look Back,* including the bit used for the "Subterranean Homesick Blues" video of Allen Ginsberg wandering around under a fire escape, were filmed in one of the narrow alleys behind this famous late-Victorian hotel. The tour broke Dylan as a major star. Others who have stayed here include Bill Haley on his 1957 tour. *The Strand at Savoy Ct., tel. 0171/836–4343. Charing Cross tube.*

ATV TIMES

Sniffin' Glue editor Mark Perry and photographer Harry T. Murlowski came up with the name for Perry's punk band, Alternative TV, while strolling down bustling St. Marlin's Lane In 1977. Murlowski wondered why so many people went to the theater. Perry explained that it was an alternative to TV.

Covent Garden–Denmark Street

*Just 'round the corner from old Soho/There's a place where the publishers go—*The Kinks, "Denmark Street"

For much of this century tiny Denmark Street—about 14 storefronts long—was Britain's Tin Pan Alley, the nerve center of British showbiz, where publishers, promoters, managers, and songwriters were billeted. With the rise of Merseybeat in the early '60s, bands started to write their own songs (or rework R&B numbers), and many of the songwriting teams became unnecessary. Yet the street is more a music center than ever, with most of the premises now occupied by musical instrument stores. Many of the big names of British music, including the Rolling Stones, David Bowie, Elton John, and the Sex Pistols, have had close associations with Denmark Street.

Today, if you keep your eyes open, it shouldn't be too hard to spot a top musician wandering in and out of the stores along this buzzing little street. As well as the instrument stores, Denmark Street has a couple of daytime cafés, London's only specialized music bookstore, and the cozy little 12 Bar Club. At the start of 1997, a developer bought most of the area on the north side of Denmark Street in order to tear it down and build a £20 million venue and hotel, possibly in conjunction with the House of Blues group. Tottenham Court Road is the tube for all Denmark Street sites.

ANDY'S GUITAR CENTRE

In 1978 Andy Preston took over a fruit shop in these wonderfully old-world premises and soon gained a

Andy's Guitars, 1996

stellar reputation. Besides regularly repairing the favorite six-strings of the likes of Jeff Beck and Jimmy Page, Andy sells vintage and used guitars. Other customers include Liam and Noel Gallagher, the Kinks, Steve Howe, Chrissie Hynde, and Aswad. On Andy's Internet site you can explore a guitar-finding service for rare models, as well as a second-hand guitar sales service. *27 Denmark St., tel. 0171/916-5080; http://www.atlas.co.uk/andysguitarslondon/.*

DENMARK PRODUCTIONS (BOOGIE MUSIC STORE)

In the '60s Denmark Productions, which managed the Kinks and the Troggs, was based here, as was Gordon Mills, who guided the career paths of Engelbert Humperdinck and Tom Jones toward Vegas. The ground floor is now Boogie Music Store, one of the few independent instrument retailers left on the street. *25 Denmark St., tel. 0171/240-3309.*

LA GIOCONDA RESTAURANT (BARINO SANDWICH BAR)

There's been a basic little eatery here for decades, with many name changes along the way. David Bowie (then Jones) met his mid-'60s backing band, the Lower Third here, when the restaurant was known as La Gioconda. Bowie and his vampish girlfriend at the time, Dana Gillespie (later an unsuccessful glam act), used to have a bite here. Over a decade later it was a popular hangout for the punks, as the Pistols and Banshees rehearsal room was just three doors away. *9 Denmark St.*

MERIDIAN STUDIO (WORLD OF PIANOS)

Donovan recorded his first demos, as well as his early hits, in a studio based here in 1965. His first two singles, "Catch the Wind" and "Colours," both reached No. 4 in the U.K. charts. The studio was owned by Southern Music publishers, who occupied the entire building at that time. Others who recorded here include the Pretty Things and Yes; the Flowerpotmen did their Summer of Love cash-in hit, "Let's Go to San Francisco," here. The major occupant is now World of Pianos, who have on display the upright piano on which John Lennon wrote "Imagine." *8 Denmark St., tel. 0171/240-5555.*

MILLS MUSIC (ARGENT'S MUSIC)

Elton John worked as an office boy for Mills Music publishers in the early '60s and toward the end of that decade wrote "Your Song" (his breakthrough single) on the roof with Bernie Taupin—hence the line "I sat on the roof." In the mid-'60s, keyboardist Rod Argent bought the retail premises. Although he later sold out to World of Music, the store still bears his name and stocks mostly sheet music. *20 Denmark St., tel. 0171/379-6690.*

NME FIRST ADDRESS/LORNA MUSIC

Britain's best-selling rock weekly, *NME* (*New Musical Express*), started out on an upper floor of this building in 1952 and stayed here for over a decade. On the top floor was Lorna Music, a publishing company whose clients in the early '60s included Paul Simon. The office space is now occupied by Associated International Management and the ground floor by Roka's Acoustic Services, a guitar store. *5 Denmark St.*

[REGENT SOUND STUDIOS (HELTER SKELTER)]

The Helter Skelter cash desk stands on the former site of the mixing desk for Regent Sound Studios. The studio's clients included the Kinks, the Dave Clark Five, and the Tremeloes, as well as a young Reg Dwight (né Elton John), who made his living in those days doing covers for Top of the Pops compilation albums.

Britain's only bookstore dedicated to rock opened in August 1995 and immediately built up a reputation as the best (and first) place to find anything interesting and unusual. Virtually every music book in print in Great Britain is stocked, plus around 100 of the latest imports from the United States, a selection of rare used books, and back issues of magazines. Staff are extremely helpful; they produce a free catalog and do mail order. Julian Cope and Dave Davies have been here for book signings, as well as Clinton Heylin and other biographers. *4 Denmark St., tel. 0171/836–1151.*

Owner Sean Body (left) with former Sex Pistol Glen Matlock at Helter Skelter, 1996

RHODES MUSIC/TIN PAN ALLEY STUDIOS

A major-league guitar store that, like most of the outlets on the street, is now under the World of Music banner, Rhodes has done business with all the big players since the '70s, when John "music was my first love" Miles worked here and sold axes to Pete Townshend, Jeff Beck, Eric Clapton, and others. More recently Chuck Berry has popped in for repair jobs when in England, as has Bryan Adams. Customers also include Gary Moore, plus members of Oasis, Elastica, Pulp, and most of the current crop of Brit bands.

The studio in the basement, for years known as the Tin Pan Alley Studios, was where Manfred Mann, the Small Faces, and Jimi Hendrix did some work. At the start of the '90s the Acid Jazz label (based next door at the time) used it as the house studio, recording Jamiroquai, Mother Earth, Corduroy, and other acts. It recently changed its name to Denmark Street Studios, an independent concern. *22 Denmark St., tel. 0171/836–4656.*

ROSE-MORRIS MUSIC

The Rose-Morris name has been around the area since the early '20s. It was a private concern until a management buyout in the early '80s. Taken over by the IMP wing of Warner Bros. later that decade, it is currently the largest store on the street, with four floors of instruments and an abundance of sheet music. Many big names have shopped here; as part of the Warners' opening ceremony, Joan Armatrading and a couple of members of Level 42 embedded their handprints on the step outside. *11 Denmark St., tel. 0171/836–0991.*

SEX PISTOLS' FLAT AND REHEARSAL ROOMS

Just after the Sex Pistols formed, manager Malcolm McLaren found digs for half the band—Messrs. Cook and Jones—in the flat above Zeno's Greek Bookshop. The full quartet also practiced in the rehearsal room at the back of the store prior to their first gigs in late 1975. By June 1976 they recorded rough demos of several songs, including "Anarchy in the U.K." and "Pretty Vacant," in this space. In 1977 Siouxsie and the Banshees wrote "Love in a Void" in the rehearsal room, leaving the line "Too many Jews for my I-I-I-liking" out of the recorded version.

By 1980 Cook and Jones were back here meddling with their Professionals outfit. They let two hard-up girls—Keren Woodward and Sarah Dallin—stay for free. The girls soon got together with another friend, Siobhan Fahey, to work out some ideas in the room below. The result was the unpunk Bananarama. *6 Denmark St.*

THE 12 BAR CLUB

This great little venue opened in early 1995 in a building that dates from the 17th century. It holds around 80 people and has music seven nights a week. Despite its size, it has managed to pull in such performers as Robyn Hitchcock, Roy Harper, and Bert Jansch, as well as special appearances by virtuosos such as Clyde Stubblefield, the drummer in James Brown's band. *Denmark Pl. off Denmark St., tel. 0171/916–6989.*

Flyer for South London favorites Past Caring at the 12 Bar Club, 1996

Fitzrovia, W1

Those who work in the West End and want to escape touristy, overcrowded Soho have recently begun colonizing the less-frequented and less expensive bars, cafés, and restaurants of Fitzrovia on the north side of Oxford Street. The Victorian neighborhood has managed to retain the shabby bohemian air that attracted such writers as Dylan Thomas and George Orwell in the '40s to the Fitzroy Tavern. Nowadays rag-trade sweatshops sit happily alongside sleek PR companies and media offices. The music monthlies *Select, Q, Kerrang!,* and *Mojo* are based in the EMAP company offices (4 Winsley St., near Oxford Circus tube), while the listings weekly *Time Out* (251 Tottenham Court Rd.) is published farther east. In between, pockets of interest can be found wherever you look: Whitfield Street has **CYBERIA** (36 Whitfield St., tel. 0171/209–0982), the city's first Internet café, as well as several weird little stores. Song references about the area include Donovan's "Sunny Goodge Street" and Lloyd Cole and the Commotions' "Charlotte Street." The madcap Beatles scenes from *A Hard Day's Night* were shot on tiny Charlotte Mews.

Fitzrovia–Around Tottenham Court Road

Fitzrovia's eastern boundary, Tottenham Court Road, is a busy, traffic-choked thoroughfare flanked by many of London's best-value electrical stores; it's largely dead at night, despite the proliferation of pubs.

Near Tottenham Court Road tube station you can find Hanway Street, a short, curvy alleyway with a treasure trove of record shops and cheap eateries, of which the best are Indian. **ON THE BEAT** (22 Hanway St., tel. 0171/637–8934), an untidy used-record store with lots of '70s rock and punk, also stocks back issues of music weeklies and magazines. **SOHO RECORDS** (3 Hanway St., tel. 0171/580–4805) specializes in collectible vinyl of '60s and '70s America, particularly country rock, singer-songwriter recordings, and psychedelia. **UFO MUSIC** (18 Hanway St., tel. 0171/636–1281 or 0171/637–1771), the largest of the Hanway Street stores, used to be called Vinyl Experience, but the vinyl stocks (annoyingly sealed in plastic covers) have diminished of late. **VIBE!** (36 Hanway St., tel. 0171/580–8898), a small store with some ultrarare records displayed high on the walls and behind the counter at inflated prices, is sometimes referred to as Rocks Off, the name the store held in the late '70s when Shane MacGowan, then in the Nips, worked here.

CBS STUDIOS/THE HIT FACTORY

The Clash recorded their early singles and debut album in Studio 3, the same place where four years earlier, in 1973, Iggy and the Stooges had cut the punk/metal prototype *Raw Power*. More recently, the Lightning Seeds (*Jollification*) and Plant and Page (*Unledded*) have used the facilities in this sleek wood-and-glass building. The Hit Factory also specializes in mainstream movie soundtracks. *31–37 Whitfield St., tel. 0171/636–3434. Tottenham Court Rd. tube.*

THE ROEBUCK (CANON'S CAFE BAR)

In 1966 David Bowie and his group at the time, the Lower Third, auditioned for new manager Ralph Horton here. A former British rail clerk, Alan McGee, set up a club, the Living Room, in this pub in 1982 before starting the Creation Records label the following year. It became the '90s' most successful indie label, with Oasis, Primal Scream, and Teenage Fanclub. *108 Tottenham Court Rd., tel. 0171/387–6199. Warren St. tube.*

Vinyl Experience, 1997

SCIENTOLOGY/DIANETICS CENTRE

Before his 1983 gigs at the nearby Dominion Theatre, Van Morrison would drop in here at a time when his religious curiosity was taking him through a brief Scientology phase. There is a dedication of special thanks on his 1983 *Inarticulate Speech of the Heart* to Scientology supremo L. Ron Hubbard. *68 Tottenham Court Rd. Tottenham Court Rd. tube.*

UFO (1966–67)

It lasted for less than a year and only on Friday nights, but the UFO remains one of the most legendary of '60s London clubs. It was instrumental in breaking Pink Floyd as the capital's top psychedelic act. Run by *IT*'s John Hopkins and producer Joe Boyd (Fairport Convention, R.E.M., and others), UFO stood for Unlimited Freak Out. It took place in the basement, decked out in psychedelic trimmings for each show, of a rough Irish dance hall called the Blarney Club. UFO was popular with musicians, who felt that the crowd was full of appreciative, knowledgeable types and not weekend hippies. At the opening night, December 23, 1966, Pink Floyd played during underground films, poetry readings, and plotless impromptu theater pieces. Floyd (the bulk of whom met while studying at Regent Street Polytechnic, now the University of Westminster, at nearby 309 Regent St.) acted as a kind of house band and experimented at will.

Among other psychedelic bands who played here were Soft Machine, the Move, Procol Harum, the Incredible String Band, Fairport Convention, and Arthur Brown, who swung from a trapeze wearing a flaming helmet. American visitors included Phil Ochs, who did some spoken-word performances. The fun ended when it closed in October '67. The block was knocked down in the '70s; an ABC cinema now stands on the site. *30/1 Tottenham Court Rd. Tottenham Court Rd. tube.*

Fitzrovia–Around Great Portland Street

BBC BROADCASTING HOUSE

Coinciding with the band's 20th anniversary, Iron Maiden and some 70 biker fans congregated outside BBC Radio's headquarters in September 1996 in a "friendly protest" to publicize their claim that Radio 1FM had banned Maiden's songs and were playing too little metal. They blared the band's newly released *Best of the Beast* album over speakers until police moved them on. The stunt had little effect on actual Radio 1FM decision-makers; that studio is based a five-minute walk away from here along Portland Place. *Portland Pl. at Langham Pl., tel. 0171/580–4468. Oxford Circus tube.*

BBC Headquarters, 1997

IBC STUDIOS

The Rolling Stones did their first demos at the International Broadcasting Company (IBC) studio, based in this elegant Georgian terrace, in January 1963, cutting "Diddley Daddy," "Road Runner," and "Crackin' Up" (all Bo Diddley songs), plus some Jimmy Reed and Willie Dixon numbers. In January 1964 the Stones started work on their first album here, joined by Phil Spector and Gene Pitney. To use up some spare moments on the disc, they all collaborated on the throwaway track "Now I've Got a Witness Like Uncle Phil and Uncle Gene." The Who recorded many of their early songs at the studio, including their first two singles, "I Can't Explain" (December 1964) and "Anyway Anyhow Anywhere" (April 1965). The band's rhythm section—Keith Moon and John Entwistle—collaborated with various Yardbirds, including Jeff Beck and Jimmy Page, to cut "Beck's Bolero," one of 1967's most exciting instrumentals. The building is now occupied by a firm of architects. *35 Portland Pl. Oxford Circus tube.*

SPEAKEASY (CAMEO)

In the wake of the success of the Bag O' Nails off Carnaby Street (*see* Soho—Carnaby Street and Around, *below*), this club, drenched in gangster memorabilia, opened at the tail end of 1966 and soon attracted the swinging London glitterati. David Bowie met his first wife, Angie, here in 1967; Keith Moon and Vivian Stanshall liked to come here to go wild; and Eric Clapton, Jack Bruce, and Jimi Hendrix would often drop by to do impromptu sets (Hendrix did a 30-minute version of "Auld Lang Syne" on New Year's Eve 1967). King Crimson came here for their first gig (April 9, 1969); a few months later, on July 10, Deep Purple unveiled their Blackmore/Paice/Evans/Lord/Gillan lineup; and in September 1970, 36 hours before he died, Jimi Hendrix had a good feed here. Another who downed his final drinks at the Speakeasy was New York Doll Billy Murcia, who spent his last night here in November 1972.

By the mid-'70s the big-spending stars had largely deserted the place. Nevertheless, Pete Townshend was a regular, and one night after an alcohol marathon, he stumbled out of the Speakeasy to sleep it off in a nearby doorway. In the early hours, he was awakened by a cop who told him he was free to go if he could "get up and walk away," a story recounted on the Who's 1978 single "Who Are You?"

During the punk era, the club attracted some of the stars of the day. Joe Strummer was beaten up by some Teds in the toilets. In March 1977, Johnny Rotten, Sid Vicious, and pals confronted "Whisperin' " Bob Harris, presenter of BBC television's *Old Grey Whistle Test* (the best serious rock music program in the '70s), over his refusal to have them perform on the show. A row followed, Vicious threatened Harris's friend, and someone said they'd "kill" Harris. Unfortunately for the Pistols, Harris's management was also responsible for Peter Frampton, then A&M's top-selling performer. Frampton wrote to A&M chiefs saying he didn't want to be on the same label as such awful people, and A&M subsequently dropped the band.

During the '80s and the first half of the '90s, the club was called Bootleggers. It is now the Cameo, a handbag (chart-friendly house music) nightclub. *48–50 Margaret St., tel. 0171/636–6787. Oxford Circus tube.*

King's Cross, EC1, N1, NW1, WC1

Dear old streets of King's Cross—The Pogues, "Transmetropolitan"

The zone around the three main line railroad stations of Euston, St. Pancras, and King's Cross, sometimes known as Somers Town, is central London's seediest, full of shabby hotels and rough pubs, although there are some great curry houses around Drummond Street, just west of Euston station. Although a couple of good clubs and bars have moved into King's Cross, it's still known mostly for its panhandlers, pimps, and street people.

EATINGDRINKINGDANCINGSHOPPINGPLAYINGSLEEPING

A relatively new arrival on the live music scene is the **RED EYE** (105 Copenhagen St., N1, tel. 0171/837–1514), which provides a good space for punk metal bands to play. **THE CROSSBAR** (*see below*) provides a late-night drinking spot at reasonable cost. **FILTHY MCNASTY'S** (*see below*) is as good as the name suggests. In the '90s the squatted old warehouses of Pancras Street have hosted many parties; the area also has two of the city's most important clubs. **BAGLEY'S** (Kings Cross Freight Depot off York Way, N1, tel. 0171/278–2777) is massive but still pays attention to the quality of music. Much smaller is the **CROSS** (Goods Way Depot off York Way, N1, tel. 0171/837 0828), mainly known for great house sounds. **STERN'S AFRICAN RECORD CENTRE** (293 Euston Rd., NW1, tel. 0171/387–5550) is the best source for records from that continent and stocks worldbeat sounds from around the globe.

CAPITAL RADIO

Capital, in tune with nothing—The Clash, "Capital Radio"

London's first commercial station had only been on air a few years when the Clash savaged its unimaginative playlist with a marvelous put-down, also called "Capital Radio," which was released on the EP given free with some copies of their first album in 1977. That March the band spray-painted WHITE RIOT on the station's foyer window. Capital's output has barely improved since then, but somehow it's the most-listened-to station in London. The station recently moved to Leicester Square. *Euston Tower, Euston Rd., NW1, tel. 0171/608–6080. Warren St. tube.*

THE CROSSBAR

In September 1995, soon after this big late-night bar (run by the Mean Fiddler organization of Forum and Reading Festival fame) opened, Liam Gallagher was involved in a scuffle. The Oasis singer apparently headbutted a smaller guy and was thrown out by bouncers while the DJ appropriately played Oasis's "Roll With It" single. *257 Pentonville Rd., N1, tel. 0171/837–3218. King's Cross tube/BR.*

[FILTHY MCNASTY'S AND THE WHISKEY CAFÉ]

Filthy McNasty was the fictional name the girlfriend of gangster Bugsy Siegel used for running business interests after he died. Irishman Gerry O'Boyle picked up on the name for this cool bar in an effort to supply London's alternative arts-and-music crowd with a hangout similar to the Rainbow Bar and Grill (on L.A.'s Sunset Strip). A sign over the bar reads, "Oh Lord Make Me Be Pure, But Not Just Yet," and other decor includes a cardboard cutout of the boxer featured on the front of the Pogues' *Peace & Love* LP; gold discs from the Pogues; and photos on Gaelic and Americana themes. Shane MacGowan often drinks here.

Will Self reading at Filthy McNasty's

Regular live performances include the Vox n Roll series of spoken-word nights, which has featured Nick Cave, Richard Hell, and Shane MacGowan. At other times, you may find live Irish music or the occasional band of interest, such as David Berman's Silver Jews. Such contemporary writers as Will Self have also done readings at Filthy's. *68 Amwell St., EC1, tel. 0171/837–6067. Angel tube.*

KING'S CROSS RAILWAY STATION

The Pet Shop Boys closed their 1987 album, *Actually,* with a song called "King's Cross" that forecast apocalyptic doom for the area. A few months later a horrific fire broke out in the tube station concourse, killing scores of people. The Clash were photographed behind the station for the cover of *Sandinista!* The Proclaimers acknowledged the station's role as the terminus for the London–Edinburgh rail route on "It Broke My Heart."

THE PINDAR OF WAKEFIELD (WATER RATS)

Bob Dylan appeared at this pub's Singer's Club Christmas party in 1962, during his first visit to Britain. Ewan MacColl and Peggy Seeger were in the audience. In 1983 the Pogues made their debut here as Pogue Mahone (Irish for "kiss my butt").

From 1992 to summer 1996 the pub, with its cozy little back room, was called the Splash Club, the best pub venue for indie music in the capital, with new bands playing six nights a week. Oasis made their London debut here in January 1994; 200 people were turned away. The eager band showed up too early for the soundcheck and were sent away by a Splash employee. Skunk Anansie played around 20 times (mostly as Mama Wild) before hitting the charts, Kula Shaker (when they were called the Kays) did eight shows, and others to play include Bush (both before and after *Sixteen Stone* was released), Reef, Supergrass, Gene, and Echobelly. Weezer played its first U.K. show here, as did the likes of Kelley Deal 6000, Seven Mary Three, and Soul Coughing.

When the owners, the Grand Order of Water Rats (a showbiz charity that's headed by magician Paul Daniels), decided in September 1996 to change the pub's image, Splash was given 10 days to quit (they're now at the Falcon in Camden Town—*see* Camden Town *in* Outer London, *below*—under the name Barfly Club). Water Rats still has live music and is hoping to reestablish itself in indie circles. *328 Gray's Inn Rd., WC1, tel. 0171/837–7269. King's Cross tube/BR.*

SCALA

Of the few gigs that have taken place in this ornate former cinema, one that quickly passed into legend was an Iggy and the Stooges show in 1972 (the band's only-ever U.K. gig). A teenage Johnny Rotten attended. A photo from the gig of a heavily made-up, bare-chested Iggy leaning on the mike (taken by Mick Rock) made the front cover of their

Gretschen Hofner playing at the Splash Club, 1997

1973 LP, *Raw Power.* The cinema has since been downgraded to the King's Cross Snooker Hall. *King's Cross Bridge at Pentonville Rd., NW1. King's Cross tube/BR.*

THAMES TV

The Sex Pistols were catapulted to national fame after a chaotic and hilarious prime-time TV interview on December 1, 1976, with Bill Grundy, presenter of the station's *Today* show. When Grundy asked them what they had done with EMI's £40,000 advance, guitarist Steve Jones replied, "We fucking spent it." Grundy then turned to the "girls behind," who included Siouxsie Sioux, as well as other members of the Bromley contingent. When Sioux told Grundy she had always wanted to meet him, Grundy naively replied, "We'll meet afterwards, shall we." Jones quickly intervened with, "You dirty sod, you dirty old man." Grundy then became bullish and provocative, taunting Jones to say something outrageous in the last few seconds, and Jones retorted, "You dirty bastard," and "You dirty fucker." When Grundy responded with, "What a clever boy," Jones hit back with a memorable, "You fucking rotter." Britain had never experienced such an outburst, even on late night shows, let alone at half past six in the evening.

The incident backfired for both parties. Within hours, Malcolm McLaren's office had calls from venues around the country pulling out of the group's first major national tour, a problem intensified by local councillors' instigating a ban. BBC radio took the group's "Anarchy in the U.K." single off their playlist, and warehouse workers at EMI's distribution plant refused to handle the disc. Just over a month later, EMI kicked the Pistols off their roster. Meanwhile Grundy, accused of deliberately winding up the band, was suspended and his career never recovered. Thames lost the TV franchise for the London area in the mid-'90s; the site is now being redeveloped. *306 Euston Rd., NW1. Warren St. tube.*

Marylebone, W1

This quiet, well-to-do area is wedged between the westerly stretch of Oxford Street and the Regent's Park; four tube stations—Oxford Circus, Marble Arch, Baker Street, and Regent's Park—form its four corners. The most exclusive patch is Harley Street, home of

Britain's highest-paid medical practitioners, while the busiest bit is around Baker Street, where tourists flock for Sherlock Holmes-related attractions and where the Beatles shot many movie scenes.

Baker Street Station and Around

Fertile earth mother, your burial mound is 50 feet down in the Baker Street underground—Jethro Tull, "Baker Street Muse"

A traffic-choked one-way street on the western edge of the West End, Baker Street is best known as the home of fictional detective Sherlock Holmes and, since 1978, for Gerry Rafferty's overplayed song named for the street.

EATINGDRINKINGDANCINGSHOPPINGPLAYINGSLEEPING

The Beatles "In My Life Walk" leaves from the Baker Street entrance of Baker Street tube station Tuesdays and Saturdays at 11 AM. It costs £4.50 (students £3.50). There is no need to pre-book; for further information, contact **LONDON WALKS** (tel. 0171/624–3978; http://www.bogo.co.uk/London.Walks).

NO SHIT, SHERLOCK!

The quirky New York pop band They Might Be Giants took their name from a 1972 comedy starring George C. Scott about a lawyer who thought he was Sherlock Holmes. The fictitious detective's famous address, 221b Baker Street, has been subsumed into the head office of the Abbey National Building Society, which now takes up numbers 215 to 229.

APPLE BOUTIQUE

Owned by the Beatles, the Apple Boutique was opened on December 5, 1967, with a party where apple juice was the only drink served. According to Paul McCartney, the boutique was to be a "beautiful place to buy beautiful things, run by Western communism principles." It would be "generous, liberal and youth-friendly." It was also a financial disaster. Lots of clothes were stolen, and on the day it shut, July 30, 1968, all £15,000 worth of remaining stock was given away to anyone who asked for it. The building is now occupied by an employment agency. *94 Baker St. Baker St. tube.*

Jam 45, Down in the Tube Station at Midnight

BAKER STREET STATION

The cover photograph of the Jam's 1978 single, "Down in the Tube Station at Midnight," was taken on one of the platforms of this busy underground station.

On "Protex Blue" the Clash are "standing in the carriage of the Bakerloo" when they test a packet of contraceptives. In a live transmission for BBC radio in March 1973, Can performed a number called "Up the Bakerloo Line." The chords for Wire's "106 Beats That" were based on the letters of the Bakerloo line stations between Queens Park and Harrow and Wealdstone.

JOB CENTRE

*In 1977, I hope I go to heaven, I've been too long on the dole—*The Clash, "1977"

Joe Strummer used to sign on at this unemployment office in 1976 shortly before forming The Clash. The fortnightly visits doubtless provided him with material for Clash standards such as "Career Opportunities" and "1977." *22 Lisson Grove, NW1. Marylebone tube.*

MADAME TUSSAUD'S

This waxworks museum, one of London's most tourist-choked attractions, dates from the 1830s, when Mme. Tussaud learned her trade making death masks of victims during the French Revolution. The Beatles (in March 1964) were the first rock stars to be installed; the dummies later appeared on the front cover of the *Sgt. Pepper* album. These days, most of the rock dummies have been sent off to the awful Rock Circus in Piccadilly (*see* Soho—Piccadilly Circus, *below*). *Marylebone Rd. opposite Luxborough St., NW1, tel. 0171/935–6861. Baker St. tube.*

MARYLEBONE MAGISTRATE'S COURT

In October 1968 John Lennon and Yoko Ono were charged here with possessing pot; the Beatle was fined £150 plus costs. A photo of Lennon being escorted away by scores of cops was used on the back cover of his *Life with the Lions: Unfinished Music #2* LP. Other rock stars who have appeared here include Keith Richards, charged in June 1973 with possessing a gun, and Sid Vicious, who turned up in a suit with silver lamé thread on a charge of possessing speed. *Oz's* "schoolkids" edition was prosecuted

John Lennon and Yoko Ono outside the Marylebone Magistrates' Court, 1968

on the grounds of obscenity, and the magazine's editors showed up for the preliminary hearing here in October 1970 dressed in schoolboy outfits. *181 Marylebone Rd. at Seymour Pl., tel. 0171/706–1261. Baker St. tube.*

RUN FOR YOUR LIFE

Several early Beatles movie scenes were shot in this well-touristed stretch of London.

In the opening bit of *A Hard Day's Night,* the Beatles run down Boston Place, which borders the eastern side of Marylebone Station.

Other opening scenes from *A Hard Day's Night* were filmed at Marylebone railway station in April 1964. In one of the shots, the group runs into the station trying to catch a train leaving from Platform 1. A hundred fans were paid to chase after the band.

In *Help!* the Beatles are seen entering an Indian restaurant, the Rajahama (6 Blandford St., off Marylebone High St.), as the screen fills with the caption, "Seeking enlightenment as to rings they approached the nearest oriental." The Rajahama never existed; a sign was simply placed in front of what was then The Dolphin restaurant and is now CJ's wine bar.

Paul McCartney and assorted non-Beatle passengers joined the coach for the *Magical Mystery Tour* on Allsop Place, just northeast of Baker Street station, in September 1967. Allsop Place is where most of the tourist coaches drop visitors to the London Planetarium and Madame Tussaud's.

MARYLEBONE REGISTRY OFFICE (CITY OF WESTMINSTER REGISTRY OFFICE)

Paul McCartney married Linda Eastman here on March 12, 1969, with his brother, Mike McGear (né McCartney) of Scaffold, acting as best man. On April 27, 1981, Ringo and

Linda's daughter, Heather, accompanies Paul McCartney and Linda Eastman to their wedding, 1969

Barbara Bach were married at the same office by the same registrar. The event brought the three surviving Beatles together for first time since Lennon's death. Back then, St. Marylebone was a separate borough; now it is part of Westminster; hence the change of name. On April 7, 1997, Liam Gallagher and Patsy Kensit carried on the tradition here. *Westminster Council House, Marylebone Rd. at Gloucester Pl., tel. 0171/798–1161. Baker St. tube.*

Around Harley Street

Harley Street is where the nation's most expensive private physicians and dentists operate, and more than a few shades-wearing rock stars and industry moguls have darted in here for some detox treatment. The upper echelons of British society have long lived in these fine Georgian streets.

APPLE (ORIGINAL HEADQUARTERS)

The Beatles opened their Apple business here in April 1968, but moved after six months on account of complaints from neighbors about loud records being played. It's now offices. *95 Wigmore St. Oxford Circus tube.*

[EMI]

They only did it for the fame; who? EMI—The Sex Pistols, "EMI"

From 1960 to 1995 EMI (Electrical and Mechanical Industries), Britain's biggest record company thanks to the Beatles (who recorded for the Parlophone subsidiary until forming Apple), Pink Floyd, and scores of other megaselling acts, was based in this square. Along the way EMI made plenty of stupid decisions, like originally turning down the Beatles in 1961 and sacking the Sex Pistols 15 years later (*see* Thames TV *in King's Cross, above*). The Pistols took their revenge on the closing track of *Never Mind the Bollocks* with the sarcastic gibe, "EMI." The label soon signed another McLaren act, Bow Wow Wow, who gratefully trashed the place and threw gold discs out the window after their 1981 home-taping-is-good single, "C30, C60, C90, Go!" flopped. One-time Rolling Stones manager Andrew Loog Oldham was banned from the building in 1968—even though EMI distributed his Immediate label—for putting Seconal in the soup at a conference.

No recording was done in this building—the label's home away from home is Abbey Road studios in St. John's Wood—but a February 1963 picture of the Beatles looking down from the stairwell near the entrance was used on the front cover of "Please Please Me" and later reused for the 1962–66 singles compilation. An identical shot of the group six years later, with hippie beards and flared suits, taken for an album that never materialized, appeared on the 1967–70 companion compilation. In 1995 EMI moved out to Hammersmith. *20 Manchester Sq. Bond St. tube.*

PAUL MCCARTNEY ADDRESS, 1963–66

While dating actress (and now successful cookery writer) Jane Asher in the early '60s, Paul McCartney stayed in the attic room of the house where she and her parents lived, surrounded by his gold records. He wrote, "I Want To Hold Your Hand" here; the hand-written lyrics are in the British Museum. *57 Wimpole St. Bond St. tube.*

POLYDOR STUDIO

The Clash made their first recordings—"Career Opportunities," "1977," "London's Burning," "Janie Jones," and "White Riot"—in November 1976 at this studio opposite Bond Street tube, with Guy Stevens producing. Polydor had hopes of signing the band, who, amazingly enough, were still without a label even though no-hopers like the Vibrators had been picked up, but the tapes were not a success. Told to intone more clearly, Strummer deliberately set out to "sound like Matt Monro" (a Sinatra-style crooner known for the theme tune of *From Russia with Love*). *17–19 Stratford Pl. Bond St. tube.*

Around Marble Arch

The name of both a major London monument and a busy traffic rotary, Marble Arch marks the end of the main Oxford Street shopping drag. The arch itself was built in 1821 and stood outside Buckingham Palace until being moved here 24 years later. Marble Arch also marks the site of Tyburn, the capital's main execution spot until 1783, with space to hang up to 21 lawbreakers. The public executions turned out to be gin-swigging occasions accompanied by the music of the day—London's first death metal gigs, if you like. The spot is marked on the sidewalk by the arch. Marble Arch tube is the station for all landmarks.

"THERE'S A RED HOUSE OVER YONDER"

Jimi Hendrix had a number of addresses in this desirable part of London in the late '60s.

Jane Hancer

34 MONTAGU SQUARE. Hendrix moved into his first private address in London, what was formerly Ringo's apartment, in December 1966. Soon after, he wrote "The Wind Cries Mary" for girlfriend Kathy Etchingham, who had walked out after a row. When he played her the song, she, understandably, returned. After Hendrix moved out of this smart Georgian square in 1967, John Lennon and Yoko Ono moved in. Lennon had just split with his first wife, Cynthia; the following summer, he and Yoko were photographed in the basement butt-naked for the cover of *Two Virgins*. In October 1968 the cops called to visit with a sniffer dog, who uncovered some marijuana, and John and Yoko were busted. Ringo moved back in but was soon forced out by the landlords, pissed at having to put up with police raids.

43 UPPER BERKELEY STREET. Hendrix lived in this small, bland-looking apartment block for a short while around March 1967.

Jimi Hendrix's house at 34 Montagu Square in London

CUMBERLAND HOTEL. In his final months, Hendrix had a suite in this hotel overlooking Marble Arch. He broadcast his last radio program (for BBC Radio 1) here in September 1970, just before he died. Since then, the busy Cumberland has been redesigned, and the Hendrix room is now No. 5008, a normal double that costs £180 a night. *Great Cumberland Pl. at Oxford St., tel. 0171/262–1234.*

Mayfair, W1

They had a meeting in Mayfair—The Clash, "Remote Control"

Dominated by million-pound Georgian town houses, Mayfair, bordered by the main roads of Oxford Street, Regent Street, Piccadilly, and Park Lane, is a quiet, peaceful, mainly residential neighborhood that reeks of old money. Statesmen, military leaders, royal mistresses, and even the odd rock star (Keith Moon), have made Mayfair their home.

Mayfair–New Bond Street and Around

Near the center of Mayfair, Berkeley Square, immortalized in the Tin Pan Alley standard, "A Nightingale Sang in Berkeley Square," but spoiled by pre-war office blocks, is not one of London's prettier Georgian enclaves. To the east lies New Bond Street, one of Mayfair's main north–south routes, crammed with wealth-dripping jewelry stores such as Asprey's (No. 165), which featured in the Beatles' *Help!* movie. A little farther east is Savile Row, the most prestigious name in British gentlemen's tailoring. Savile Row's traditional conservatism—the Kinks sang of getting no kicks walking down Savile Row on "End of Season" from the 1967 album *Something Else by the Kinks*—was dashed when Tommy Nutter arrived in 1969 to set up shop at 35a and sold the Beatles the suits they wore on the cover of *Abbey Road*. Savile Row is now ultrarespectable once again.

⌐ APPLE CORPS, 1968–72 ⌐

The Beatles played their last gig, captured in the *Let It Be* movie, on the Apple roof on January 30, 1969. At the lunchtime performance, the group—augmented by Billy Preston on organ on the point of breaking up, generated little warmth and perfunctorily ran through the songs that formed the bulk of their last album, also called *Let It Be*. After 40 minutes, the show was broken up by cops because of complaints of noise from nearby office workers, and at the end John Lennon deadpanned, "I'd like to thank you on behalf of the group and myself and I hope we passed the audition," a sarcastic reference to the Beatles' failed audition for Decca Records in 1962. Lennon went back on the roof that April to announce formally that he had changed his middle name from Winston to Ono.

In July 1968 the group's Apple organization had moved from its original Wigmore Street base to this large Georgian house. Ringo used a photo of the door for the front cover of his 1976 album, *Rotogravure*. Soon afterward, the graffiti'd door was shipped out to Lennon and Yoko Ono to furnish their New York apartment. Apple moved out in 1972. *3 Savile Row. Oxford Circus tube.*

JIMI HENDRIX ADDRESS

When he came back to England in late 1968 after a long U.S. tour, Hendrix and his girlfriend Kathy Etchingham ("My Yoko Ono from Chester" as he called her) lived in an apartment in this fairly ordinary Georgian house. The guitarist was then at the peak of his career, the star turn jamming at late night parties in clubs like the Speakeasy. This stretch of Brook Street is currently being redeveloped, and a row has broken out between fans of Hendrix and those of George Frideric Handel (1685–1759), who lived next door at No. 25. Hendrix backers want a blue commemorative plaque placed outside No. 23, but the Handel House Trust wants to build a museum that would cover both houses and snootily deem that a plaque to Jimi would be inappropriate. When told that Handel had lived next door, Hendrix had said, "I haven't heard much of the guy's stuff, but I dig a bit of Bach now and again." *23 Brook St. Oxford Circus tube*

SOTHEBY'S

Many rock mementoes have been traded for multifigure sums at Sotheby's, London's most prestigious auction house. Much of the memorabilia has been Beatle associated. The record sum to date was £161,000 in 1996 for Paul McCartney's handwritten lyrics to "Getting Better," scrawled on Roundhouse notepaper. This beat the previous best for a rock artifact, also set for Beatles lyrics, for "A Day in the Life," which went for £48,000 in 1992. Scenes from the Ringo Starr/Peter Sellers movie *The Magic Christian* were filmed here. *34–35 New Bond St., tel. 0171/493–8080. Bond St. tube.*

WESTBURY HOTEL

Jerry Lee Lewis was staying in this just-built hotel in May 1958 when news broke that his 13-year-old female companion, Myra, was not just his cousin but his wife. After a hostile press reaction led by the *Daily Mirror,* Lewis was forced to leave Britain and abandon the rest of what was his first British tour. A double room now costs £200 a night; a honeymoon suite more than twice that amount. *Conduit St. at New Bond St., tel. 0171/629–7755. Oxford Circus tube.*

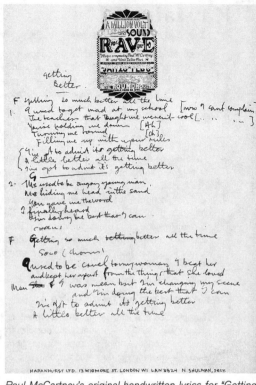

Paul McCartney's original handwritten lyrics for "Getting Better," 1967

ZIGGY STARDUST COVER

The old-style red telephone kiosk on the back cover of David Bowie's *The Rise and Fall of Ziggy Stardust and the Spiders from Mars* is no longer here. It was removed in the late '70s, sold at auction, and replaced by a tasteless open-air stand-up metal model. But this hasn't stopped hundreds of mostly Continental Bowie fans from daubing the surrounding walls with barely legible graffiti—lots of "love on ya"s and Aladdin and Ziggy logos. The phone booth is at the northwestern end of this horseshoe-shape street. *Heddon St. Piccadilly Circus tube.*

Mayfair–Park Lane and Around Grosvenor Square

Park Lane, a divided highway that is part of the main north–south route from the M1 to the south side of the Thames, is often one of London's most snarled-up thoroughfares. On one side is Hyde Park; on the other stand some of the most expensive hotels and properties in Europe. To the east on Piccadilly is the original branch of the Hard Rock Cafe.

AMERICAN EMBASSY

Mick Jagger attended what turned out to be a violent anti-Vietnam War demonstration here in May 1968 when police on horseback weighed into the crowd. The event (at

The Who visiting the Hard Rock Cafe, 1990s

which Malcolm McLaren claims to have burned Old Glory) inspired Jagger to write "Street Fighting Man," which was banned by many U.S. radio stations, who felt that it might incite violence. *24–31 Grosvenor Sq., tel. 0171/499–9000. Bond St. tube.*

BEATLES ADDRESS, 1963–64

The only time all four Beatles lived together was from fall 1963 to spring '64 in this five-story Victorian villa. *Flat L, 57 Green St. Marble Arch tube.*

[HARD ROCK CAFE]

In June 1971 two young Americans—Isaac Tigrett and Peter Morton—fed up with being unable to get a decent burger in London, decided to open their own place. They decked the joint out with rock memorabilia and advertised for "matronly women" in their forties and fifties to capture that essential diner atmosphere. After almost three decades, the Hard Rock (now part of the Rank Organization, with recent operating profits of $02 million) has more than 60 branches worldwide. Inside this original branch are some 300 items of rock history—plenty of Beatles, Rolling Stones, Hendrix, and Zeppelin mementoes. Legend has it that the Harley Davidson was ridden into the café and left there by Keith Moon. Although the over-touristy feel may be off-putting, the Hard Rock still has the best burgers in the city. Vegetarians have to make do with burgers from a recipe by (who else but) Linda McCartney. *150 Old Park La, tel. 0171/629–0382. Hyde Park Corner tube.*

HMV (ORIGINAL STORE)

Now claiming to be the largest music retailer in the world, HMV opened its empire in style in July 1921, with British composer Edward Elgar cutting the ribbon. Back then, the store sold mostly sheet music, though it had a few wind-up gramophones in stock and some 78 rpm discs to play on the new-fangled machines. As the amount of recorded material available grew, the store continued to thrive. In 1962 Brian Epstein walked in with a demo of a band he was managing but for whom he was having trouble getting a recording deal. HMV buyers put him in touch with George Martin at Parlophone, and within a few weeks the Beatles-led pop revolution was beginning to happen for real. Though most in-store performances happen at the larger 150 Oxford Street branch (see Oxford Street in Soho, below), this store has had a few rooftop gigs: Echo and the Bunnymen played in July 1987 and Blur stopped traffic with a 20-minute set in September 1995. *363 Oxford St., tel. 0171/629–1240. Bond St. tube.*

One of the first neon signs in the U.K.: HMV at 363 Oxford Street, 1920s

LONDON HILTON ON PARK LANE

The Beatles first heard the Maharishi Mahesh Yogi lecture on transcendental meditation in this 30-story hotel, famed for its rooftop restaurant, in August 1967.

Elvis Costello busked outside on the pavement during a CBS conference in July 1977. He was arrested and fined £5 for obstruction, but CBS signed him up later in the year. In the late '80s, the Beastie Boys were said to have drilled a hole through the floor here so they could reach the room below; they received a worldwide ban from the chain for their efforts. Rooms are £200-plus per night. *22 Park La., tel. 0171/493–8000. Hyde Park Corner tube.*

KEITH MOON/MAMA CASS DEATH SITE

Two rock deaths occurred here. Mama Cass Elliott of the Mamas and Papas choked on a sandwich and died of swallowing vomit on July 29, 1974. On September 7, 1978, Keith Moon overdosed on pills that had been prescribed to cure his alcoholism. A few hours beforehand, Moon had told his girlfriend that if she didn't want to cook him any more meals, she could "fuck off!" Apparently he cooked himself a steak breakfast, gobbled some pills, and did just that. *Flat 12, 9 Curzon Pl. Hyde Park Corner tube.*

VIRGIN—MARBLE ARCH BRANCH

Most of Virgin's central London in-store appearances take place at the megastore, but recent visitors to this branch have been the Black Crowes, Grant Lee Buffalo, Terrorvision, and Tori Amos. Evan Dando of the Lemonheads joined Oasis here for an impromptu acoustic gig in August 1994, when the Manchester band premiered the "Whatever" single. Dando, whose songwriting ability was beyond dispute at the time, would seem to have been a welcome guest in any emerging band, but the Gallaghers seemed to disapprove of the uninvited American, giving the xenophobic elements of the music press an excuse to boost Britpop. *527 Oxford St., tel. 0171/491–8582. Marble Arch tube.*

Soho, Mostly W1

I met her in a club down in old Soho—The Kinks, "Lola"

Unlike the geographical derivation of its namesake in New York, the name Soho comes from an old hunting cry dating back to a time when this square mile of 24/7 activity was prime hunting land. The area has no formal boundaries, but the four tube stations of Tottenham Court Road, Leicester Square, Piccadilly Circus, and Oxford Circus are generally considered to form its four corners.

For most of this century Soho been the most exciting nighttime area in London. When youth culture took a real grip in the '50s, dozens of coffee bars (of which Bar Italia is the best remaining example) with their steaming espresso machines cropped up alongside cellar bars and smoky jazz dives. Today it buzzes with pubs, trendy bars, cafés, brasseries, restaurants, jazz clubs, Chinese eateries, discos, coffee bars, strip clubs, members-only clubs, exclusive small hotels, major movie houses, and theaters, not to mention some of the best specialty stores in the city, including some dozen or so great record retailers. The range of music venues remains pretty good, from the Astoria, which holds 2,000 and puts on touring rock bands, to little dives like the 100 Club and the jazz magnet Ronnie Scott's.

Soho's clubs have been at the center of every new rock trend, from the first British rock & rollers at the 2i's coffee bar in 1956 through the folk revivalists in tiny basement bars and psychedelic undergrounders of the '60s at the world-famous Marquee. The punk scene exploded out of the 100 Club and the turn of the '70s saw the New Romantic movement boom at several hangouts on Greek Street. The '90s brought the easy-listening craze centered around Madame Jo Jo's, and though Camden Town stole much of the credit, Britpop sounds were played here in clubs like Smashing and the Wag.

Soho also has sex shops aplenty and horrible smelly unlicensed clubs that induce gullible foreign businessmen and out-of-town soccer fans to see a mild strip show and pay hundreds of pounds for the privilege of drinking nonalcoholic cocktails. If people start fussing about the rip-off charges, very burly and persuasive customer service staff make sure the bill is paid in full.

Soho, or to be precise Old Compton Street, also sees the most visible expression of London's gay community, with all-night cafés and other gay-owned businesses. Even more colorful is Chinatown, fanning out from Gerrard Street, which has cafés and restaurants to satisfy everyone from Chinese workers to expense-account business people and tourists. Soho has been home to literary and bohemian types for centuries and, despite all the bright lights and office space, is still a residential area with a good community feel. And of course there's the fashion element, though Carnaby Street is a sad little shadow of its mid-'60s heyday.

EATING DRINKING DANCING SHOPPING PLAYING SLEEPING

THE LONDON WALKS COMPANY (tel. 0171/624–3978) runs two walking tours through Soho that deal with rock. The *Beatles Magical Mystery Tour* meets outside the Tottenham Court Road tube (entrance next to the Dominion Theatre) on Thursday and Sunday at 11 AM. It's led by the president of the London Beatles Fan Club, as is the *Swinging '60s Pub Walk*, which sets off from the same spot on Wednesdays at 7 PM. Tours last around 2¼ hours and cost £4.50 (£3.50 for students).

Soho Songs

Booker T and the MGs, "Carnaby Street" (1967)
Al Stewart, "Old Compton Street Blues" (1969)
Jethro Tull, "Jeffrey Goes to Leicester Square" (1969)
Al Stewart, "Soho (Needless to Say)" (1973)
The Jam, "Carnaby Street" (1977)
The Jam, "A Bomb in Wardour Street" (1978)
Television Personalities, "Oxford Street W1" (1978)
Secret Affair, "Soho Strut" (1979)
The Ruts, "West One (Shine on Me)" (1980)
Phil Lynott, "Solo in Soho" (1980)
Stiff Little Fingers, "Piccadilly Circus" (1981)
Squeeze, "Piccadilly" (1981)

The Pogues, "A Rainy Night in Soho" (1986)
Everything But the Girl, "Oxford Street" (1988)
Morrissey, "Piccadilly Palare" (1990)

Soho can be explored on a wandering tour running more or less west–east from Carnaby Street to Leicester Square, then up Charing Cross Road, and along Oxford Street westward back to Carnaby Street.

Soho–Carnaby Street and Around

Everywhere the Carnaby-tion army marches on—The Kinks, "Dedicated Follower of Fashion"

Now a sad little anachronism, Carnaby Street was *the* symbol of mid-'60s Swinging London. During the '50s it was just one of plenty of Soho side streets full of clothing sweatshops with a couple of small stores selling flamboyant clothes to the gay and theatrical communities. Then in 1959 along came John Stephens, who set up the **His Clothes** store at 41 Carnaby (now a Cobra sports clothes branch) and sold gear that was outrageous for the time to young men keen to ape the rock & roll style introduced by America. By the mid-'60s, anyone who was anyone shopped here or just hung out to get a glimpse of the big-spending mod stars. Soon, numbers of boutiques opened and quantity replaced quality. The Kinks' "Dedicated Follower of Fashion" satirized the bandwagon nature of the scene in 1966.

Several important rock types had offices on the street in its heyday. Don Arden signed the Small Faces to a shackling management contract here that allowed them a £20-per-week salary and an account for clothes at every boutique on the street. It was not a happy liaison. Arden had a heavy reputation—one of his minders once dangled a young Robert Stigwood out of a 4th-floor window to get him to tear up his contract with the band.

Chris Stamp and Kit Lambert, managers of the Who, set up Track Records on Carnaby to establish tighter control of the band's product. Their first big success was not with Townshend and company but with new boy in town Jimi Hendrix, whom Lambert signed on the spot after seeing him at Westminster's Scotch of St. James club in September 1966. The label's first release was Hendrix's "Purple Haze" in March 1967. Along with albums by the Who and Arthur Brown, it made Track one of the most important U.K. labels for alternative acts until Island came along.

Gross commercialism killed off the Carnaby scene within a couple of years, but the street had a brief revival as a hangout zone during the post-punk days. The modish Jam named a B-side "Carnaby Street" and were photographed here for the cover of the later "News of the World" single. These days, it's just a cheesy pedestrianized street full of cash-in (cashing in on tourist trends) stores.

EATINGDRINKINGDANCINGSHOPPINGPLAYINGSLEEPING

Since opening in 1993, the **Ain't Nothin' But Blues Bar** (20 Kingly St., tel. 0171/287–0514) has put on all styles of that genre seven nights a week in a cozy juke-joint setting. Club nights at the swanky **Hanover Grand** (6 Hanover St., tel. 0171/499–7997 or 0171/629–0049) have of late attracted soap opera stars, footballers, and sundry B-list celebrities. **Eve's** (189 Regent St., W1, tel. 0171/734–4252) was one of the hottest Britpop hangouts in 1995. **Voltaro** (11 Kingly St.) ranks as one of London's best greasy spoons; Shane McGowan reminisced about "a fried egg in Voltaro's" on the Pogues' "Transmetropolitan."

Keith Richards and friend outside the courthouse after he was charged with drug and weapons possession

BAG O' NAILS (MIRANDA CLUB)

John Gunnell, manager of Georgie Fame, Chris Farlowe, Geno Washington, and others, opened this small basement club with its tiny dance space in November 1966. It became one of the elite joints of the swinging '60s and only let the right people in. The Beatles and the Stones hung here, as did Jimi Hendrix; one of the best-remembered impromptu jams teamed Stevie Wonder, Mick Jagger, and Eric Clapton. Paul McCartney met Linda Eastman for the first time here in May 1967 at a Georgie Fame gig, and John McVie proposed to Christine Perfect here. It is now the Miranda Club—"Private. Members Only." *9 Kingly St. Oxford Circus tube.*

GREAT MARLBOROUGH STREET MAGISTRATES' COURT

The Rolling Stones had various encounters with this court at the top end of Carnaby Street. Brian Jones made a 10-minute appearance in May 1967, along with his noble Swiss friend Prince Stanislas Klossowski de Rola, after 11 items were taken away from his flat for examination. He was back a year later for possessing cannabis and was bailed for £2,000 before attending trial at the Inner London Sessions court.

In December 1969, Jagger and Faithfull were called here for having some pot. He was fined £200; she was acquitted. In October 1973, it was Keith's turn: a £200 fine for four drug and three firearm offenses, a relatively light punishment, probably because the police had crassly tried to stick a charge of possession of an antique shotgun on him as well. Another rock star called before the bench here was Johnny Rotten, in March 1977, who was fined £40 for possessing amphetamine sulphate, the defining punk accessory. *20 Great Marlborough St. Oxford Circus tube.*

PALLADIUM THEATRE

Britain's favorite live television variety show of the '60s and '70s, *Sunday Night at the London Palladium*, as well as having old-hat comedians and raconteurs, presented some of the biggest new bands of the day. The Beatles' performance on the show on October 13, 1963, saw them adopted as media darlings in the next day's papers. The Rolling Stones were less loved when they broke the tradition of getting up on the revolving stage to wave at the audience in January 1967.

Back in the '30s, 10-year-old Ahmet Ertegun saw Cab Calloway and Duke Ellington at the Palladium. These days, the staple fare is musicals such as *Oliver!*, but in between shows rock gigs do take place. Some of the more notable gigs over the years include Marvin Gaye in 1977, when he cut his *Live at the London Palladium* album; Kate Bush, who did a five-night run in 1979; the Smiths (a photo of Morrissey onstage here is on the cover of his debut single, "Suedehead"), Tori Amos, whose 1994 show was heavily bootlegged; and a variety performance the same year for the Stonewall gay rights group that had the Pet Shop Boys headlining. *7 Argyll St., tel. 0171/494–5020. Oxford Circus tube.*

Soho–Piccadilly Circus

And a foreign student said to me, was it really true, there are elephants and lions too in Piccadilly Circus?—Jethro Tull, "Mother Goose"

Neon-lit, traffic-clogged Piccadilly Circus is perhaps London's most famous meeting spot, especially for foreign visitors, who mingle under the aluminum Eros statue. Increasingly over the past few years, Piccadilly has become a pedestrian bottleneck, with parties of tourists moving in slow-motion crocodile formation. What brings them here, other than tradition, are such attractions as Sega World, the Rock Circus (more on that below), and theme restaurants in the London Pavilion and Trocadero developments.

Piccadilly is also the center of the city's rent-boy (homosexual prostitute) trade, which is touched on in a couple of songs: Morrissey's "Piccadilly Palare" is about gay cruising in the '50s, when local homosexuals spoke in "polari," a slang they used to size up likely clients, while in the Pogues' "Old Main Drag," an impressionable 16-year-old comes to London for the bright lights and ends up as a rent boy, going "down to the 'dilly to check out the scene."

In June 1967, 300 hippies staged an all-night vigil in support of busted Rolling Stones Mick Jagger and Keith Richards after a march from the UFO club on Tottenham Court Road, close to a mile north.

THE CAFÉ ROYAL

This hangout, recently refitted, was where David Bowie chose to have his celebrity-infested Ziggy Stardust "retirement" party in July 1973 after he killed the character off at the Hammersmith Odeon (*see* Hammersmith *in* Outer London, *below*). Among the hundreds of guests were the Jaggers, the McCartneys, the inevitably drunk Keith Moon, Barbra Streisand, and Lou Reed. The Royal occasionally has top-drawer cabaret; in summer 1994, reflecting the boom in easy-listening clubs throughout the city, Jimmy Webb (writer of such standards as "Up Up and Away" and "MacArthur Park") had a three-week residency. Ex-Animal Alan Price did an 11-night run during the 1996 Soho Jazz Festival. *68 Regent St., tel. 0171/437–9090. Piccadilly Circus tube.*

Courtesy of The Café Royal

The Three Degrees at the Café Royal

ROCK CIRCUS

This spin-off from Madame Tussaud's Waxworks Museum opened in 1989. The £7.50 admission would be better spent on something at Tower across the way. The place, however, is on the site of a movie house where the world premieres of *A Hard Day's Night*,

Help!, and *Yellow Submarine,* all of which the Beatles attended, were held. The movie theater closed in the early '80s; the facade was retained and the inside rebuilt in 1989 as the Trocadero, which, besides the Rock Circus, has other stores and attractions, including the '50s-style Rock Island Diner, with singing and dancing wait staff. *London Pavilion, 1 Piccadilly Circus, tel. 0171/734–8025. Piccadilly Circus tube.*

TOWER RECORDS

The major U.S. retail record store opened up in this three-story landmark location in 1986. It stays open to the reasonable hour of midnight six days a week, and although it doesn't have as much space as the HMV and Virgin stores on Oxford Street, it does stock a better range of import mags and fanzines and is very strong in the alternative and roots departments. Performances by Luciano Pavarotti and Bon Jovi, both in 1990, made so much noise and caused such long lines outside that distracted drivers caused wrecks. When Mariah Carey came for a signing, the divine Ms. C had a rider that stipulated that every place with which she came in contact had to be specially painted pink. *1 Piccadilly Circus, tel. 0171/439–2500. Piccadilly Circus tube.*

Soho–Around Berwick Street

The stretch around Berwick Street between Carnaby and Wardour streets is the center of London's sex industry, with strip clubs, porn mag shops, illegal drinking clubs, and hidden-away brothels, especially around Walker's Court. *The Wire* magazine, the excellent monthly round-up of new and experimental music, is based at 45 Poland Street.

EATING DRINKING DANCING SHOPPING PLAYING SLEEPING

These streets have a few specialty record stores selling the latest club sounds. **BLACK MARKET RECORDS** (25 D'Arblay St., tel. 0171/437–0478), with its stylish metallic interior, prides itself on getting import techno and house sounds fastest and has built up a clientele of top DJs. **MR. BONGO** (44 Poland St., tel. 0171/287–1887) has funk, jazz, and hip-hop; upstairs offers one of the city's widest ranges of Latin sounds. **SOUL JAZZ RECORDS** (12 Ingestre Pl., tel. 0171/494–2004), just south of Poland Street, sells what its name suggests. **THE VINTAGE MAGAZINE SHOP** (39 Brewer St., tel. 0171/439–8525) stocks mostly movie mags but also has some good rock posters, T-shirts, and back issues.

MADAME JO JO'S

Set up in 1985 for a still-thriving drag cabaret that takes place Thursday through Saturday, the club became famous in the indie world when Count Indigo and Felchy B. Hawkes produced their Indigo club night of kitsch easy-listening sounds from 1994 to '96. Tony Bennett, riding a wave of popularity that started when he appeared on the American MTV Awards with the Red Hot Chili Peppers, played a "secret" show here after his run at the Palladium in 1995. The following June, the scene's number-one icon, Burt Bacharach (whose image appears

Courtesy of Madame Jo Jo's Cabaret Club

Girls at Madame Jo Jo's

on the front of Oasis's *Definitely Maybe*), did a similar show. Indigo is on Tuesdays; on Wednesdays is a more recent Britpop night called It. *8–10 Brewer St., tel. 0171/734–2473. Piccadilly Circus tube.*

SCENE CLUB

So many tickets down the Scene, honey, they'll likely blow a fuse—The High Numbers, "I'm the Face"

In the early '60s the Piccadilly Jazz Club changed hands and became the Scene, a mod hangout co-owned by Ronan O'Rahilly, who managed Alexis Korner's Blues Incorporated and founded Radio Caroline. One of the DJs was Guy Stevens, who also ran Sue Records, which released rare R&B classics that would probably have been otherwise unheard in Britain. Stevens later went on to produce albums by Mott the Hoople, the Clash, and others. The Who played here when they were still known as the High Numbers, but today the site is a parking lot. *Ham Yard, 41 Great Windmill St. Oxford Circus tube.*

(WHAT'S THE STORY) MORNING GLORY?—RECORD STORES OF BERWICK STREET

For decades Berwick Street has been home to some of the city's best record vendors. Oasis chose wisely when they used it for the cover of their second album *(What's the Story) Morning Glory?* to signify that they had left behind the parochial stage of Manchester and were now a truly national band. The area is not as quiet as the Oasis shots might suggest: As well as music blasting from the doorways of the record stores, the sounds of central London's busiest fresh produce street market fill Berwick Street. On the back of the lyric sheet is another photo taken near the junction of Berwick Street and Noel Street—there are no Liam Streets or Bonehead Roads in London.

AMBIENT SOHO. All sorts of electronic and dubby spacey sounds blast into trip-hippie decor. *4 Berwick St., no phone. Tottenham Court Rd. tube.*

DADDY KOOL. A much-respected store going since the mid-'70s stocks everything from traditional roots reggae and ska to the latest ragga club sounds. It has great stock, lots of vinyl, and a used section, too. *12 Berwick St., tel. 0171/494–1081. Tottenham Court Rd. tube.*

RECKLESS RECORDS. Entirely used stock of all genres, great turnover, and reasonable prices make this store (with branches in Islington and San Francisco) an essential visit. It's especially good on indie. *30 Berwick St., tel. 0171/437–4271. Tottenham Court Rd. tube.*

MR CD. The tiny store sells only CDs, with current releases for just £10—up to an incredible £5 less than the big record stores. The small drawbacks are that the discs are chaotically racked and the store is always packed with bargain hunters. *80 Berwick St., tel. 0171/439–1097. Tottenham Court Rd. tube.*

MUSIC & VIDEO EXCHANGE. A branch of the used-sounds empire that started off in Notting Hill, it stocks quite a bit of vinyl. *95 Berwick St., tel. 0171/434–2939.*

SELECTADISC. This is the store on the left side of the Oasis *(What's the Story) Morning Glory?* cover. It has an excellent stock of new and old CDs, an interesting selection of hard-to-find vinyl, and some fanzines. *34 Berwick St., tel. 0171/734–3297.*

SISTER RAY. It's good for the latest indie imports and dance sounds, plus some great old punk recordings. *94 Berwick St., tel. 0171/287–8385.*

Soho–Wardour Street

I found you shopping in Europa/On Wardour Street—Underworld, "stagger"

Wardour does have a serious claim on being one of the most important streets in London's rock history thanks to clubs like the now-gone Marquee and Vortex, the grand old St. Moritz, and the still-surviving Wag (all detailed below). Pete Townshend lived on the street in the late '60s at No. 87.

FLAMINGO CLUB (O'NEILL'S PUB)

Opened at the start of the '60s, this basement dive played heavy jazz and R&B sounds that appealed to both a predominantly black audience and the burgeoning mod movement. Georgie Fame and the Blue Flames (with John McLaughlin on guitar) were the house band in the early days, followed by Zoot Money's Big Roll Band (with Andy Summers, later of the Police, on guitar). It was also in this heavy, often violent atmosphere that Simon & Garfunkel made their first U.K. appearance in summer 1964. The club is currently the basement bar of yet another Irish theme pub, but the upstairs Wag Club (*see below*) is still going strong. *35 Wardour St. Piccadilly Circus tube.*

THE INTREPID FOX

This loud, dark bar with rock posters on the wall and a good varied jukebox has provided a watering hole for Metallica and hundreds of other visiting rockers and Soho regulars alike. It has a deliberate gothy feel, with metal gargoyles over the bar and the windows blacked out in the upstairs room. *99 Wardour St., tel. 0171/ 287–8359. Piccadilly Circus tube.*

LA CHASE (MEZZO)

An upstairs drinking club in the '60s, La Chase was where Yes was conceived in June 1968. Vocalist Jon Anderson, a barman, met drinker and bassist Chris Squire and decided on a lineup of Tony Kaye on keyboards, Bill Bruford on drums, and Peter Banks on guitar. Now the Mezzo, a jazz bar with some live stuff, it's part of Terence Conran's development. *100 Wardour St., tel. 0171/314–4000. Tottenham Court Rd. tube.*

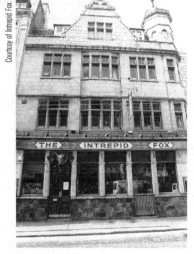

The Intrepid Fox, 1997

MARQUEE, 1964–88

For more than 20 years this claustrophobic dive was London's most prestigious rock venue, helping break the Yardbirds, the Who, David Bowie, Pink Floyd, Led Zeppelin, Yes, Genesis, the Police, the Sex Pistols, and even Guns N' Roses. The Marquee moved from its original Oxford Street site (*see* Oxford Street, *below*) into this former warehouse on March 13, 1964. It started off catering to the mod/R&B scene. In fall 1964 the Who had a Tuesday residency called "Maximum R&B," while the Yardbirds recorded their debut album, *Five Live Yardbirds.*

By 1966 a typical week's bill might include the Move, Manfred Mann, the Spencer Davis Group, John Mayall's Bluesbreakers, the Yardbirds, the Hoochie Coochie Men (with Rod Stewart), or Bluesology (with Elton John playing piano). The club bookers, ahead of the times, started the "Spontaneous Underground" sessions on Sunday afternoons in early 1966. While musicians, poets, artists, filmmakers, and magicians performed, the audience dressed in bright, proto-psychedelic clothes and showed a fondness for drugs. Pink Floyd was the "Spontaneous Underground" house band, which made them kings of

Courtesy of A & M Records Ltd.

Police at the Marquee in 1977

the U.K. underground. Not all the Marquee management approved of a group doing 20-minute numbers to psychedelic lights, and so the Marmalade (they of "Ob-La-De-Ob-La-Da" infamy) provided support. Schoolboy Phil Collins helped put the chairs out (and a few years later was teamed up with Genesis here for the first time). Fire-loving Arthur Brown was another favorite with the underground scenesters but was too much for the girlfriend of a *Melody Maker* reviewer one night: She fainted when the lanky singer took his clothes off.

A 1966 Sunday afternoon slot went to David Bowie for his three-hour "Sunday Show-boat," at which he first began wearing full make-up and doing mime in front of about 20 people. In contrast, one of the most oversold shows took place the following year when Jimi Hendrix played his only-ever gig at the Marquee. On only their second and third U.K. gigs, Led Zeppelin, billed as the New Yardbirds, got more than a thousand in for their shows in October 1968.

Things sloped off during the early '70s, though bands such as Zeppelin and Genesis came back long after they had reached arena-filling status. The venue largely sidestepped the punk movement, but the Pistols played their seventh gig and their first at a bona fide rock venue here on February 12, 1976, opening for Eddie and the Hot Rods (who released a *Live at the Marquee* EP later in the year). The club preferred more traditional up-and-coming acts like Dire Straits, the Pretenders, and AC/DC, who had a Monday-night residency in summer 1976. Next, some new-wavers, such as the Jam, who played in 1977, crept in. The Damned, Adam and the Ants, and the Boomtown Rats were among others to play around this time.

The club's importance declined in the '80s, as there was greater competition. Visiting Americans loved to come to pay homage. Among them were ZZ Top, the Bangles, and Metallica (who made their U.K. debut here in March 1983). Guns N' Roses also chose the venue for their first gigs in England, in June 1987. They were greeted with a head-line in the tabloid *Daily Star* that read "A Band Even Nastier Than the Beastie Boys Is Heading for Britain!" In 1988 the club moved on to its third location at Charing Cross Road (*see* Soho—Charing Cross Road, *below*). The building is now owned by the Manhattan Loft Corporation. *90 Wardour St. Tottenham Court Rd. tube.*

ROUNDHOUSE PUB (O-BAR)

The London Skiffle Centre started out in a room above the pub (not to be confused with the Roundhouse venue in Camden) in 1952. Under the direction of Alexis Korner and other British R&B pioneers, it segued into the Blues and Barrelhouse Club a couple of years later, getting in Muddy Waters, Big Bill Broonzy, and other respected names from the United States. By the early '60s it was changing with the times and had become an R&B club and the home venue of Blues Incorporated, the first big-name R&B band in Britain, featuring Korner, Cyril Davies, and an ever-changing roster of others, including drummer Charlie Watts and later some of the other future Rolling Stones. Nowadays, the place has been yuppified as the trendy O-Bar, with cocktails aplenty, funk music, and lines outside. *83 Wardour St., tel. 0171/437-3490.*

ST. MORITZ CLUB

The St. Moritz Club and its sibling restaurant of the same name, which still serve the national Swiss staples of cheese and meat dishes, were opened in 1960 as hangouts for the city's Swiss community by Armin "Mr. Sweety" Loetscher. There's been live music on the club's incredibly cramped little stage since the beginning. Among the bands who played in the '60s were the Kinks, Episode Six (with Roger Glover and Ian Gillan in pre-Deep Purple days), and the Sweet.

The '70s saw Joe Strummer's band, the 101ers, onstage and propping up the bar on several occasions when the club had punk disco nights. The bondage brigade were followed by the New Romantics, who had a club night here in the early '80s. The rest of the decade saw heavy-drinking metallurgists, including Lemmy of Motörhead, and many visiting U.S. bands, who came in after playing the Marquee—but not Slash of Guns N' Roses, who was barred and kicked in a window in protest.

These days, the cozy, cavernlike club room still rocks most nights of the week to a range of sounds from drum & bass to good-time R&B. Thursday nights is "Gaz's Rockin' Blues," a mix of ska, dub, blues, rockabilly, and a live set presented by Gaz Mayall, son of British blues veteran John. The junior Mayall started the club night back in 1980, and it moved here in 1995 after many successful years at what is now Gossips. *159 Wardour St., tel. 0171/734-0525. Tottenham Court Rd. tube.*

VORTEX (VOGUE)

I'm stranded on the Vortex floor—The Jam, "A Bomb in Wardour Street"

Out of the ashes of the soulboy Crackers disco, the Vortex started as a Monday night club on July 4, 1977, with a night featuring Manchester punk bands. The Buzzcocks headlined; also on the bill were John Cooper Clark and the Fall, making their first London appearance. Throughout the summer the Vortex Monday night shows headlined Siouxsie and the Banshees, the Slits, Steel Pulse, and Wayne County, among others.

The club soon built up enough momentum to spread to other nights of the week and open 24 hours so the young suburban punks did not have to cope with the capital's transport vagaries. On September 23, 1977, bands were scheduled to play both in the club and on the street for the benefit of camera crews. Sham 69 drew the straw of playing outdoors; they thought arrest was less likely if they played on the roof of the adjoining building rather than on the sidewalk. Unfortunately, after just a couple of numbers, the cops came and took them away.

At the height of the club's popularity, Keith Moon turned up in a Rolls-Royce (he had just been to see a gig by the Worst at the Marquee) and shouted at the people waiting in line that if they were real punks they would just barge in. The Vortex lasted another few months, during which time Spizz 77, the Lurkers, the Police, the U.K. Subs, and Eater played. After the Vortex, the place became Vespers, a mod revival joint; after several other name changes it became the Vogue around 1992 and now plays disco and dance music. It's not to be confused with a more cutting-edge club called Vortex in Stoke Newington. *201 Wardour St., tel. 0171/434–3084.*

THE WAG CLUB

Upstairs from The Flamingo (*see above*) was the Whisky A Go Go club, which opened in 1962 and later attempted to draw a more hip clientele with various Stones and such artists as David Bowie. It hosted Bernie Rhodes's Club Left for a while and changed its name to the Wag Club (a reference to the jovial party type rather than an abbreviation of the old name) at the start of 1982. Just before the official opening, it started one of the very first rap nights, bringing over Grand Master Flash and the Furious Five, Afrika Bambaataa and the Soul Sonic Force, and others, with the Futura 2000 crew doing hip-hop murals on the walls.

The Raincoats' Gina Birch

All this helped the Wag become one of the best-known '80s venues in the country; it soon started a celebrated rare groove night on Fridays and on Thursdays had live sets featuring Sade, the Pogues, Terence Trent D'Arby, and the Fine Young Cannibals before they all hit it big. Eclectic jazz, Chicago house, and the best London DJs, including Mark Moore of S'Express and the M/A/R/R/S crew appeared.

The '90s have brought with them more competition for venues of this size (it holds 500), but the Wag has kept its reputation through several club nights such as the "Leave My Wife Alone" soul club and Asian dub-hop nights that featured appearances by the likes of Apache Indian. By the end of 1996 the Wag was catering to Britpop and New Romantic fans on different nights of the week. *35 Wardour St., tel. 0171/437–5534.*

Soho–Old Compton, Dean, and Frith streets

These heaving streets are probably the liveliest in Britain, packed night and day with a highly cosmopolitan crowd. Old Compton Street has recently seen several all-night cafés open to cater to the gay community. Past residents of the area include Mozart (20 Frith St. in 1764–65), Karl Marx (28 Dean St. in the 1850s), and Wagner (52–3 Old Compton St. in 1839).

EATING DRINKING DANCING SHOPPING PLAYING SLEEPING

On and around Dean Street are numerous private members' clubs frequented by literary and journalistic types. At the **GROUCHO CLUB** (44 Dean St., tel. 0171/439–4685), pop stars of the caliber of Alex James (Blur) and Jarvis Cocker (Pulp) are permitted admission and the tales of their wacky doings get reported in *Melody Maker* ad nauseam. The best-known pub around here is the **COACH & HORSES** (29 Greek St., tel. 0171/437–5920) a bit of a bohemian haunt. **PIZZA EXPRESS** (10 Dean St., tel. 0171/437–9595) is the flagship branch of this extremely reasonably priced pizza chain started by jazz buff Peter Boizot. Downstairs is a cozy basement that, thanks to the owner's contacts, puts on big-name jazz. Mose Allison plays regularly, and in August 1996 Van Morrison joined him on the tiny stage. This is one of the main venues for the **SOHO JAZZ FESTIVAL,** which has now been going since 1986 each late September/early October in local pubs, clubs, restaurants, and sometimes bigger halls. Trad jazz is the mainstay; don't expect too much freeform experimental stuff.

Dire Straits mention two Soho landmarks on the "Wild West End" track off their self-titled debut album: The classy, old-fashioned **ANGELUCCI COFFEE MERCHANTS** (23b Frith St., tel. 0171/437–5889) is where Knopfler stepped out for some coffee beans. **THE BAROCCO BAR** (13 Moor St., tel. 0171/437–2324) was where the waitress watched him crossing the road. The Pogues, on "London Girl," mention the cheapo Italian restaurant **CENTRALE** (16 Moor St.).

BAR ITALIA

It opened in 1949, and the decor style is still in place. This 24-hour Italian bar gets trendies sipping cappuccino on the sidewalk during the day and garrulous post-clubbers during the early hours. Just about everyone who has been famous has stepped into this long, narrow room with its mirrors, huge TV screen, and predictable photo of an Italian hero (in this case, Rocky Marciano, who actually made a visit). Such a place could not go unnoticed to those commentators on British life, Pulp, who closed their 1995 album *Common People* with a track called "Bar Italia." More important to popular culture is the fact that in 1926 John Logie Baird first unveiled his new invention—the television—to fellow scientists in the attic here. There's a blue plaque on the outside wall to mark it. *22 Frith St., tel. 0171/437–4520. Leicester Square tube.*

BILLY'S (GOSSIP'S)

When this venue was known as Gargoyle's, it hosted several important club nights, not to mention Noel Coward and Francis Bacon doing their things here in the '30s and '50s respectively. In 1978 Steve Strange (later a member of Visage and boss of the Camden Palace venture) and Rusty Egan ran a successful night playing Bowie and Roxy Music records that more or less created the New Romantic scene in London. After that, Perry "What Is Funk?" Haines's "i-D" night attracted a similar posse of posers. Around this time the place also hosted the "Comedy Store," which did much for the re-emergence of stand-up comedy.

On Wednesdays in 1982 and 1983 the "Batcave" night played gothic punk by Siouxsie and the Banshees, Bauhaus, and so on. Alien Sex Fiend was one of the most prominent bands to come out of this particular scene. The longest-running night of all was Gaz Mayall's "Gaz's Rockin Blues," which started in 1980 when he was 22 years old and continued until 1995, when the club became Gossip's and no longer put on live music. Mayall now has his weekly night at the St. Moritz (*see above*). *69 Dean St., tel. 0171/434–4480. Tottenham Court Rd. tube.*

RONNIE SCOTT'S

Britain's most famous jazz club has been running since 1959, when it opened at nearby 39 Gerrard Street (now a Chinese restaurant) before settling here six years later. Oscar Peterson, Count Basie, Chick Corea, and Sarah Vaughan have all played this cramped little

Sarah Vaughan at Ronnie Scott's

club, but occasionally some rockers have hosted special events. The Who premiered *Tommy* for the rock press here in May 1969; just over a year later, Jimi Hendrix jammed here the night before he died—his last public performance—with Eric Burdon and War.

Van Morrison also chose the venue to do a special preview of his *Avalon Sunset* LP before a selected media crowd in June 1989. Half an hour before the gig, he decided to go shopping and kept the hacks waiting. Eventually, when he did decide to come on, Morrison enthusiastically delivered his new collection of songs for precisely 30 minutes, at which point he stopped in midsong, told the band to cease playing, looked at his watch, and announced, "It's half past seven, so it is," and headed off without another word.

In 1992 the Lemonheads did a free lunchtime show to coincide with the release of *It's a Shame About Ray*; the line stretched the whole way down Frith Street. *47 Frith St, tel. 0171/439–0747. Leicester Square tube.*

TRIDENT STUDIOS (SOUND STUDIO)

The Beatles didn't record the *Abbey Road* LP solely at Abbey Road Studios. "I Want You (She's So Heavy)" was done at this then state-of-the-art studio in the heart of Soho café land. The group had also done a number of tracks for *The White Album* here, including "Dear Prudence" and "Martha My Dear." David Bowie's "Space Oddity" single was also cut here, as was the Genesis album *Nursery Cryme*. The place, now called the Sound Studio, deals with TV and movie production. *17 St. Anne's Ct, tel. 0171/734–6198. Tottenham Court Rd. tube.*

2i'S COFFEE BAR

Often cited as the birthplace of British rock & roll, this coffee bar opened in 1956 in the heart of Soho. Owned by the Irani brothers (hence the two *i*s), the basement bar started putting on skiffle bands with 200-plus people cramming into a space where passive smoking alerts would kick in with 50. During this decade Tommy Steele, Cliff Richard, and Vince Taylor, whose band wore leather jackets and whose song "Brand New Cadillac" was covered by the Clash, performed here. Taylor himself was the model for David Bowie's Ziggy Stardust character. Just starting out at the time was 14-year-old Paul Gadd (later Paul Raven, later still Gary Glitter), who pestered the manager enough to let him do three numbers one night. Man mountain ex-wrestler Peter Grant worked the door here before getting into management with Led Zeppelin, and Marc Bolan served coffee after school; Ritchie Blackmore played in the house band at the start of the '60s. The place has gone through a multitude of name changes since then. It's currently a café-bar in the Dome chain; every time there's a new owner, aficionados of early British pop try to get them to preserve the basement as some sort of shrine. *59 Old Compton St, tel. 0171/287–0770. Leicester Square tube.*

Soho–Greek Street and Soho Square

Home of some of the area's priciest restaurants, Greek Street runs north from Shaftesbury Avenue into Soho Square, a sweet little park surrounded by the offices of film, book, and music companies. A couple of past residents of the street are Giovanni Giacomo Casanova, who lived here in the 1760s, and Thomas De Quincey, who described his life in *Confessions of an English Opium Eater* and had a place here in the mid-19th century.

GAY HUSSAR

An old-school Hungarian restaurant with wood paneling and red velvet upholstery, the Gay Hussar has for many years been a place for leftist politicians and writers to chatter and dine. In 1969 Labour MP Tom Driberg (a signatory of the Beatles-sponsored full-page *Times* ad calling for marijuana to be legalized), Paul Foot (still one of the country's foremost journalists), Marianne Faithfull, and Mick Jagger (who around this time in the midst of the Vietnam War was making some socialist noises, had been at the big anti-war demonstration outside the American Embassy the previous year, and was contemplating a run for Parliament) had an informal discussion here about creating a new left-wing party. *2 Greek St., tel. 0171/437–0973. Tottenham Court Rd. tube.*

LE BEATE ROUTE (ECLIPSE)

An early '80s New Romantic hangout, this was where Spandau Ballet recorded "Chant No. 1 (I Don't Need This Pressure On)," a No. 3 hit in the United Kingdom, live. The lyrics even gave directions on how to get here. It's now called the Eclipse disco. *17 Greek St. Tottenham Court Rd. tube.*

MPL COMMUNICATIONS

Paul McCartney's working headquarters include a basement studio done out like the Abbey Road No. 2 recording suite: Apparently, he wanted to use it but found it booked, so he recreated it here. The former Beatle can occasionally be seen nipping out for a sandwich, accompanied at all times by a burly minder. Just a few yards north on Soho Street is the Radha Krishna Temple and restaurant, often visited by devotee George Harrison. *1 Soho Square. Tottenham Court Rd. tube.*

Soho–Leicester Square and Chinatown

One evening as I was lying down by Leicester Square/I was picked up by the coppers and kicked in the balls—The Pogues, "Old Main Drag"

Apart from the little splash of green in its center, everything about pedestrianized Leicester Square is big: big movie houses, a big (and awful) disco called the Hippodrome, and big American restaurant chains. Leicester Square is a place for star-spotting when the big names come out for movie premieres. In the '60s its clubs and restaurants were hangouts for pop celebrities, from the Beatles on down.

Just off the Square, the small Soho Market area is not as much of a musicians' hangout as it was in the '70s, when Rock On records was here. Adjacent Chinatown is more low-rent, with dozens of tiny little cafés and some posh ones for the tourists along Gerrard Street.

EATING DRINKING DANCING SHOPPING PLAYING SLEEPING

The classy **CAFÉ DE PARIS** (3 Coventry St., tel. 0171/437–2036), where the Queen had her 23rd birthday party, currently hosts a club night run by the people who made Indigo (*see* Madame Jo Jo's in Soho—Around Berwick Street, *above*) such a splash. **CHEAPO CHEAPO RECORDS** (53 Rupert St., tel. 0171/437–8272) looks good and does have loads of very cheap (for London) vinyl, but the quality of stock is poor. **STEVE'S SOUNDS** (20 Newport Ct., tel. 0171/437–4638) has been here since the mid-'70s with a large supply of cheap vinyl and CDs and some genuine bargains.

Julie Oram

NOTRE DAME HALL

For a time during the mid-'60s the downstairs room of the parish hall belonging to the Notre Dame de France church (itself a former the-

Jitterbug dancers at Notre Dame, 1997

ater built in the 1850s) was the Cavern Club. Mod bands keen to follow in the path of the Who dominated the scene. One such outfit, the Small Faces, made their debut here in summer 1965 and went down well enough to be offered a residency.

In the church itself, the Sex Pistols were filmed for a documentary slot on Janet Street Porter's *London Weekend Show* in November 1976. The following March, with the Pistols finding themselves banned by local councils up and down the country, Malcolm McLaren was able to get the nod from the church priests to put on the band's first gig of 1977. It was also the first time that Sid Vicious had played with them in public, and although the gig was announced just a few hours ahead of time, the numbers locked out were enormous. The Pop Group did a benefit—for themselves—here, after having been declared bankrupt in July 1979, the same month that the Clash previewed material here from the *London Calling* album before an audience of specially invited journalists. Also that month Wire, playing behind a wire mesh fence, recorded seven of the eight tracks that appeared on the limited edition mini-LP that accompanied *Document and Eye Witness.*

Rock gigs take place very occasionally here now; the hall hosts mostly jazz gigs, ethnic music, and private functions. *5 Leicester Pl., tel. 0171/437–5571. Leicester Square tube.*

WHITE BEAR PUB (POLAR BEAR)

Some say this is where the embryonic Rolling Stones first rehearsed in 1962. It still has music connections, but now it's a big, brash, smelly place full of jazz and reggae sounds and tourists. *30 Lisle St., tel. 0171/437–3048. Leicester Square tube.*

Soho–Charing Cross Road

Charing Cross Road is the center of the British bookselling industry. The small antiquarian stores cluster around Leicester Square tube station, while the big stores are up toward Tottenham Court Road, where there are also several musical instrument retailers.

EATINGDRINKINGDANCINGSHOPPINGPLAYINGSLEEPING

Most of London's best midsize venues are on the north side of town, but Charing Cross Road boasts the two halls at the **LONDON ASTORIA** (*see below*), as well as the **BORDERLINE** (*see below*), which manages to get some good scoops. Also around here is the **ACOUSTIC CAFÉ** (17 Manette St., tel. 0171/439–0831), licensed until 3 AM, which has blues, country, and folk.

BORDERLINE CLUB

The Borderline veers toward indie and country rock music and puts on many North American and Australasian bands making their first performances in the United Kingdom, often at record company showcases. Just one of the platinum-selling artists to make their European debut in this 275-capacity club with a low-slung ceiling and Tex-Mex effects was Counting Crows, in 1994. R.E.M. played their only British show in 1991 here as Bingo Hand Job. They were joined

Bill Janovitz at the Borderline, 1996

onstage by Billy Bragg, Robyn Hitchcock, and ex-The dBs Peter Holsapple, while Stipe showed his scintillating wit by insisting on being addressed as Reverend Bingo for the duration of the proceedings. The following February Pearl Jam played before a pre-dominantly invite-only audience when Britain was starting to warm to the grunge boom. Even though their first album had yet to be released in the United Kingdom, the line of fans outside stretched onto the main street; the band came out and gave away some Pearl Jam freebies. *Orange Yard, Manette St. just off Charing Cross Rd., tel. 0171/734–2095. Tottenham Court Rd. tube.*

CENTRAL ST. MARTIN'S COLLEGE OF ART AND DESIGN

While he was a student here, Glen Matlock managed to get his new band, the Sex Pistols, their first gig, on Thursday, November 6, 1975. Fronted by Johnny Rotten wearing a torn Pink Floyd T-shirt with the words "I hate" scrawled over it, they did mostly covers but were so awful the union's events officer pulled the plug halfway through the set. The Pistols were supporting a band called Bazooka Joe that featured Stuart Goddard. More impressed than the union official, Goddard left that band and re-emerged as Adam Ant. Other students at various points have included Nirvana (U.K.) pair Patrick Campbell-Lyons and Alex Spyropoulous, Lora Logic of X-Ray Spex, and Pulp's Jarvis Cocker, who attended at the beginning of the '90s, making a few videos, including one for the Aphex Twin. Among those drafted as models for the students to draw have been Chrissie Hynde and Sid Vicious. *107 Charing Cross Rd., tel. 0171/494–0553. Tottenham Court Rd. tube.*

LONDON ASTORIA

The busiest large venue in the city, right next to Tottenham Court Road tube station, has two halls: the London Astoria, which holds 2,000, and LA2, which holds half that number. The place started out as a jam factory and became a theater before being converted for live music and club nights in 1986. Since then, practically everyone has played here.

Nirvana played three of only four London performances here. The first, in December 1989, finished with Kurt Cobain throwing his guitar to Krist Novoselic, who batted it away with his bass, baseball-style. Nirvana also headlined in 1990 and again in November 1991, when Britain was going mad for *Nevermind.*

In March 1995, while Prince was in town playing arena shows and supervising the opening of his now-defunct store in Camden Town, he decided he would like his own London club. So, for a week, he had the Astoria converted into the Glam Slam, flying in a produc-tion team from Minneapolis to

Motörhead at the Astoria

make everything purplish. With great pre-publicity, he announced that he would play here at a special party on the final night. When he finally took to the stage it was 3 AM, the bar was closed, and most people were either bored or had gone home.

The Astoria is also where Richey Edwards of the Manic Street Preachers appeared onstage for the last time (December 1994). Two months later, he disappeared (*see* Bayswater *in* Outer London, *below*).

Other significant gigs include Radiohead's recording their *27.5.94 The London Astoria Live* longform video, and Oasis's first show at a major London venue, in August 1994. In October 1994 there was a heavily bootlegged Green Day gig. In August 1995 Metallica played one of only four shows in the world that year as a warm-up for the Monsters of Rock Festival at Donington.

Although sight lines and acoustics are fine here, it gets a thumbs down for clearing the place to run a club night with an admission charge as soon as the gig finishes. *157 Charing Cross Rd., tel. 0171/434–0403. Tottenham Court Rd. tube.*

MARQUEE, 1988–96

The club moved to its third premises in 1988, with an opening night headed by Kiss. Prodigy, the Wildhearts, S*M*A*S*H, and Biohazard were some of the top names to play before the lease ran out. By that time it seemed to be making most of its money on indie club nights and as a ticket agency. A theme pub has replaced it; by the start of 1997, the Marquee was still looking for its fourth address. *105 Charing Cross Rd., tel. 0171/437–6601. Leicester Square or Tottenham Court Rd. tube.*

Oxford Street

I've got blisters on my feet/Trying to find a friend on Oxford Street—The Jam, "Strange Town"

Oxford Street is often touted as the busiest shopping street in the world, but on this easterly stretch it's mostly chain stores or outlets that sell supposedly discount clothing to tourists. Apart from visiting two of the biggest music stores in the world (HMV and Virgin) and the historic 100 Club, it's never that pleasurable going onto its crowded sidewalks. Liam Gallagher was found in possession of a few wraps of cocaine along this street in December 1996; he later was given a caution by the police, which upset the anti-drugs lobbyist who wanted to see him jailed or, better, hanged.

AIR STUDIOS, 1975–93

Now operating out of a converted church in Hampstead, this major studio was based on the top floor of this building facing Oxford Circus. It was busy in post-punk days; some of the albums recorded here include Heaven 17's *How Men Are,* the Teardrop Explodes's *Kilimanjaro* and *Wilder,* Japan's *Tin Drum,* and the last studio album by the Jam, *The Gift.* The front cover of the Pretenders' *Learning to Crawl* LP was shot on the roof. This building is now office space. *214 Oxford St. Oxford Circus tube.*

HMV

Opened in 1986, this is what HMV claims is the world's biggest record store. HMV is certainly the best laid-out of the three big stores in the capital, and staff are helpful, considering the size of the place. The most disruptive in-store appearance was that of teen band Bros in 1988, when 5,000 fans caused traffic chaos on central London's busiest street. That same year, Prince (as he was known at the time) came to promote his *Lovesexy* album but refused to talk to anyone and signed his albums "Love God '88." Sheryl Crow, Kiss, and Pulp have appeared more recently; Michael Jackson came here to shop in 1995. *150 Oxford St., tel. 0171/631–3423. Oxford Circus tube.*

MARQUEE (ORIGINAL SITE)

The most famous venue in London rock lore, the Marquee first opened as a coffee bar and jazz club on December 5, 1958, without an alcohol license, underneath what was the Academy Cinema. In those early pre-rock-group days the regular acts were jazzers like George Melly and Chris Barber.

Billed as the "home of the new sound," it began to attract a new, wider nonjazz audience. Management started booking more R&B and gave Blues Incorporated, featuring Alexis Korner, a Thursday night residency in 1962. With the lineup in constant flux, some of the new young musicians on the London R&B scene began to turn out with the group, including Jack Bruce, Ginger Baker, Brian Jones, and Mick Jagger.

On the evening of July 12, 1962, Blues Incorporated were booked for a BBC radio session. Korner decided not to take along Jones or Jagger, so the pair hauled in a group of friends with whom they had been jamming in Soho pubs—Keith Richards, Dick Taylor (later to found the Pretty Things), Ian Stewart (the "Stu" of Led Zeppelin's "Boogie With Stu"), and Mick Avory (later of the Kinks)—and took the stage at the Marquee under the name "Brian Jones, Mick Jagger and the Rollin' Stones." When Korner found out, he fired Jagger and Jones from Blues Incorporated, but the Stones played several more times. The club moved out, taking most of the fixtures and fittings to a new site at 90 Wardour Street in March 1964. The original Marquee has now been subsumed into a branch of Abbey National Bank. *165 Oxford St. Oxford Circus tube.*

100 CLUB

Then you said we were going out, to the 100 Club—The Clash, "Deny"

This small basement club, along with New York's CBGBs one of the most celebrated venues in punk rock, has actually had relatively little to do with guitar-based sounds over the years. During World War II, it was Feldman's, Britain's only wartime jazz club, and then became the Humphrey Lyttleton Club before adopting its street
address as its name in 1963. The
deep-red downstairs room kept to
its trad jazz format at least three or
four times a week throughout the
'60s (as it still does), but some rock
bands—notably the Who and the
Animals—did play here.

It started a brief flirtation with punk
in 1976. One of the earliest shows
starred the Sex Pistols, who played
here in front of around 50 people on
March 30, 1976, and began a Tuesday night residency in May. The
Damned played their first "proper"
gig at one such night on July 6,

Jimi Tenor at the 100 Club

1976. The early Pistols gigs were known for their violent air. Much of this was contrived by the management, but on June 29, 1976, *NME* critic Nick Kent was kicked and pushed at various points throughout the night by one of the Pistols' hangers-on. When Kent asked him to stop, the guy attacked him with a bicycle chain. The assailant was Johnny Rotten's pal John Beverly, a.k.a. Simon Ritchie, already known in the Pistols camp as Sid; this incident helped him attain the handle of Sid Vicious.

In retrospect, one of the most important events in British rock history was the 100 Club Punk Festival, held over two nights on September 20 and 21, 1976. Headlining the first night were the Sex Pistols, supported by the Clash and two bands making their debuts:

Suzie (sic) and the Banshees and Subway Sect. The Banshees had only just formed out of a group of Pistols fans known as the Bromley contingent. Ex-Chelsea guitarist Marco Pirroni was the only one in the band who could actually play. As they had no drummer, Malcolm McLaren suggested Sid Vicious. The Banshees' set mostly consisted of a half-hour of guitar white noise (which allegedly was a version of "Sister Ray"), over which Suzie (as she was then known), wearing Nazi armbands and a see-through plastic rain-coat, recited the Lord's Prayer.

On the second night the Buzzcocks made their London debut, with support coming from old hands the Vibrators (an out-of-place Chris Spedding on guitar), plus the Damned and the Stinky Toys, an early French contribution to the punk scene. During the Damned's set, someone threw a beer glass, which shattered. Part of it hit a girl, who lost her eye. The police arrested Sid Vicious. He was found not guilty of the crime but was later fined for being in possession of a flick-knife. After that, 100 Club managers (like many other club owners throughout the country) were less keen to put on punk or new-wave gigs, though the Jam recorded "Sweet Soul Music" and "Back in My Arms Again" (for the B-side of "This Is the Modern World") here. To this day, the name of the 100 Club remains synonymous with English punk. When a group wants to gain kudos for an event or movement, they use the venue.

In spring 1978 the club reverted to a heavily jazz-biased program, though from time to time it hosted prestigious gigs, such as warm-up shows by the Rolling Stones in 1976 and 1982 (which also celebrated their 20th anniversary). Nowadays the club hosts jazz most nights, but rock usually has a window once a week, with BabyBird, the Dharmas, and (London) Suede among those who have played in the '90s. Caroline, the indie label that put out early recordings of Smashing Pumpkins and Hole, announced the creation of its Caroline U.K. subsidiary with a sold-out showcase gig here in May 1996, featur-ing sets from Ben Folds Five, Sincola, and Engine 88. *100 Oxford St., tel. 0171/636–0933. Tottenham Court Rd. tube.*

VIRGIN MEGASTORE

Richard Branson has been selling records here since the late '60s, when he ran a mail-order business in a room above a shoe store that was previously on part of this huge site. When the postal strike of 1970 prompted him to think about starting a retail outlet, he opened his first Virgin record store here. Since then, it's gobbled up more and more space, to the point where in June 1995 it took on the current Megastore format. The company claims that it is the biggest home entertainments store in the world, but there's so much merchandise crammed in here and so many people stocking up on CDs that it seems claustrophobic.

There's usually an in-store appearance once a week; in April 1995, when Hole played an acoustic set, an estimated 2,000 fans and just plain curious people locked outside caused no end of traffic congestion. During the performance, Courtney Love spotted one kid wearing a Pearl Jam T-shirt, gave him $20 for it, and threw it away, telling him to keep his Pearl Jam and Nirvana albums separate. A lower-key affair took place in October of that year when three-fifths of Oasis—just the Gallaghers and Alan White—did a midnight acoustic set to help launch the *(What's the Story?) Morning Glory* album before 300 fans, with Liam not quite sober enough to get the words out properly. Dur-ing the so-called Britpop boom, albums by Cast, Kula Shaker, Ocean Colour Scene, and (London) Suede were launched here. Having learned from the Hole experience, the store now holds most personal appearances and live performances after hours.

The Megastore site takes in what was until recently the Cannon Classic movie theater, where just after Metallica's U.K. debut in 1983 a booze-filled James Hetfield climbed onto the roof and attempted to take down the neon sign. He was arrested but was let off with a warning. *24 Oxford St., tel. 0171/631–1614. Tottenham Court Rd. tube.*

Waterloo, SE1

As long as I gaze at Waterloo Sunset, I am in paradise—The Kinks, "Waterloo Sunset"

This lively area on the south bank of the Thames, just a 10-minute walk from Leicester Square, might lack the gentility of Georgian London but offers some great views across the river—"Waterloo Sunset" can be easily spotted from Waterloo Bridge—and boasts the amazing South Bank arts complex.

The South Bank, the collective name given to the cultural buildings between the river and Waterloo station, started coming together for the 1951 Festival of Britain. Here stand the Royal Festival Hall and the Queen Elizabeth Hall, both of which put on predominantly classical concerts but do have one or two experimental or rootsy rock things each month. The complex also includes the National Film Theatre (a rep cinema), MOMI (the Museum of the Moving Image), the Royal National Theatre, and the Hayward Art Gallery. Two other famous theaters, the Young and Old Vics, are nearby. Regardless of what's on, the South Bank is great for hanging, watching the skateboarders, browsing through the used bookstalls outside the NFT, or having a coffee on the balconies overlooking the Thames.

Just south of Waterloo is Vauxhall, as in the 1994 Morrissey album *Vauxhall and I*. The track "Spring-Heeled Jim" contains a sampling from the pioneering '50s TV documentary, "The Lambeth Boys," set in local streets. All landmarks can best be reached from Waterloo station, except where stated.

EATING DRINKING DANCING SHOPPING PLAYING SLEEPING

Apart from the occasional rock concerts at the South Bank Centre, there's no place to see live music in the area. Near the Imperial War Museum is **THESE RECORDS** (112 Brook Dr., SE11, tel. 0171/587 5349; Lambeth North tube), which specializes in weird stuff like the Residents and Henry Cow.

NEW MUSICAL EXPRESS AND MELODY MAKER

Britain's two rock and pop weeklies—*NME* and *Melody Maker*—are both owned by IPC magazines and based in this tower block. *King's Reach Tower, Stamford St. NME: 25th floor, tel. 0171/261–6472; http://www.nme.com. Melody Maker: 26th floor, tel. 0171/261–5670.*

QUEEN ELIZABETH HALL

Pink Floyd's *Games for May* concert at this 1,100-seat hall on May 12, 1967, was the first use of quadraphonic sound at a live gig. The establishment was shocked by the use of a classical hall for "pop," but management were even more pissed when the hall was filled with millions of bubbles that stained the seats; the group was subsequently banned. In July 1968 Tim Buckley made his London debut here. The recorded concert was released as *Dream Letter—Live in London 1968* 22 years later, by which time Buckley was long dead. In the hall's smaller Purcell Room, David Bowie launched his eponymous 1969 album, now called *Space Oddity*, on November 20. Everyone reckoned it was an excellent gig; when an excited Bowie came off stage, he asked his manager which journalists had been watching, only to be told that the invitations to the press hadn't been sent out. *Belvedere Rd., tel. 0171/960–4242.*

[ROYAL FESTIVAL HALL]

Despite being banned from the Queen Elizabeth Hall, Pink Floyd was allowed to play the larger, 3,000-seat Royal Festival Hall on April 14, 1969, in a show called "More Furious Madness from the Massed Gadgets of Auximenes." The band hired an actor who dressed up as a sea monster and ran up and down the aisles and on and off the stage

Courtesy of MTV Europe Networks

Oasis plays Festival Hall, 1996

teasing the crowd. The same year, Fairport Convention debuted *Liege and Lief,* the most celebrated album in the history of British folk-rock, here.

David Bowie's big breakthrough came after he performed at a Friends of the Earth benefit with Mott the Hoople in the RFH in July 1972. Lou Reed joined him onstage and rave reviews in the music papers helped turn him into one of the biggest U.K. stars by the end of that year. In October 1985, New Order, at a benefit for victims of an earthquake in Mexico, did "Decades," the first time they had performed a Joy Division song since Ian Curtis had died. Bobby McFerrin, who had enjoyed a reasonably successful career as a soul singer in the '80s, conducted the London Philharmonic at the hall in September 1995. It was the first time a black man had conducted here or in front of the orchestra.

In August 1996 when Oasis came to record an MTV Unplugged set here, Liam Gallagher, who had a sore throat, and his girlfriend, sat out the gig in one of the boxes. Meanwhile Noel took the stage with the other band members, explained the situation, and quipped, "You'll have to put up with the four ugly ones." Although the elder Gallagher writes all the songs and often sings a couple of numbers at each gig, the MTV chiefs, who had plowed a lot of money into the event, were less than pleased and threatened to sue the band unless they re-recorded the acoustic session. *Belvedere Rd., tel. 0171/960–4242.*

A TOUCHING DISPLAY

Wire chose to play their final gig under the railway arches next to the South Bank Centre in May 1995, when they were in the public eye thanks to Elastica's acknowledged indebtedness to their sound. The punk-era legends (who for part of the '90s had shortened their name to Wir when one of the original quartet left) didn't believe in saying long goodbyes—they played just one song, although the feedback-punctuated effort did last 15 minutes.

WATERLOO RAILWAY STATION

This is where "Terry," supposedly actor Terence Stamp, meets "Julie," believed to be Julie Christie, in the Kinks' "Waterloo Sunset." The two actors had just starred together in

Ministry of Sound's logo projected onto the wall of Buckingham Palace, 1996

John Schlesinger's *Far from the Madding Crowd*. Waterloo, recently refurbished to incorporate the spectacular glass-roofed Eurostar terminal, was better known throughout the '80s for the legions of homeless who slept around the approaches and arches of the station in what was called Cardboard City. *Waterloo Rd. at York Rd.*

Westminster

The area wedged between Piccadilly and the river, although comprised mostly of state buildings, including Buckingham Palace and the Houses of Parliament, has seen some often-hilarious rock activity over the years. The pompous 1977 Silver Jubilee celebrations provided fertile ground for prankster punks to play on. A short walk northeast from Buckingham Palace and its surrounding parks is the St. James's area, with its exclusive gentlemen's clubs along the little streets of Pall Mall.

Buckingham Palace and St. James's, SW1

BUCKINGHAM PALACE

God save the Queen, because tourists are money—The Sex Pistols "God Save the Queen"

Rock's first visitors to the home of Queen Elizabeth II were the Beatles, who came to collect their MBEs (Member of the British Empire)—awards that acknowledge outstanding achievement to the nation—at an ever-so-formal ceremony here on October 26, 1965. In subsequent interviews, the blissed-out four claimed they had shared a joint in the toilets before receiving the award. At the time, the decision to honor the Beatles caused a ruckus among members of the establishment. John Lennon later returned his MBE in protest against "Britain's involvement in Biafra, against our support of America in Vietnam, and against 'Cold Turkey' slipping down the charts." Other similarly honored rock stars include Elton John, Eric Clapton, Cliff Richard, and Van Morrison. In 1985 Bob Geldof (an Irish citizen) received the rare distinction of an honorary knighthood. In March 1997 Paul McCartney was knighted and is now a "Sir."

On March 10, 1977, just two months after they had been released by EMI (with their £40,000 advance intact), the Sex Pistols held an outdoor signing ceremony to A&M just across the street from the front gates to the Palace. The signing—done at a cheap trestle table—was rushed in case cops should move them on. Barely a week later, A&M executives, worried about bad publicity, let the band go, and this time they kept a £75,000 advance.

The palace and its residents have figured in numerous songs. The Beatles ended their final album with a track called "Her Majesty." Jamaican toaster U Roy outspliffed the Beatles by claiming that he shared a joint with the Queen in the song "Chalice in the Palace." Morrissey has visited the palace twice in song, bragging about dropping his trousers to the Queen on "Nowhere Fast" off *Meat Is Murder* and imagining breaking in with a "sponge and a rusty spanner [wrench]" on "The Queen Is Dead."

In September 1996, the original superclub, the massive Ministry of Sound (*see* Southeast London *in* Outer London, *below*), advertised its fifth birthday bash by beaming its logo onto a wall of the palace. *Queen's Gardens at The Mall and Constitution Hill. Victoria BR.*

ICA (THE INSTITUTE OF CONTEMPORARY ARTS)

Since it opened in 1947, the ICA has been staging photographic exhibitions, avant-garde art shows, and offbeat film seasons. It's also had more than a fair few rock and off-the-wall events. An October 1976 party to launch Throbbing Gristle's multimedia exhibition, "Prostitution," raised questions in the House of Commons. The party, funded with help from the public purse, was a reaction to the cutesy opening nights at most cultural institutions: They had no wine (just beer), there was a stripper, and the support band was the noisy Chelsea who, especially for the occasion, performed under the pseudonym LSD.

In October 1976 the Clash headlined for the first time, supported by Subway Sect. A photo of the show that did the rounds of the papers pictured an overenthusiastic girl punk trying to bite a guy's earlobe off. She later joined the Mo-Dettes, and he turned out to be Shane MacGowan. The brief notoriety in the rock press that the event gave MacGowan spurred him on to form a punk band, the Nipple Erectors (the Nips), and then in the early '80s to form the Pogues, whose lyrical journey through London, "Transmetropolitan," briefly mentions the ICA. Patti Smith also got into the performance so much that she danced onstage. The following year, on May 10, Adam and the Ants made their live debut in the café, having secured the gig by saying that they were a country band. They were thrown off stage after a couple of numbers, when Adam Ant put on a leather mask for "Beat My Guest."

One of the furious riots at Jesus and Mary Chain gigs took place at the ICA in late 1984. The group was banned from the venue. Also that year, Genesis P-Orridge, Stevo, and Frank Tovey staged their Concerto for Voices and Machinery here, during which they destroyed part of the stage using electric saws, generators, and torches before the management put a stop to their efforts.

Nothing so wild happens these days, though the ICA still puts on events with a rock edge. Tindersticks did a five-night residency, incorporating different films and support bands each night, in November 1996. *12 Carlton House Terr., The Mall, tel. 0171/930–0493. Charing Cross tube.*

(NEW) SCOTLAND YARD

Interpol und Deutsche Bank, FBI und Scotland Yard—Kraftwerk, "Computer World"

Kraftwerk's 1981 tribute to binary technology wasn't rock's earliest mention of the Metropolitan Police headquarters. In his 1973 track from *A Wizard a True Star,* "When the Shit Hits the Fan/Sunset Boulevard," Todd Rundgren eerily anticipated three decades of bombs on London streets in the line "The IRA have just hit London; they blew up half of Scotland Yard." The building, well known to TV viewers from its appearance in countless cop shows, has never actually been hit. *Victoria St. at Broadway. St. James's Park tube.*

SCOTCH OF ST. JAMES (DIRECTOR'S LODGE CLUB)

For almost two years after it opened in spring 1965, this posh drinking club with its tartan-styled soft furnishings was the prime London hangout for rock's top names. The Byrds whooped it up on a marathon drinking session here during their 1965 tour. The Beatles, the Stones, and the Animals were regulars, and the Who bassist John Entwistle wrote "Boris the Spider" here after a drunken argument with his Stones counterpart, Bill Wyman.

Jimi Hendrix played here shortly after arriving in London in September 1966 and won over an enthusiastic crowd. He returned three nights later and jammed with an obscure group called the VIPs, which included Greg Ridley (later of Humble Pie), Jerry Harrison (later of Spooky Tooth), and Luther Grosvenor (who became Mott the Hoople's Ariel Bender). After the jam he was pursued at length round the club by the Who manager Kit Lambert, who wanted to sign him for his new label, Track. Hendrix agreed when Lambert offered him an immediate appearance on the *Ready Steady Go* TV program. A month later, on October 25, 1966, Hendrix returned with Mitch Mitchell and Noel Redding for what was the debut performance of the Jimi Hendrix Experience.

Also that fall, Atlantic Records boss Ahmet Ertegun, in London to find out why there was so much fuss being made about British rock, hosted a party at the Scotch for Wilson Pickett. With his back to the stage, Ertegun remarked to Pickett that the guitarist jamming onstage was so good he had to be out of Pickett's backing band. The soul singer explained that his guitarist was at the bar having a drink. They turned round to see that the mystery guitarist was Eric Clapton. Ertegun couldn't believe that a white British kid could play so well and immediately recommended that Atlantic's British distributors, Polydor, sign him up. Atlantic went on to release Cream's first album, which Ertegun didn't like—it wasn't bluesy enough for him. Nevertheless Cream sold 15 million records for Atlantic in the United States. The venue is now the Director's Lodge club. Outside in Mason's Yard is where Gered Mankowitz shot the front cover of the Rolling Stones' *Out of Our Heads. 13 Mason's Yard, tel. 0171/930–2540. Piccadilly Circus tube.*

VICTORIA RAILWAY STATION

After touring the USSR, David Bowie arrived in central London for a series of shows at Wembley in May 1976, his first U.K. appearance in almost three years. In front of the press, Bowie got into a waiting limo, and as it pulled off he gave what looked like a Nazi salute. Lambasted for being totally insensitive at a time when the extreme right-wing National Front were particularly active, Bowie later claimed it was nothing more than a wave. Many nevertheless pointed out the coincidence between this incident and the time when customs officials at the Polish border found Nazi literature in his baggage; Bowie later maintained it was research for a movie project. *Platform 8, Buckingham Palace Rd. at Grosvenor Gardens.*

"GOING UNDERGROUND"—THE CIRCLE LINE

In the early '70s the Moody Blues held a lavish press reception for a few hours aboard the Circle Line, which loops around central London stations from Victoria. Generation X sang about "office workers going round and round on the Circle Line" on "Day by Day." Tony Parsons interviewed the Clash using a cheapo cassette recorder while riding around the Circle Line for an hour. The interview was included on the free *Capital Radio* EP that accompanied early pressings of their first album.

Whitehall, SW1

Whitehall is the broad thoroughfare that connects the Houses of Parliament with Trafalgar Square, a route along which rock and politics have collided on several occasions.

BIG BEN

The cover shot for *The Who Sings My Generation* (the quaintly retitled American version of the *My Generation* album) was taken of the band looking all moddish with the clock tower behind them. Eleven years later, the Jam, in their mod phase, copied the pic. In between, the Newcastle folk-pop outfit Lindisfarne posed for the cover of their 1970 *Nicely Out of Tune* album with Big Ben in the background. On a pedantic note, the name Big Ben refers only to the bell—heard throughout the world daily on BBC radio—and not the clock or the tower. *Bridge St. Westminster tube.*

[HOUSE OF COMMONS]

Who needs the Parliament, sitting making laws all day?—The Clash, "Remote Control"

From time to time, the nation's legislators have sought rock crossover appeal. In 1955 Labour MP Christopher Mayhew announced that he would gulp some mescaline and describe the effects on TV. The Shamen sampled his speech for their 1987 single "Christopher Mayhew Says." Arty party-going Labour MP Tom Driberg asked the House to "deplore" the magistrate who'd called the Rolling Stones "complete morons who wear filthy clothes" in September '66. Driberg and another Labour member, Brian Walden (now a right-of-center political commentator), were the only MPs to sign the June 1967 *Times* ad calling for more liberal marijuana laws. It was Driberg as well who was involved with Mick Jagger's short-lived attempt to become an MP (*see* Gay Hussar *in* Soho—Greek Street and Soho Square, *above*).

Blah, blah, blah...the House of Commons in session

MPs, like their U.S. counterparts, have spent much time knocking rock. This started back in the '50s, when debates in the Commons touched on the horrors of Teddy Boys slashing seats at venues on Bill Haley's U.K. tour. In 1958 the storm over Jerry Lee Lewis's marriage to his 13 year-old cousin broke while he was touring the United Kingdom, and horrified politicians had things to say about that, too. In the '60s the danger of drugs was often the order of the day, and in the '70s, when Labour was in power, their MPs took a moral stand against punk. One of their number, James Dempsey, misguidedly tried to get the Ramones' first LP banned on grounds that it encouraged sniffing glue—he had missed the irony of the track "Now I Wanna Sniff Some Glue." Marcus Lipton, Labour MP for nearby Lambeth Central, condemned punk when the Sex Pistols' "God Save the Queen" was racing up charts to the No. 2 slot during the Queen's jubilee week celebrations, saying, "If pop music is going to be used to destroy our established institutions, then it ought to be destroyed first." The previous year, Tory grandee Nicholas Fairbairn had condemned the ICA for "wasting" its grant monies by allowing the likes of Throbbing Gristle to play surrounded by bondage pictures of singer Genesis P-Orridge's girlfriend, Cosi Fanni Tutti.

During the Thatcher-Major Tory years, rock has gained more acceptance; coincidentally, Thatcher's Attorney General, Michael Havers, had been Mick Jagger and Keith Richards's defense counsel during their 1967 drug bust. More recently, in 1996, Michael Howard, the Tory minister in charge of law and order, stood up and condemned Oasis after they cursed and pretended to stick things up their butts at the BRITS awards. In January 1997, Gallagher spoke out about the hypocrisy surrounding drugs, saying that there were lots of cocaine and heroin users among the MPs. His outburst was debated with some fervor, with MPs naturally denying everything.

MPs can hold functions in the House of Commons' many rooms and bars. In summer 1980, Tory arts minister Norman St. John Stevas facilitated a pop-book launch party to which all artists who had had a No. 1 U.K. hit were invited. Into this bastion of closeted homosexuality wandered the Village People in their full stage regalia, while Elton John turned up in the out-of-bounds parliamentary chamber, slouching in the Speaker's Chair.

A few years later Billy Bragg, Tom Robinson, and Jerry Dammers attended the opposition Labour Party's Red Wedge initiative press launch, which was chaired by party leader and reggae "fan" Neil Kinnock. In 1994 the Stonewall group also had a press launch here to bolster their campaign to lower the age of homosexual consent to 16; members of (London) Suede attended. *Bridge St. by River Thames, tel. 0171/219–3000. Westminster tube.*

[10 DOWNING STREET]

To promote their third single, "Flowers in the Rain," the Move sent out a postcard bearing a nude caricature of then Prime Minister Harold Wilson in the tub. Wilson successfully sued the band, winning an injunction that gave part of the royalties from the disc to charity. The single got to No. 2 in the U.K. charts and was the first record to be played when BBC Radio 1 went on air on September 30, 1967.

Screaming Lord Sutch was arrested here in July 1972 after leaping from a bus (whose passengers included four nude women) on Downing Street to tell the PM about his upcoming tour. Sutch was charged with insulting behavior, but the case was later thrown out. In 1989 the street was closed off behind iron railings for security reasons, thereby bringing an end to stunts like these.

The Troggs did a song called "Number 10 Downing Street" in 1967, but most lyrical references concerning the place involve Margaret Thatcher, its incumbent from 1979 to 1990. First to tackle the controversial PM were the (English) Beat, whose anthemic "Stand Down Margaret" was a No. 22 hit in summer 1980. The Smiths were going to call their 1986 LP *Margaret on the Guillotine* but decided on tackling the monarchy instead and called it *The Queen Is Dead.* "Margaret on the Guillotine" was later used by Morrissey for the closing track on his first solo album, *Viva Hate.* In 1989 Elvis Costello also had a swipe against Thatch in "Tramp the Dirt Down" (off *Spike the Beloved Entertainer*). Also, Richard Thompson got pretty brutal with her on "Mother Knows Best" (*Rumour and Sigh,* 1991). *10 Downing St., Westminster tube.*

WESTMINSTER SCHOOL

Shane MacGowan won a semi-scholarship to this prestigious public school at age 12. Remembered as shy, he was nevertheless expelled a few years later after being found with some dope. Another star who calls Westminster School his alma mater is Bush lead singer Gavin Rossdale. *Little Dean's Yard, tel. 0171/222–5516. Westminster tube.*

East London

The capital's toughest quarter, east London embodies many of the city's most clichéd qualities, especially that of the chirpy Cockney. In rock speak, the derisive "mockney" term has been applied to those who overdo Cockney affectations, starting with early British idols like Tommy Steele and Adam Faith through to the Small Faces (who really were from east London) and more recently Blur (from Essex and points south). Iron Maiden makes less fuss of their early days spent in east London.

Songs of East London

Ian Dury, "Plaistow Patricia" (1977)
Cockney Rejects, "I'm Forever Blowing Bubbles" (1980)
XTC, "Towers of London" (1980)
ABC, "Tower of London" (1985)
Frank Tovey, "Bethnal Green Tube Disaster" (1989)
Pulp, "Mile End" (1995)
Edward Ball, "Docklands Blues" (1996)

A GEOGRAPHICAL NOTE

East London is defined here as places within the E1 to E18 postal codes (these numbers appear on the name plates of virtually every street).

The East End, E1, E2, E3

East End heroes got to score—Genesis, "The Battle of Epping Forest"

East London's spiritual heart, the East End comprises Bethnal Green, Whitechapel, Stepney, Mile End, and Docklands. Over the centuries successive waves of immigrants—Huguenots, Irish, and Jews—settled here, but by the 19th century the East End was synonymous with the capital's worst slums. Despite wartime bombings and '50s slum clearance, things haven't improved, except on the fringes like Docklands. The old tight-knit communities have been broken up and the area is now an uneasy mix of poor whites and poorer Bangladeshi living mostly in grim apartment towers.

From Jack the Ripper (who was the inspiration for a 1992 Morrissey B side) to the '60s gangsters the Krays (another Morrissey fixation), the East End's violent edge has been written and sung about—at least by Morrissey. The East End has also been a breeding ground for far-right politics: In the '30s, '70s, and '80s there were pitched battles on the streets between fascists and anti-racists. Many of the East End's neighborhoods have figured in song. Shabby Stepney, for example, is the place where the heroine of the Rolling Stones' 1965 "Play With Fire," no longer able to cut it in posh Knightsbridge, ends up.

EATINGDRINKINGDANCINGSHOPPINGPLAYINGSLEEPING

There are a couple of good spots on the fringe of the City of London on Charlotte Road, Shoreditch: the **BRICKLAYERS' ARMS** (63 Charlotte Rd., tel. 0171/739–5245), which plays loud crossover dance sounds, and the more yuppie **CANTALOUPE** (35 Charlotte Rd., tel. 0171/613–4411). **SPITZ** (109 Commercial St., tel. 0171/247–9747), nearby in the marvelous covered Old Spitalfield Market, is a new live venue for jazz, experimental sounds, and Latin. The cozy and friendly **BLUE NOTE** (1 Hoxton Sq., tel. 0171/729–8440, Old St. tube) has long been known for its acid jazz nights, as well as Asian dub.

The area's main tourist attraction remains the busy **Petticoat Lane Market** (Middlesex St., Liverpool St. tube) every Sunday. Some clothes bargains can be found, but don't bother looking for records.

THE BASS CENTRE

The self-proclaimed "world's biggest store for bassists" is an impressive sight, with more than 200 models in stock and the ceiling plastered with photos of famous customers. The list of those who have done a deal here since it opened in 1983 reads like a Who's Who of British bass players, including Bill Wyman and John Entwistle; Bootsie Collins and Pearl Jam's Jeff Ament have also been in. Under the same roof is the Acoustic Centre, with a similarly grand display of guitars and clientele. *131 Wapping High St., E1, tel. 0171/ 265–1567. Wapping tube.*

James Cumpsty

The Bass Centre

MILE END STADIUM

Dominated by poverty and ugly apartment towers, Mile End draws mid-'90s Britpop bands keen to establish some laddish credentials. Blur, at the crest of their popularity, chose this little-used space to bolster their mockney image before 25,000 fans in June 1995. They were back again in September for the first Music Industry Soccer Six Challenge Cup, to raise money for the Nordoff Robbins Music Therapy charity. Again in May 1996 they were mad for it in the second soccer tournament, scoring a rare win over Oasis to decide last place. *Rhodeswell Rd., E3, tel. 0181/980–1885. Mile End tube.*

PROFESSION OF VIOLENCE

Reggie Kray, do you know my name? . . . Ronnie Kray, do you know my face?– Morrissey, "The Last of the Famous International Playboys"

In an area rich with lore and lawlessness, no East End myth is more powerful than that of the Kray twins, Reggie and Ronnie. They ran the area's most powerful gang in the '60s from a mundane council flat at 178 Vallance Road, Bethnal Green. The pair were given life sentences in 1969 for murdering fellow gangsters George Cornell in the Blind Beggar pub on Whitechapel Road and Jack "The Hat" McVitie in Stoke Newington. In 1990 Spandau Ballet's Kemp brothers, Gary and Martin, played the twins in Peter Medak's movie The Krays. Ronnie is now dead,

but various showbiz figures, including Roger Daltrey, support calls for his brother's release. Morrissey has also shown a strange fascination. He sent an *R*-shaped bouquet to Ronnie's funeral and sang about the Krays on "The Last of the Famous International Playboys." Once the Krays were jailed, the East End became the main stomping grounds of the skinhead and suedehead (Morrissey again), some of whom grew up to invent the area's particularly aggressive version of punk, Oi.

SARM STUDIOS (EAST)

Dub giant Lee "Scratch" Perry came to London to record with Bob Marley in 1977, but after hearing the Clash's version of his own "Police and Thieves," he took a day off to team up with them in this studio. They cut one reggae song, the unreleased "Pressure Drop," and one punk number, "Complete Control." Sarm is based in a particularly dismal part of the East End, below a cash-and-carry clothing warehouse. *9–13 Osborn St., Whitechapel, E1, tel. 0171/247–1311. Aldgate East tube.*

TOWER BRIDGE

To promote Michael Jackson's *HIStory* album in 1995, Sony floated a huge statue of El Loco on a barge up and down the Thames, with the bridge having to be opened to let it through. One of London's best-known landmarks, the bridge has also appeared on a number of album covers, including the Jam's *Snap!* and Wings' *London Town*. Arch Stranglers fan Dagenham Dave—irreverently remembered by name on the song off *No More Heroes*—committed suicide by leaping from the bridge in 1977. *Tower Bridge, E1. Tower Hill tube/Tower Gateway DLR.*

Hackney, E8, E9

Marc Bolan was born Mark Feld in Hackney Hospital on Homerton High Street in 1947, but no major bands have emerged from this project-blighted land. Spinal Tap, however, claimed that they came from Squatney. There's no such place; the word is a portmanteau of "squat" (of which there were many here in the '70s, the area still being a popular place with crusties) and Hackney. Sid Vicious briefly attended Hackney Community College before joining McLaren's cabaret.

EATINGDRINKINGDANCINGSHOPPINGPLAYINGSLEEPING

Hackney's entertainment options tend to be local affairs with a high community input. **THE HACKNEY EMPIRE** (291 Mare St., E8, tel. 0181/985–2424; Bus 253), a refurbished music hall, hosts ragga, reggae, worldbeat, and comedy shows. The **SAMUEL PEPYS** (289 Mare St., E8, tel. 0181/533–7709) is a busy pub with occasional live music. **CHAT'S PALACE** (42 Brooksby's Walk, E9, tel. 0181/986–6714), a neighborhood arts project in operation since 1975, has live bands once or twice a week. Over in Dalston, to the northwest, is the popular **PRINCE GEORGE** (40 Parkholme Rd., Dalston, E8, tel. 0171/254–6060), a big pub with some good R&B on the jukebox.

VICTORIA PARK

This bland park just north of the East End was the setting for the first Rock Against Racism rally, on April 30, 1978, when some 100,000 people watched Steel Pulse, Tom Robinson, X-Ray Spex, the Ruts, and others. The Clash grabbed the headlines after Strummer, in a successful attempt to shock, wore a T-shirt favoring Brigade Rosse, the Italian paramilitary outfit that had killed hapless former prime minister Aldo Moro the previous year. The event started with a march from Trafalgar Square, which in itself was the largest anti-fascist event of its kind through the area since the '30s.

The RAR movement began in 1976 soon after Eric Clapton made racist comments on stage in Birmingham and David Bowie flirted with Teutonic motifs. RAR's aim was to stop rock's being used as a fascist medium—including squashing the swastika insignia of some punk bands—and to expose white audiences to black music, particularly reggae and ska. Those who turned out for the cause included Pete Townshend, the Specials, Sham 69, and many more. RAR lasted about five years, but its umbrella organization, the Anti-Nazi league, was revived in the early '90s. *Grove Rd., E9. Cambridge Heath BR.*

Val Wilmer/courtesy of Redferns

Shoreditch, E1

An area full of character and tragic history—Jack the Ripper murdered many of his victims here—Shoreditch, in the shadow of the city and the East End, has become a major haunt for artists and designers in recent years, mainly due to the plentiful supply of cheap warehouse space. It is also a major clubbing area.

Mick Jones of the Clash on stage at the Rock Against Racism rally, London, 1978

ELVISLY YOURS

Sid Shaw has been running this memorabilia store, devoted to the cheeseburger king, since 1982. As well as the kitsch—decks of cards, magic mugs, soaps, flags, auto plates and Vegas-period sunglasses—there are collectibles including first-day covers and old newspapers. In the mid-'80s the Presley estate trademarked the Elvis name and put an injunction on his exporting to the United States, meaning American fans are unable to buy his stuff, even by mail order. In March 1997 Shaw won a High Court ruling permitting him to sell Elvis goods. The business is primarily mail order, though the store is a little shrine to Presley, with a full-size Vegas-era statue on display. *107 Shoreditch High St., E1 6JN, tel./fax 0171/ 729–4217. Liverpool St. tube or BR.*

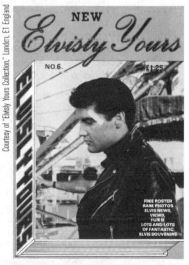

Courtesy of "Elvisly Yours Collection," London, E1 England

Stratford and East, E7, E12, E15, E16

But London Bridge is falling down/there ain't no gold in Silvertown—Carter U.S.M, "Every Time a Churchbell Rings"

Elvisly Yours *fanzine*

London continues to sprawl east of the River Lea, soaking up the badlands of Stratford, West Ham, East Ham, Canning Town, and Silvertown, which makes for a glum end to the North London rail line. Forest Gate and Manor Park are slightly more suburban.

THE BRIDGE HOUSE HOTEL

In 1980 Mute Records founder Daniel Miller discovered Depeche Mode playing in this forlorn-looking pub, one of the few traditional buildings still standing here. Nowadays there's nothing doing. *23 Barking Rd., Canning Town, E16, tel. 0171/476–0948. Royal Victoria DLR.*

THE ELVIS SHOP

A record store for 20 years, the Elvis Shop for the last 15 years has sold nothing other than records by the King, which, as well as the usual, means Yugoslavian imports of the *King Creole* album and Japanese pressings of *50,000,000 Elvis Fans Can't Be Wrong. 400 High St. North, East Ham, E12, tel. 0181/552–7551. East Ham tube.*

THE UPPER CUT (ACE OF CLUBS)

Jimi Hendrix wrote "Purple Haze" in December 1966 in the dressing room of this club owned by boxing champ Billy Walker. The boxer's chums, The Who, had opened the joint earlier in the month. Despite Walker's fame, the place wasn't all that successful and later became a bingo hall. It is now the Ace of Clubs, a hairspray disco. *15 Woodgrange Rd., Forest Gate, E7, tel. 0181/519–8700. Forest Gate BR.*

Walthamstow, E17

An almost agreeable but faded suburb on the fringes of Epping Forest, Walthamstow is now famous for its postal code, East 17, the name used by the local chart-topping boy band. The district is also the home of the Bevis Frond, Nick Saloman's 1990s kitsch-psychedelic one-man cottage industry.

EATINGDRINKINGDANCINGSHOPPINGPLAYINGSLEEPING

There's been live music at the **STANDARD MUSIC VENUE** (1 Blackhorse La., E17, tel. 0181/527–1966) since the '60s. These days it's a mix of original and tribute bands with, from time to time, someone big on the way up, such as the Spin Doctors and Little Angels. The **HOUSE OF RHYTHM** (95 Wood St., tel. 0181/520–3584) sells secondhand vinyl, cassettes, and CDs, including lots of 12-inchers.

SMALL WONDER

The punk indie label was based above this record store in 1977. Small Wonder's early releases included the Fall, Crass, the Leyton Buzzards, the Zeros, and the Cure's debut single, "Killing an Arab." Among punk poet Patrik Fitzgerald's recordings with the label was his 7-inch EP, "Safety-Pin Stuck in My Heart." Driving school offices now occupy the space. *162 Hoe St., E17. Walthamstow Central tube.*

Patrik Fitzgerald's 7-inch "Safety-Pin Stuck in My Heart" EP

Middlesex

This huge, largely characterless sprawl of divided highways, white-collar housing developments, reservoirs, and chemical works used to be the county that, more than a hundred years ago, incorporated and ran London. Now, because nobody has ever found a better way of describing the outer bits of north and west London, the name lives on—in postal addresses, sports clubs, and local usage. Middlesex no longer has towns these days—they've all been eaten up by the growth of London—just suburbs, like Wembley, home of the famous sports stadium, and Twickenham, scene of various Who and Beatles movie projects.

Harrow

Best known for the exclusive public school whose alumni include Lord Byron, Winston Churchill, one-time Manfred Mann singer Mike D'Abo, and Island Records founder Chris Blackwell, Harrow incorporates a number of contrasting suburbs—bourgeois Pinner, where Elton John was born as Reg Dwight on March 25, 1947, and shabby Wealdstone, a mile east, pocked with run-down houses and take-out restaurants. All the members of Episode Six, a band from nearby Hatch End, attended Harrow County School; their bass player was Roger Glover, and later they took on a teenage Ian Gillan as singer.

RAILWAY HOTEL (RAILWAY TAVERN)

It was at a Who gig in this grotty pub in fall 1964 that Pete Townshend first smashed up his guitar. During the band's first set, Townshend jumped up while experimenting with feedback and the neck accidentally hit the low ceiling, producing a weird sound. During the band's second set the same night, fans challenged Townshend to do it again. This time when he bashed it, the neck caught in the ceiling and the guitar broke. The audience began laughing, so Townshend smashed up the rest of the instrument to give the impression that he had intended to destroy it all along. After that, there was no turning back, and audiences would shout for Townshend to smash up his six-string everywhere the Who played; it was still a highlight of their set in the '70s.

For much of 1964 the Who had a residency, just as the Yardbirds had here a year earlier. The Who's gigs were promoted by Townshend's flatmate, Richard Barnes, who turned up the heating to make the place more sweaty and took out all the light bulbs except a few that he painted red. The venue was supposed to hold only 200, but nearly 1,000 would often turn up. One visitor, who stood out from the mainly blue-collar teenage crowd, was Kit Lambert, son of classical music critic Constant Lambert. He arrived by chance one night, looking for a band to feature in a movie he was making about soon-to-be-swinging London. He liked the Who so much that he gave up the project to manage them. The Who honored the place with a picture of the pub on the inside sleeve of their compilation album, *Meaty Beaty Big and Bouncy. The Bridge/Station Approach, tel. 0181/427–0459. Harrow and Wealdstone tube/BR.*

Heathrow Airport

Through Southern snow to Heathrow—(London) Suede, "Black or Blue"

At the height of Beatlemania, thousands of teenies would besiege Heathrow, Britain's largest airport, to greet the Beatles on their departure for and arrival from foreign tours. Jimi Hendrix Experience drummer Mitch Mitchell had a tear gas gun confiscated by customs officials in August 1967 after flying in from New York and being strip searched. The authorities found some smack on Clash drummer Topper Headon in 1981. He was arrested and charged but not jailed after admitting at Uxbridge Magistrates to being an addict ready to clean himself up. In spring 1992, Customs and Excise seized an aromatic package sent by jazz eccentric Sun Ra to techno artists The Grid when it arrived at Heathrow. They opened it up only to find a tape covered in patchouli oil.

New York Doll Johnny Thunders barfed in the departure lounge once in the mid-'70s, exacting some media coverage, but this was nothing compared to what the Sex Pistols got in January 1977. On a flight to Amsterdam, accompanied by EMI label executives, they allegedly swore at staff, caused a general rumpus in the lounge, and puked. Sid Vicious wasn't then in the band, and so wasn't at the airport, but he is now—permanently. His mom dropped the urn containing his ashes when she passed through, and they blew into the air-conditioning system.

The airport has also inspired a number of songs. Van Morrison did a track called "Heathrow Shuffle" on *How Long Has This Been Going On?*, the jazzy 1995 collaboration with Georgie Fame. The Byrds' "Eight Miles High" is often cited as a typical druggy number, but the group has always maintained it was inspired by their first air trip to England in 1965, when they landed at Heathrow. Ritchie Blackmore used to work here as a radio operator. *Off A4/A30, Heathrow. Heathrow tube.*

Hounslow

A mix of shopping malls, industrial parks, storage depots, housing projects, and residential neighborhoods on the Piccadilly tube line just before Heathrow Airport, Hounslow has produced hitmakers from the earliest days of rock & roll right through to the Britpop crop of today. In the early '60s locally based Dave "Screaming Lord" Sutch had in his band, the Savages, a 16-year-old Hounslow kid named Ritchie Blackmore. Other early Hounslow rockers were Mick Underwood and Cliff Bennett of the Rebel Rousers.

A&M Records

Ian Gillan lived on Brabazon Road in West Hounslow opposite the busy intersection of routes A4 and A30. He played with his first band, Garth Rockett and the Moonshiners (a loose ensemble that also included Chris Aylmer of Samson), in early 1962 at St. Dunstan's Youth Club in nearby Cranford, where in exchange for free rehearsal space they had to do regular gigs.

The early '80s punkers Actifed were based here; more recent successes have come in the form of Dodgy, who moved to Hounslow

Dodgy, 1996

from Birmingham, writing and rehearsing their *Homegrown* album of 1994 in the garage of their house (187 Brabazon Rd.). As soon as the trippy, soulful popsters moved out, the Bluetones took up residence and worked out their debut album in the same garage.

Hounslow's one true old-school rock landmark, the Attic Club, which put on R&B and underground acts, including Cream and Pink Floyd, in the mid-'60s, stood just across the road from the town's main bus station but has been wiped off the map by '90s property developers. Still here, though, is the main shopping drag along the Bath Road (A4) in West Hounslow where Depeche Mode shot the video to their 1982 No. 8 U.K. hit, "See You"; businesses that were shown include the local Woolworth's store and a coin-op launderette.

Sunbury-on-Thames

A suburb on the north bank of the Thames a few miles west of Richmond, Sunbury is home to the Shepperton movie studios and Kempton Park racecourse, where the 1968 National Jazz and Blues Festival (the forerunner of the Reading Festival) was held.

SHEPPERTON STUDIOS

The Who have helped produce two movies—*Quadrophenia* and *The Kids Are All Right*—at these long-running studios. For *The Kids Are All Right*, the Who played before a selected crowd on May 25, 1978. It was Keith Moon's last appearance on stage before he died.

Another Shepperton movie with rock connections is *The Man Who Fell to Earth*, starring David Bowie and directed by Nic Roeg, the subject of Big Audio Dynamite's 1986 Top 20 U.K. single, "E=MC²." Led Zeppelin went to great expense to mock up their favorite New Orleans bar, the Absinthe, in Shepperton for the cover of their last studio album, 1979's *In Through the Out Door*. While the band was rehearsing inside, a priest spotted the clapped-out bread van John Bonham was driving around in, got hold of some holy water, and blessed it on the spot. *North end Littleton La., tel. 01932/562611. Shepperton BR.*

Twickenham

Middlesex's smartest suburb, home of the world's most famous rugby stadium, sits on a picture-pretty bank of the Thames just north of Strawberry Hill (from which the Strawbs, formerly the Strawberry Hill Boys, took their name), and a mile or so southwest of touristy Richmond (*see* Surrey *in* the Home Counties and the South).

EEL PIE ISLAND

Pete Townshend's publishing company and recording studio (*see below*) are named for this small, leafy island in the River Thames some 10 miles southwest of central London. Previously known as Goose Eyte and Twickenham Ayte it became known as Eel Pie Island in the 19th century when the now-demolished island pub began serving up pastry dishes containing the slippery fish.

By the 1060s Eel Pie had a thriving bohemian community. The 1000 built Eel Pie Island Hotel on the far side, away from the bridge, began putting on shows by the Yardbirds, the Rolling Stones, the Who, and other rock acts. The only way the bands could get their equipment onto the island was by wheeling it over a tiny bridge that is now so rickety only three people are allowed on it at a time. The venue closed in 1967 and was immediately squatted by hippies. It reopened two years later as Colonel Barefoot's Rock Garden, putting on bands from the new underground scene; Genesis played a very early gig here in 1969. After the building burnt down in suspicious circumstances in 1972, an apartment block was erected on the site. The island has become simply a residential place popular with boatmakers; the bohemian tradition remains in the number of artists' studios it now harbors. *Water La. at the Embankment. Twickenham BR.*

EEL PIE RECORDING PRODUCTIONS LTD.

In this Pete Townshend-owned studio, set on the left bank of the Thames near Richmond Lock, the Who leader has recorded a number of his solo albums, including *All the Best Cowboys Have Chinese Eyes* and *White City—A Novel*. Townshend also records demos for his albums on a barge moored here that he takes up and down the river. *The Boathouse, Ranelagh Dr., tel. 0181/891–4630. St. Margaret's BR.*

PETE TOWNSHEND HOME

One of five sumptuous residences owned by the Who guitarist, this one was inhabited by the poet Alfred Lord Tennyson, a Dylan favorite, from 1851 to 1853. *Chapel House, Montpelier Row. St. Margaret's BR.*

TWICKENHAM FILM STUDIOS

Studio shots for the Beatles' *A Hard Day's Night* and *Help!* movies, as well as videos for various singles, including "Ticket to Ride," "Day Tripper," and "I Feel Fine" were shot at Twickenham Film Studios. The Beatles came here for the last time in January 1969 to work on the *Let It Be* movie. More recently, Genesis has come to Twickenham studios to shoot videos and rehearse before touring. *The Barons at Kelvin Dr., tel. 0181/892–4477. St. Margaret's BR.*

"ACT NATURALLY"

Various scenes from *Help!* and *A Hard Day's Night* were shot in and around Twickenham.

- In one scene from *Help!,* the Beatles get out of their Rolls-Royces and enter a stretch of terraced houses on Ailsa Avenue off St. Margaret's Road. Ringo goes into No. 5, John No. 7, George No. 9 and Paul No. 11. The inside, done up as one huge room, was a Twickenham Studios set.

- The scene, from the same movie, in which Ringo posts a letter and nearly has his wedding band snatched off by a man hidden inside a postbox, was shot outside No. 1 South Western Road, just south of the Turk's Head pub (28 Winchester Rd.), which was used in *A Hard Day's Night.* The post box was a prop.

- In one scene from *A Hard Day's Night,* Ringo trashes the Turk's Head pub, a few hundred yards west of St. Margaret's Station.

- In the same movie, the Beatles frolic in a field by a helicopter launch pad while "Can't Buy Me Love" plays. Part of this scene was shot at Gatwick Airport in Sussex and the rest at Thornbury playing fields (London Rd. at Bridge Rd.) in Isleworth, a mile north of Twickenham.

TWICKENHAM RAILWAY STATION

Rod Stewart's drunken bawling of some old blues songs on the platform after a hard night's local gigging in January 1964 was heard by Long John Baldry, who asked him to join his group, the Hoochie Coochie Men. It was Stewart's big singing break. *London Rd. at Mary's Terrace.*

Wembley

A small suburb of Harrow until the growth of the railways at the end of the 19th century, this cosmopolitan area 8 miles northwest of central London is now best known as the home of the sports stadium (and occasional rock venue) built in the 1920s on land that had been intended for a British version of the Eiffel Tower. Keith Moon grew up here on Chaplin Road. His first job was delivering papers, including to the house where Twiggy and her parents lived.

WEMBLEY ARENA

A scarcely believable bill offering the Beatles, Bob Dylan, the Rolling Stones, and the Who played an *NME* poll-winners' concert at this venue (then known as the Wembley Empire Pool) on May 1, 1966; it was the Beatles' last-ever U.K. gig. *NME* poll-winners' contests were held here regularly in the '60s until tours by individual acts made the package show redundant.

The New York Dolls made their British debut at a charity gig here in October 1972, supporting Rod Stewart. A&R men sent by Mercury Records agreed that the Dolls were the worst band they'd ever seen, but signed them to the label soon after negotiations with Atlantic Records broke down. A week after the Wembley gig, the Dolls' drummer, Billy Murcia, choked to death on a cup of coffee poured down his throat in an unsuccessful attempt to revive him from a drugged stupor.

In 1977 the Empire Pool became the Wembley Arena, and for 20 years has put on some of the biggest names in rock, despite the poor sound quality. The likes of David Bowie, Bruce Springsteen, and Prince have been among those to do multinight stands here. Blur and the Smashing Pumpkins have played here more recently. In December 1995 the Manic Street Preachers gave their first gig after the disappearance of Richey Edwards here, supporting the Stone Roses. In September 1996, Sleeper, Björk, Ocean Colour

Jarvis Cocker at Wembley Arena

Scene, Sheryl Crow, and the Bluetones were among those who played here as part of a special *Top of the Pops* benefit for the Childline charity. *Empire Way at Lakeside Way, tel. 0181/900–1234. Wembley Park tube.*

WEMBLEY STADIUM

The world-famous 75-year-old stadium, home of soccer's FA Cup Final since 1923, has also put on its fair share of major rock gigs since an August 1972 rock & roll revival festival with Chuck Berry, Bill Haley, Billy Fury, and, somewhat incongruously, the MC5, before a crowd of 50,000. In June 1975 a massive 120,000 crowd turned up to see Elton John, the Eagles, and the Beach Boys, the latter stealing the show.

On July 13, 1985, Wembley hosted Live Aid, the first of several mega benefit gigs it staged in the '80s. Live Aid drew another six-figure crowd and more than a billion people on TV. The bill assembled the biggest, if not the best, acts on the planet—Queen, George Michael, Sting, Elton John, David Bowie, Dire Straits, a re-formed Who, U2, Phil Collins (who then crossed the Atlantic on the Concorde to play the Live Aid concert at the old JFK Stadium in Philadelphia), and Paul McCartney (whose mike quit during the opening bars of "Let It Be"). Over £50 million was raised and event instigator Bob Geldof got an honorary knighthood from the Queen.

Another bunch of superstars—Whitney Houston, George Michael, Simple Minds, and Dire Straits again—was hired to celebrate the 70th birthday of Nelson Mandela on June 11, 1988 (while he was still imprisoned), and this concert was shown on TV in 64 countries. The then-unknown Tracy Chapman, a late replacement for Stevie Wonder and one of the few black acts, became a household name overnight after a strong performance. The event was organized by Artists Against Apartheid, a collective of musicians kick-started by Jerry Dammers, who wrote the single, "Free Nelson Mandela" that his band, the Specials, took into the charts in 1984. A few months later, Wembley was the chosen venue for the first gig in the worldwide Amnesty tour. Ticket prices to watch Bruce Springsteen, Peter Gabriel, Sting, Tracy Chapman, and Youssou N'Dour were astronomical. The show began with all the performers uniting on stage for a version of Bob Marley's "Get Up, Stand Up." The stadium also hosted the concert in April 1990 to celebrate the release of Nelson Mandela. Neil Young turned in an awesome version of "Rockin' in the Free World." Others who appeared included the Neville Brothers, Lou Reed, Bonnie Raitt, Aswad, and veterans of the 1988 concert, Tracy Chapman and Peter Gabriel.

Two years later, another gaggle of names assembled here for a tribute concert to Freddie Mercury, with proceeds going to AIDS research. As well as sets by Metallica, Def Leppard, Extreme, and Guns N' Roses, the three remaining members of Queen were on stage accompanying the guest artists for much of the night. This part of the show had several duets, including the unlikely pairing of Elton John and Axl Rose. Organizers claimed that this event attracted a larger worldwide TV audience than Live Aid.

In recent years Wembley gigs (those who have filled the place have included U2, Guns N' Roses, and the Eagles) have tailed off due to competition from other open-air venues such as Milton Keynes Bowl, Finsbury Park, and Knebworth. Fans became fed up straining their necks to spot tiny specks on the distant stage and paying over the odds for burgers and drinks. The stadium is due for a major overhaul in 1998/99. *Empire Way, tel. 0181/900–1234. Wembley Park tube.*

North London

Running north from dynamic Islington through genteel Highgate and yuppie Crouch End on to seedy Tottenham, north London is where the Kinks were raised and pub rock flourished in the Hope and Anchor and other similar venues. It's also where Joy Division, the Clash, and the Sex Pistols cut many of their best-known records.

Songs of North London

The Kinks, "Muswell Hillbilly" (1971)
The Kinks, "Holloway Jail" (1971)
The Nipple Erectors, "Stavordale Rd, N5" (1977)
Marillion, "Holloway Girl" (1989)
St. Etienne, "Archway People" (1993)
My Life Story, "Angel" (1994)

A GEOGRAPHICAL NOTE

North London is defined here as places within the N1 to N22 postal codes (these numbers appear on the name plates of virtually every street).

Angel/Islington, N1

Islington, close to the West End, is immensely fashionable. In rock terms, it boasts the famous Hope and Anchor pub, the Garage venue, and Nick Mason's Britannia Row studio. Rolling Stones drummer Charlie Watts was born in the district in 1941 and grew up here. The place is dominated by yuppies and Labour Party hacks. Wine bars, fancy restaurants, antiques stores, and more antiques stores sprout along the main drag of Upper Street.

EATINGDRINKINGDANCINGSHOPPINGPLAYINGSLEEPING

The mile-long stretch between Highbury Corner and the district known as the Angel is great for drinking, eating, and shopping. You don't need to pay a lot of money to eat well at such places as **ALFREDO'S** (6 Essex Rd.), a great breakfast and lunch café. For live music, the main spot is the **GARAGE** (*see below*), north London's most important indie venue. The **HOPE AND ANCHOR** (*see below*) provides some historical interest, while the **WEAVERS** (*see below*) is the best place for roots in the capital. The Angel's main club is the huge **COMPLEX** (1–5 Parkfield St., tel. 0171/288–1986). **DISGRACELAND** (196 Essex Rd., tel. 0171/354–3369) is a great little pub/club that is strong on dub crossover sounds. Sporting industrial decor with some wild, kitschy trimmings, it puts on house/techno/jungle with regular live dance acts.

Brasseries, wine bars, and bistros of every nationality spoil the choice for something to eat. Sitar-player Ravi Shankar owns the vegetarian restaurant **RAVI SHANKAR** (422 St. John St., tel. 0171/833–5849).

RECKLESS RECORDS (79 Upper St., tel. 0171/359–2222), which has branches in San Francisco and in central London, has a basement with rare '70s albums on vinyl.

BRITANNIA ROW STUDIOS

Major albums recorded in this studio owned by Pink Floyd's Nick Mason include his band's *Animals* (1977), the Damned's *Music for Pleasure* (which Mason produced the same year), Joy Division's *Closer* and their "Love Will Tear Us Apart" single (both 1980), and New Order's 1983 LP, *Power, Corruption and Lies,* which singer Bernard Sumner wanted to call *Piss Off, You Lot. 35 Britannia Row, tel. 0171/226–3377. Angel tube.*

THE GARAGE

Behind a horrible purple paint job, right outside Highbury and Islington tube, lies London's best venue of its size. This old train shed was taken over in 1993 by the Mean Fiddler organization; since then it's been filling the space with the best alternative and indie acts. Particularly strong on U.S. bands, the Garage has hosted Boss Hog, Belly, Man or Astroman?, Matthew Sweet, Dinosaur Jr, and Rancid, and most of the bands on the Epitaph label have been here. Booker Jim Benner raves about the wild performances the Jesus Lizard have thrown in here and is particularly proud of nabbing Rocket From the Crypt's first U.K. gig. Britpop headliners have included Elastica, Echobelly, and Supergrass; interesting nuggets in recent years include Arthur Lee's Love and El Vez, who made his British stage debut here in July 1996. Dodgy also had a residency for its Dodgy Club, which featured guest appearances by many others, from Transglobal Underground to Ralph McTell.

A smaller auditorium—Upstairs at the Garage—that holds 200 is used mainly for acoustic players; some key performances here have been by Jeff Buckley, Dick Dale, and Grant Hart. *20–22 Highbury Corner, tel. 0171/607–1818. Highbury and Islington tube.*

HIGHBURY CORNER

In February 1996, former Wire guitarist Bruce Gilbert blasted his work out of speakers linked to three cars circling this busy rotary to promote his latest electronic recordings. One car provided the treble, one the middle, and one the bass. *Outside Highbury and Islington tube.*

THE HOPE AND ANCHOR

At first glance, it's hard to believe that this nondescript Victorian local was London's leading mid-'70s pub rock venue, breaking such groups as Dr. Feelgood, the Stranglers, and Graham Parker and the Rumour. Gigs were put on in the basement room, which was barely large enough to contain a handful of musicians, let alone an audience, generating an atmosphere that electrified even the most mundane of gigs. Down here, too, Stiff Records' Dave Robinson ran a recording studio and put out the *Hope and Anchor Front Row Festival* LP in November 1977, featuring the Stranglers.

The Hope and Anchor

The Hope and Anchor missed out on the main punk bands, like the Sex Pistols and the Clash, but was soon booking the best of the so-called new wave acts. XTC played in June 1977, Joy Division made their London debut in December 1978 playing to just 20 people (mostly journalists), Dexy's Midnight Runners did likewise six months later, and U2 came for what was only their fourth London gig the following December. Madness didn't play their first gig here; that took place right across the street in 1977 in the back garden of a sumptuous Georgian house at 8 Compton Terrace.

The pub stopped putting on bands in 1984, when the live music scene in London was at a low ebb, but it is now booking again, with new band, unplugged, rock, punk, and club nights; those who have played recently include Penthouse, Sidi Bou Said, Livingstone, and Terry Edwards. The pub itself is a major disappointment, with a jukebox you can find in any dive. Its importance in rock history is barely reflected by a few tatty plaques to the likes of Graham Parker and the Rumour, Eddie and the Hot Rods, Racing Cars, McGuinness Flint, and, surprisingly, Tim Hardin. *207 Upper St., at Islington Park St., tel. 0171/ 354–1312. Highbury and Islington tube.*

SCREEN ON THE GREEN

The Clash played their first official London gig, and the Buzzcocks their first outside Manchester, supporting the Sex Pistols at this popular artsy cinema in August 1976. The gig, billed as the Midnight Special, took place after the feature film was finished. The Clash's performance did not impress the *NME*'s Charles Shaar Murray, who, in an infamous review, described them as the "kind of garage band that should be speedily returned to the garage, preferably with the motor still running." Upset by his vitriol, the Clash responded by writing "Garageland"—which closed their debut album, *The Clash*—and Murray soon started to see their potential. *83 Upper St., tel. 0171/226–3520. Angel tube.*

THE WEAVERS

This unassuming pub has been putting on the best roots and serious country music in the capital since 1988, often bringing over artists from Texas and Louisiana for their first U.K. appearances. Butch Hancock, Jimmie Dale Gilmore, Flaco Jiminez, Junior Brown, Rattlesnake Annie, and Guy Clark are among the big names to have come here. Cajun is popular: Steve Riley and the Mamou Playboys have played here recently. Irish roots music also has an important place at the Weavers, with performers such as Altan, Sharon Shannon, and Davy Spillane. In 1992 Weaving Records was established; to date it has released a handful of compilation CDs featuring both the established and local artists who have taken the Weavers' stage. It's only coincidence that it shares its name with the '50s folk group; the pub has had this title for more than 200 years. *98 Newington Green Rd., tel. 0171/226–6911.*

Crouch End/Hornsey, N8

Little more than a few streets around a traffic junction based on old ley lines, Crouch End has recently become a hip residential district for music biz and media types who have migrated from nearby Highgate (too expensive), Tottenham (too rough), and Camden Town (too tacky).

EATING DRINKING DANCING SHOPPING PLAYING SLEEPING

The best hangout is the **WORLD CAFÉ** (130 Crouch Hill, tel. 0181/340–5635), a wonderfully laid-back little place just across the street from Church Studios; it's a favorite stop for Dylan when he's in town. The mumbling one has also acquired a taste for curry at **SHAMRAT OF INDIA** (34 Broadway Parade, tel. 0181/341–5461), where he orders chicken vindaloo. At **BANNERS** café-bar (21 Park Rd., tel. 0181/348–2930), the food is pretty lousy, but there's much rootsy American music memorabilia on the walls and sometimes live music. Well-stocked **TERRAPIN RECORDS** (15 Park Rd., tel. 0181/292–0085) is one of the best places for Grateful Dead-type music in the country.

CHURCH STUDIOS

One of London's very best-equipped studios was converted from an old church in the mid-'80s by the Eurythmics pair, Dave Stewart and Annie Lennox. They recorded much of their output here. When the band split, Stewart took sole control, and the studio now operates on a fully commercial basis. Like everyone else, Stewart has to book studio time. Church is perhaps most famous for Bob Dylan, who comes in and strums whenever he's in town, though top albums by Therapy?, the Boo Radleys, Nick Cave, the Divine Comedy, and Alicia's Attic have been recorded here, and Lou Reed, Paul McCartney, and Bryan Ferry have also been recent visitors. *145H Crouch Hill, Crouch End, N8, tel. 0181/340–9779. Crouch Hill BR.*

MIXED-UP CONFUSION

Sometime in the mid-'80s, Bob Dylan and Dave Stewart struck up what was to be a close friendship. The British producer suggested that Dylan look him up whenever he next came to London, saying, "The address is 145 Crouch Hill. Call in anytime." Sure enough, Dylan came to London, decided to look up his buddy, and journeyed up to Crouch End. Confusingly for Dylan (and probably many others), though, there is also a major street called Crouch End Hill, and it was at 145 Crouch End Hill where Dylan knocked on the door and said, "I'm here to see Dave." The woman who answered said that her husband Dave was out but to come on in. Not long afterward, the husband came home, and the wife said, "Your friend Bob is in the living room." The husband, a local plumber, thinking this wasn't weird, as indeed he had a friend called Bob, walked into the room and found Dylan sipping a cup of tea. After the initial shock, he, unlike his wife, realized he had one of the world's most famous people in his front room and managed to sort out the confusion.

HORNSEY COLLEGE OF ART

Past students include the Kinks' Ray Davies and Deep Purple bassist Roger Glover, both of whom attended in the early '60s. Adam Ant (a.k.a. Stewart Goddard) attended in the mid-'70s, along with a couple of Raincoats and a Slit. The Stranglers played here in 1976 (with the Vibrators making their debut performance) a few weeks before the big gig at the 100 Club with the Pistols. The building is now the Trades Union Congress National Education Centre. *77 Crouch End Hill.*

KONK STUDIO

Ray Davies built this studio onto a house in 1976. The Kinks have recorded here ever since, and much of the action in Davies's quasi-autobiographical *X-Ray* takes place here. Other users have been as varied as the Bay City Rollers and Nick Cave. More recently, Britpop bands have been lining up to use the space, including Elastica, Echobelly, Skunk Anansie, and Supergrass. *84 Tottenham La., tel. 0181/340–7873. Hornsey BR.*

Finsbury Park, N4

This gray part of north London is dominated by railway lines and the unattractive park that gives the area its name. The park is now the main green space in the capital for one-day concerts. The neighborhood's most famous live music landmark, the former Astoria/Rainbow, is now a church, but the Powerhaus gets in bands on the way up. The local tube station is also the site of one of the most bizarre rock deaths in Britain.

[THE ASTORIA/THE RAINBOW]

Down at the Astoria the scene was changing...we were the first band to vomit in the bar—The Who, "Long Live Rock"

A major rock venue in the '60s (as the Astoria) and in the '70s (as the Rainbow), this was where the Beatles played their last English gig (on December 11, 1965) and where Jimi Hendrix first doused his guitar with gasoline before lighting it (March 31, 1967) on the opening night of the Experience's first tour. The Experience was sharing a bill with the Walker Brothers, Cat Stevens, and Engelbert Humperdinck, and it wasn't a spontaneous event—Hendrix felt he needed a stunt to take attention away from the Walkers.

The Astoria became the Rainbow after refurbishment in 1971. Frank Zappa and the Mothers of Invention were billed to play two shows on December 10, 1971, but only managed one. During the encore, a fan pushed Zappa off stage; he fell into the orchestra pit unconscious. He had broken a leg and couldn't tour for a year.

Pink Floyd showcased *Dark Side of the Moon* over four nights in February 1972, a year before it was released. Floyd returned on November 4, 1973, with a spectacular show in which a 4-foot model airplane zoomed through the auditorium and exploded upon reaching the stage. Weirder still was Can's February 18, 1973, gig, one of the few London dates they ever played. The first 15 minutes took place in complete darkness. When the lights eventually came on, the by-then restless audience was even more perturbed to find Holger Czukay fiddling with a transistor radio. The rest of the gig was of their usual high standard.

Steve Morley/courtesy of Redferns

Dire Straits plays the Rainbow

Also in 1973, two of the best-known of the handful of live albums recorded at the Rainbow were cut. A Pete Townshend—organized Fanfare for Youth concert in January 1973 was supposed to celebrate Britain's entry into the European Economic Community, but it received more hype for marking Eric Clapton's return to the stage after three years' absence due to heroin addiction. Clapton, wearing a white suit and white boots, was joined by Rick Grech, Ronnie Wood, and Stevie Winwood, among others, and the gig was recorded as *Eric Clapton's Rainbow Concert.* That July Van Morrison (playing with the Caledonia Soul Orchestra) invited his six-year-old daughter onto the stage during gigs that were being recorded for the live double, *It's Too Late To Stop Now.* Other albums recorded here include Spirit's *Spirit Live,* in March 1978, and the Ramones' *It's Alive,* from 1979. In January 1977 the Stranglers' Hugh Cornwell came on stage wearing a "Fuck" T-shirt, the oath designed in the style of the Ford logo. Officials from the Greater London Council, watching—with binoculars—from the back of the hall, sent the band's manager onstage to get Cornwell to remove the shirt, threatening to pull the plug. Cornwell turned the shirt inside out; the men from the council were not satisfied, and they pulled the switch: cue miniriot.

More trouble came on May 9, 1977, when the White Riot tour—the Clash, the Jam, the Slits, the Buzzcocks, and Subway Sect—ended its run here. When the Clash asked the venue's management to take the seats out, they refused, so the band urged the crowd to do the job for them and stage a riot of their own.

By the '80s, the Rainbow was in such disrepair it was no longer profitable for promoters to put on gigs. Promoter Harvey Goldsmith considered buying the place until he found the basement flooded before a gig. It closed down and the building continued to fester. In 1995 it was bought by the Brazilian-based Universal Church of the Kingdom of God after they unsuccessfully bid to buy the Brixton Academy. *232 Seven Sisters Rd. Finsbury Park tube.*

FINSBURY PARK

During the '90s this large but unattractive park has proved an unlikely rival to Wembley Stadium for a big music day out. Finsbury one-dayers usually offer anything from 5 to 25 bands and a greater sense of camaraderie. The biggest success story of all is the annual Irish-themed Fleadh (pronounced "fla" and meaning "party" in Irish), started in 1988 by Irish-born Vince Power of the giant Mean Fiddler organization. It was a great piece of niche marketing, given the large

Fleadh, 1995

number of young Irish (not to mention romantic second-generation types) in London. The bill has become increasingly less Gaelic—Sting and Crowded House have been recent headliners—but Christy Moore is a hardy perennial; the program is packed with crossover Irish acts such as Clannad and Altan. Van Morrison has also played several times, as has Shane MacGowan. U2 are about the only big name from Ireland never to have done the event. It's reckoned one in every 12 pints of Guinness sold in Britain on that day is drunk in this field.

In August 1992 Madness organized Madstock at Finsbury Park, a reunion gig where they were supported by Flowered Up, Ian Dury, and Morrissey, who draped himself in the Union Jack during "National Front Disco," despite a strong presence of Front (National

Front, a small but extreme right-wing party—a skinhead, less-organized version of the KKK in the United States) supporters in the crowd. After being pelted with coins and weapons during the next number, he left the stage and refused to come back, pulling out of the next day's event as well.

The busiest year yet for the park was 1996, with Fleadh VIII, Madstock III, the Sex Pistols reunion on June 23, 1996 (where the *Filthy Lucre Live* album was recorded), and an event headed by Paul Weller a few weeks later. Kiss was one of the big names in 1997. *Seven Sisters Rd. Finsbury Park tube.*

FINSBURY PARK TUBE STATION

British R&B innovator Graham Bond—whose band, the Graham Bond Organisation, included Jack Bruce, Ginger Baker, and John McLaughlin—died beneath the wheels of a train at this tube station in May 1974. After the short-lived GBO split up in 1967, Bond developed a huge drug appetite. The 36-year-old Bond's reliance on drugs is usually put forward as the explanation for his death, but Bond, who was also well into the occult, had just performed an exorcism during which a demon supposedly invaded him, dragged him to the station, and forced him in front of the train.

POWERHAUS/THE GEORGE ROBEY

Those who liked their live music environs rough, ready, and a bit dirty were sad to see the demise of the George Robey, as this venue was called until March 1, 1996. Johnny Rotten's local in the early '70s, it was popular with crusties—they even had posts for gig-goers to tie their dogs to—particularly on weekend club nights when they tried to re-create a slice of Glastonbury in Finsbury Park. The eclectic range of music covered the punk end of indie (S*M*A*S*H, Done Lying Down) plus reggae, folk, and dance. The Mean Fiddler organization took the place over in March 1996 and renamed it the Powerhaus. Indie hopefuls Salad played the opening night. It now sports spanking-new decor and a quality sound system, but the dog posts are gone. The music, too, is more geared toward guitar bands; recent bookings in the club have

Massachusetts's alt-country Scud Mountain Boys play the Powerhaus, 1996

included Die Cheerleader and Southern Culture on the Skids, plus a secret show by the Butthole Surfers. *240 Seven Sisters Rd., tel. 0171/561–9656. Finsbury Park tube.*

Highbury, N5

Perched between the expensive bit of Islington and seedy Finsbury Park, Highbury is one of the few districts of North London that has retained a villagey feel. It has proved a good location for two successful studios.

ARSENAL FOOTBALL CLUB

London's most successful soccer club enjoys many rock & roll connections. Fans include the Kinks' Ray Davies, a season-ticket holder; Spandau Ballet's Martin Kemp, who was a schoolboy trainee; and John Lydon, who used a photo of the Arsenal crowd at a match on the inside cover of his autobiography, *Rotten: No Irish, No Dogs, No Blacks.* Pink Floyd originally planned to call "Echoes," the lengthy piece that takes up side two of 1971's *Meddle*, "We Won the Double" in honor of the club's trophy-winning 1971 season. Morrissey, who supports Manchester United, called his 1993 album *Your Arsenal. Avenell Rd., tel. 0171/226–0304. Arsenal tube.*

MATRIX-WESSEX STUDIOS

Many of the Sex Pistols' and the Clash's most important tracks were recorded in this former Rank Charm School behind a church on elegant Highbury New Park. The Pistols first visited in fall 1976 to work on "Anarchy in the U.K.," for which producer Chris Thomas, who had worked alongside George Martin on the Beatles' "Helter Skelter" and "Octupus's Garden," needed 29 guitar overdubs. Thomas had also mixed Pink Floyd's *Dark Side of the Moon* at Abbey Road, which was ironic, as Johnny Rotten used to wear a Pink Floyd T-shirt embellished with the words, "I hate."

The Clash came here in January 1979 to cut the "Cost of Living" EP, which featured "I Fought the Law," and returned in August 1979 to start work on *London Calling*. To get here from his apartment in World's End, Chelsea, Strummer used to take Bus 19, hence the line, "Sing Michael sing, on the route of the 19 bus," on "Rudi Can't Fail."

The Clash also recorded most of *London Calling*'s overblown follow-up, the triple *Sandinista!* set at Wessex, during which Ian Dury's backing band, the Blockheads, stormed the studio dressed as the cops and caused near heart attacks all round. In 1982 the Clash returned to remix *Combat Rock*, with ex-Who producer Glyn Johns at the controls. Matrix-Wessex continues to be one of London's major studios, having recently recorded Dodgy and (London) Suede. *106 Highbury New Park, tel. 0171/ 359–0051. Canonbury BR.*

Pathway Studios

PATHWAY STUDIOS

This studio right in the heart of bedsitland was a major player in the early days of punk. Records cut here include the Police's first single, "Fall Out"; Squeeze's "Packet of Three" EP; Siouxsie and the Banshees' "Hong Kong Garden"; and Sham 69's debut, "I Don't Wanna." Although nowadays Pathway serves mostly local blues, cajun, and ethnic acts, some of the old names have returned in the '90s. Nick Lowe (who did the first single on Stiff Records, "So It Goes," here in 1976) has been in; so has Elvis Costello, to do some tracks on 1993's *Brutal Youth* album, 16 years after he recorded his debut LP, *My Aim Is True*, here. *2a Grosvenor Ave., tel. 0171/359–0970. Canonbury BR.*

Holloway, N7, N19

The kind of neighborhood Holloway is can be gauged from Jimmy Lydon, John's brother and member of the punk band the Bollock Brothers, who claimed in *Rotten: No Irish, No Dogs, No Blacks* that Queensland Road, near where the Lydons were brought up in the late '50s/early '60s, was the roughest street in London. When John Lydon was six (in 1962), brother Jimmy brought home a policeman's helmet that kids had been kicking around and a gun; the copper they belonged to had just been killed by local Teds. The Victorian tenement, on Benwell Road between Queensland Road and the main Holloway Road drag, where the Lydons were raised had no inside toilet. Conditions were so bad that John caught spinal meningitis from drinking contaminated water. By the '70s the Lydons' slum had been demolished, but on the same road, the music paper *Sounds* was based (at No. 1). Killing Joke's Jaz Coleman once emptied a bucket of offal over the reception area after a bad review. The magazine, a sturdy rival to *Melody Maker* and the *New Musical Express* in punk days, ceased publishing in the late '80s.

EATINGDRINKINGDANCINGSHOPPINGPLAYINGSLEEPING

Although cheap rents mean lots of young people, the bars are at best dull. **THE ROCKET** (166 Holloway Rd., N7, tel. 0171/700–2421) has of late been putting on some good dance crossover all-nighters. **THE DOME** (178 Junction Rd., Tufnell Park, N19, tel. 0171/272–8153) is a scruffy joint that puts on a mixed bag of live and DJ music.

ARCHWAY TAVERN

The Kinks were photographed leaning against the bar of this rough pub for the front cover of *Muswell Hillbillies.* The pub is one of the few local buildings to have survived the rebuilding of the last 30 years. Ray Davies later claimed that the Tavern was chosen because in the early '70s when the Kinks were working on the album, it had the world's worst country & western band. *Archway Close, tel. 0171/272–2840. Archway tube.*

The Kinks, Muswell Hillbillies

HOLLOWAY PRISON

When child killer Myra Hindley, one of the "Moors Murderers," was incarcerated here in summer 1966, other prisoners chanted the biblical line, "Suffer little children to come unto me," at her when she walked past. Morrissey, obsessed with the grisly murders that had taken place just outside Manchester in the '60s, used "Suffer Little Children" as the name of the first song he and Johnny Marr worked on. The jail also inspired two more direct references—"Holloway Jail" and "Holloway Girls"—by the Kinks and Marillion respectively. *Parkhurst Rd. at Dalmeny Ave. Tufnell Park tube.*

JOE MEEK'S STUDIO

Above what is now a cycle store on busy Holloway Road, Joe Meek, Britain's first independent rock & roll producer, ran the tiny studio where then-unknowns such as Tom Jones and Rod Stewart made some of their earliest records. Here Meek also cut an impressive string of hits in the early '60s, including Johnny Leyton's eerie "Johnny Remember Me" and the Tornados' "Telstar," the first record by a British group to top the U.S. charts (it was also a No. 1 in Britain).

Paranoid about the possibility of others, particularly Phil Spector (!) stealing his work, Meek would incessantly search the place for bugs and lost his temper at the slightest thing, flinging pieces of equipment across the room. He once threatened drummer Mitch Mitchell (who later joined the Jimi Hendrix Experience) with a shotgun for playing the wrong rhythm.

From being one of the most powerful men in British pop in the early '60s, Meek soon dropped to obscurity once the Beatles and other beat groups took hold of the charts. This sent him into further bouts of melancholy. On February 3, 1967, the ninth anniversary of Buddy Holly's death, Meek shot his landlady after an argument and then turned the gun on himself. On the wall above the store, a black plaque reads: "Joe Meek, record producer, the Telstar Man, 1929–1967, pioneer of sound and recording technology, lived, worked, and died here." If Meek could speak from the grave, he'd probably still claim that he never received a penny of royalties for the record that made him famous. *304 Holloway Rd. Holloway Rd. tube.*

NORTH LONDON POLYTECHNIC
(UNIVERSITY OF NORTH LONDON)

On March 15, 1985, at a Jesus and Mary Chain concert advertised under the title "Art As Terrorism" and oversold, many ticket holders were left outside. Bobby Gillespie (JAMC's stand-up drummer at the time) tried to remedy the problem by kicking down the main doors. When JAMC took to the stage an hour after the final support band, one irritated guy tried to drag guitarist Jim Reid off stage. The band left the stage for a bit, but when a PA stack was knocked over by some punters, the band had had enough. Some angry types got backstage but couldn't find the dressing room; the law arrived just in time to stop the crowd from trashing the whole college. An estimated £8,000 worth of equipment was wrecked, and four fans were taken to the hospital. Swansea-based Fierce Records later released "Riot," a 7-inch limited-edition recording of the event *Holloway Rd. Holloway Rd. tube.*

PENTONVILLE PRISON

Stranglers singer Hugh Cornwell spent two months inside for possession of heroin early in 1980 after being arrested in Hammersmith. He wrote the book *Inside Information* about his experiences. *Caledonian Rd. at Wheelwright St. Caledonian Rd. tube.*

Muswell Hill, N10

Muswell Hill is known in rock circles for being the Kinks' much-loved home. The Kinks, together with a band called the Ethnic Shuffle Orchestra, featuring a pre-Fairport Convention Ashley Hutchings, used to play the North Bank Youth Club in Muswell Hill in the early '60s. In 1971 Ray Davies called a Kinks album *Muswell Hillbillies*. This pun on the Beverly Hillbillies referred to families forced out of their neighborhood in the '60s when the busy Archway traffic junction, a mile and a half south, was developed without any regard to the existing community. (*See also* the Archway Tavern, *above.*)

"FAIRPORT"

Fairport Convention took their name from this large detached house, "Fairport," where they rehearsed in 1966. It was owned by guitarist Simon Nicol's parents. *Fortismere Ave. at Fortis Green. East Finchley tube.*

Stoke Newington/ Stamford Hill, N16

A haven for refugees and other immigrants for much of this century, Stoke Newington has become popular with students, bohemian types, and media people over the last decade despite having no tube station and appalling bus service to central London.

Stoke Newington Church Street, the main east–west route, is packed with quality, inexpensive restaurants, including Georgian, Turkish, and Malaysian. There are many popular bars, including **BAR LORCA** (175 Stoke Newington Church St., tel. 0171/254–2266), which has good tapas and live Latin music. **THE VORTEX** (139 Stoke Newington Church St., tel. 0171/254–6516) has a bookshop, a café, and a venue dealing mostly in jazz and worldbeat in the same building. As for more conventional drinking spots, the spit-and-sawdust **SHAKESPEARE** (57 Allan Rd., tel. 0171/254–4190) attracts a lively, studenty crowd despite being off the main drag. **TOTEM** (168 Stoke Newington Church St., tel. 0171/275–0234) is a reasonably priced general secondhand vinyl store.

MARC BOLAN'S ADDRESS, 1947–62

A plaque commemorates the fact that Marc Bolan, born Marc Feld in Hackney Hospital 2 miles away on September 30, 1947, was raised in this shabby terrace. *25 Stoke Newington Common.*

Wood Green, N22

This shabby suburb is dominated by the Victorian monstrosity Alexandra Palace, set on one of north London's loftiest hills. The Palace was the scene of a defining hippie-era event, the 14-Hour Technicolor Dream. The district also has some pub rock history and is the unlikely setting for the recording of one of R.E.M.'s better albums.

ALEXANDRA PALACE

In November 1936 the world's first public television broadcast was transmitted from this 19th-century folly, which had been used as a POW camp during the first world war. By the mid-'60s, however, Ally Pally, as it is affectionately known, was being used for some of the first rock concerts to break the sterile package tour mold. The first was a June 1964 "all night rave" organized by the Rolling Stones' fan club that also featured John Lee Hooker. The high point was the April 1967 benefit for *International Times* (*see below*). New Year's Eve 1968 saw the last-ever show by the Small Faces, while one of the major events in the following decade was a three-night stand by the Grateful Dead in fall 1974.

The building was gutted by a near-disastrous fire two weeks after it was built in 1873 and again in 1980. Now restored, it is used as a conference and exhibitions center. Few gigs take place, though there have been shows in recent years by the Stone Roses (1989), Blur, who shot their *Showtime* video here (1994), and Orbital (New Year's Eve 1996). It was also where the awkwardly run MTV Europe Awards were held in late '96. *The Avenue at Duke's Ave., tel. 0181/365–2121. Alexandra Palace BR.*

SUMMER OF LOVE N22

The most famous event held at Alexandra Palace was the 14-Hour Technicolor Dream benefit for the underground *International Times* magazine on April 29, 1967. *IT* had been threatened with closure after their offices were raided by the vice squad, who took away literally every scrap of paper—including phone directories—from their offices. The April 1967 event, attended by 10,000 people, is now seen as one of the defining moments of the hippie era in Britain. Performers included Mick Farren and the Deviants, Alex Harvey, Graham Bond, the Pretty Things, John's Children (featuring Marc Bolan), Tomorrow (with a pre-Yes Steve Howe), Pink Floyd, Soft Machine, and the Crazy World of Arthur Brown—known pyromaniac Brown came on in a helmet and long flowing robe screeching "I am the God of hellfire, and I bring you . . . fire!!!"

Nonmusic performers included British beat poet Michael Horovitz and Yoko Ono, who performed an act called Cut Piece, in which she invited a girl on stage and asked members of the audience to come up and cut off pieces from her clothes until she was naked. When the girl was down to her bra and knickers, a bouncer came on stage and carted her off in a blanket to audience groans.

But it was the Soft Machine who won all the plaudits for costumes. Kevin Ayers sported glider wings on top of his cowboy hat, Daevid Allen wore a miner's helmet—supposedly to stop his brains from falling out—while Robert Wyatt came on in a suit and tie with a short back and sides haircut: It was his protest against what he called the Californianization of the U.K. rock scene. Pink Floyd, who topped the bill, came on as dawn broke and sunlight streamed through the glass roof. It was one of their last gigs with Syd Barrett, who was out of it on acid and lasted about four numbers.

LIVINGSTON STUDIOS

The Livingston operation moved to this converted church in 1980 and soon built on its reputation for folk-rock developed during the '60s and '70s. R.E.M. traveled the whole way from Georgia to this obscure part of north London to record their *Fables of the Reconstruction* in March 1985 just so that they could team up with producer Joe Boyd, whose work with Fairport Convention and Nick Drake they so admired. A few weeks later 10,000 Maniacs followed suit for *Wishing Chair,* their first album for Elektra. Recent years have seen the production of Everything But the Girl's *Amplified Heart* album, which included the zillion-selling "Missing," while parts of Björk's first LP, *Debut,* were done at the now-closed annex in nearby Guillemot Place. *Brook Rd, off Mayes Rd, tel. 0181/889-6558. Wood Green tube.*

Northwest London

In rock terms, northwest London is dominated by brash Camden Town, crammed with music venues, clubs, bars, and street markets selling alternative wares. A little farther west is exclusive St. Johns Wood, home of London's best-known rock landmark, the Abbey Road studio. If all the rock stuff gets to be too much, there's always London Zoo to visit, where Bon Jovi have sponsored a ruffled lemur.

Songs of Northwest London

Donovan, "Hampstead Incident" (1966)
Al Stewart, "Swiss Cottage Manoeuvres" (1967)
Bee Gees, "Kilburn Towers" (1968)
Nirvana, "St. John's Wood Affair" (1968)
The Kinks, "Willesden Green" (1971)
Madness, "Primrose Hill" (1982)
Microdisney, "Singer's Hampstead Home" (1988)
Gallon Drunk, "Arlington Road" (1992)
The Popinjays, "Kentish Town" (1994)
Suggs, "Camden Town" (1995)
Ed Ball, "The Mill Hill Self-Hate Club" (1996)

Northwest London is defined here as places within the NW1 to NW11 postal codes, north of the Thames (these numbers appear on the name plates of virtually every street). Some of NW1 falls in King's Cross/Euston (*see* Central London).

Camden Town, NW1

I got the ticket from some fucked-up guy in Camden Town—Pulp, "Sorted For E's and Whizz"

Over the last two decades Camden Town has overtaken Notting Hill, Chelsea, and Soho as London's hippest hangout area. On weekends it's downright claustrophobically crowded with tourists and shoppers. It wasn't always this way; built up around the canals, during the 19th century it was a cheap area for Irish immigrants to settle. To this day the place, particularly just off the main drags, has a rugged working-class feel.

Camden Town's popularity in the rock world dates from the late '60s, when every head in the capital would descend on the Roundhouse to see groups like the Soft Machine or Led Zeppelin. In the mid-'70s Camden Town attracted punks in search of records in Camden Market, and Dingwalls started putting on new bands. The district's dive bars also achieved a reputation for heavy drinking: Bon Scott downed his last liquor here, Shane MacGowan of the Pogues helped boost bar profits at several establishments, and his buddy the Texan country-rocker Steve Earle gave a nod to the place on "Johnny Come Lately," with the line, "I'm gonna drink Camden Town dry tonight if I have to spend my last pound." Cheap rents and bountiful squats provided a good base for bands, including Gallon Drunk and the country-rock outfit the Rockingbirds.

In recent years Camden has been the center of the Britpop explosion. It became a regular stomping ground for the likes of Blur, Menswear, and Lush, plus their mainly teenage fans. Noel Gallagher of Oasis, just like the Beatles had before him, moved down to London as soon as he had made it, and lives round here, as does Morrissey (who has a £650,000 luxury house in very exclusive Regents Park Terrace). The industry has also moved in gradually. MTV Europe is based here, as are Creation Records and the Food label.

For all landmarks, unless otherwise stated, use Camden Town tube.

EATING DRINKING DANCING SHOPPING PLAYING SLEEPING

Camden Town has it all, from smoky old guys' pubs to swanky designer joints. The **ENGINE ROOM** (*see below*) is probably the best and the most unusual pub. The **GOOD MIXER** (*see below*) was the hub of the Britpop scene of the mid-'90s. When the Mixer got too crowded, the "stars" and the industry movers slunk off to the **SPREAD EAGLE** (141 Albert St., tel. 0171/267–1410), where fewer annoying teenies are to be found. **THE HAWLEY ARMS** (2 Castlehaven Rd., tel. 0171/485–2855) is a comfy place with a wildly eclectic jukebox. The modern, plate-glass-fronted **WKD CAFÉ** (18 Kentish Town Rd., tel. 0171/267–1869) plays jazz, soul, and reggae sounds—both live and DJ'd—in the evening, has decent food, and is open late.

On a good night, it's possible to choose from as many as 10 live music bills in Camden Town. In 1995 the first Camden Live series of gigs was broadcast on Radio 1FM. There's also the Camden Crawl, a night of some 15 bands (headliners have included the Wedding Present) playing in five venues for a flat £5 fee. The coolest place of late has been the seven-nights-a-week Barfly Club at the **FALCON** (*see below*). **CAMDEN PALACE, DINGWALL'S, DUBLIN CASTLE,** and the **ELECTRIC BALLROOM** (*see below*) often have something

Steve Gillett

Drugstore performing at the Underworld

to offer. The **Laurel Tree** (113 Bayham St., tel. 0171/485–1383) is by day a quirky boozer, but on weekends it has Britpoppish disco nights and the occasional live band. **The Jazz Café** (5 Parkway, tel. 0171/916–6060), another outfit run by the Mean Fiddler organization, has throughout the '90s showcased the best names in modern jazz. **The Monarch** (49 Chalk Farm Rd., tel. 0171/916–1049), putting on gigs since 1991, has already proven itself to be one of the top breaking grounds for new bands in the area. **The Underworld** (174 Camden High St., tel. 0171/482–1932), in a labyrinthine basement under the World's End pub, puts on predominantly indie bands and club nights.

Camden's reputation as a tourist magnet—it is officially the fourth-largest attraction in London—rests largely with its markets; on a Sunday in summer, it's shuffling pace only. The real in-yer-face place to be is the covered **Camden Market** (open Thurs.–Sun.), 50 yards north of Camden Town tube station on Camden High Street. This hectic jumble of some 120 stalls is best for alternative trendsetting clothing and jewelry and has some good record stalls as well. **Camden Lock** (Chalk Farm Rd. at Regent's Canal; open Thurs.–Sun.), farther north up Camden High Street, consists of warehouses that were carefully redeveloped in the early '90s into a three-story indoor market with antiques, clothing, book, and ethnic food stalls. **The Electric Market** in the Electric Ballroom (184 Camden High St., tel. 0171/485–9006) has good alternative designer stuff on weekends and lots of record stalls. At **Stables Market** (Chalk Farm Rd.; open weekends), even farther north, outlets selling antiques, clothes, and New Age stuff are built into old warehouses, one of which was where the Clash formulated their sound (*see* Rehearsal Rehearsals, *below*).

Camden Town teems with record sellers, from hawkers selling bootlegs on the sidewalk, through the dozens of stalls in the markets, to some of the most established secondhand stores in the city. There are also record fairs most Saturdays in the Electric Ballroom (184 Camden High St., information tel. 0116/271–1977), with more than 50 dealers. The Camden branch of the **Music & Video Exchange** (229 Camden High St., tel. 0171/267–1898; open daily until 8 PM), has a good stock of secondhand CDs and vinyl, though prices tend to be tourist-level. The friendly but pricey **Out on the Floor** (10 Inverness St., tel. 0171/267–5989) is well stocked with blues, rock, '60s obscurities, funk, and jazzy stuff on vinyl and secondhand singles in the basement. **RHYTHM RECORDS** (281 Camden High St., tel. 0171/267–0123) holds an eclectic range of most genres and is particularly good on indie, hardcore, and progressive countryish stuff. **SHAKEDOWN** (24 Inverness St., tel. 0171/284–2402) sells used rock, reggae and punk on vinyl and CD. For drum & bass, house, and garage dance stuff, **DEEP FREEZE** (63 Camden Rd., tel. 0171/424–0572) has all the latest releases. **ZOOM** (162 Camden High St., tel. 0171/267–4479) gets in lots of dance imports from the States. **THE FOLK SHOP** (2 Regent's Park., tel. 0171/284–0534), located in Cecil Sharp House, which puts on live folk events, sells traditional sounds from around the world and is particularly strong on English and Celtic artists. For **ROCK ON,** see below.

ARLINGTON HOUSE

This monstrous-looking Victorian hostel for homeless people, next to the Good Mixer pub, featured in Madness's wistful 1984 single, "One Better Day," in the lines, "Arlington House, address, no fixed abode/An old man in a three-piece suit/Sits in the road." The Pogues also gave it a reference that year—"from Arlington House with a two bob bit"— in "Transmetropolitan." Nine years later, Gallon Drunk dealt with similar circumstances in their song, "Arlington Road." Arlington Rd. at Inverness St.

MUSIC MACHINE (CAMDEN PALACE)

Formerly a grand music hall, once used by the BBC, it was a popular venue and club in the late '70s and early '80s, when it was known as the Music Machine. On August 17, 1978, the Human League played here behind riot shields to protect their equipment, and in December that year the Clash played a benefit for the recently dead Sid Vicious. On February 19, 1980, AC/DC's Bon Scott downed his last drinks here before heading for southeast London, where he died while sleeping in a car (see Southeast London, below).

During the romantic early '80s, the venue became the Camden Palace, hosting a narcissistic club run by Steve Strange, which the Pogues put down in "Transmetropolitan" with a line about "scaring the Camden Palace poofs." In 1988 Prince staged a special invitation-only party here with guest appearances on stage from Eric Clapton, Boy George, Ron Wood, and actor Mickey Rourke. More recently it's been best known as home to the teen-friendly Feet First indie club, which puts on live bands at midnight. 1a Camden High St., next to Mornington Crescent tube station, tel. 0171/387–0428 or 0171/387–0429.

CREATION RECORDS

Named for one of founder Alan McGee's favorite U.K. '60s psychedelic bands, Creation, started in 1983 from a house in Tottenham, has become one of the most successful British independent labels ever. The label earned critical acclaim with discs by Primal Scream and McGee's old friends the Jesus and Mary Chain. Although JAMC soon left for a major label, new successes in the late '80s arrived in the form of the House of Love, My Bloody Valentine, and Ride. McGee then picked up Teenage Fanclub and the Boo

Giles Duley

Super Furry Animals

Radleys from other labels. The big coup came when he signed a little-known Manchester band who turned out to be Oasis. More recent signings include trippy Welsh rockers Super Furry Animals and the punky Three Colours Red. *109 Regents Park Rd., tel. 0171/ 722-8866.*

DINGWALLS

Now mainly used as the Jongleurs comedy venue, Dingwall's was one of London's leading clubs in the '70s and '80s. Hawkwind recorded "Silver Machine" here in 1972. It was with punk that the place took off; the Stranglers namedropped the place in "London Lady."

Dingwalls was popular with rock writers; *NME* used to hold their Christmas parties here, with entertainment by groups such as the Flamin' Groovies, the Clash, the Ramones, Motörhead, Thin Lizzy, and Ian Dury. After a Ramones/Stranglers/Flamin' Groovies punk special in August 1976, Clash bassist Simonon had a famous fight with his Stranglers counterpart, Jean Jacques Burnel, outside the building. It quickly turned into a mass brawl involving an A to Z of London punk, including Johnny Rotten, Sid Vicious, and arch-Stranglers fan Dagenham Dave. There were no arrests that time, but Joe Strummer was picked up by the law in May 1977 for spraying THE CLASH on the wall outside.

In May 1980 Alex Chilton recorded his *Live in London* album here, and eight years later Dingwall's was the setting for the first gig that any of Blur can remember playing. They were then known as Seymour and were bottom of a bill that included the New Fast Automatic Daffodils and Too Much Texas. The group ended their set on a high note—sprayed with Mace by killjoy bouncers.

After a lay-off from live music for several years to make way for comedy, the club has brought in Steve Earle, Ian McNabb, Tarnation, Deus, and My Life Story for recent gigs. *Middle Yard, Camden Lock, Camden High St., tel. 0171/267-1999.*

DUBLIN CASTLE

You'll find live music seven nights a week in the back of this dark, ordinary-looking pub. Its 150 capacity was more often than not exceeded at early Madness gigs. That band later returned here to shoot footage for their movie, *Take It or Leave It.* Several different promoters use the space to put on the best new indie bands; in the early '90s Club Zitt presented the first shows by Gene and Delicatessen; in 1996 the Liverpool band Space played here well before they had a hit. The Castle also got worldwide attention when Blur, at the height of the Britpop peak, played a secret show in May 1995. *94 Parkway, tel. 0171/405-1773.*

ELECTRIC BALLROOM

When former Lizzy tour manager Frank Murray converted and refurbished this old Irish dance hall, opening night, July 28, 1977, featured the Greedy Bastards with a lineup of Thin Lizzy (the Lynott, Moore, Gorham, Downey format), Jimmy Bain, Chris Spedding, Paul Cook, Steve Jones, and many others. It was at this dive venue that Sid Vicious gave his last live performance, on August 22, 1978, playing in a punk "supergroup" with Rat Scabies and Glen Matlock. Half of A Certain Ratio's 1980 cassette-only release on Factory, called *The Graveyard and the Ballroom,* was recorded here supporting Talking Heads. The Electric Ballroom still puts on a few gigs; recent ones have included Moby, Menswear, and Ocean Colour Scene, who played in spring 1996 cheered along from the floor by the brothers Gallagher. The Electric Ballroom also hosts a hip market on weekends. *184 Camden High St., tel. 0171/485-9006.*

ENGINE ROOM

With dark wood floors, ripped seating, and walls plastered with posters, the Engine Room is a big fave of Shane MacGowan. As it's out from the main Camden hub, it's not besieged by autograph-hunting kids. Since May 1994, the pub has hosted a monthly pop quiz attended by all the Camden music types—press officers, rock journos, record label people, and pop stars. Morrissey has popped in a few times, as have producer Steve Lillywhite and Liam Gallagher. Top prize is usually six cans of lager, while the team with the wittiest name gets T-shirts.

The jukebox is stuffed with classic R&B; since around 1991, a banner has flown from the top of the building claiming that it is the headquarters of the Keep Britain Vinyl party. *Chalk Farm Rd. opposite the Roundhouse* (see below*), no phone.*

THE FALCON

(London) Suede's spring 1992 gig in this pub's cramped little gigging room helped break the band. Morrissey was watching them and started backing them, covering their song, "My Insatiable One," before it had even been recorded. Lush did their first gig here in 1988. In November 1996, the Splash Club (now known as the Barfly Club)—one of the best forums for new bands in the country—moved here to take over the bookings after being forced to leave the Water Rats in King's Cross. Courtesy of the Splash people, the pub now has three buzz bands every night of the week. Those who have headlined include The Egg, Embrace, and Gravity Kills. *234 Royal College St., tel. 0171/485–3834 (pub), 0171/482–4884 (24-hr Splash info).*

THE GOOD MIXER

*Gotta get out of these smoky clothes/Rid myself of this Camden filth/Drinking at the Mixer with Mark and Keith—*The Boo Radleys, "Charles Bukowski Is Dead"

In the mid-'90s Britpop bands such as Blur, Menswear, and nearly everyone else associated with the tag, decided this shabby pub was the place to meet, and soon it was packed every night with hangers-on. The sudden shift in ambience didn't please the local working-class clientele (nor the genuine boho band, the appropriately named Gallon Drunk, who used to hang here), unimpressed at the "irony" of middle-class boys roughing it in an old geezers' pub. Nevertheless, the pub has begun cashing in on its fame by selling Good Mixer T-shirts and keeping the jukebox well stocked. Now the word is that the music types have moved on to the Spread Eagle. In previous rock eras the Mixer was a local for Mark Knopfler (in the '70s) and Madness (in the '80s). *30 Inverness St., tel. 0171/916–7929.*

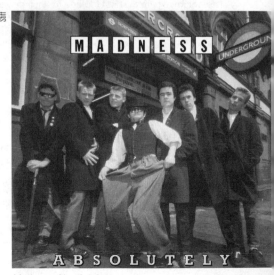

Madness, *Absolutely*

MADNESS'S *ABSOLUTELY* ALBUM COVER

The so-called nutty boys are pictured acting nutty outside the brown-tiled Chalk Farm tube station on the cover of their 1980 LP, *Absolutely. Chalk Farm Rd., NW3.*

MORNINGTON CRESCENT

This scruffy Victorian district, a transition zone between King's Cross and Camden Town, where the Camden Palace club and the busy Southampton Arms pub can be found, was the title of the debut 1994 album by the orchestral indie types, My Life Story. Their label, Mother Tongue, set about a citywide poster campaign advertising the album using the London underground logo (Mornington Crescent is also the name of a tube station at Hampstead Rd. at Eversholt St.), but transport chiefs didn't see the funny side and ordered a halt.

NIKI AND GEORGE'S RESTAURANT

At the height of Britpop in the mid-'90s, this licensed traditional English food joint—referred to by Camden scenesters as Niki and George's, after its owners—was almost as celebrated as the Good Mixer pub for attracting the "right" clientele, such as members of Elastica and the Verve; there are even pictures of B-list celebrities on the walls. Besides the music associations, it's worth a visit for the huge all-day breakfasts and the decent vegetarian choice. *38 Parkway, tel. 0171/485-7432.*

PRIMROSE HILL

I dreamed I saw a tree full of angels up on Primrose Hill Billy Bragg, "Upfield"

Photographer Gered Mankowitz shot a picture of the Rolling Stones for the cover of their 1967 *Between the Buttons* LP in this northern tip of Regents Park, smearing the lens with petroleum jelly to hide the bags under their eyes. Fifteen years later Madness were photographed in a similar spot for their *Rise and Fall* LP, which included a track called "Primrose Hill." Madness also name-dropped the park on the "Driving in My Car" single.

This grassy promontory, which offers a good view of the London skyline (or what there is of a skyline) also has connections with two Beatles songs. In 1967 Paul McCartney took his dog for a walk here and wrote "Getting Better" in his head before making a quick demo at his St. John's Wood home in Cavendish Road. On other dog-walking excursions, McCartney noticed someone who hung round the park a lot acting strange enough to inspire the melancholic "The Fool on the Hill," on the "Magical Mystery Tour" EP. *Regent's Park Rd., NW3. Chalk Farm tube.*

REHEARSAL REHEARSALS

The center of all things Clash in 1976, this disused two-story railway warehouse just north of the main Camden Town drag was where the band rehearsed and wrote much of their first album. Here the just-formed band came up with the name "The Clash" by flicking through headlines in the *Evening Standard,* and here they played their first London gig, on August 13, 1976, in front of a hand-picked audience of journalists, promoters, and producers. They also posed in an alleyway by the side of the building for the front cover photo of their debut album. Manager Bernie Rhodes, who sold used cars two doors down, had chosen the building as a base. It was damp and draughty—not that that stopped Simonon from using it as a crash pad—but Rhodes installed a jukebox filled with cult singles. For decor they splashed paint everywhere and wrote agit-prop slogans along the lines of "Face of the Assassin," "Hate and War," and "London's Burning." Another new band rehearsed here in the summer of 1976: the Flowers of Romance; their line-up included various future Slits and Sid Vicious—on sax.

The Clash left the premises in 1978 following an acrimonious bust-up with manager Rhodes, but not before the bizarre pigeon-shooting incident of March 30, 1978. Paul Simonon and Nicky Headon were testing out a friend's air rifle by firing at pigeons from the roof of the building when a police helicopter suddenly zoomed into view and a cop told them to desist immediately. The pair had no idea that opposite the building, on the other side of the railway tracks, were the offices of the Transport Police, who thought that they were terrorists aiming at trains. Simonon and Headon were charged with criminal damage and spent a night in the cells. They recounted the incident in the song, "Guns on the Roof." The building is now part of Stables Market. *Arch 15, Chalk Farm Rd.*

ROCK ON

For many years this small store, opened by Ted Carroll and Roger Armstrong in August 1975, was one of only a handful of places in Britain where you could buy vintage U.S. punk, '60s garage stuff, obscure soul, and early rock & roll. The pair also ran pioneering Chiswick Records, a rare U.K. indie that recorded the cream of the mid-'70s pub rock scene, such as the Count Bishops and the 101ers (with Joe Strummer), their singles wrapped in then rarely seen picture sleeves. Competition has overtaken Rock On in some cases, but it is still good on rare and secondhand rock & roll, rockabilly, and '70s punk. *3 Kentish Town Rd., tel. 0171/485–6469.*

THE ROUNDHOUSE

This just-about-standing former train shed built in 1846 became one of London's best-loved rock venues in the '60s and '70s. On October 11, 1966, Pink Floyd played their first major show here at a fancy-dress party to launch *International Times* (*IT*). It was billed as the "All-Night Rave Pop Op Costume Masque Drag Ball Et Al." *IT* editor (Barry) Miles was on the door, handing everyone who entered a sugar lump (which, of course, contained absolutely no acid). Avant-garde films such as

The Roundhouse, 1996

Kenneth Anger's *Scorpio Rising* showed all night, while there was a room with a tub of jello for those who were affected by the sugar cubes. First prize in the fancy dress was won by Marianne Faithfull, clad in a nun's habit that just failed to cover her butt.

Supporting Pink Floyd (who were paid £15 for the night) was Soft Machine, who played with a motorbike on stage on which members of the group took girls from the audience on rides around the circular gallery. Soft Machine returned a few months later to play an all-night New Year's Eve rave alongside the Who and the Move. (A poster for that gig on the back of which Paul McCartney wrote the lyrics to the Beatles' "Getting Better" was sold at Sotheby's in 1995 for a record £161,000; *see* Mayfair *in* Central London, *above*).

Within a couple of years the Roundhouse was putting on Sunday afternoon shows that started at 3 PM and finished by midnight. The Doors chose the venue to stage their European debut in August 1968, while in November of that year Led Zeppelin played their first-ever London show.

David Bowie met his future wife, Angie Barnett, when he performed here as part of a mixed-media troupe called Feathers (along with his then girlfriend, Hermione Farthingale). Three years later, in August 1971, the Roundhouse put on the Andy Warhol play, *Pork,* at which Bowie met Warhol for the first time, the singer having just recorded his tribute to the artist, "Andy Warhol," on the *Hunky Dory* LP.

In the late '70s the Roundhouse won a new lease on life as a punk venue. When the Ramones made their British debut here on July 4, 1976, (supported by the Stranglers and Flamin' Groovies) as part of the American Independence Day bicentennial celebrations, they were the first new-wave American punk group to play in the United Kingdom.

The Clash played their last gig with Keith Levene (who went on to form PiL) here on September 5, 1976.

From the mid-'80s on, no gigs took place here until the Mean Fiddler booked in shows in 1996 by Elvis Costello, Billy Bragg, and (London) Suede. The future is very uncertain, as there are plans to renovate the Roundhouse as an architecture library. *100 Chalk Farm Rd.*

Hampstead, NW3

Greetings from Shitsville...NW3—The Wildhearts, "Greetings From Shitsville"

Hampstead's lofty position above the London smoke and its proximity to the city have made it London's most desirable suburb, a haven for moneyed folk since the 18th century and for many rock stars, including the Beatles, the Rolling Stones, and the Sex Pistols, who squatted in the heart of the village. More recent rock residents have included Shaun Ryder of Black Grape, George Michael, and Boy George, the subject of Microdisney's scornful, "Singer's Hampstead Home." Hampstead has been named in few rock songs but has earned two mentions on Jethro Tull's *Aqualung,* in which Ian Anderson sings of coming upon Mother Goose "as I did walk by Hampstead Fair" and of Cross-Eyed Mary dining in Hampstead Village "on expense account gruel." The truly massive and rambling Hampstead Heath is where the cover photo of the Kinks' *Village Green Preservation Society* LP was taken.

ROLLING STONES ADDRESS (1964–65)

Mick Jagger and Keith Richards lived in the basement of this gingerbread cottage in 1964 and early 1965. Manager Andrew Loog Oldham locked them in, forcing them to write some hits so that they wouldn't have to keep on doing covers. After a couple of weeks, they came up with "The Last Time," which became their first self-penned single. *10a Holly Hill. Hampstead tube.*

SEX PISTOLS ADDRESS (1976)

Hampstead isn't quite all executive houses and desirable villas. John Lydon and John Beverly shared a tiny flat in this still grubby-looking building while they were waiting for things to hit the big time and reputedly wrote "God Save the Queen" here. *42a Hampstead High St.; entrance at side on Flask Walk.*

Kentish Town, NW5

More scruffy than neighboring Camden Town, this district nevertheless has had a strong tradition of live music venues, both large and small.

BULL AND GATE

In the mid-'80s Jon "Fat" Beast, who would later find fame as a cult MC with Carter U.S.M, started putting on indie nights in this ragged little boozer. Over the next few years, Nirvana, (London) Suede, Teenage Fanclub, PJ Harvey, and the Manic Street Preachers played from the tiny stage, while important club scenes such as the Timebox Club promoted new bands, including the ex–One Little Indian records band, the Popinjays. Shed Seven were spotted at the Bull and Gate and signed by Polydor. In the mid-'90s the Bull and Gate continued to promote new bands—Bawl and The Pod both made significant early appearances here—but it tended to be eclipsed by venues in the resurgent Camden, even though it now has a better PA and has been cleaned up a bit. *389 Kentish Town Rd., tel. 0171/485-5358.*

THE FORUM (TOWN & COUNTRY CLUB)

An Art Deco cinema from its opening in 1934 until 1970, this stylish big venue became an Irish dance hall for a few years and then lay vacant. In 1986 it was converted into a live music venue called the Town & Country Club, presenting virtually all of the top touring acts. Van Morrison played the last-ever gig under the T&C name in early 1993. Mean Fiddler, who had taken over the lease, reopened the place in May 1993 as the Forum, booking as the opening act—Van Morrison. Since then, it has competed with the Brixton Academy (and more recently the Shepherds Bush Empire) to put on the biggest names in rock, with Prince, Oasis, Björk, and Sonic Youth among the many who have headlined. One sad incident occurred in 1994 when a Motörhead fan allegedly headbanged himself to death at the band's gig. *9–17 Highgate Rd., Kentish Town, NW5, tel. 0171/ 344–0044. Kentish Town tube.*

Sleeper at the Forum

Kilburn, NW6

London's largest Irish center, Kilburn is a vibrant but featureless suburb on the main Edgware Road/A5 northwest route out of London. Before going solo in 1977, Ian Dury sang with the no-hope pub group Kilburn and the High Roads.

KILBURN NATIONAL BALLROOM

At their playing peak in October 1986, the Smiths recorded their live album, *Rank,* in this former cinema. Six years later the Manic Street Preachers' Nicky Wire caused a stir when he announced on stage: "I hope Michael Stipe goes the same way as Freddie Mercury." He later apologized. Problems over its license caused the National to slip from prominence on the gig circuit during the '90s, though '96 and '97 saw the return of some big names. *234 Kilburn High Rd., tel. 0171/328–3141. Kilburn tube.*

St. John's Wood, NW8

Your mother is an heiress, owns a block in St. John's Wood—The Rolling Stones, "Play With Fire"

Almost as exclusive as Hampstead but lacking its charm, St. John's Wood is the home of Lord's, the world's most famous cricket ground, and the legendary Abbey Road studios.

EATINGDRINKINGDANCINGSHOPPINGPLAYINGSLEEPING

There's not much nightlife around here; the nearest bar of any excitement is the big, modern **CUBE BAR** (135 Finchley Rd., NW3, tel. 0171/483–2393) in neighboring Swiss Cottage, which has jazz and funk DJs weekends and good food.

Abbey Road's recording history is dominated by two groups, the Beatles and Pink Floyd. The Beatles recorded almost their entire body of work in Studio 2, beginning on June 6, 1962, when they demoed for George Martin. They started cutting "Love Me Do" on September 4. They ended on August 25, 1969, when the last touches were put to the *Abbey Road* album. There's a story that Ringo wasn't considered up to scratch when it came to drum on the Beatles' debut single, "Love Me Do." The group was called back to cut it again, this time with session man Andy White on drums and Ringo on tambourine. Nevertheless, the earlier version with Ringo was put out as the single, while the White cut went out on the *Please Please Me* album.

On June 25, 1967, the Beatles recorded the worldwide televised performance of "All You Need Is Love" here, helped out by Mick Jagger, Keith Richards, Keith Moon, and Eric Clapton, and seated in a circle of flower-power children. This was after Pink Floyd had appeared in a similar setting on Top of the Pops to perform "See Emily Play."

For many, the peak of the Beatles' Abbey Road endeavors was the *Sgt. Pepper* album, which was recorded in February and March 1967. At the same time the then little-known Pink Floyd were here making the more daring *The Piper at the Gates of Dawn.* Floyd returned to Abbey Road on many occasions. On November 2, 1967, they cut one of British psychedelia's most out-to-lunch singles, "Apples and Oranges," which featured Syd Barrett nonsense lines made up on the spot, like, "Thought you might like to know, I'm a lorry

Graffiti at Abbey Road Studios

driver man." When Floyd came to Abbey Road in spring 1968 to cut their second album, *A Saucerful of Secrets,* the by-then estranged Barrett sat around the studio reception area for weeks hoping to be asked to play but was largely ignored by the group. At the last minute, they relented and allowed him to include one of his songs, "Jugband Blues." Around this time, drummer Nick Mason shot some film of Barrett out of his head on acid prancing around in the street outside the studio. A rare video, *Syd's First Trip,* was made from it.

In 1972 Floyd were here to record *Dark Side of the Moon* (a shot of the band working on it in the studio appears in the Pink Floyd *Live at Pompeii* movie) and roped in doorman Jerry Driscoll to utter the line, "There is no dark side of the moon, really; matter of fact, it's all dark." During the recording of *DSOTM*'s follow-up, *Wish You Were Here,* in 1975, Syd Barrett wandered into the studio unrecognized by keyboard player Rick Wright.

Other studio regulars during the '60s were EMI acts Cliff Richard, Manfred Mann, and the Hollies. Even George Martin had time to do other things, like come up with the original Radio 1 theme tune, arranged by Led Zeppelin's John Paul Jones. In recent years Abbey Road has been used by Kate Bush, Massive Attack, the Red Hot Chili Peppers, and Oasis, who recorded the "Supersonic" and "Shakermaker" singles in 1994, with Noel Gallagher returning a year later to do his bit on *Help,* the Bosnian children charity record. *3 Abbey Rd., tel. 0171/286-1161. St. John's Wood tube.*

WHY DON'T WE DO IT IN THE ROAD?

Tourists continue to flock to the Abbey Road Studio (during the '60s it was known as EMI Studios—the name was only changed after the success of *that* album) to add to the voluminous graffiti that mark the walls and to the zebra crossing to pose in Beatle fashion—often in the early hours when there are fewer vehicles. The Red Hot Chili Peppers used the shot for the picture sleeve of their "Abbey Road" EP.

Abbey Road, a leafy and pleasant turning in the heart of St. John's Wood, runs north–south for nearly a mile from Quex Road near Kilburn at the northern end to Grove End Road, near Lord's cricket ground, at the south, which is where the studios can be found. The zebra crossing the Beatles used is just south of the studios. The photo that appeared on the front cover of the *Abbey Road* album was taken by Iain MacMillan, who was positioned on a stepladder in the middle of the road, just before noon on August 8, 1969.

It's no good looking for the tile street sign featured on the back of the album. The building it was fixed to, which stood on Alexandra Road, has been demolished, and all similar signs have either been stolen or replaced by Westminster council. Indeed Alexandra Road has all but vanished, replaced by Rowley Way, which Richard Thompson used for the cover of his *Sunnyvista* album.

PAUL MCCARTNEY ADDRESS (1965–PRESENT)

Paul McCartney bought this huge villa in 1965 so that he could walk to the Abbey Road studios. A regular group of teeny fans started to keep vigil outside, and one June night in 1969 a group of them took advantage of a ladder lying next to his Meditation Dome and entered the house through an open window. All they took were some dirty shirts—because they smelt of McCartney. The Beatles' bassist recorded his debut solo album, *McCartney,* here in 1970. He still owns the house but doesn't live in it, though he has had Noel Gallagher round for a "cup of tea." *7 Cavendish Ave. St. John's Wood tube.*

West Hampstead, NW6

The only similarity West Hampstead shares with Hampstead is the name. Though only just over a mile west of the village, this part of Hampstead is characterized by noisy railway lines, litter-strewn streets, and shabby bedsits.

DECCA STUDIOS (ENGLISH NATIONAL OPERA)

Decca Records is famous for turning down the Beatles after the group auditioned in Studio 3 on New Year's Day 1962. They thought that Brian Poole and the Tremeloes had what the kids wanted and signed them up instead. Although Decca later signed the Rolling Stones and the Who, both groups did their recording elsewhere.

One of the few important albums that was cut here was John Mayall's *Bluesbreakers,* featuring Eric Clapton, in 1966. Thin Lizzy held auditions for new guitarists here in March 1974. They chose Scott Gorham and Brian Robertson. The building is now used by the English National Opera. *165 Broadhurst Gardens. West Hampstead tube.*

RAILWAY HOTEL (THE RAT AND PARROT)

In the '60s the pub's upstairs club was a popular R&B venue known as Klooks Kleek. Decca recorded a live album with John Mayall, *John Mayall Plays John Mayall,* here in March 1965 by dangling wires from the upper windows to the label's studios, next door (*see above*). In December 1979, when the pub was still known as the Railway Hotel, U2 made their London debut in the room upstairs (then known as the Moonlight Club) supporting the Dolly Mixtures. They were billed as Capital U2. In April 1980, Joy Division played here, only an hour after supporting the Stranglers at London's Rainbow Theatre. Singer Ian Curtis had an epileptic seizure on stage and three days later tried to commit suicide. On May 18 he succeeded. There has been no live music here for a long while. *100 West End La. West Hampstead tube.*

Willesden/Harlesden, NW10

A grotty blue-collar slice of northwest London, Willesden incorporates the even more dismal Harlesden, which inspired the wacky punk group Splodgenessabounds to write, "I Fell in Love with a Female Plumber from Harlesden." Other groups from the area include reggae veterans Aswad and the hip-hop band Eusebe. The area is also home to Ace Records (http://www.acerecords.co.uk), which started out in 1978 as the reissues arm of the Chiswick label. Among the gems in their vaults is the entire Modern catalog (containing titles by B.B. King, Elmore James, and Ike Turner), which they bought outright in 1990, and licensed material from Stax and Fantasy labels, as well as dozens of Grateful Dead discs. Also in the north part of the neighborhood, behind Willesden Green Station, you can find Lennon Road and Elvis Road, both of which lead onto the Marley Walk Estate.

[MEAN FIDDLER]

The little venue that spawned the massive Mean Fiddler organization, which now operates over a dozen venues and almost as many festival events, was opened on December 9, 1982, by Vince Power, whose previous business foray had been owning a secondhand furniture store. Billing Mean Fiddler as "London's Newest Country Nightclub," Power aimed to re-create the feel of a Nashville honky-tonk. Noticing that country bands could not fill the place during the week, he started booking Irish bands, including De Dannan. The acts grew more radical and diverse in 1984, when they had Pogue Mahone (a name that meant "kiss my ass" in Irish and would soon be shortened to the Pogues), Bo Diddley, and Lloyd Cole. The following year saw the arrival of American bands, including Los Lobos and Lone Justice, while indie bands were also booked: Some of the first to play were That Petrol Emotion and the House of Love. During the late '80s the venue's program mixed it up with some of the most cutting-edge alternative bands (Sonic Youth, the Butthole Surfers—whose Gibby Haines set fire to his clothing and then later in the set was attacked by a fan for the sloppy playing of "Jimi"), country icons (Charlie Louvin, Johnny Cash), and Irish favorites of every hue (Rory Gallagher, Davy Spillane). Eric Clapton joined Robert Cray onstage for a jam in 1986. The following November witnessed Roy Orbison's last solo appearance in the United Kingdom; 1988 saw the first British appearances of both the Red Hot Chili Peppers and the Pixies. In 1992 the venue

Mary Coughlan at Mean Fiddler

celebrated its 10th anniversary with a month of gigs featuring Bob Geldof, Green on Red, the Pogues, Belly, and the Chieftains, among many others. Since then, the Fiddler has continued to draw in a mixed bunch of key acts. As the parent organization has grown, the Fiddler has had to share its billings with other venues in the Mean Fiddler empire. *22–28a High St., tel. 0181/963–0940. Willesden Junction tube/BR.*

Southeast London

While the bad things about east London make it somewhat interesting, the sprawling southeast—a patchwork of both scuzzy and wealthy neighborhoods—is, for the most part, plain boring. The underground system virtually ignores the place, local trains travel with the velocity of a milk float, and packed buses meander around the twisting roads at leisure. Not surprisingly, with few live music venues, it's thrown up few rock connections, save for Bon Scott ending his days here and a few musicians attending Goldsmith's College. Similarly, few bands have emerged from here other than Alternative TV, Squeeze, and Carter U.S.M.

A GEOGRAPHICAL NOTE

Southeast London is defined here as places south of the Thames within the SE1 to SE27 postal codes, apart from the area around the South Bank and Waterloo, which are in Central London (these numbers appear on the name plates of virtually every street).

EATINGDRINKINGDANCINGSHOPPINGPLAYINGSLEEPING

The only significant place for live rock in the southeast is the **VENUE** in New Cross (2a Clifton Rise, SE14, tel. 0181/692–4077), an old upstairs ballroom that used to put on decent indie bands but of late has been leaning toward tribute bands. Each May the London Blues Festival takes place at **BLACKHEATH CONCERT HALLS** (23 Lee Rd., SE3, tel. 0181/463–0100); the 1996 line-up included such acts as Clarence "Gatemouth" Brown, the Fabulous Thunderbirds, Keb Mo, and Magic Slim. Out east in Woolwich (near Greenwich) the **TRAMSHED** (51 Woolwich New Rd., SE18, tel. 0181/854–2828) is a cool new venue that mixes name touring bands and top jungle nights. The **HALF MOON** (1 Half Moon La., Herne Hill, SE24, tel. 0171/274–2733) had one of U2's earliest U.K. dates, but nowadays bands are mostly unknown locals. One of London's top clubs, the huge **MINISTRY OF SOUND** (103 Gaunt St., SE1, near Elephant and Castle, tel. 0171/378–6528), opened in September 1991 and boasts a superb sound system. All the top DJs have played here, but to date the only live performance has been by the Cocteau Twins in May 1996. For entertainment of a different kind, there's Paul Chan—the "Chinese Elvis"—at the **ELVIS GRACELANDS PALACE** (881–883 Old Kent Rd., SE15, tel. 0171/639–3961).

Songs of Southeast London

Julie Driscoll, Brian Auger and the Trinity, "Vauxhall to Lambeth Bridge" (1969)
Desperate Bicycles, "New Cross New Cross" (1978)
Nick Nicely, "Hilly Fields (1891)" (1981)
Linton Kwesi Johnson, "New Cross Masahkah" (1984)
The Bible, "Crystal Palace" (1988)
Big Audio Dynamite, "London Bridge" (1989)
Carter U.S.M, "The Taking of Peckham 123" (1990)
Carter U.S.M, "24 Minutes to Tulse Hill" (1990)
Carter U.S.M, "The Only Living Boy in New Cross" (1992)

Camberwell/Kennington, SE5, SE11, SE17

Scruffy Camberwell is popular with young boho types and technoheads because of its cheap rents and excellent night bus service. It took on significant cachet after drug-loving Danny, in the cult British road movie *Withnail and I,* called his monstrously huge spliff the "Camberwell Carrot." In the early '60s Syd Barrett attended Camberwell School of Arts and Crafts. The KLF based their Transcentral Studios here in the late '80s/early '90s.

LABOUR PARTY HEADQUARTERS

Unlike in the United States, where singers since Sinatra had been keen to endorse political candidates, British artists kept to single-issue campaigns until Margaret Thatcher came along. In 1985 numerous rock stars gave concerts and sound bites to raise support for the Labour Party under the banner of the Red Wedge organization, which had an office here. Supporters included Madness, Alison Moyet, Frankie Goes to Hollywood, ex-Special Jerry Dammers, and ex-Tory Paul Weller. Red Wedge toured nationally but petered out when Labour lost the 1987 election. The most active and vociferous Red Wedger was Billy Bragg, who nowadays disagrees with the very soft socialism espoused by Prime Minister Tony Blair (who sang with Ugly Rumours, a Deadhead-style band at Oxford University in the early '70s and, like the man on Capitol Hill, didn't inhale). Oasis's Gallagher brothers nevertheless vociferously support Labour. *150 Walworth Rd., SE17, tel. 0171/701–1234. Elephant & Castle tube.*

Sniffin' Glue *cover, 1976*

MI6 HEADQUARTERS

Britain's conspicuous new spy headquarters completed in 1990 takes the form of a cream-and-green riverside mass that looks like an iced layer cake and a bulky battlement. On Valentine's Day 1995, Portishead, noted for the spy-movie-score element in their music, chose it as the appropriate spot on which to project a light show from across the Thames. *Albert Embankment at Vauxhall Bridge, SE11.*

Deptford, SE8

This forgotten corner of London, defaced by unimaginative council buildings and thrift stores, was where Mark Perry founded the *Sniffin' Glue* punk fanzine in the early '70s and then formed the punk band Alternative TV in 1977. The district produced one other major local band, Squeeze, who, like Alternative TV, started out on Miles Copeland's Deptford Fun City label.

ALBANY THEATRE

Dire Straits' first gig under that name took place in August 1977, supporting Squeeze, when this theater was on the corner of Deptford Church Street and Albury Street. Mark Knopfler lived nearby at the time in a flat in Farrer House on Deptford Church Street. The Albany moved to its present dull location in 1981; two years later a musical based on Squeeze songs was performed here. *Douglas Way, tel. 0181/692–4446. Deptford BR.*

Greenwich, SE7, SE10

On a night when the lazy wind is wailing around the Cutty Sark—Dire Straits, "Single-Handed Sailor"

The *Cutty Sark,* a dry-moored 1869 sailing clipper that carried tea from China to Greenwich, and the Royal Observatory attract thousands of tourists here each week. Greenwich also capitalizes on the setting of the 0° meridian here and attempts to put forward a village atmosphere with lots of quasi-trendy cafés and pubs (as well as plenty of "ye olde" tearooms and crummy bookstores).

New Cross/Lewisham, SE14

The cover of Sham 69's debut single in October 1977, "I Don't Wanna," carried a picture of cops on Lewisham High Street carting off an anti-National Front demonstrator during a march. Those born in the Lewisham area include Bill Wyman, Ginger Baker, and Sid Vicious. Although neighboring New Cross has large numbers of students, it has few night spots and is frustratingly boring—as described in Carter U.S.M's 1992 single, "The Only Living Boy in New Cross."

GOLDSMITH'S COLLEGE

John Cale learned many of the ideas he later deployed with the Velvet Underground when he studied avant-garde classical composition at this university college in the early '60s. Cale left in 1963 when he won a Leonard Bernstein scholarship and went to study composition at Tanglewood in Massachusetts. All of Blur (except the drummer) went to Goldsmith's in the late '80s; when the band was still called Seymour, they played a gig here in 1988 at which they met Damien Hirst, the avant-garde artist. Hirst later declared Blur the best band since the Beatles and directed their "Country House" video. Another recent past-pupil was Brian Molko of Placebo, who studied drama but dropped out to concentrate on the band. *Lewisham Way at Dixon Rd., tel. 0181/692–1406. New Cross tube/BR.*

Mick Gold/courtesy of Redferns

John Cale

Dulwich, SE22

Well-to-do Dulwich likes to think of itself as village England, whereas really rich people refer to it as "Brixton Borders." Roxy Music guitarist Phil Manzanera was in a prog rock band called Quiet Sun while he was a student at the posh Dulwich College in the late '60s.

BON SCOTT DEATH SITE

After a heavy night's drinking in Camden Town on February 20, 1980, AC/DC singer Bon Scott was offered a ride home by an acquaintance, Alistair Kinnear. Scott was so drunk that instead of going to his central London apartment, they went to Kinnear's flat on the crest of a windswept hill just a short walk from cutesy Dulwich village, arriving some time after 3 AM. The story goes that Scott couldn't be budged, so Kinnear put a blanket over him and left a note in the car with directions to his third-floor flat in this blond-brick bunker. When the singer hadn't appeared by early evening of the next day, Kinnear went to see what was wrong, found his worst fears confirmed, and rushed him to King's College hospital, where Scott was declared DOA. *Outside 65 Overhill Rd., Dulwich, SE22.*

Southwest London

The southwest is where many artists live after they've made it. It has always had a good number of live music venues, from bars like Putney's Half Moon to the huge Brixton Academy. In swish Chelsea, Jagger, Richards, and co. did much of their swinging in the '60s. The Sex Pistols formed here in the following decade. Elsewhere on the north side are swanky Belgravia, ostentatious Knightsbridge, scruffy Earls Court, and likeable Fulham. Counterculturally dominating the south side is big, bad Brixton, with its late-night divebars and clubs. Neighboring Clapham has a vast common and pretentious bars. Past the wastelands of Wandsworth are the very desirable riverside Barnes and suburban Wimbledon.

A GEOGRAPHICAL NOTE

Southwest London is defined here as places within the SW1 to SW20 postal codes (these numbers appear on the name plates of virtually every street). The area covers both sides of the Thames, although some of SW1 falls in Westminster (*see* Central London).

Songs of Southwest London

The Lurkers, "Fulham Fall-out" (1977)
Elvis Costello, "I Don't Want to Go to Chelsea" (1978)
The Clash, "Guns of Brixton" (1979)
Simple Minds, "Chelsea Girl" (1979)
Angelic Upstarts, "Flames of Brixton" (1982)
Eddy Grant, "Electric Avenue" (1983)
Hanoi Rocks, "Tooting Bec Wreck" (1983)
Faith Brothers, "Fulham Court" (1985)
The Pogues, "Misty Morning Albert Bridge" (1989)
Ride, "Chelsea Girl" (1990)

Barnes, SW13

Occupying a glorious stretch of the Thames, Barnes is the unlikely setting for one of Britain's most successful studios, Olympic, as well as the place where Marc Bolan died in a car wreck.

EATINGDRINKINGDANCINGSHOPPINGPLAYINGSLEEPING

There are few better locations for neighborhood drinking in London than Barnes; the riverside **BULL'S HEAD** (373 Lonsdale Rd., tel. 0181/876–5241) is a top pub jazz venue.

[MARC BOLAN DEATH SITE]

T. Rex's Marc Bolan was killed on the night of September 16, 1977, when the purple Mini in which he was being driven by his girlfriend, Gloria "Tainted Love" Jones, coming over the bridge from the east, crashed into a horse chestnut tree; it was the third wreck involving the tree that year. Neither was wearing a seat belt and the impact at 45 mph flattened the engine compartment and forced the steering wheel up to the roof. Jones got a broken jaw and facial lacerations, but the singer died instantly. He was cremated at Golders Green Crematorium in northwest London.

Fans have a gathering each September 16, and the tree is always smothered with flowers, ribbons, and graffiti, plus oddments along the lines of a cigarette stuck to a note that reads: "Me and Max decided to give you a fag as you might need it in the afterlife." Press reports in 1993 claimed the tree was to be felled to protect a nearby house, but the local council has insisted it won't be. *Queen's Ride at railway bridge, Barnes Common.*

OLYMPIC STUDIOS

Built into an Edwardian theater, Olympic is one of London's major studios, run by Who collaborator Glyn Johns during the '60s and '70s and responsible for Family's *Music in a Doll's House,* Traffic's and Blind Faith's self-named albums, the Who's *Who's Next,* and Hawkwind's *Hall of the Mountain Grill.*

Olympic Studios, 1997

In August 1967 the Rolling Stones cut their "We Love You" single, a thank-you to fans who stuck by them when they were jailed for possessing drugs, at Olympic. The Beatles supplied backing vocals, the only time the two groups recorded together. The following year, during the making of the *Beggars Banquet* album here, nouvelle vague French movie director Jean-Luc Godard came by to film the Stones for his *One Plus One* movie.

Also that year, Led Zeppelin made their debut album, called simply *Led Zeppelin,* at a cost of £1,750; within 10 years it had grossed £7 million. While Family cut the intensely psychedelic *Music in a Doll's House* album that year, they spent hour after hour at the studio watching the Walt Disney movie *Fantasia.*

The Stones were working on new material here in 1969 on the night that Brian Jones died in his country mansion. In 1971 Derek and the Dominos disbanded during the recording of their never-completed follow-up to the *Layla* album. The building was bought by Virgin in the mid-'80s (themselves since bought out by EMI), and since then the Stones have been back (to mix *Steel Wheels*), as has Eric Clapton. Younger users include ex-Waterboy Mike Scott, Marcella Detroit, and (London) Suede. *117 Church Rd., tel. 0181/748-7961. Barnes Bridge BR.*

Battersea, SW8, SW11

All over Battersea, some hope and some despair—Morrissey, "You're the One for Me, Fatty"

Battersea, sprawling out from the south bank of the Thames across from Victoria rail station, is best known for the beautiful, disused Battersea Power Station and the Battersea Dogs' Home. It was from the latter that the Who had their van stolen while they were inside selecting a guard dog in 1965; the visit might well have given them the idea for their ridiculous B-side of 1969's "Pinball Wizard," entitled "Dogs Part 2," that was just several minutes of barking. Apart from the areas around Battersea Park, Battersea is mostly concrete towers, and rough.

[BATTERSEA POWER STATION]

This remarkable-looking former electricity depot, like a chunky upside-down table, has long attracted photographers. It has been particularly associated with Pink Floyd ever since the farce of the flying hog that broke free during the December 1976 cover shoot for the band's *Animals* LP. The pink 40-foot-long inflatable animal broke free from its moorings above the chimneys and soon made off over London. Scores of people phoned the papers in amazement, and an airline pilot had a hard time trying to convince air traffic control that he wasn't seeing things. It eventually landed some 30 miles east, and the band had to superimpose a photo of the hog on the cover. Floyd also held the press launch for *Animals* here the following month.

Others who have made use of the building include the Beatles (in the *Help!* movie); the Who, who used a picture of the station in the booklet that accompanied the *Quadrophenia* album; Morrissey, pictured on the back cover of his 1990 *Bona Drag* collection; the Orb, whose *Live '93* album parodied the Floyd shot, using a sheep floating over a similar looking model; and the Boo Radleys, who became the first band to film inside the station's rotting shell when they made the video for "Wake up Boo" in 1995.

Orb, Live '93

The building, designed in the 1930s by Giles Gilbert Scott of red telephone box fame, can be viewed best from the bridge on Ebury Road by the Victoria rail station on the north side of the river. It's sadly lying disused; to date none of the many plans to convert it—including one by the producer Youth (ex-Killing Joke), who to wants to turn it into a multimedia complex—have come up with the finance. *Off Nine Elms La. at Victoria Railway Bridge, Nine Elms, SW8. Battersea Park/Queen's Rd. Battersea BR.*

RAMPORT STUDIOS

The Who installed a hi-tech studio in this former church building in 1972 so that they could record *Quadrophenia* in authentic mod surroundings: Thessaly Road is full of the kind of bleak, pre-war housing that fit in with mod romanticism. During rehearsals for the *Quadrophenia* tour at Ramport in fall 1973, Daltrey and Townshend had their worst-ever fight. Townshend was punched unconscious and had to be taken to a hospital, accompanied by a hysterical Keith Moon. The Who recorded their next two albums, *The Who by Numbers* and *Who Are You*, here and were photographed for the cover of the latter slouching against their stacked equipment shortly before Keith Moon's death. Ramport is now disused. *115 Thessaly Rd., Nine Elms, SW8. Battersea Park/Queen's Rd. Battersea BR.*

Belgravia and Pimlico, SW1

The sumptuous Georgian terraces of Belgravia are consulate land; it's one of London's most expensive districts for living and shopping. Belgravia's most-hyped and best-known address is Sloane Square (from where Kings Road darts through Chelsea), but most rock stars who've lived here were based closer to Victoria station at the opposite end of the area.

IN THE CITY

Pete Townshend had three addresses in fashionable Belgravia, near Victoria station, while '60s London swung.

* **84 Eaton Place (1964)**

The Who's management installed the guitarist in this cream-color Georgian villa in 1964 to poshen him up. After hearing the Kinks' "You Really Got Me" at Keith Moon's pad, he returned home and upped the stakes with "I Can't Explain."

* **8 Chesham Place (1965)**

Deep into the Who's pop-art period, Townshend decorated this flat with pages ripped out of arty magazines.

* **20 Ebury Street (1965)**

Townshend wrote "Anyway Anyhow Anywhere" while living in this five-story Georgian house listening to Charlie Parker. The song's title is his description of Parker's style.

PRETTY THINGS ADDRESS, 1965

In their early R&B days, the Pretty Things were billeted in this luxury block, only yards from Beatles manager Brian Epstein's pied-à-terre and Buckingham Palace. They recorded a song also called "13 Chester Street" on their debut album. Brian Jones lived in the flat above. *13 Chester St. Victoria tube/BR.*

SLOANE SQUARE

Hairdresser on fire, all around Sloane Square—Morrissey, "Hairdresser on Fire"

Around the first anniversary of Sid Vicious's death, a thousand or so punks in full regalia marched from here to Hyde Park in his memory. In the '80s Sloane Square came to epitomize London yuppiedom as the supposed spiritual home of the toffish Sloane Ranger.

Brixton, SW2, SW9

D. Wayne's ladies, chillin' with the Brady's Massive, Brixton Acid Posse—Alabama 3, "Ain't Goin' to Goa"

The youth of Brixton they put down their .45 Smith & Wesson pistol—Black Uhuru, "Youth of Eglington"

No need for the Black Maria, Goodbye to the Brixton Sun—The Clash, "The Guns of Brixton"

Said I'd return but I gotta fight the Brixton riot—2Pac, "I Ain't Mad at 'Cha"

Much-mentioned in song, Brixton's place in London lore still rests with the riots of summer 1981, when local youth and the cops fought lengthy battles. One of Britain's most established centers of Caribbean culture and an area of cheap rents for young people, Brixton is radical, underground, multiracial, and boho. It's also got something the media-favorite hangout of Camden Town hasn't: a venue as big and credible as the Brixton Academy (*see below*).

David Bowie was born here (*see below*), as was the Clash's Mick Jones. X-Ray Spex's Poly Styrene worked in the local Woolworth's; Nico shared a flat on Effra Road with punk poet John Cooper Clarke in the mid-'80s. Other bands with connections to the place include Carter U.S.M and Skunk Anansie. Saffron, the singer with Republica, lives here. Indigenous acts tend to be experimental: The Alabama 3, with their acid country blues, are the current local heroes, along with the punky guitar techno guys, Headrillaz, and the acoustic moodmasters, Past Caring.

Larry Love, Alabama 3 singer, chillin' at Brady's saloon

EATING DRINKING DANCING SHOPPING PLAYING SLEEPING

There's more to Brixton than the **ACADEMY** (*see below*). **BRADY'S** (Electric La., SW9, tel. 0171/274–4396) is a classic dive bar where parts of the Clash's *Rude Boy* movie were filmed and the Alabama 3 made their name, but it has been quiet recently. The **LOUGHBOROUGH HOTEL** (Loughborough Rd. at Evandale Rd., SW9, tel. 0171/498–6450) presents mostly Latin sounds, as well as occasional classic R&B nights. The **CANTERBURY ARMS** (9 Canterbury Crescent, SW9, tel. 0171/274–1711) attracts customers with local punk bands and cheap beer nights. In nearby Stockwell, Celtic rock and country sounds are the staple at the relatively expensive **SWAN** (215 Clapham Rd., SW9, tel. 0171/978–9778). The most famous of the clubs is the massive **FRIDGE** (Town Hall Parade, SW2, tel. 0171/326–5100), started in the late '80s by Jazzy B of Soul II Soul; this wildly successful place puts on mostly mixed gay nights, with a few live band nights; the adjacent Fridge Bar stays open late. The **DOGSTAR** (Coldharbour La. at Atlantic Rd., tel. 0171/733–7515) is an amazingly busy bar where techno, acid house, and all types of dance sounds are spun; it charges entrance at night. The **BRIX** (at St. Matthew's Church, Brixton Hill, SW2, tel. 0171/274–6470) puts on a variety of live and DJ nights; it also has the area's best-value restaurant, **BAH HUMBUG**. A couple of miles farther south, in Streatham, **LA PERGOLA** (66 Streatham High Rd., SW16, tel. 0181/769–2601) is a likeably kitsch Italian restaurant owned by a Turk that has belly-dancing and other suitably cheesy entertainment.

If Brixton could ever be said to have a tourist attraction, it is its **ETHNIC MARKET,** which sprawls around several side streets and alleys. Food stalls proudly show their wares, including pigs' feet and weird-looking fish. Several stalls sell mostly reggae and drum & bass tapes. **RED RECORDS** (500 Brixton Rd., SW9, tel. 0171/274–4476) blasts out its inventory of hip-hop, jungle, and reggae onto the main drag. **SUPERTONE** (110 Acre La., SW2, tel. 0171/737–7761) looks after the rootsier side of reggae. Unfortunately, Brixton is set for a massive "face-lift"—the council wants to rip the heart out of the area with a mall—and things could go downhill fast as trendies from other parts of the city start to discover the "scuzzy end of town."

BOB MARLEY WAY

A two-minute stroll from Brixton's market area leads to the first street in London named for a contemporary music star. On a thoroughfare next to Marcus Garvey Way, the name is a political gesture to please the local black community. The street lies a few yards from where the riots kicked off in 1981. *Off Railton Rd., SE24.*

DAVID BOWIE BIRTHPLACE

Bowie was born David Robert Jones in this shabby Victorian terrace on January 8, 1947, to unmarried parents—his father was still waiting for his divorce to come through. When he was three years old, the infant Bowie discovered the joys of makeup. The Joneses lived here until young David was eight. *40 Stansfield Rd., SW9. Brixton tube/BR.*

[BRIXTON ACADEMY]

One of Britain's best venues, the Academy earned a unique niche in rock history in 1995 when local people and politicians campaigned successfully to stop its being turned into a church. This huge auditorium (capacity 4,400) opened as a cinema around 1930. It was vacant and decaying in 1983 when Simon Parkes bought it for £1 and turned it into a suc-

Photographed by David Corio

Bob Marley

cessful live music venue. Since then, everyone who is anyone in rock has played here, including Bruce Springsteen and the Rolling Stones; the Ramones did what could well be their last gig here in February 1996. Motörhead, Faith No More, and Brian May have cut live albums here; scores more have released tracks and video segments from Academy shows.

In 1995, after a small but wealthy Brazilian Pentecostal sect's offer of £4.5 million for the building set off fan and community protests, Break for the Border (who also run the Borderline and the Shepherds Bush Empire) offered around £2 million and Parkes accepted. The new owners have left things alone. The Academy is still putting on a roster that reads like an A-to-Z of contemporary rock music. It also presents an increasing number of crossover dance acts, and all-nighters are becoming common. *211 Stockwell Rd., SW9, tel. 0171/924–9999. Brixton tube/BR.*

BRIXTON PRISON

While spending a night in this gruesome Victorian fortress in summer 1967 after a drug bust, Mick Jagger wrote "2,000 Light Years from Home" and "We Love You," which begins with the slamming of a prison door and was intended as a thank-you to fans who stuck by him. Local reggae poet Linton Kwesi Johnson told the story of a young black man and the treatment he got in this prison in the forceful "Sonny's Lettah." *Jebb Ave., Brixton Hill, SW2. Clapham South tube.*

ELECTRIC AVENUE

We're gonna rock down to Electric Avenue—Eddy Grant, "Electric Avenue"

The busy fruit and veg section of bustling Brixton market runs along this crescent, which can be, well, seedy (not to mention smelly) at night. Former Equals member Grant wrote a hit song in its honor to show solidarity with the area after the 1981 riots. *SW9. Brixton tube/BR.*

RAM JAM CLUB

London's top late-'60s soul club took its name from Geno Washington's backing band. When the singer performed here, the crowd would chant "Geno, Geno," as Dexy's Midnight Runners later recalled on the 1980 single, "Geno." A wealthier regular was Peter Gabriel, who saw Otis Redding here in 1966 and had what he referred to as a "rock epiphany." The building is now occupied by Lambeth Social Services. *390 Brixton Rd., SW9. Brixton tube/BR.*

Chelsea–King's Road, SW3, SW10

King's Road, which cuts through the heart of Chelsea from Sloane Square in the east to Putney Bridge two miles west, a haven for creative types since the last century, is central to rock myth. In the '50s King's Road teemed with then-risqué jazz clubs and coffee bars. In 1955 Mary Quant opened Bazaar, declaring it the country's first boutique. Hers was soon joined by other clothes stores selling outrageous gear. In psychedelic times, it was the place to come to for Regency jackets, tie-dyed shirts, and Chelsea boots. In the early '70s attention focused on No. 430, where Vivienne Westwood and Malcolm McLaren opened their Sex boutique (where the Sex Pistols later formed). During punk's 1977 heyday, fights between Teddy boys and punks took place almost every Saturday afternoon. By the '80s the street was full of mohawked punks posing for tourists' cameras. *Landmarks run east–west from Sloane Square tube station. Landmarks in the high numbers are nearer Fulham Broadway tube station.*

EATINGDRINKINGDANCINGSHOPPINGPLAYINGSLEEPING

You can head for the covered markets, like **THE ORIGINAL GARAGE** (Nos. 181–183, tel. 0171/351–5353), a miniature version of Kensington Market; the **CHELSEA ANTIQUES MARKET** (No. 245a), where Boy George once worked on a clothes stall and which is good for movie ephemera; or the secondhand American clothing place, **PHLIP** (No. 191, tel. 0171/352–4332). There's also a bunch of pricey American clothing stores, bars, and diners.

CHELSEA DRUG STORE (MCDONALD'S)

This is where the subject of the Rolling Stones' "You Can't Always Get What You Want" supposedly got her prescriptions. The chemist has since become a branch of McDonald's. *49 King's Rd.*

ERIC CLAPTON'S APARTMENT (1967)

Eric Clapton shared an apartment in the Pheasantry in 1967 with artist Martin Sharp, who wrote the lyrics to Cream's "Tales of Brave Ulysses." While Clapton was living here,

Det. Sgt. Norman Pilcher, whose mission in life seemed to be busting rock stars for drugs, buzzed the intercom, shouted "Postman, special delivery!" and burst in—only to find that Clapton, who suspected a raid, had nipped out the back. The Pheasantry is now a swish bar with a cool courtyard. *152 King's Rd.*

SGT. PEPPER PHOTO SHOOT

The Beatles came to these photographic studios in 1967 to help Peter Blake design the sleeve of *Sgt. Pepper's Lonely Hearts Club Band*. It was here that they posed in military gear for the photo that adorns the gatefold inner sleeve. *Chelsea Manor Studios, 1 Flood St., at King's Rd., SW3.*

The Beatles, Sgt. Pepper's Lonely Hearts Club Band

THE ROEBUCK (THE DOME)

John Lydon was introduced to the rest of the future Sex Pistols in this pub in August 1975, a few days after meeting Malcolm McLaren at Sex (*see below*). It's now the Dome, one of a chain of reasonably priced café-restaurants. *354 King's Rd.*

[SEX (WORLD'S END)]

British punk can be traced back to 1971, when left-field fashion designer Vivienne Westwood and art student Malcolm McLaren took over the premises of a '60s boutique. The pair quickly stamped their identity on the place by installing a pastiche of a '50s living room and renaming it Let It Rock, in homage to teddy boy culture. They began selling period records, winkle-picker shoes, and drape jackets designed by Westwood. Impressed Teds were soon joined by rock stars—Bowie, Bolan, and Roxy Music—looking for chic revivalist gear. In spring 1972 McLaren and Westwood had had enough of reactionary Teds and changed the store's name to Too Fast to Live Too Young to Die (a slogan McLaren had spotted on a biker's jacket) and began selling '40s zoot suits. New customers included the New York Dolls, who dropped in while touring Britain and met McLaren, who eventually became their manager.

In 1974 McLaren and Westwood again remodeled the interior, this time to resemble a womb, daubed the walls with situationist graffiti, and called it Sex: "specialists in rubberwear, glamourwear, and stagewear." This sort of gear was sold by new assistants, including Chrissie Hynde, who had just arrived from Ohio, and the outrageously dressed Pamela Rooke, a.k.a. Jordan, who would turn out for work in leotards and fishnets way before anyone dressed like that. A photo in the porn mag *Forum* showed four store workers, including Ms. Hynde, baring their backsides daubed with lipstick.

After a visit to New York in 1974, McLaren began selling torn T-shirts and clothes decorated with safety-pins. This version of the store attracted an inordinate number of hangers-on, including John Beverly (Sid Vicious), who occasionally helped out here wearing a padlock over his crotch, and John Lydon, who wore a Pink Floyd T-shirt with the words "I hate" scrawled over the group's logo. Then there was a band called the Strand, named after Roxy Music's "Do the Strand," consisting of Steve Jones, Paul Cook, and Wally

Nightingale. They asked McLaren to find them a bass player and he suggested a Sex employee, Glen Matlock. McLaren's assistant, Bernie Rhodes (later manager of the Clash), also suggested that Lydon had just the sort of "attitude" needed to front a band. McLaren asked him to join, arranging a meeting at the nearby Roebuck pub (*see above*). When they returned to Sex after a few pints, Lydon sang along to Alice Cooper's "(I'm) Eighteen" on the jukebox and won the audition to join what soon became the Sex Pistols.

In late 1976 Sex was renamed Seditionaries, and Ben Kelly, who later did Manchester's Hacienda Club, redesigned it: The new brilliant white decor showed deliberately provocative photos of the Dresden bombing and had a hole punched in the ceiling (to resemble bomb damage). But when punk broke in 1976, the various Pistols, Chrissie Hynde, and many of the other key movers were long gone. During the King's Road style wars of summer 1977, teddy boys, who had never forgiven McLaren for getting rid of Let It Rock, kicked the windows in, for old time's sake.

Now known as World's End, named for the unfashionable part of King's Road in which it is situated, the store is still part of the Westwood empire and is identifiable by its back-ward-moving clock above the awning. *430 King's Rd., tel. 0171/352 6551.*

GRANNY TAKES A TRIP

One of London's top psychedelic '60s boutiques—commemorated in song by the Purple Gang—Granny Takes a Trip attracted top rock names by the limo load. Mick Jagger, Keith Richards, Syd Barrett, and the rest used to drop by to pick up their caftans, velvet trousers, and satin jackets or just soak up the hazy atmosphere, incense, and patchouli oil. The place was run by tailor John Pearse, whose girlfriend, Sylvia, was pictured on the front cover of Lou Reed's 1972 *Transformer* album. Others who regularly hung out here included Cher and Salman Rushdie, who lived in the flat above the store. It's now the Entre Nous coffee bar. *488 King's Rd.*

THE WETHERBY ARMS (TIGER LIL'S)

The Rolling Stones, then called Little Boy Blue and the Blue Boys, rehearsed and regu-larly drank at the Wetherby in 1962 when they lived on nearby Edith Grove. After bassist Dick Taylor left to attend the Royal College of Art, they auditioned prospective replace-ments here. The successful applicant was Bill Perks, who changed his name to the more rock & roll–sounding Bill Wyman on joining the embryonic Stones. The pub is now called Tiger Lil's. *500 King's Rd., tel. 0171/376–5003.*

"LONDON CALLING" INSPIRATION

Joe Strummer got the idea for "London Calling"'s chorus, "London is drowning and I live by the river," when he lived in an upper level apartment of this ugly and, for Chelsea, incongruous-looking project of high-rises halfway along King's Road. The murder of the estate's parking attendant while being robbed of a few quid was recounted in the *Sandinista!* song "Somebody Got Murdered." *World's End Estate, King's Rd. at Edith Grove.*

Chelsea, off King's Road, SW3, SW10

They call her Natasha when she looks like Elsie, I don't want to go to Chelsea—Elvis Costello, "I Don't Want to Go to Chelsea"

No longer a center for bands, Chelsea—which is heavily residential away from the noise of King's Road—is still fashionable with the literary/media crowd. Elvis Costello took a swipe at the cynicism behind the swinging London facade in his bile-ridden 1978 sin-gle, "I Don't Want to Go to Chelsea." Chelsea was also the name given to the ropey punk group formed in summer 1976 by Gene October, John Towe, Tony James, and Billy Idol. The latter three then quit to form Generation X.

APPLE CORPS LTD.—CURRENT LOCATION

The Beatles empire, still run by the band's former road manager, Neil Aspinall, occupies a suite in this smart villa. After a quiet early '90s, Apple generated much frantic activity in 1995 to organize the release of the *Anthology* CDs. *27 Ovington Sq., SW3, tel. 0171/ 225–1700. South Kensington tube.*

LIVE WITH ME

Chelsea's elegant riverside stretch, Cheyne Walk, has long been popular with creative folk, including George Eliot, who lived and died at No. 4. Jagger and Richards bought expensive properties here in the '60s, a step up from their previous Chelsea address on shabby Edith Grove.

- **Mick Jagger Address, 1967–78**

Jagger bought this 1711 Queen Anne town house for £40,000 in 1967 and lived here with Marianne Faithfull. "Street Fighting Man" was written in this distinctly nonrevolutionary setting. A frequent visitor was Labour MP Tom Driberg, whom they invited for dinner when Jagger toyed with running for parliament on the Labour ticket. Jagger and Faithfull were busted by cops here in May 1969 for possession of a quarter of cannabis and fined £200 plus £50 costs. When Jagger married Bianca Perez Morena de Macias, he made this their home but moved out in 1978 when they divorced. *48 Cheyne Walk, SW3.*

- **Keith Richards Address, 1969–78**

Keith Richards and Anita Pallenberg moved into this luxury six-story 1876 residence overlooking the Thames and promptly installed a shrine to Jimi Hendrix in one of the rooms. In June 1973 the place was raided by cops, who discovered Richards, Pallenberg, and society chum Prince Stanislaus Klossowski de Rola with an assortment of pharmaceuticals and some firearms. The guitarist was subsequently convicted and fined £200. A year later future Sex Pistol Steve Jones burgled the house and took a color TV. *River House, 3 Cheyne Walk, SW3.*

- **Jagger, Richards, and Jones's Address, 1962**

These three Stones shared a squalid apartment in this shabby house in summer 1962, at the time when Jagger was studying at the London School of Economics. Richards's mum would often drop by to take away the boys' dirty washing. The fourth tenant was an oddball known only as Phelge who scared the tyro Stones by parading around wearing only a pair of dirty underpants—on his head. Richards later adopted the name Phelge as an early songwriting pseudonym alongside Jagger's Nanker ('60s slang for a gurn). *102 Edith Grove, SW10.*

- **Brian Jones's Apartment, 1966**

Jones lived here for a few months at the height of his powers, just after the *Aftermath* album, on which he shows his pedigree as a multi-instrumentalist, was released. *7 Elm Park La., SW3.*

STEVE CLARK DEATH SITE

Def Leppard guitarist Steve Clark died in his sleep in this cozy three-story house on January 8, 1991. Age 30, he was, according to band biographer Dave Dickson, an extreme alcoholic; the hospital autopsy registered an alcohol level in his blood of 0.59. *44 Old Church St. Sloane Square tube.*

Clapham, SW4, SW11

Cheer up, it might never happen/Drive-by shootings on the streets of Clapham—Carter U.S.M, "Cheer Up, It Might Never Happen"

The various Claphams—North, High Street, Common, Junction, and South—form a 2-mile-long belt west of Brixton. The district tries to compete with Brixton, and it's at the point closest to Brixton—Clapham High Street—that you'll find most of the semitrendy bars and an art-house cinema. Over on the west, grubby Clapham Junction has the major live venue, the Grand, and loads of fast food joints.

EATINGDRINKINGDANCINGSHOPPINGPLAYINGSLEEPING

Clapham lacks any consistently good live venues. Even the **GRAND** (*see below*) has a very patchy program. **DUB VENDOR** (274 Lavender Hill, SW11, tel. 0171/223–3757), near the Grand, imports all the latest reggae sounds from Jamaica and carries a huge back catalog. They do mail order, too.

CLAPHAM COMMON

This big, sprawling park, where grown men assemble to sail radio-controlled boats in a pond, appears on Squeeze's well-known and overplayed 1979 single, "Up the Junction," named for the novel by Nell Dunn and the '60s kitchen-sink movie of the same name, shot in the Clapham area. It also gets a mention from Morrissey—"4 AM, Northside, Clapham Common"—on "Mute Witness."

Like most of London's major parks, Clapham Common usually hosts some rock events each year. The biggest-ever attendance, rumored at a quarter of a million, was in July 1986, when Sting, Peter Gabriel, and others did a fund-raiser for the Anti-Apartheid Movement. The past few years have seen an annual May Day Festival, with Billy Bragg a common fixture, but it moved to Finsbury Park in 1997.

THE GRAND

This beautiful '30s theater that holds 1,800 has not, despite the efforts of the Mean Fiddler, which has run the place since 1992, been able to compete with the Academy. Big Star, Gil Scott-Heron, Jethro Tull, Sebadoh, Pavement, and Hole have played here in the '90s, as well as (London) Suede, who headlined a Red Hot Aids charity gig here in August 1993, hosted by Derek Jarman, who died soon after. Recently, however, the

Jane Hancer

Shane MacGowan and the Pogues at the Grand

Earl's Court, 1996

venue has turned to doing club nights on weekends, and the only live acts are swing-beat groups brought in by outside promoters. *St. John's Hill, SW11, tel. 0171/738–9000. Clapham Junction BR.*

Earl's Court, SW5

Why do you smile when you think about Earls Court?—Morrissey, "Piccadilly Palare"

Antipodeans favor this busy and scruffy sector of southwest London for its low rents and cheap eats. Not that much goes on at night, save for a few days of the year when there is a gig in the local hangar, Earls Court stadium.

EARL'S COURT EXHIBITION CENTRE

One of Britain's main exhibition halls for trade and consumer shows, Earl's Court is also a major gigging venue, proof that a band has reached the top. Led Zeppelin and the Rolling Stones were among the first groups to do multinight stands. David Bowie introduced his Aladdin Sane persona for the first time in 1973 at Earl's Court, having arrived in London from Japan the long way, via the Pacific and the Trans-Siberian Express. Unfortunately, the gig was a bit of a disaster despite the then-record 18,000 audience. Fights broke out and fans danced naked in the aisles and pissed wherever they wanted; Bowie canceled the second show.

Pink Floyd, who have performed *Dark Side of the Moon* and *The Wall* here, saw their 1994 tour get off to a bad start when the lighting rig collapsed and the show had to be abandoned. More recently, Oasis have stamped their name on the place. In November 1995 their two shows sold out in record time; they were back the following January to pick up several prizes at the annual BRITS awards ceremony. The band was on their best rock & roll behavior—Liam Gallagher stuck the statuette up his arse and refused to get off the stage. The biggest drama, however, was a bizarre incident involving Michael Jackson and Jarvis Cocker of Pulp. During Jacko's rendition of "Earth Song," complete with Christlike affectations on a stage packed with child actors and a rabbi, Cocker got on stage, turned round and wiggled his butt at the audience. Security heavies threw him off, and in the chaos, some of the kids got hurt. Cocker was arrested, carted off to Kensington Police Station, and later cleared of wrongdoing. *Warwick Rd., tel. 0171/373–8141. Earl's Court tube.*

THE TROUBADOR

A friendly licensed coffee house, decorated with antiques and musical instruments, the Troubador has been running a folk night since the early '60s. When the emcee one night in 1963 asked for volunteers, a shambling-looking figure insisted on having a go—Bob Dylan. A week later folk guitar master Bert Jansch, just down from Edinburgh, made his London debut here. *265 Old Brompton Rd., SW5. West Brompton tube.*

Fulham, SW6

Archetypal southwest London suburbia, Fulham has some attractive, well-kept residential neighborhoods and fine views over the Thames. The politically informed soul-tinged Faith Brothers lived and worked here in the mid-'80s.

EATINGDRINKINGDANCINGSHOPPINGPLAYINGSLEEPING

After the closure of some venues, the live-music scene is in the hands of the **KINGS HEAD** (*see below*). For record shopping, there's a branch of secondhand merchants **MUSIC & VIDEO EXCHANGE** (400 Fulham Rd., tel. 0171/385–5350).

FULHAM BROADWAY TUBE STATION

This is where Ian Dury claimed that he could have been a ticketman on his 1978 single "What a Waste."

FULHAM ROAD

There was a rush along the Fulham Road—Jethro Tull, "A Passion Play"

John Lydon had to make his way down here in his pajamas at 4 AM after cops busted him for drugs in 1978. They searched his flat and failed to find anything, but refused to take him back home in a squad car.

Senser playing at the Kings Head

KINGS HEAD

Since 1989, the McKibben brothers have been putting on live music four nights a week in this standard old pub. Most of the groups are obscure local bands—Senser has come through the ranks—but from time to time there are secret charity gigs by big names—Plant, Page, Bruce Dickinson, Eric Bell, Francis Dunnery—who have also used the upstairs room as a practice space. *4 Fulham High St., tel. 0171/736–1413. Putney Bridge tube.*

Knightsbridge, SW7

In 1977...it's so lucky to be rich, Sten guns in Knightsbridge—The Clash, "1977"

Knightsbridge, with its grand Georgian terraces, stuccoed villa mews, major-league museums, and top-rank department stores, has it all (if you're rich), including plenty of rock & roll landmarks.

DAVID BOWIE ADDRESS, 1969

For most of 1969, Bowie lived in a three-story Victorian house on this quiet road with Hermione Farthingale. He wrote two songs about the relationship, "Letter to Hermione" and "An Occasional Dream," that were included on 1969's *David Bowie,* which was later re-released as *Space Oddity. 22 Clareville Grove. Gloucester Rd. tube.*

BROMPTON ORATORY

The memorial service for Rory Gallagher, who died in June 1995, was held in this Italianate church on November 8, 1995. Van Morrison and Bob Geldof turned up, as did former Fleetwood Mac leader Peter Green in one of his rare public appearances. The church was, until the ending of the Cold War, the site of a KGB drop (behind a column near one of the altars). *Brompton Rd. at Thurloe Pl., tel. 0171/589-4811. South Kensington tube.*

CHRISTIE'S

Most auctions of expensive rock memorabilia are held at Sotheby's in Mayfair, but in September 1995 the pot John Lennon kept his marijuana in was sold here for £4,500. In the same lot, a Beatles fan from Japan paid £18,000 for a kimono given to Lennon by a Japanese airline, while Bill Clinton's sax fetched £3,600. *85 Old Brompton Rd., tel. 0171/581-7611. South Kensington tube.*

GORE HOTEL

The Rolling Stones held a party to mark the release of *Beggars Banquet* in the hotel's Elizabethan Rooms in December 1968. Liveried waiters brought out roast suckling pigs on silver trays, which they placed on crisp white tablecloths, but a food fight predictably ensued. It costs £150 or more to stay at this Victorian hotel, whose Restaurant 190 is one of the most acclaimed in the capital. *190 Queens Gate, tel. 0171/584-6601. Gloucester Rd. tube.*

HARRODS

This Edwardian store, supposedly London's, if not the world's most prestigious, must also rank as one of the snootiest. Door staff are permanently on guard to bar undesirables, and one who came in for this treatment was the Go-Gos' Jane Weidlin, in February 1995, because she had blue hair. Back in the run-up to Christmas 1965, they closed the store so that the Beatles could buy their presents in peace. *87 Brompton Rd. SW1, tel. 0171/730-1234. Knightsbridge tube.*

ISLAND RECORDS FIRST ADDRESS, 1962

Chris Blackwell, a white Jamaican, set up his outstandingly successful label while living in this pretty little house near the Albert Hall in the first months of 1962. Early releases were mainly bluebeat, aimed at London's growing West Indian market—the label's first release was Lord Creator's "Independant [sic] Jamaica Calypso," which came out to coincide with the island's independence from Britain. By the fall, Blackwell had moved on to Bayswater. *4 Rutland Gate Mews. Knightsbridge tube.*

The National Sound Archive

[**NSA—BRITISH LIBRARY NATIONAL SOUND ARCHIVE**]

Opened in 1955, this mesmerizing bank of over a million records, 160,000 tapes, and a huge consignment of videos and books covers all types of 20th-century music from all over the world. All new releases are collected on all formats, and the pop collection grows by approximately 15,000 recordings per year. The NSA also offers the only public access to all those BBC radio sessions and interviews. The knowledgeable staff can help you find your way around. While use of the listening and viewing booths is free of charge, you do need to make an appointment. The reference library, which includes back issues of all the major pop music magazines and papers, requires no pre-booking. *29 Exhibition Rd., tel. 0171/412–7440. Open Mon.–Wed. and Fri. 10–5, Thurs. 10–9. South Kensington tube.*

[ROYAL ALBERT HALL]

Now they know how many holes it takes to fill the Albert Hall—The Beatles, "A Day in the Life"

When rock bands play at Britain's most prestigious classical music concert venue—all velvet curtains, luxury boxes, and ornate fittings—they tend to bill it as a special event. In reality, the Albert Hall has a long history of rock events. Built in 1871 and named for Queen Victoria's dead husband, the 8,000-seat hall put on its first rock & roll show, the Pop Prom, in September 1959 with Bert Weedon, Billy Fury, and Marty Wilde. The Proms were repeated for most of the '60s, and crooners were soon edged out by the beat bands. The '60s witnessed several groundbreaking rock events in the hall. The 1963 Proms had the Stones and the Beatles. Some of the other key dates of this era are:

MAY 1966. Disgusted folkies shouted: "Go home Dylan, drop dead. Get the group off," to which the singer coolly replied: "Oh you beautiful people... folk was just an interruption and was very useful." Fights broke out in the auditorium between pro- and anti-electric camps, and when hecklers persisted, a pissed off Dylan dared one fan to come up on stage and repeat his words.

SEPTEMBER 1966. The Rolling Stones recorded their American LP, *Got Live If You Want It*, here.

DECEMBER 1966. Pink Floyd played an Oxfam benefit, their first gig in a large venue.

JULY 1968. The Nice burned the American flag during a version of Bernstein's "America." They were banned from the hall for life.

NOVEMBER 1968. Cream's farewell gig also signaled the arrival in the big time of their support act Yes.

FEBRUARY 1969. Jimi Hendrix's last-ever mainland U.K. gig.

SEPTEMBER 1969. Deep Purple's best-forgotten "concerto" for rock band and orchestra was performed with the Royal Philharmonic. The album of the show had an interior shot of the hall on its cover, but rehearsals didn't go smoothly, with one member of the string section saying she didn't want to play with second-rate Beatles.

OCTOBER 4, 1970. Deep Purple put in a more typical show and were included in the *Guinness Book of Records* as the loudest band in the world.

The likes of the Byrds and Zeppelin continued to play the hall, but the Purple performance made management less keen to book rock bands. In February 1971 they canceled a Frank Zappa and the Mothers of Invention gig at the last minute after finding the lyrics to *200 Motels* obscene. Hall officials had furnished the band a list of 12 objectionable words they couldn't say on stage, including "brassiere."

By the '80s fewer major rock events were held here, although Siouxsie and the Banshees recorded a live album, *Nocturne*, in 1983, the same year that Echo and the Bunnymen had a picture of the hall on the cover of their "Never Stop" single. Creation Records' 10th anniversary party, Undrugged, took place here in fall 1994. The cult '60s psychedelic band, the Creation, inspiration for the label's name, starred, and Oasis debuted "Live Forever," "Whatever," and "Shakermaker." Nowadays, while bands like

(London) Suede and Gene might do single shows, the place is best known for hosting Eric Clapton's seemingly interminable annual season, which runs for about 24 shows. *Kensington Gore, tel. 0171/589–8212. South Kensington tube.*

Steve Gillett

Eric Clapton at Royal Albert Hall

Putney, SW15

Putney is a desirable residential area wedged between Wandsworth and Barnes. The district was known for live music when the Pontiac bar had a fine stretch in the '60s and '70s, staging a rare Byrds appearance at a small venue in the United Kingdom and one of the Police's earliest shows, but the club, now called the Railway, no longer has bands.

EATING DRINKING DANCING SHOPPING PLAYING SLEEPING

SOUL BROTHER RECORDS (1 Keswick Rd., tel. 0181/875–1018) stocks lots of rare soul and jazz.

THE HALF MOON

This pub, with room for 200 people, has been putting on music seven nights a week for the past two decades. In the '70s Richard Thompson, Dr. John, and Wilko Johnson appeared; the '80s saw early appearances by U2 and kd lang; more recent gigs have included Fairport Convention and Mike Flowers Pops. *93 Lower Richmond Rd., tel. 0181/780–9383.*

ST. MARY'S BALLROOM

Now boarded up, this regular early '60s venue for the Detours, the band that metamorphosed into the Who, was where Pete Townshend developed his windmill guitar technique. Townshend admitted he got the idea from watching Keith Richards when the fledgling Who shared a bill with the Rolling Stones in 1964 here, but the Stone claimed no recollection of ever doing it. *Hotham and Charlwood Rds. East Putney tube/Putney BR.*

Wimbledon and around, SW17, SW19, SW20

Home of British tennis, Wimbledon, a well-to-do suburb deep in south London, is taken up on its western side by Wimbledon Common. Marc Bolan and his wife June lived rough in a van on the common in 1967. A mile or so east of the park is the Merton Park suburb, from which the dreadful mod revivalist band, the Merton Parkas, took their name. A little farther east, by Morden tube station, the southernmost stop on the Northern Line, is Morden Hall Park, also known as Deer Park, after which the Fall named a track on *Hex Enduction Hour.*

GRANADA

Jerry Lee Lewis was booed by the 2,000-plus crowd when he played an uproarious gig here in May 1958. When he retorted: "I'm alive, I sure hope y'all ain't as dead as you sound," someone shouted back, "Go home baby snatcher"—a dig prompted by newspaper revelations that his 13-year-old female companion, Myra, was not only his cousin but also his wife. A year later Gene Vincent opened his British tour here. At a Jimi Hendrix Experience gig here in April 1967, Mitch Mitchell annoyed the support act, Cat Stevens (now Yusef Islam), by placing a toy robot on stage that "machine-gunned" Stevens as he sang "I'm Gonna Get Me a Gun." The venue is now a bingo hall. *50 Mitcham Rd., Tooting, SW17, tel. 0181/672–5717. Tooting Broadway tube.*

West London

From Hyde Park, West London sprawls outward toward Heathrow Airport. In between are areas of wealth (Kensington), dodgy districts (White City), and fairly sleepy suburbs (Ealing). While there is much for Who fans to scrape over throughout the west side, the most appealing area for music fans is Notting Hill and around Ladbroke Grove. Exciting and seedy in equal degrees, this multiethnic zone is home to the Notting Hill carnival, which attracts more than 1 million partyheads each August bank holiday. The area also has loads of bars and numerous record stores. Major venues are dotted throughout the area, with emerging Hammersmith the site of several key joints.

Songs of West London

Cat Stevens, "Portobello Road" (1967)
Pink Fairies, "Portobello Shuffle" (1972)
The Clash, "(White Man) in Hammersmith Palais" (1978)
Dire Straits, "Portobello Belle" (1979)
Pete Townshend, "White City Fighting" (1985)
Tangerine Dream, "Hyde Park" (1985)
Art Of Noise, "Acton Art" (1987)
The Pogues, "White City" (1989)

A GEOGRAPHICAL NOTE

West London is defined here as places within the W2 to W14 postal codes (these numbers appear on the name plates of virtually every street). W1 is very much the West End (*see* Central London).

Acton, W3

Stardom in Acton, that's all they got—Pete Townshend, "Stardom in Acton"

Pete Townshend claims this gray, soulless suburb of railway lines and shabby terraced houses as his "manor." The Who guitarist was actually brought up a few miles west, in Ealing, but the band went to school in Acton and played their first gigs locally. Deep Purple also has associations with the area, and early Brit pin-up rock & roller Adam Faith was born here on June 23, 1940.

ACTON COUNTY GRAMMAR SCHOOL (ACTON HIGH SCHOOL)

Pete Townshend and John Entwistle formed the Confederates, a trad jazz band, at this school in 1958. Townshend was on banjo and Entwistle, the school's star musician—he was the only student asked to play for the Middlesex Youth Orchestra—on French horn, an instrument he later used on many Who songs. Roger Daltrey also attended here—in a younger class. One day when Entwistle saw him carrying a bass guitar to school, he stopped and asked him: "Do you play bass...do you want to be in my group?" Also in Townshend and Entwistle's class was future Deep Purple singer Ian Gillan. *Gunnersbury La. Acton Town tube.*

CLASH BIRTHPLACE

The Clash formed in this squat—it still looks like the worst house on the street—in summer 1976. Strummer, who had just left the 101ers, had been introduced to Mick Jones and Paul Simonon, who were squatting here with future Slit Viv Albertine. After forming the band, they rehearsed regularly at Davis Road for a few months. Only one song from that period, "1-2, Crush on You," eventually found its way onto a Clash record (as the B-side of "Tommy Gun"). *22 Davis Rd., off The Vale. Acton Central BR.*

DEEP PURPLE ADDRESS (1968)

This ordinary-looking house was briefly home to the pioneering heavy metal band in its first incarnation—Ritchie Blackmore, Jon Lord, Ian Paice, and the soon-displaced Nick Semper and Rod Evans. *13 2nd Ave., off The Vale. Acton Central BR.*

Bayswater, W2

Hotel and embassy land, Bayswater is full of streets of cream-color stucco villas plus some very cosmopolitan stretches like Queensway, a lively street of all-night stores that Van Morrison sings of walking down on the *Them* track, "Bring 'Em on In."

COLUMBIA HOTEL

Built in the 1850s as separate luxury town houses, this is now one of London's premier rock & roll hotels for bands on the way up. Management actually encourages rock types to stay and is happy to cater to most of their whims. For instance, when the Teardrop Explodes stayed in 1980, on their first visit to London, Julian Cope wrecked his comfy bed, bunged the mattress on the floor, and threw some favorite books, bottles of booze, discarded record sleeves, and other ephemera around it so that it would remind him of the bohemian squalor of his own Liverpool pad. Hotel staff carefully kept it like that for him while he stayed in London. Not so welcome, though, is Oasis, banned for lobbing furniture through the manager's Mercedes in June 1994, the day after they had won over the crowd at the Glastonbury festival. They named a track on *Definitely Maybe* "Columbia," after the hotel, however. Slade's Noddy Holder has been a resident here. Rooms come at £65. *95 Lancaster Gate, tel. 0171/402–0021. Lancaster Gate tube.*

EMBASSY HOTEL

Richey Edwards of the Manic Street Preachers was last seen on February 1, 1995, when he stayed in Room 561 of this £120-a-night Victorian hotel. Edwards left a note on his pillow for his girlfriend, Lori Fidler, that said, "I love you," checked out at around seven in the morning, and drove off in his silver Vauxhall Cavalier. The car was later discovered abandoned at a service station on the Welsh border (*see* Out from Bristol *in* the West). At the time of writing, the singer has still not been found. *150 Bayswater Rd., tel. 0171/229–1212. Queensway tube.*

HYDE PARK

A welcome chunk of green amid the bustle of west London, this large park has appeared regularly in rock history, mainly for celebrated open-air mega-gigs, usually held in the Cockpit next to the Serpentine lake. The first Hyde Park gig took place on June 29, 1968, with Pink Floyd, supported by Jethro Tull and Roy Harper. Only 8,000 turned up for that one, yet around 150,000 gathered on June 7, 1969, to see the Third Ear Band, the Edgar Broughton Band, Richie Havens, and Donovan support Blind Faith, the Eric Clapton–Stevie Winwood–Ginger Baker–Rick Grech supergroup, who were making their debut.

Blind Faith's success in drawing the crowds prompted the Rolling Stones to play the park on July 5, 1969, in what was their first gig in two years, and allow them to "introduce" Mick Taylor (who had just replaced Brian Jones) to fans. Three days before the gig, Jones was found dead at his Sussex farm and the concert was turned into a memorial to the guitarist. Jagger, in a white smock, read from Shelley's "Adonais"—"Peace, peace, he is not dead, he does not sleep, he has awakened from the dreams of life"—and then released thousands of mainly dead butterflies into the air during the Stones' opening number, a version of Johnny Winter's "I'm Yours, and I'm Hers." One newspaper report put the crowd at 650,000, and none went below the quarter-million mark, making it the biggest-ever rock event in the United Kingdom. The gig was stewarded by Hells Angels, who did what was generally considered an efficient job.

Mick Jagger of the Rolling Stones singing at Hyde Park, 1969

(rotated caption at left of image) Peter Sanders/courtesy of Redferns

Bob Dylan and John Lennon were filmed engaged in surreal conversation while being driven through the park in a cab in May 1966 for the rarely seen *Eat the Document* movie. On a cold Friday (payday) morning in 1969 Island Records gathered together the cream of the label—Traffic, Jethro Tull, Fairport Convention, Free, Spooky Tooth, and Nirvana (U.K.), who came straight from the Speakeasy—for the cover shoot of the compilation *You Can All Join In.* Another album cover shot here was the Beatles' *Beatles for Sale* in 1964. Joe Strummer worked here cutting the grass in 1975 and Jimmy Somerville was arrested for gross indecency in 1985.

Gigs tailed off in the '70s and no more concerts took place until July 1996, when a Prince's Trust festival gathered together Bob Dylan, Eric Clapton, Alanis Morissette, and an all-star cast featuring Pete Townshend, Roger Daltrey, Dave Gilmour, Gary Glitter, and others for a first-ever stage adaptation of the Who's *Quadrophenia* following the success of the *Tommy* stage show in the West End.

SPEAKER'S CORNER

In the northeast corner of the park, near Marble Arch, is Speaker's Corner, where generations of orators have waged war against the evils of society. Dire Straits sang of going "down to Speaker's corner" where "two men say they're Jesus" on "Industrial Disease" from 1982's *Love over Gold.* In 1992 pop rockers Dodgy played from the back of a van before a crowd of 200 in protest against the poll tax. The cops turned up, spelt out that amplified music was not allowed on the corner, and arrested two of the band but not singer Nigel Clarke, who escaped into McDonald's.

....

HYDE PARK TOWERS HOTEL

Jimi Hendrix wrote two early songs, "Stone Free" (the B-side of "Hey Joe") and "Love or Confusion" (included on *Are You Experienced?*) while staying here in fall 1966. He had arrived in the United Kingdom for the first time under the auspices of former Animals bassist Chas Chandler. *41–49 Inverness Terr., off Bayswater Rd., tel. 0171/221–8484. Queensway tube.*

LONDON SS HANGOUT

Around 1975 the greasy-spoon Praed Street Café was where the London SS, the much talked about but unrecorded punk band, hung out and practiced in the basement. Put together by Malcolm McLaren and Bernie Rhodes (who went on to manage the Clash), the group's ever-fluctuating lineup consisted, at one time or another, of Mick Jones (later of the Clash), Tony James (later of Generation X and Sigue Sigue Sputnik), and Brian James and Rat Scabies (both Damned). The band never got around to doing a gig, yet their legend spread, thanks to mysterious write-ups in the rock press, T-shirts worn by the right people, and so on. They also managed to attract hundreds of wanna-bes including Morrissey—by correspondence—and Chrissie Hynde, who joined a London SS offshoot—Mike Hunt's Honourable Discharge. The place is now a Chinese restaurant. *113 Praed St. Paddington tube.*

MICK JONES ADDRESS 1974–79

It certainly boosted the punk credentials of the Clash's Mick Jones when he falsely told the *NME* in 1977: "I ain't never lived below the 17th floor." High-rise blocks, along with the Queen's silver jubilee, were one of punk's most potent symbols. The Warwick Estate, where Jones lived with his grandmother, is a mass of housing projects overlooking the main Paddington railway line and the Westway, central London's only highway, which regularly appeared in Clash imagery. *111 Wilmcote House, Woodchester Sq., Warwick Estate. Royal Oak tube.*

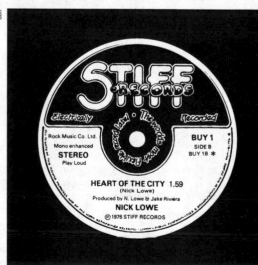

STIFF RECORDS

Britain's pioneering punk-era label, formed in 1976 by Dave Robinson and Andrew Jakeman (a.k.a. Jake Riviera), was based in this elegant street near Notting Hill. Robinson had managed Brinsley Schwartz, and Jakeman, Dr. Feelgood (whose Lee Brilleaux had lent him £400 to get the thing going). Stiff quickly capitalized on the then-booming pub rock scene. The label's first release was ex-Brinsley Schwartz member Nick Lowe's double A-side, "So It Goes"/"Heart of the City." Other quality early records include Lew Lewis's "Boogie on the

Stiff Records' first release

Street" and the Yachts' "Suffice to Say." But Stiff struck gold with the Damned (who released "New Rose") and Elvis Costello, whose debut album *My Aim Is True* was a major breakthrough; they put a huge cardboard cutout of him in an upper window. Another key single in the early Stiff years was Richard Hell's "Blank Generation."

Stiff paved the way for the DIY indie label boom that has dominated the '80s and '90s, putting considerable effort into packaging, sleeves, and devising wacky slogans. They even revived the package tour idea, sending their artists round the country on Stiff showcases. The label suffered the departure of three of its leading figures in 1978— Jakeman, Nick Lowe, and Elvis Costello, who formed Radar Records—but kept up the hits for a few years, mainly through Ian Dury, Lene Lovich, Tracey Ullman, and Madness, who had 18 U.K. hits with them. Stiff also issued U.S. acts in Britain, including Devo (who released a single, "Be Stiff") and the Plasmatics. In 1984 Stiff was absorbed by Island and signed up the Pogues, but it reverted to independent status two years later. Madness moved on in 1985, and nowadays the Stiff marque is a re-issue label. The building is now a private residence. *32 Alexander St. Royal Oak tube.*

Chiswick, W4

This slice of suburbia with some grand Georgian houses lent its name to Chiswick Records, a pre-punk indie label that preceded Stiff and Rough Trade. Artists included the 101ers (Joe Strummer's pre-Clash band), the Count Bishops (whose "Speedball" EP was the first release, in November 1975), Radio Stars, Irish punkers the Radiators from Space, and the Damned. The label was actually run out of the Rock On store in Camden Town. A label with a current presence in the neighborhood is Caroline U.K., the British subsidiary of the label that introduced the Smashing Pumpkins and Hole.

Steve Marriott lived in a posh apartment on Chiswick Mall overlooking the river in 1966. He annoyed his neighbors by throwing noisy parties and allowing his dogs to shit every-where. Pissed off with their complaints, he wrote the song "Lazy Sunday Afternoon," which began: "Wouldn't it be nice to get on with me neighbours."

EATINGDRINKING**DANCING**SHOPPING**PLAYING**SLEEPING

SPINNING DISC (54 Chiswick High Rd., W4, tel. 0181/994–4606) stocks '50s and '60s singles in meticulous order.

CHISWICK HOUSE

The Beatles filmed the promo film for the "Paperback Writer"/"Rain" single in the lavish gardens of this 18th-century Palladian villa in May 1966. Paul McCartney apparently was in great pain during the shoot; he had just chipped a tooth in a moped accident. There's a charge to get into the house, but the grounds are open to the public. *Burlington La., tel. 0181/995–0508. Chiswick BR.*

Ealing, W5, W13

Mick Jagger made his name playing Ealing Blues Club in the early '60s. Around this time, Pete Townshend, who studied at Ealing Art College, was developing the Who sound in various Ealing addresses.

EALING ART COLLEGE (THAMES VALLEY UNIVERSITY)

Students at this art school in the late '50s/early '60s included Ronnie Wood, Freddie Mercury (né Bulsara), and Pete Townshend, who learned about pop art and autode-struction, things the Who later dabbled in. Townshend was taught by lecturer Gustav Metzke, who destroyed a double bass in a tutorial and would dip paintings in acid to see how long they took to decompose, photographing the results. *St. Mary's Rd., tel. 0181/ 579–5000. South Ealing tube.*

EALING BLUES CLUB

Mick Jagger made his singing debut at England's first R&B club on March 17, 1962, but with Blues Incorporated, not the Rolling Stones. The club had been set up by Alexis Korner in a former jazz club, below the ABC Tea Rooms (now a property company offices) in the center of the district. Blues Incorporated, who were club regulars, were formed by guitarist Korner and harp player Cyril Davies to showcase Delta and Chicago blues for the English. The band also included Dick Heckstall-Smith (sax), Jack Bruce (bass), and Charlie Watts (drums) and they were soon joined by another blues freak who came in from Cheltenham, 100 miles west. He called himself Elmo Lewis, because it sounded more authentically bluesy, but soon revealed that his real name was Brian Jones. Mick Jagger took over as singer from Long John Baldry after sending Korner a demo tape but started pretty low down the pecking order. Patrick Campbell-Lyons from Nirvana (U.K.) remembers Jagger cleaning out his harp in the club toilet with the excuse "Brian says it's my job." Until recently the venue was still a jazz club. It has now closed down. *42a Broadway. Ealing Broadway tube.*

PETE TOWNSHEND ADDRESS (1945–64)

The Who leader was born into a musical home; his father Cliff had played sax and clarinet in a dance band. When Pete was in his late teens, he moved back into the house, occupying the attic, after a spell at Sunnyside Road (*see below*). He tried unsuccessfully to build a studio by laying down a two-inch-thick concrete floor, but when the ceiling below started to sag, he was told to go. *20 Woodgrange Ave. Ealing Common tube.*

PETE TOWNSHEND ADDRESS (1964)

While attending Ealing College of Art in 1964, Townshend moved into this house. It was here that he and Roger Daltrey decided on the Who as the new name for their group, which had alternated between the Detours and the High Numbers. On "Somebody Saved Me," from his 1982 solo album *All the Best Cowboys Have Chinese Eyes,* Townshend sings of how it "always rains in Sunnyside Road." *35 Sunnyside Rd. South Ealing tube.*

Hammersmith, W6

A dynamic area that has recently attracted big firms and exciting new buildings, Hammersmith is now becoming a major U.K. base for record companies, including Polydor, Mercury, London, and EMI.

HAMMERSMITH ODEON (LABATT'S APOLLO)

A major rock venue, with 3,000 seats, it still tends to be called by its former name, Hammersmith Odeon, by Londoners. David Bowie killed off his Ziggy Stardust alter ego here on July 4, 1973. Watching the performance were future Sex Pistols Steve Jones and Paul Cook who, the legend goes, after the gig nipped backstage while no one was looking, hid themselves away, and at dead of night made off with a stack of expensive microphones, which they loaded into a waiting van (itself stolen). Much of the Pistols' equipment was accumulated in this manner over the next few years.

Eric Clapton made a fool of himself at the Odeon in December 1974. As he came out on stage, a voice from the crowd shouted, "Clapton is God," referring to graffiti scrawled around London in the late '60s. After the applause died down Clapton went up to the mike and announced: "I'm not God, just the greatest guitarist in the world." Fee Waybill of the Tubes didn't come out of a 1978 gig looking too clever either—while wielding a whirling chainsaw over his head, he fell off the stage and broke a leg (another who fell off the stage was Siouxsie Sioux in 1985, dislocating her kneecap). Two years later Black Sabbath played their first show following Ozzy Osbourne's sacking from the band. When his replacement, Ronnie James Dio, started to do his thing, someone shouted

David Bowie at the Hammersmith Odeon

"Ozzy Ozzy Ozzy," and soon the whole audience joined in. They almost managed to drown out Black Sabbath, not exactly one of the world's quietest bands. In December 1993 Jethro Tull were joined onstage by former guitarist Mick Abrahams, for the first time in 25 years. The following summer one-time Fleetwood Mac frontman Peter Green made one of his very rare public appearances on stage to thank ex-Thin Lizzy guitarist Gary Moore for making the *Blues for Greeny* tribute album.

Recordings made here include parts of Thin Lizzy's *Live and Dangerous* (November 14– 16, 1976); Motörhead's *No Sleep Til Hammersmith* (June 27, 1980); and parts of Public Enemy's *It Takes a Nation of Millions to Hold Us Back* in 1988. Since the place received a makeover in the early '90s, bookers have shunned noisy metal and rap acts, preferring smoochy soul singers and MOR. *Queen Caroline St., tel. 0171/416–6080. Hammersmith tube.*

HAMMERSMITH PALAIS

The Palais was an obscure dance hall until the Clash released the 1978 single "White Man in Hammersmith Palais." In the song Joe Strummer recounts the story of a reggae all-nighter in June 1977. Naively expecting a radical bill and a radical all-black crowd, Strummer was subjected to a night of old-fashioned entertainment from Leroy Smart, Dillinger, and Delroy Wilson and some hassle from dreads amazed to see a white face.

These days the place masquerades under the name of Le Palais (its original name from the mid-'20s was Le Palais de Dance; the original stone plaque bearing that name is still here), but most people still use the Hammersmith prefix. Live music ranges from soul stars through ethnic music festivals to the occasional rock band; (London) Suede, Massive Attack, and Supergrass have been recent headliners, while in punk days the Damned and the Jam also performed here. *242 Shepherd's Bush Rd., tel. 0181/748– 2812. Hammersmith tube.*

RIVERSIDE STUDIOS

Once Europe's largest TV studios, Riverside, on a dreary part of the Thames, is now west London's leading arts center, putting on avant-garde exhibitions and films. While rehearsing a prototype Clash here in early 1976, Mick Jones and Keith Levene (who later helped found PiL) wrote "What's My Name," the Clash's first song and one of their greatest. In December 1986 the Fall's Mark E. Smith directed his play, *Hey Luciani,* based on Pope John Paul I, at Riverside. *Crisp Rd., tel. 0171/254-6485. Hammersmith tube.*

Kensington, W8

A classy area, Kensington is one of London's main shopping stretches—proprietors past and present have included Jimmy Page, who ran a black magic bookshop in the '70s, and Bill Wyman, who owns a restaurant.

EATINGDRINKINGDANCINGSHOPPINGPLAYINGSLEEPING

Bill Wyman's likeable **STICKY FINGERS** restaurant (1a Phillimore Gardens, tel. 0171/938-5338), just off Kensington High Street, has lots of Stones memorabilia on the walls and serves up good burgers and salads. **CUBA** (11 Kensington High St., tel. 0171/582-6437) has live funk with top session players each Tuesday; on other nights DJs spin cutting-edge latin and soul sounds. In West Kensington (W14), where Marcus Garvey died, you'll find the **ORANGE** (3 North End Crescent, W14, tel. 0171/371-4317), a long-running pub venue that puts on a wide range of music every night of the week.

Courtesy of Sticky Fingers

Bill Wyman at Sticky Fingers

HOLLAND PARK

A picture of Van Morrison next to one of the statues in Holland Park's walled garden was used on the front of 1986's *No Guru, No Method, No Teacher,* and there's one of him sitting on a bench on the cover of the 1991 double album, *Hymns of the Silence. Off Abbotsbury Rd. Holland Park tube.*

KENSINGTON MARKET

In the early '70s stallholders included Queen's Freddie Mercury and Roger Taylor, while in the early '80s Billy Duffy worked here before joining the Cult. The market covers two floors, with stalls, crammed together along rickety passages, selling every kind of fashion from goth to techno. It's popular with tourists and has prices to match. *49 Kensington High St., tel. 0171/938-4343. High St. Kensington tube.*

NASHVILLE ROOMS

Wire made their stage debut at this popular punk venue, now the Three Kings pub, in December 1976, supporting the Derelicts. A year previously, in July 1975, Eddie and the Hot Rods were signed to Island after a storming gig here. In April 1976 a Sex Pistols gig here was marred by fighting after fashion designer Vivienne Westwood tried to enliven a dull night by attacking a girl in the crowd. When the girl's boyfriend intervened, members of the group bowled off stage and waded in. Mayhem ensued for a few minutes until the Pistols went back on stage and finished their set. The incident made them as infamous for violence as for music—which is exactly what McLaren and Westwood wanted. It was also at this gig that Mick Jones convinced Paul Simonon to join him in the Clash.

At an August 1977 Elvis Costello show here, hundreds were turned away at the door and missed the singer recording the live versions of "Blame It on Cain" and "Mystery Dance" used on the B-side of "Watching the Detectives." *171 North End Rd., W14. West Kensington tube.*

OLYMPIA

This massive '30s exhibition hall has only occasionally been used for gigs. Syd Barrett's last show with Pink Floyd, billed as "Christmas on Earth Revisited," took place here on December 22, 1967. In June 1970 Syd returned to play a rare solo gig, at a fashion festival, backed by his Floyd replacement, Dave Gilmour, and Humble Pie's Jerry Shirley. *Hammersmith Rd., W14, tel. 0171/603–3344. Kensington Olympia tube.*

JIMMY PAGE ADDRESS, 1973–CA. 1980

Jimmy Page bought this Victorian Gothic pile from actor Richard Harris for £350,000 in 1973, outbidding David Bowie. Architect William Burges modeled each room on a different theme from nature—the sea, animals, the stars, time, love. Page used the house as a babe magnet. Cult moviemaker Kenneth Anger occupied the basement while applying the finishing touches to *Lucifer Rising* in 1974. *Tower House, 29 Melbury Rd. High St. Kensington tube.*

RED COW

AC/DC played their first British gig at this pub rock venue early in 1976, with Bon Scott carrying Angus Young on his shoulders out into the crowd. Photos for the front cover of the Jam's *In the City* debut album were taken here—the group had a residency that year. The building is now Latymer's, a pub and Thai restaurant. *157 Hammersmith Rd., W14, tel. 0181/748–3346. Barons Court tube.*

Maida Hill, W9

The W9 area has a reputation for snootiness, especially the canal-side stretch called Little Venice. The BBC has its Maida Vale Studios on Delaware Road, where just about everyone who was ever anyone has recorded a session for John Peel's radio show. The larger Maida Hill 'hood is one of west London's roughest zones. Slum clearance and wartime bombing made it ripe for squatting during the '60s and '70s. The squats attracted a wide cross-section of malcontents, including ex-public school types like Joe Strummer.

Jane Hanser

Strummer's squat

SQUATNEY CALLING

- **23 Chippenham Rd.** Strummer kipped here, within earshot of the Westway, for a week in spring 1974.

- **101 Walterton Rd.** In 1975 Strummer lived at this now-demolished squat. The street number provided the name for his band the 101ers.

- **36 St. Luke's Rd.** After being kicked out of Walterton Road in 1975, Strummer dossed in this filthy four-story terraced house. His flatmates included future Slit Palmolive and Clash debut album producer Mickey Foote.

- **7 Foscote Mews.** When an ice cream company moved out of this dive in December

The Notting Hill Carnival

1976, Strummer moved in, and wrote the song "Hate and War," which ended up on the Clash's first album.

"PROTEX BLUE" INSPIRATION

The Clash song "Protex Blue" was written about buying contraceptives in this hulking pub. *The Windsor Castle, 309 Harrow Rd., tel. 0171/289–7039. Westbourne Park tube.*

Notting Hill, W10, W11

I took a walk down W11. I had to wade through 500 European punks—The Fall, "Deer Park"

An exciting, cosmopolitan, and densely populated area, Notting Hill could claim to be the spiritual home of British rock. Hundreds of rock stars—Van Morrison, Jimi Hendrix, Hawkwind, the Clash, and newcomers like Brett Anderson of (London) Suede and Justine Frischmann of Elastica—have come to Notting Hill. Mark Knopfler likes the place so much he named his upmarket skiffle outfit the Notting Hillbillies. Virgin founder Richard Branson also has a mansion here. Depending on the stage of their careers, rock stars make for the "lively" squats north of the Westway (the raised highway that runs east–west through the area), the down-at-heel but still classy-looking bedsits around Portobello Road market, or the gorgeous stuccoed villas nearer Holland Park.

In the '50s West Indians moved into Notting Hill, the first large-scale black immigration into England. The West Indians' small-scale annual festival has since blossomed into Europe's largest street carnival (held over the last weekend in August). In the '60s the northern parts of the area were savaged by the wrecking ball. Street after street became prime territory for squatters like members of Hawkwind and radicals; the underground paper *Oz* was based on Princedale Road.

In punk days Notting Hill became *the* place to hang out. Fans and bands would stroll down Portobello Road market, drop in at Rough Trade Records, and then move on to Kensington Park Road. Around the same time, a huge underground reggae scene bloomed around Ladbroke Grove, the main north–south route through the area. These days London's rock epicenter has moved to Camden Town, but Notting Hill still buzzes. Record companies both large (Virgin) and small (Wiija) are based here, and it is one of London's hippest places to live, eat, and club.

EATINGDRINKINGDANCINGSHOPPINGPLAYINGSLEEPING

The major venue in this part of town is dance-oriented **SUBTERANIA** (*see below*), and the area is packed with bars, from fashionable new arrivals to grubby old hangouts. **THE MARKET BAR** (240A Portobello Rd., tel. 0171/229–6472) combines both trendy and scruffy elements and pumps out reggae. London's first Internet bar is **PORTOBELLO GOLD** (95 Portobello Rd., tel. 0171/460–4900). The music industry hangout **PARADISE BY WAY OF KENSAL GREEN** (19 Kilburn La., W10, tel. 0181/969–0098) also serves great modern dishes. The area has some superb Portuguese bakeries: **LISBOA** (57 Golborne Rd., tel. 0181/968–5242), the best of the lot, draws rock stars, from the Bad Seeds to Pulp, for coffee and pastries.

A favorite hotel for everyone from Tina Turner to Guns N' Roses and Oasis is the **PORTOBELLO** (22 Stanley Gardens, W11, tel. 0171/727–2777). There are only 22 bedrooms or suites, and a double costs around £150.

Portobello Road, the trendiest street market in London, overflows with stalls and small stores selling quality antiques, alternative clothes (near the Westway), ethnic foods, and interesting junk. The ever-growing **MUSIC & VIDEO EXCHANGE** (38 [the best], 34, and 56 Notting Hill Gate, 28/30 Pembridge Rd., tel. 0171/243–8574) empire is one of London's largest secondhand chains, selling cameras, vintage clothes, bikes, and books as well as records. Other notable local record stores include **INTOXICA!** (231 Portobello Rd., W11, tel. 0171/229–8010), which is good on soul and '60s psychedelia rarities; **SHAKEDOWN** (297 Portobello Rd., W10, tel. 0181/964–5135), for a selected range of secondhand rock and punk vinyl; and **STAND OUT COLLECTORS RECORDS** (2 Blenheim Crescent, W11, tel. 0171/727–8400), with real collector stuff, specializing in albums from the '60s to punk. **HONEST JON'S** (276–278 Portobello Rd., W10, tel. 0181/969–9822) has great soul, jazz, and Latin, with a "Reggae Revive" section in the back. **DUB VENDOR** (150 Ladbroke Grove, tel. 0181/969–3375) is a reggae specialist. The most famous of all the local stores is, of course, **ROUGH TRADE** (*see below*).

All landmarks are W11 except where stated.

A RIOT OF MY OWN

There's rarely any trouble these days at the August Notting Hill carnival, now Europe's biggest street party, but in the '70s it often brought serious violence. Cops charged youth in August 1976 and this led to a battle between black youth and the police, the worst riot since 1958. The fighting inspired the Clash's debut single, "White Riot," which began with a police siren taped at the carnival. Some thought the band was being racist, but the Clash were simply saying that they, as white people, wanted a riot of their own, "a white riot."

ALL SAINTS CHURCH HALL

Pink Floyd made their debut under that name at this small venue, then home for the London Free School's Light and Sound Workshop, on October 14, 1966. The flyer for this gig read: "Announcing pop dance featur-

Courtesy of Halcyon Hotel

Halcyon Hotel

ing London's furthest-out group, the Pink Floyd in Interstellar Overdrive, Stoned Alone and Astronomy Domini (an astral chant) and other numbers from the space age book." At this gig they introduced U.K. audiences to psychedelic light shows; while the band messed around with lengthy jams like "Interstellar Overdrive," a couple of American lights wizards projected slides onto the bodies of the musicians. The gigs became so popular they had to move the show to the UFO on Tottenham Court Road (see Fitzrovia—Around Tottenham Court Road in Central London, above). The last one held here was on November 29, 1966. *Powis Gardens. Westbourne Park tube.*

HALCYON HOTEL

Only a few months after Oasis had booked in for £375 a night, running up a record mini-bar bill and shooting the cover of "Cigarettes and Alcohol," the band's label, Creation Records, returned for their 1995 Christmas party. Dressed as Father Christmas, company boss Alan McGee declared that '95 had been the most successful year in the label's history, thanks to Oasis, and handed out presents to the band. The best, a chocolate brown Rolls-Royce, went to songwriter and nondriver Noel Gallagher. Singer Liam Gallagher is a regular visitor to the hotel's bar. The restaurant is one of the most popular for showbiz types in the capital. Standard rooms are £200 a night. *81 Holland Park, tel. 0171/727-7288, W11. Holland Park tube.*

[JIMI HENDRIX DEATH SITE]

Jimi Hendrix died while staying in this former residential hotel (now private apartments) on Friday September 18, 1970. Hendrix returned from Mike Nesmith's party at 3 o'clock on the Friday morning, ate a tuna sandwich, told girlfriend Monika Danneman he needed a lie down and took a sleeping tablet. It didn't help, because he talked to her until 7 o'clock before falling asleep. At 10:30 Danneman woke and went to Portobello Road to get some cigarettes, but she couldn't wake the guitarist when she came back. Danneman noticed Hendrix had been sick and taken about 10 of the pills. She called an ambulance, which took him to St. Mary Abbot's Hospital in Kensington, where he was pronounced dead.

There has been some confusion over the exact manner of his death ever since. Ambulance staff later said that Hendrix was covered in vomit and was dead. The doctor at St. Mary Abbott's said Hendrix had drunk so much red wine he drowned trying to regurgitate it. The official reason given at the time was "inhalation of vomit due to barbiturate intoxication," but even this was later changed to an open verdict. *Samarkand Hotel, 22 Lansdowne Crescent. Holland Park tube.*

ISLAND/ZTT/SARM WEST

Home of Island Records during the '70s, here Black Sabbath recorded *Paranoid,* Traffic *John Barleycorn Must Die,* and the Clash *Give 'Em Enough Rope.* By the '80s Island had moved out and a new label, ZTT, had moved in. ZTT, steered by producer Trevor Horn and former *NME* journalist Paul Morley, made a big splash with Frankie Goes to Hollywood, the Art of Noise, and Propaganda. Roy Orbison and Grace Jones signed up for a couple of releases, but the label suffered a huge setback after a court case with Frankie's Holly Johnson. In the studio in 1984 a cross section of the nation's biggest-selling stars, including Sting, Phil Collins, and Duran Duran, came together for the Band Aid "Do They Know It's Christmas" charity single. It is now the four-room Sarm West studios, one of the largest and busiest in the capital. *8 Basing St., tel. 0171/229-1229. Ladbroke Grove tube.*

LADBROKE GROVE

This lengthy road, Notting Hill's main north–south route, takes in sumptuous villas at its southern end near Holland Park and decaying estates around the Westway at its northern end. Van Morrison, who lived in the area in the mid-'60s, mentions Ladbroke Grove on "Slim Slow Slider," from 1968's *Astral Weeks*. Sting, being photographed for *Q* magazine in Ladbroke Grove tube station in March 1993 busked "Every Breath You Take" and other well-known songs. Passersby, assuming he was just another bad Sting impersonator, ignored him. *Ladbroke Grove tube.*

THE MOUNTAIN GRILL

Hawkwind and other heads, known as the London Groovers, hung out in this greasy spoon (now George's Fish Bar takeout) in the early '70s. Hawkwind honored the place by naming their 1974 album *Hall of the Mountain Grill*. *275 Portobello Rd. Ladbroke Grove tube.*

MUTE RECORDS

Electronics dabbler Daniel Miller wandered into Rough Trade's (*see below)* Kensington Park Road store in 1978 with a single he had made at home, "TV OD"/"Warm Leatherette." When store owner Geoff Travis heard it, he was so impressed he asked Miller to press more, let him hang around the store dealing with record biz people, and encouraged him to set up his own label, Mute. Miller hit gold by signing Depeche Mode in 1980, and since then hits have followed with Yazoo, Erasure, Nick Cave, and Moby. Mute keeps up the experimental end with artists as varied as Diamanda Galás, Einstürzende Neubaten, and Barry Adamson. The company also owns the Nova Mute electronic dance label and the Rhythm King imprint that has had British dance hits with Bomb the Bass and S-Express. Through the Blast First subsidiary, they have introduced the likes of Sonic Youth, the Butthole Surfers, and Afghan Whigs to British ears. A more recent addition, the Grey Area of Mute, re-releases classics by Cabaret Voltaire, Can, and the like. At street level the company has a retail and mail order store that stocks many rarities and limited issue discs, as well as T-shirts, books, and Mute accessories. They can be e-mailed at mutebank@muteliblech.com. *429 Harrow Rd., W10 4RF, tel. 0181/964-0029. Westbourne Park tube.*

PORTOBELLO ROAD MARKET

Island Records founder Chris Blackwell sold the label's early singles, mainly bluebeat stuff, from a stall in this market in the mid-'60s. High on pills, Free guitarist Paul Kossoff smashed up four cars driving down the road in 1975. Legend has it that Mick Jones, Paul Simonon, and Keith Levene bumped into the 101ers' Joe Strummer in the market in 1976 and told him that while his band was a waste of time, he was a star and should join them in a new group...who became the Clash. In 1993 Kurt Cobain dropped into Ana da Silva's antiques store and asked the incredulous former Raincoat whether the band wished to support Nirvana on their forthcoming tour. *Notting Hill Gate and Ladbroke Grove tube.*

ROCK ON

Rock 'n' Roll/I get my records at the Rock On stall/Rock 'n' Roll/Teddy boy he's got them all—Thin Lizzy, "The Rocker"

When Ted(dy boy) Carroll opened his oldies stall (basically a couple of tables in the back of a mini-marketplace) here in 1972, it was just about the only place where British fans could pick up original U.S. releases, especially early rock & roll numbers. Rock On was popular with Teddy Boys, who would congregate here in the afternoons when the pubs weren't open. The store moved to Soho and then to Camden Town in 1975. There is now a junk shop on the premises. *93 Golborne Rd., North Kensington, W10. Ladbroke Grove tube.*

ROUGH TRADE

A major record store and punk-era meeting place, Rough Trade also became one of Britain's leading indie record labels in the '80s. Founder Geoff Travis (who has since managed the Cranberries and Pulp) began selling records at 202 Kensington Park Road, just south of Ladbroke Grove station, in February 1976 after running a stall in nearby Portobello Road market. Over the next few years it was the best place in the land for picking up hard-to-find reggae and U.S. psychedelic/garage stuff like Roky Erickson, the Seeds, and the MC5.

When British punk bands started putting out their own material, Rough Trade ensured it had all the required pressings and sleeves, one of which would be fastened to

Interior at Rough Trade Records, Talbot Road

the wall for posterity. No Stranglers records were sold here, however, because bassist Jean-Jacques Burnel had beaten up store friend and rock writer Jon Savage, whose fanzine, *London's Outrage*, was sold here alongside *Sniffin' Glue* and scores of others.

The store was always full of a bizarre cross section of heads, dreads, bands, and hangers-on—the Clash's Mick Jones, PiL's Keith Levene, and Chrissie Hynde were regulars—and when visiting U.S. acts like Patti Smith, the Ramones, and Talking Heads came to Britain, they dropped by.

In 1978 Rough Trade started its own record company. Founded on strong socialist feelings, it was run, like the store, as a co-op, with everyone on the same wages. Bands were signed because they fit the label's philosophy rather than because they could make the owners a quick buck. So Blondie were rejected for being too commercial (but not Stiff Little Fingers) and early releases were by left-field acts like Metal Urbaine (whose "Paris Maquis" in 1979 was Rough Trade's first release), the Swiss girl group Kleenex, Essential Logic, the Raincoats, and Pop Group, who had an album track called "Amnesty International Report on British Army Torture of Irish Prisoners."

Yet even though Rough Trade seemed more concerned with politics than music, they put out gem after gem: Spizzenergy's "Soldier Soldier," Cabaret Voltaire's "Nag Nag Nag," and the Fall's "How I Wrote Elastic Man." There were hits as well, from Aztec Camera and Stiff Little Fingers. In the early '80s Rough Trade set up a distribution wing with other indies, the Cartel, but success led to the introduction of capitalist practices, like profit-sharing. Rough Trade kept well in with new indie trends, signed the Smiths, and by the end of the decade had a turnover topping £40 million. It was this boom that caused cracks in the structure. "You can't sign a band by committee," Travis famously announced. Executives were appointed, they quarrelled, and they made bad decisions like buying a dodgy computer system and moving the company to an unsuitable warehouse in Finsbury Park. The company also had bad luck with creditors. When in 1991 the whole thing seemed in danger of a collapse that could have brought down the entire indie network, RT was bailed out by a consortium that ironically included some of the labels it had helped spawn, like Mute and 4AD.

The record label went bust in May 1991 but has since been revamped as Rough Trade 2 with Boutique and Spring-Heel Jack. The retail side flourishes, thanks to its knack of staying several steps ahead of trends, with other branches in Tokyo and Paris, and Slam City Skates in Covent Garden. The Kensington Park Road main store moved to Talbot Road in 1982 and is still very much at the cutting edge of the indie scene, great for rarities, exotica, techno, trance, thrash, and underground sounds of every description. The original Kensington Park Road site is now occupied by Cheeky Monkeys—haircuts, shoes, clothes, toys. *130 Talbot Rd., tel. 0171/229–8541; e-mail: shop@roughtrade.com. Open Mon.–Sat. 10–6:30. Ladbroke Grove tube.*

SUBTERANIA/ACKLAM HALL

In the mid-'70s, when it was the Acklam Hall, many bands associated with the burgeoning scene around Rough Trade records played at this decrepit punk venue right underneath the Westway. The Fall recorded a cassette-only album, *Live at the Acklam Hall.* The Hall also hosted many ska acts: the Mo-Dettes formed for a one-off gig here and then kept going a bit longer. The North London Invaders, a beta version of Madness, played here in late 1978, as Chas Smith, whom they had earlier fired as bassist, invaded the stage and pranced around so impressively that they invited him back into the band. His invention became the band's trademark "Nutty Dance."

Overhauled and renamed Subterania, the venue was chosen by Rough Trade to host their 20th anniversary week of six shows—under the title of "The Acklam Hall Revisited"—in March 1996. Among those who appeared were Tindersticks, the Cocteau Twins, Drugstore, and the Raincoats, plus artists from the Mo-Wax label. For the rest of the time however, Subterania, part of the Mean Fiddler organization since 1989, concentrates on acts such as Ice T, the Red Hot Chili Peppers, the Pharcyde, as well as techno club nights. *12 Acklam Rd., tel. 0181/960–4590. Ladbroke Grove tube.*

THE SOUND OF THE WESTWAY

Up and down the Westway, in and out the light—The Clash, "London's Burning"

West London's only highway, which runs above house level between Shepherd's Bush and Edgware Road, featured heavily in early punk mythology symbolizing the speed and adrenalin rush of the music. The Westway was particularly meaningful for the Clash, whose Joe Strummer and Mick Jones lived in earshot of it for much of the '70s. Their early records were promoted as "the sound of the Westway." There was even a punk fanzine called *Sounds of the Westway.*

On the track "London's Burning" from their debut album, *The Clash,* they sing of driving up and down the highway in boredom. The Jam were photographed under the Westway near Latimer Road for the cover of *This Is the Modern World,* in an attempt to outpunk the Clash.

Shepherds Bush, W12

Shepherds Bush—dirty, rough, with little charm, but a popular place to live as it's not too far from the center and cheaper than Notting Hill—has gone down in Mod folklore as the place where the Who did many of their earliest gigs. More recent bands to come out of the area include funksters Jamiroquai and Bush, who got into trouble with politically correct America over the genitalia-linked nature of their name (plus the image on their debut CD cover), though they insist it comes from this area where they used to live. The area is also home to teen power-poppers Symposium.

EATINGDRINKINGDANCINGSHOPPINGPLAYINGSLEEPING

Apart from the Shepherds Bush Empire (*see below*), there is not much to recommend the area. **PECKINGS** (142 Askew Rd., tel. 0181/749–4517) sells only reggae stuff made at Studio One (Coxsone Dodd's studio in Jamaica, West Indies).

Cyndi Lauper sings at the Shepherds Bush Empire

Justin Thomas

BBC TELEVISION CENTRE

The corporation's main television studios are based, somewhat surprisingly, in one of London's most miserable spots, between a tube train depot, Wormwood Scrubs prison, and a nasty council estate. For decades it was home to Britain's longest-running pop program, Top of the Pops, a tacky half-hour show that concentrates on the singles charts but effectively dictates what is likely to be a hit anyway. The show is now recorded in Elstree, Hertfordshire (*see* Hertfordshire *in* the Home Counties and the South). *Wood La., tel. 0181/743–8000. White City tube.*

SHEPHERDS BUSH EMPIRE

This three-tiered Edwardian arena, until recently used by the BBC to record episodes of TV programs, was converted in the early '90s for use as a rock venue. Maintaining its original fittings, it's topped some polls for best venue in the city; the views from the circles are good, and there is standing room downstairs. With a capacity of 2,000, it competes with the Forum. The Sex Pistols had a hugely successful gig here in July 1996. With several gigs per week, the Empire has hosted some of the biggest names on the circuit, including Hole, the Smashing Pumpkins, Soul Asylum, Alanis Morissette, and Patti Smith. *Shepherds Bush Green, tel. 0181/740–7474. Shepherds Bush tube.*

WHITE CITY ESTATE

The White City, that's a joke of a name—Pete Townshend, "White City Fighting"

The Who's leader named his 1985 solo album after this rough pre-war estate near Queens Park Rangers' football ground and included pictures of various sites on the back cover and sleeve. Townshend was raised in middle-class Ealing, a few miles west, but the estate had always fascinated him. Townshend claimed in the blurb on the back cover: "The White City might not be perfect, but it's survived the fall of the British Empire. Everyone seems to know each other's names, even if they don't actually get on well."

WORMWOOD SCRUBS PRISON

They smelt of pubs and Wormwood Scrubs and too many right-wing meetings—The Jam, "Down in the Tube Station at Midnight"

Keith Richards was sentenced to a year in this jail that is just as gruesome as the name suggests in June 1967 after a drug bust. After a successful appeal, Richards, Prisoner 7855, stayed only one night, during which inmates kept asking him if he wanted some hash. Another Stone, Brian Jones, spent a night here that October for possessing cannabis. He had been sentenced to nine months, but the sentence was commuted on the recommendation of a psychiatrist who claimed that Jones was "an extremely frightened young man." *Du Cane Rd. East Acton tube.*

I could be in Berkshire where the poppies grow so pretty—Traffic, "Berkshire Poppies"

A well-heeled county into which London, to the east, is increasingly making its way, Berkshire contains a major tourist magnet in Windsor and has always been popular with upwardly mobile rock stars like John Lennon and Mick Jagger. Members of Traffic also came out here, but lived in less salubrious circumstances. Their song about times spent out here—"Berkshire Poppies"—was written in and about a village that has since been redrawn into the boundaries of Oxfordshire (*see Out from Oxford in the West*). More important, Berkshire's the site of the annual Reading Festival, for many years, now, one of Europe's top rock festivals.

Pangbourne

A boating village where the Pang meets the Thames, Pangbourne was in 1980 the scene of Led Zeppelin's greatest tragedy. A few years beforehand, when Ian Gillan first left Deep Purple, he amused himself by turning out for the local police soccer team.

JOHN BONHAM DEATH SITE

Led Zeppelin drummer John Bonham died of alcohol poisoning at this Jimmy Page–owned house on September 25, 1980. The 31-year-old Bonham, who had just come off heroin, had been drinking heavily all day. He then passed out and died in the morning. At the inquest, it was discovered that Bonham had knocked back 40 measures of vodka in 12 hours, excessive even by his standards, and then choked on his own vomit à la Hendrix. The more excitable sections of the media blamed Jimmy Page (who had bought the house from Michael Caine for a million pounds in 1979 in order to build a home studio) for dabbling in the occult. *Old Mill House, Old Mill La., 5 mi northwest of Reading.*

Reading

Berkshire's major town is best known for the end-of-August festival that has become Britain's most important annual outdoor rock event. World of Music Arts and Dance (WOMAD) also stages its biggest event of the year in Reading.

EATINGDRINKINGDANCINGSHOPPINGPLAYINGSLEEPING

Outside of festival times, touring indie bands play the downtown three-level **ALLEY CAT** (5/6 Gun St., tel. 01734/561116), which also holds popular techno club nights and puts on a range of other bands, from the acid jazz of Corduroy to the veteran Squeeze.

BLACK SABBATH COVER

The grainy cover of Black Sabbath's self-named 1969 debut album was shot outside the 15th-century water mill in the grounds of this redbrick mansion near Reading. *Mapledurham House, Mapledurham Village, 5 mi northwest of Reading, tel. 01734/723350.*

[READING FESTIVAL]

The annual Reading festival, the most important outdoor event in the British rock calendar, has taken place here more or less every year since 1971. It was then known as the

National Jazz, Blues and Rock Festival and moved here after spending 10 years in other locations.

At the first Reading bash, plainclothes cops, easily identifiable by their dogs, almost outnumbered the fans who had come to watch Wishbone Ash, Rory Gallagher, Genesis, Colosseum, and Lindisfarne. The next few years saw Genesis, the Faces' 1973 farewell, 10cc, Yes, Thin Lizzy, and AC/DC. The organizers barely noticed the advent of punk in 1977, although they did book Wayne County, who performed "If You Don't Wanna Fuck Me Baby Fuck Off" only for the crowd to bombard him with missiles.

The following year Reading acknowledged the new wave but with a safe bill of the Jam, Tom Robinson, and Patti Smith alongside the more typical Reading bands Gillan and Status Quo. In 1979 Peter Gabriel came here to make his solo debut, but by the start of the '80s metal had arrived in a big way with Def Leppard, Whitesnake, Ozzy Osbourne, Gillan, Twisted Sister, Michael Schenker, and Iron Maiden performing. Lightning struck during Black Sabbath's set in 1983, but Armageddon was held at bay.

During the mid-'80s the festival temporarily lost its license after the Tories took over the town council. It returned in 1986. The nadir was in 1988 when the likes of Bonnie Tyler, Meat Loaf, Squeeze, and Uriah Heep performed. The event was probably best remembered for members of the crowd pissing in beer bottles and throwing them toward the stage. One of these piss-bombs hit Ms. Tyler in the face in mid-performance.

The following year the bookers (who also ran the Marquee in London) went into partnership with Vince Power, whose Mean Fiddler and Powerhaus venues were the hottest live-music joints in the capital. Out went the heavy rockers and the MOR and in came a contemporary bill headlined by New Order, the Pogues, and the Mission. The Butthole Surfers, the Sugarcubes, and Pop Will Eat Itself were also prominent. The Pixies and Iggy Pop headed affairs over the next two years, but 1992 belonged to Nirvana. Kurt Cobain virtually handpicked the main Sunday lineup, and there's famous footage of him, clad in a surgical gown, being pushed onstage in a wheelchair. This wet weekend was marked by "fans" throwing mudballs on stage...one hit the guitar of L7's Donita Sparks smack-on; she stopped playing, reached under her dress, pulled out a tampon, and threw it into the crowd with a yell of "eat my dead uterus you bastard."

By 1993 Power had gained control of the festival. Headlining that year was New Order, doing their first gig for years and possibly their last ever. In 1994 Courtney Love's wild antics (she apparently punched the Wedding Present's David Gedge for the crime of simply knowing Steve Albini) got the music press headlines. Neil Young backed by Pearl Jam turned in a worthy top-of-the-bill performance in 1995. The following year, the Stone Roses' Ian Brown's totally out-of-tune performance left half the fans in tears and the others laughing. Metallica headlined the '97 event.

Reading Festival

The three-day, four-stage Reading Festival takes place each year over the Bank Holiday weekend at the end of August. Weekend tickets cost around £60. *Richfield Ave. behind Rivermead Centre, information tel. 0181/963–0940.*

WOMAD

The World of Music Arts and Dance (WOMAD), instigated by Peter Gabriel among others, held its first festival in 1982 in Shepton Mallet, presenting a mix of well-known and obscure artists from every corner of the planet. Since then, WOMAD has staged close to 100 events in some 20 countries. One of the biggest dates in its calendar remains the annual three-day festival in mid-July that has been held in Reading since 1990. Recent years have seen performances by Thomas Mapfumo (Zimbabwe), Ali Farke Toure (Mali), Abdel Ali Slimani (Algeria), NG La Banda (Cuba), and Yungchen Lhamo (Tibet). There's also a worldbeat dance tent, with the likes of Loop Guru, System 7, Banco de Gaia, and Black Star Liner.

The festival attracts more than 20,000 fans each year to events in six arenas (WOMAD, Free Mailing List, Box, nr Corsham, Wilts SN13 8PN; http://realworld.on.net). *Richfield Ave. behind Rivermead Centre, tel. 01225/744494.*

Tiddas performing at WOMAD, Reading

Sunningdale

This desirable village is close to the Ascot horseracing course.

JOHN LENNON AND YOKO ONO RESIDENCE

Lennon wrote and recorded the "Imagine" single and album while living here—not that it was easy imagining no possessions with seven bedrooms, a swimming pool, and 50 acres of grounds. Lennon closed off the grounds to the public when he bought the place for £150,000 in May 1969. That August the Beatles held their last-ever photo session here; the result was used for the cover of the *Hey Jude* compilation.

In September 1971, the same month that *Imagine* was released, Lennon and Ono left for the United States. Ringo bought the place for £2 million in 1973 and sold it 15 years later to Sheikh Zayed bin Sultan al-Nahyan of Abu Dhabi. *London Rd., Tittenhurst Park Estate.*

One of the least spoiled counties in southern England, Buckinghamshire, northwest of London, is dominated by pretty villages and expensive villas. It also contains the concrete-and-glass monstrosity of Milton Keynes, Britain's most infamous New Town (a '60s government planning fad). Welwyn Garden City is where S*M*A*S*H, labeled as the new wave of the new wave, emerged around 1994, though they had been gigging around unsuccessfully for a decade beforehand.

Amersham

This village at the edge of the Chiltern Hills is best known as the far northwestern terminus of London's Metropolitan tube line. During the '80s, the high-tech **FARMYARD RECORDING STUDIO** was based outside the town on the way to Little Chalfont. On *The Wall,* Pink Floyd secreted a backward-masked message about the studio, which ran: "Congratulations, you have just discovered our secret message. Please send the answer to Old Pink, the Funny Farm, Chalfont." It was also in this unlikely rural setting in 1983 that Tina Turner began working on the recordings that led to her comeback, cutting "What's Love Got to Do with It?," "Show Some Respect," and "I Can't Stand the Rain" for the phenomenally successful *Private Dancer* album, her first hit album in 13 years.

Aylesbury

Marillion formed in this town, famous for its eponymous ducks, in 1978 as Silmarillion, taking their name from a Tolkien story. The band lived at 64 Weston Road until their first album, *Script for a Jester's Tear,* was released. They sang about the now-closed Seatons bar on Market Square on their debut single, "Market Square Heroes."

FRIAR'S

One of the Home Counties' best-known gigging spots during the '70s, Friar's was where Iggy Pop in 1977 played his first U.K. date after bombing at the King's Cross Scala in 1972. The keyboardist throughout the U.K. tour was David Bowie, who was annoyed that most of the fans were screaming for him, not Iggy. Friar's was then based at the now-demolished Borough Assembly Hall on Market Street, having moved from its '60s location in the British Legion on Walton Street. In the '80s it moved to the Reg Maxwell Hall in the Civic Centre. It is now an all-purpose arts center that only occasionally puts on rock gigs. *Civic Centre, Market Sq., tel. 01296/86009.*

High Wycombe

A quiet market town, High Wycombe has garnered a reputation on the live circuit with a couple of good small venues. Its most famous contributions to the music world have been '80s chart-topper Howard Jones and the loud garage sound of (Thee) Hypnotics, who formed here around 1988 and had albums released by Sub Pop and Beggars Banquet. The **WHITE HORSE** (95 W. Wycombe Rd., tel. 01494/527672) is a good small venue in town with a mix of indie and rock bands.

THE NAG'S HEAD

A live music pub since around 1970, the Nag's is well known for rock, R&B, and blues. During the '70s the promoter at the time, Ron Watts, had his own Cajunish ensemble called Brewer's Droop, which provided Mark Knopfler with his first paying role. Other big names who have passed through include Elvis Costello, the Jam, Long John Baldry, and the Tom Robinson Band. Howard Jones did his first solo gig here. Jackie, the landlady, had to throw Marillion's Fish out of the women's toilets, where he had been applying his stage makeup. The wall at the back of the stage is plastered with dedications from the hundreds of bands who have performed here. *63 London Rd., tel. 01494/521758.*

Maidenhead

The main town in southeast Bucks, Maidenhead is best known for its surrounding mansion houses, particularly the opulent Cliveden.

CLIVEDEN

This sumptuous mansion, which stood in for Buckingham Palace in the *Help!* movie, is now, handily for Beatles' fans, a hotel. It's also one of the most expensive in the country, with room rates likely to start at £250 a night, double that for a suite. Access to its 376-acre grounds costs £4.

Cliveden, which overlooks the Thames, was built by Charles Barry, who designed the House of Commons, and was the home of Lord Astor and Lady (Nancy) Astor, Britain's first female MP. The Astors substantially rebuilt the place in the 1860s. In the early 1960s the mansion was the setting for the society parties where war minister John Profumo met call girl Christine Keeler, the affair recounted in the movie *Scandal. Taplow, 3 mi north of Maidenhead, tel. 01628/665946.*

ESSEX

Good evening I'm from Essex in case you couldn't tell—Ian Dury, "Billericay Dickie"

London has exerted an enormous influence on this hard-to-love county in recent decades. Places near the London border like Barking, Dagenham, and Romford are now little more than London exurbs. Many of Essex's biggest towns, such as Harlow and Basildon, were created primarily to take the overflow from London housing projects and are now the spiritual home of the '90s comic stock-in-trades, "Essex man" and "Essex girl," stereotyped respectively for their Ford cars and white shoes. While the rest of the world tells jokes about blondes, Brits tell them about Essex types.

Keith Flint of the Prodigy, 1996

In rock & roll terms, these characters have occasionally been put into lyrics, especially by Ian Dury in late '70s songs like "Billericay Dickie." Around that time, Essex was a hotbed of musical activity, thanks to the R&B revival scene around Dr. Feelgood, which spawned Eddie and the Hot Rods and, indirectly, Talk Talk. In the '80s, as synth sounds came to the fore, Essex produced one of Britain's most successful bands, Depeche Mode, along with Vince Clarke's groups Yazoo and Erasure, and Mute labelmates Nitzer Ebb. The electronic tradition is present today in Romford's Underworld and Braintree's the Prodigy; in "Born Slippy" and "Firestarter," respectively, the two bands produced the most memorable singles of summer '96. The county also spawned Blur, whose roots lie mostly in the ancient city of Colchester.

Songs of Essex

Genesis, "The Battle of Epping Forest" (1973)
Kilburn & the High Roads, "Upminster Kid" (1975)
Ian Dury, "Billericay Dickie" (1977)
The Stranglers, "Dagenham Dave" (1977)
Ian Dury, "Lord Upminster" (1981)
Morrissey, "Dagenham Dave" (1995)
Blur, "Essex Dogs" 1997

The major venue in the county is the **ISLAND** (300–310 High Rd., Ilford, tel. 0181/514–4400); all the top-rank touring bands play its main room. Upstairs, the **REVOLUTION** caters to new and more offbeat acts.

Barking and Ilford

Barking, a run-down suburb on the London–Essex border, is the home of the sensitive socialist post-punk poet Billy Bragg, commonly called the "Bard of Barking" or the "Barking Bard" and born here on December 20, 1957. The local maternity hospital was also where David Evans of U2 was born in 1961, but his family returned to Dublin soon afterward.

BARKING TOWN HALL

Neil Young chose this offbeat venue to record two tracks with the London Symphony Orchestra, "A Man Needs a Maid" and "There's a World," for his 1972 *Harvest* album. Young, nursing a bad back, lay in a bed provided by Barking's town council during the recording session. *Broadway at Axe St.*

SJ Rumens

Basildon

In 1980 school friends Vince Clarke, Andrew Fletcher, and Martin Gore needed a singer for their twin guitar and synth band in this much-derided town. They recruited Dave Gahan from a nearby comprehensive school, stole the name Depeche Mode from a French magazine (the term means "fast fashion"), and traded in the guitars for two more synthesizers. In late 1981, just after their debut album, *Speak and Spell*, hit the U.K. Top 10, Vince Clarke, already fed up with touring, left the group. The Depeche sound got heavier while Clarke twiddled his keyboards in Yazoo, backing the bluesy vocals of Alison Moyet (another Basildonian,

Billy Bragg

though she had by this time moved to the more gigging-friendly town of Southend). After 18 months, the pair split and Clarke set up the Assembly and then Erasure.

Chelmsford

Thanks to its position at a historically important crossroads, Chelmsford is Essex's county town. Since 1994 it has hosted an annual pop festival—the Chelmsford Festival. Virgin sponsored the 1996 affair, the biggest yet, with 70,000 people attending over two days, and renamed it V96. The bill was heavy on Britpop, with Pulp, Elastica, and Supergrass among the main acts. The following year, at V97, Blur and the Prodigy headed the two days. The town's best-known export is the electronic Mute label band, Nitzer Ebb, who formed here in 1982.

CHELMSFORD PRISON

The Sex Pistols played to inmates on September 17, 1976, amid much jeering and booing. The gig was recorded for a bootleg. *200 Springfield Rd., tel. 01245/268651.*

Clacton-on-Sea

A popular seaside resort for decades, Clacton was the setting for the first Mods (lovers of sophisticated soul—James Brown and Smokey Robinson—who wore smart suits, rode scooters, and popped pills) versus Rockers (fans of earthy rock & roll—Eddie Cochran and Chuck Berry—who rode big motorbikes, wore denim and leather, and drank beer by the gallon) seafront battles, on a cold Easter weekend at the end of March 1964. The press had the most fun and portrayed the clashes as far worse than they were.

It's hard to say who had fun at the 1971 festival just outside of town in Weeley. Clacton Council had thought the idea of a progressive rock festival would be good for local trade. They had reckoned on 10,000 turning up, but closer to 140,000 came to see T Rex, Status Quo, Barclay James Harvest (complete with a full-size orchestra), and the Faces, among others. The BJH performance was one of those disrupted by fire trucks zooming through the site to put out fires when igloo-style huts that some festival-goers had made out of straw bales ignited.

Colchester

Britain's oldest recorded town, Colchester was the center of Roman pagan worship in Britain. It is also the home of Blur.

COLCHESTER ARTS CENTRE

When this former church was attacked by Roundheads in the Civil War, it was defended by a canon called Humpty Dumpty (hence the nursery rhyme). More than 300 years later, in 1988, Graham Coxon and Dave Rowntree met Damon Albarn for the first time at the latter's solo gig here and soon formed the band that became Blur. *Church St. at Head St., tel. 01206/577301.*

Liz Johnson-Artur/© 1996 EMI Records UK

Blur, 1996

ESSEX UNIVERSITY

The sleeve for Fairport Convention's *What We Did on Our Holidays* was shot at a 1968 Uni gig. Can made their British debut in less than ideal circumstances in the union cellar on May 8, 1972; the German experimentalists had been booked to follow a slapstick comedy act, and after their first number, the crowd just watched in shocked, absolute silence. *Wivenhoe Park, tel. 01206/863211.*

Dagenham

Little more than an overspill development from London's East End that has been built up around the Ford auto plant, Dagenham has given rise to two songs called "Dagenham Dave." The first, by the Stranglers, on their 1977 *No More Heroes* album, tells the story of a fanatical Stranglers follower from here who committed suicide by leaping off Tower Bridge. The other, sung by Morrissey 18 years later, uses a generic character to mock the legendary stupidity of the typical Dagenham "wide boy" in lines like, "I love Sharon, I love Karen, on the windscreen." The place is also home to the Poole sisters (Shelly and Karen), who hit the U.K. charts big time in 1996 under the name of Alisha's Attic.

Romford

Going back to Romford!/Mega! Mega! Mega!/Going back to Romford!—Underworld, "Born Slippy"

Ian Dury reminisces about "going out on the nick, South Street Romford shopping arcade" on "Razzle in My Pocket," the B side of his debut solo single, "Sex and Drugs and Rock and Roll," from 1977, just before he recruited the Blockheads. He slips a *Razzle* soft porn magazine into his pocket but gets caught and hauled in before the cops. In the '90s, Romford is better known as the hometown of Underworld, whose techno-rock "Born Slippy" was the sound of the summer for 1996.

EATINGDRINKINGDANCINGSHOPPINGPLAYINGSLEEPING

SOUNDS FAMILIAR (47 North St., tel. 01708/730737) has two floors of used vinyl and CDs and is especially good for 12-inch singles.

Southend-on-Sea

The unlikely birthplace of that most stately of prog-rock acts, Procol Harum (who emerged from the early '60s beat group the Paramounts), Southend, long a favorite Sunday afternoon destination for blue-collar east Londoners, also gave rise in the early '70s to a brief outburst of primeval R&B that galvanized Southeast England's gigging circuit and paved the way for punk. At the forefront of this scene was the local Dr. Feelgood, a rough-and-ready-looking outfit who hailed from nearby Canvey Island, a marshy tract of land reached by one tiny road over a creek.

Dr. Feelgood favored everyday blue-collar clothes over the loon pants/platform soles look of the time and was an instant live hit, thanks to the dynamic front man, Lee Brilleaux, and the manic-eyed guitarist, Wilko Johnson. Although they played mainly R&B covers—"Boom Boom," "Bony Moronie"—their own numbers, like "She Does It Right" and "Roxette," were superior. In 1976 they had a No. 1 U.K. album with the live *Stupidity.*

The Feelgoods' success prompted a host of other local acts to get going, and soon people were talking about the sound of the Thames Delta. Until 1976, Eddie and the Hot Rods, the Kursaal Flyers, Mickey Jupp, and Lew Lewis all peddled the image of the sensitive Cockney spiv to the full, and all made some spirited but only marginally successful records. The most recent band to break from here are the hardcore outfit Above All, who signed with the Roadrunner label in 1995.

THE ESPLANADE

The U.S. all-girl band the Lunachicks trashed the dressing room after a 1993 gig when they found that the staff were watching them change through a two-way mirror. Otherwise, the club does a good job of bringing up-and-coming indie/alternative bands to these reaches of Essex. *Western Espalanade, tel. 01702/460440.*

THE KURSAAL

This now-derelict building housed an amusement arcade, a funfair, and its own radio station in the '60s, when it was the most popular hang-out on the Essex coast. It also gave its name to mid-'70s pub rock act the Kursaal Flyers, a great live draw until punk put bands like them out of business. *Eastern Esplanade just west of Southend Pier.*

CLIFFS PAVILION

The mid-'90s saw Brit bands like Blur and the Stone Roses playing hitherto unfashionable seaside venues. One of the most talked-about gigs of this kind was Oasis's performance here on April 17, 1995, from which 17 tracks are featured on a long-form video. *Station Rd. at Hamlet Court Rd., tel. 01702/351135.*

In the mid-'60s it was nearly impossible to hear all but the most banal chart stuff on British radio. Numerous pirate stations (the most famous one being Radio Caroline, which hit the airwaves on March 3, 1964, with the Rolling Stones' "Not Fade Away") moored in ancient, virtually unseaworthy vessels off the Essex coast at prim and proper Frinton, began broadcasting to rock & roll–hungry audiences. The pirates adopted many gimmicks familiar to American audiences but then unheard in Britain, like jingles (as collected by the Who on the *Sell Out* LP), and knowledgeable DJs such as John Ravenscroft, who had briefly worked on stations in the United States. Ravenscroft came back to Britain, changed his name to John Peel, joined the crew at Radio London, and was instrumental in introducing U.S. folk rock (Byrds, Dylan) and early psychedelia (Velvet Underground, Captain Beefheart) to British listeners. The authorities, worried about kids being corrupted by radio advertising, outlawed the pirates in 1967. Caroline and all the other stations soon went off the air. Peel, meanwhile, was offered a job at BBC Radio 1 and has been there ever since.

© East Anglian Productions

The good ship Radio Caroline

Part of the ancient kingdom of Wessex, agricultural Hampshire has a mix of London dormitory suburbs and pretty villages, a smattering of nasty "squaddie" towns like Aldershot and Portsmouth, and some marginal rock & roll history.

Andover

This is the home of the veteran '60s proto-punk band the Troggs, led by the charismatic Reg Ball, who quickly changed his name to the more charismatic-sounding Reg Presley. The Troggs were responsible for the much-covered "Wild Thing," a live Jimi Hendrix favorite, and "Love Is All Around," a Top-10 hit for the band in 1967 but spectacularly outsold by Wet Wet Wet's version more than 25 years later. Presley earned an estimated £1 million from royalties from that cover and shocked many people when he said he was going to spend it on research into crop circles (unexplained, perfectly formed circles found cut into grain fields in western England).

Mega City Four

Farnborough

Known for its annual air show, Farnborough was for a time the base of the hard-touring indie noise band Mega City Four. After moving to the Big Life label, they rented a rehearsal space on Sebastapol Road, and the album of that name crept into the Top-30 album charts for a week in 1992.

Headley

[HEADLEY GRANGE]

Led Zeppelin recorded their third album, *Led Zeppelin III,* and their celebrated untitled fourth in this rural Victorian former workhouse. As John Paul Jones told *Mojo:* "It was an 'orrible place, dripping with damp," but the third album, recorded in 1970, gave them a whole new audience and much acclaim and sales. It took the group into a new folk direction, influenced by Fairport Convention, with covers of old songs like Fred Gerlach's "Gallows Pole."

Zeppelin returned to the Grange early in 1971 to record album number four, which contains their most-requested number, "Stairway to Heaven." Robert Plant was reading about old Anglo-Scottish battles at the time; hence the inclusion of tracks like "The Battle of Evermore." The album was cut using the Rolling Stones' mobile unit, which pianist Ian Stewart, who plays the barrel-house piano on "Rock and Roll," brought along. Headley Grange's huge hallway proved ideal for the thunderous drum sound on "When the Levee Breaks," much sampled by '80s hip-hop groups. Many tracks for *Physical Graffiti* were also recorded here in winter 1973–74. *Liphook Rd. at Hurland La., off A325.*

Portsmouth

The hometown of Manfred Mann and Joe Jackson was also the base of the weird experimental Portsmouth Sinfonia, whose ever-changing lineup in the '70s included Brian Eno and Gavin Bryars. They even managed to crack the Top 40 in 1981, when "Classical Muddley" on Island records reached No. 38. Five years earlier, Mike Oldfield's single, "Portsmouth," hit No. 3 on the U.K. charts.

Southampton

For many years Southampton was one of Britain's leading commercial ports for American ships. During World War II it was a major port of entry to Europe for GIs. Bill Haley landed here for the first tour of Britain by an American rock & roll star. The most famous band of recent times has been the punky folk-revivalist Men They Couldn't Hang, who sang about their city on the track "Dancing in the Pier."

THE GAUMONT (MAYFLOWER THEATRE)

The last-ever AC/DC gig with Bon Scott up front was at this venue on January 27, 1980. Less than a month later, Scott was found dead in a car on a south London hill. Since renamed the Mayflower Theatre, the venue still puts on the major touring bands between musicals, plays, and the like. *Commercial Rd., tel. 01703/711811.*

GARY NUMAN CRASH-LANDING SITE

In January 1982, after developing engine trouble, Gary Numan "parked" his Cessna 210 plane in a forced landing on this road just east of Southampton near the village of Botley. He narrowly missed a gasoline truck and a house. *A3051, Botley-to-Winchester Rd.*

SOUTHAMPTON DOCK

Standing in the dock at Southampton, trying to get to Holland or France—The Beatles, "The Ballad of John and Yoko"

More than 5,000 first-generation rock & rollers greeted Bill Haley as he stepped off the *Queen Elizabeth* when the liner docked here in February 1957. He continued on a train to London. When John Lennon and Yoko Ono tried to board a ship at the dock to go to France in March 1969, they were held back by passport problems and had to make alternate plans—private jet. The incident was later recalled on the Beatles' "The Ballad of John and Yoko."

The Pink Floyd track, "Southampton Dock," on *The Final Cut,* concerned the British-Argentine dispute over the Falkland Islands in the early '80s; British soldiers sailed from Southampton during the conflict.

HERTFORDSHIRE

A pleasant but characterless county north of London, Hertfordshire is occasionally besieged by a 100,000+ crowd whenever a gig is held on the grounds of Knebworth mansion.

Elstree

Over the last 50 years, what had been a tiny village in the countryside some 12 miles north of London has been eaten up by film and TV studios between here and the easterly neighbor of Borehamwood.

BBC/TOP OF THE POPS STUDIOS

After 1,438 editions, the BBC decided to spruce up its weekly pop program, Top of the Pops, and moved the filming of the show out to a purpose-built studio in its Elstree complex. The new format promised fewer videos and more "live" performances. Most bands still lip-synch, though if they choose this option they still have to record their song again prior to the show. Nirvana chose to do a deliberately out-of-tune "Smells Like Teen Spirit" live, during which Kurt Cobain kept mimicking a blowjob with his microphone. *BBC Elstree Centre, Clarendon Rd., Borehamwood, tel. 0181/953–6100.*

Knebworth

The quaint village of Knebworth is best known for its Tudor mansion, whose grounds have witnessed a number of major outdoor gigs over the years. The first starred the All-

Knebworth from the air

Alan J Millard

man Brothers in July 1974, and a year later Pink Floyd showcased the whole of *Dark Side of the Moon* for the last time. During the gig, a pair of Spitfires flew over the 75,000-strong crowd and a model plane performed a planned crash at the front of the stage. The Rolling Stones' June 1976 bash, at which they were supported by Todd Rundgren, Lynyrd Skynyrd, and 10cc, was billed as their last-ever concert. A good ruse, it drew 200,000 fans.

Led Zeppelin played here before around 200,000 fans on August 4, 1979, their first English gig since playing Earls Court four years earlier. Zep couldn't get the theremin to work on "Whole Lotta Love," as it was raining. During "Trampled Underfoot" John Bonham's 11-year-old son Jason guested on drums to allow the drummer the chance to stand aside and see Plant and the others in action. A week later Zeppelin played their last-ever U.K. concert here, after which Knebworth's owner, the Hon. David Lytton Cobbold, fined the band £150 for breaking the midnight curfew.

Holder of the attendance record for the biggest gig ever staged in the United Kingdom was Oasis, who played two largely uneventful gigs before 250,000 here in August 1996.

Watford

Hertfordshire's largest town, some 18 miles north of London, is best known as the first stop on the London–Manchester railway line. It was also home to a perennially awful soccer team that was purchased by Elton John in 1976 and transformed into one of the country's best. For years the bespectacled singing pianist was a fixture at matches and press conferences; he officially opened the new Rous Stand in 1986. He eventually began to lose interest and sold his majority share in 1990. The club slid back into obscurity, but in spring 1997 Elton once again took charge and promised to pump in some of his royalties in an attempt to get back into the big time. *Watford Football Club, Vicarage Rd.*

ISLE OF WIGHT

At the end of the '60s this sunny island was the setting for a number of major festivals. A wide cross-section of artists, including Bob Dylan, the Who, and Jimi Hendrix, performed. Previously, the nearest Wight had come to rock was during the late '50s, when John Paul Jones and his father played in a group in the summer season at the island's dance halls and camps. The future Led Zepper, then known as John Baldwin, played bass, and his dad, who unsuccessfully tried to cajole him into dropping the bass to take up sax, played piano. The twosome often appeared on the same bill as Ronnie Aldrich and the Squadronnaires; the trombonist was Pete Townshend's dad.

The most famous islanders in rock terms are Level 42, three of whom grew up here and played covers at holiday camp ballrooms before going to London in 1980 and recruiting a fourth member for their pop-funk band.

Jimi Hendrix at Isle of Wight Festival, 1969

THE ISLE OF WIGHT FESTIVALS

After a low-key opening festival before just 10,000 in 1968, with Jefferson Airplane and Arthur Brown, the Isle of Wight bash took off the following year at Wootton, when 150,000 saw Bob Dylan (backed by the Band) play his first proper gig since his Woodstock motorcycle crash. He apparently chose to do the event because it allowed a visit to the home turf of one of his poet heroes, Alfred Lord Tennyson. The fest was spoiled by atrocious hygiene, a shortage of food, and lack of enthusiasm from the supporting acts, Blodwyn Pig, the Pretty Things, Nice, and Joe Cocker, who was still on a high from his recent Woodstock festival triumph.

A year later, in August 1970, at Freshwater Farm, Afton Down, in the west of the island, Jimi Hendrix made his last British appearance, three weeks before dying in London. With nearly a quarter of a million people (double the island's population), this was the major Isle of Wight event and saw good sets from Family, Taste, and Procol Harum on the Friday; Free, ELP, and the Who on the Saturday; and Donovan, Leonard Cohen, and

141

Hendrix on the Sunday. Joan Baez topped the bill. When the Who came on, it was 3 in the morning; they used airport-style landing lights to wake up the crowd. Less inspired was Jim Morrison, who came out for the Doors set and announced, "Suck my cock." Backstage, Morrison got into an Irish whiskey drinking competition with Roger Daltrey and lost.

This third festival was notable for more than the music. Hundreds of protesters forced their way in, shouting, "Music is free!" During Joni Mitchell's set, a man leapt onstage and grabbed the mike, shouting, "This is just a hippie concentration camp," leaving Joni in tears. She was eventually booed off.

A movie of the event by Murray Lerner lay dormant for 25 years until BBC television showed it under the title *Message to Love* in 1995, the year when some promoters tried to revive the festival but found they couldn't compete with the annual Reading, Phoenix, and Glastonbury events.

QUARR MONASTERY

Scott Walker, then a 22-year-old heartthrob, was an unlikely novice at this Benedictine monastery in December 1966. Walker, desperate to disentangle himself from the music biz, had tried to commit suicide in his Marble Arch flat in London. When that didn't work, he enrolled here as a monk, with the aim of learning Gregorian chant. His bid for anonymity didn't work. The music papers blew his cover. While some fans began phoning the monastery incessantly, others besieged the place during Sunday mass. Walker reluctantly left and went back to recording. *Binstead, Ryde, tel. 01983/882420.*

Most of the rock & roll output from the so-called garden of England has been from the towns on the London border, where David Bowie was brought up. The Bromley contingent that followed the Sex Pistols around the country spawned Siouxsie Sioux and Billy Idol. The college town of Canterbury had its musical heyday in the late '60s–early '70s with the jazzy/progressive axis that grew up around Soft Machine.

Beckenham

Parts of Beckenham are barely distinguishable from the adjacent suburban mass of southeast London, while others are prime suburbia favored by sports stars. It's also where David Bowie lived during his first few years of fame at the turn of the '60s.

[BECKENHAM ARTS LAB]

David Bowie ran the rather grand-sounding Beckenham Arts Lab in a room above the Three Tuns pub in the summer of 1969. It started as a Sunday folk club, with Bowie and friends performing in a dope-filled den. Before long it was putting on arty films, poetry readings, and exhibitions with weird projections on the walls. Bowie was the resident performer, backed by an early version of the Spiders. The most amazing moment was when Bowie made an impassioned speech against taking speed (dope was considered to be OK). The club closed in 1970; the pub is now a yuppie affair. *Three Tuns pub, 157 High St., tel. 0181/658–9618.*

BECKENHAM RECREATION GROUND

To raise the profile of his Arts Lab project, David Bowie organized the Beckenham Free Festival in this park in summer 1969. His wife-to-be, Angie Barnett, flipped burgers for the crowd of 5,000 that turned up. The *David Bowie* LP track, "Memory of a Free Festival," recalls the day. *Croydon Rd. at Belmont Rd.*

DAVID BOWIE ADDRESS, 1970–73

After a brief stay in an *IT* journalist's spare room in nearby Foxgrove Road, David and Angie Bowie moved into Flat 7 of Haddon Hall at the beginning of the '70s, when Bowie was considered little more than a one-hit wonder—Bowie's producer, Tony Visconti, moved into the second bedroom to help with the rent—and stayed right up to the time when Bowie was the biggest star in the land. Previously, Flat 7 had been the home of some 20 cats, who left behind a mega stench. Bowie had the joint filled with art nouveau furniture and glass from junk shops.

Members of Bowie's band, the Spiders from Mars, soon moved into another apartment in the building and rehearsed in the basement. While living here, Bowie wrote most of the songs for the *The Man Who Sold the World, Hunky Dory,* and *Ziggy Stardust* albums and devised the Ziggy persona. The shot of him reclining on a chaise longue in a dress used on the front cover of the original release of *The Man Who Sold the World* was taken here. Haddon Hall was a huge 10th-century folly, with weathervanes and turrets, built for the Crystal Palace exhibition, but since demolished and replaced by an apartment block. *Haddon Hall, 42 Southend Rd., near Beckenham Golf Course.*

Bromley

About 10 miles southeast of the metropolis, now mainly a dormitory town for central London clerical workers, Bromley was famous in punk days for its wildly dressed, outrageous Pistols hangers-on, the "Bromley contingent." They included Susan Ballion (a.k.a. Siouxsie Sioux), Simon Barker (Berlin), Steve Bailey (a.k.a. Steve Severin, later Banshees bassist), Sue Catwoman (so named because she looked like Catwoman), and Bill Broad (a.k.a. Billy Idol, so named because he was bone idle). The Bromley contingent began following the Pistols around after a December '75 gig at the nearby Ravensbourne Art College.

DAVID BOWIE ADDRESS, 1955–69

Courtesy of Sanctuary

Bowie lived here after moving from Brixton with his family to this petit-bourgeois environment in 1955. A year after moving in, Bowie formed his first (skiffle) group. He continued to stay at Plaistow Grove on and off during the '60s, even after he had charted with "Space Oddity." Bowie moved out when his father died in 1969. You can see the Bowie bedroom from the Crown pub. *4 Plaistow Grove.*

BROMLEY CONTINGENT HOUSE PARTY

Two doors down from Bowie's teenage home, the ultrapunk Bromley contingent held a still-much-talked-about fancy dress

Siouxie Sioux

party, "Berlin's Baby Bondage Party," in May 1976, in the home of Simon "Berlin" Barker—while his parents were away for the weekend. Everybody had to come as a fetish. Johnny Rotten dressed in rubber, Steve Jones as Macho Man, and Paul Cook as a dog. Siouxsie Sioux wore just a plastic apron and tights, brandishing a leather whip. *8 Plaistow Grove.*

BROMLEY TECHNICAL HIGH SCHOOL/RAVENSWOOD SCHOOL FOR BOYS

David Jones (Bowie) and Peter Frampton both attended this secondary school in the early '60s. Frampton's father was an art teacher here. Bowie formed his first serious group, the Kon-Rads, at the school. At break times he'd mess about on the guitar, singing Everlys stuff. One day, a fight over a girlfriend ended up with his needing surgery on his left eye. *Oakley Rd. at Croydon Rd., Keston Mark, Bromley.*

Canterbury

Three key jazzy prog-rock bands—Soft Machine, Caravan, and Hatfield and the North—emerged from this ancient city, famed for its cathedral, in the late '60s–early '70s. They all had roots in a Canterbury band, the Wilde Flowers, that featured well-known Soft Machiners Robert Wyatt, Hugh Hopper, and Kevin Ayers, as well as Richard Sinclair, later of Caravan (who named their compilation album Canterbury Tales). Soft Machine, who took their name from a novel by William Burroughs, also spawned Gong, plus Kevin

Ayers and the Whole World, the backing band in which Mike Oldfield got his start on bass guitar. Ian Dury formed Kilburn and the High Roads at Canterbury Art School, where he lectured in 1973.

Chislehurst

CHISLEHURST CAVES

One of British rock's stranger venues is this series of man-made caves—a 20-mile-long system of tunnels left over from a disused chalk and flint mine. In the '60s and '70s, crowds would pile into the primitive surroundings (there is some concrete flooring and a couple of toilets) to see Pink Floyd, Hendrix, and others. Led Zeppelin's record label, Swan Song, held a riotous party at these caves on Halloween 1974 to mark its first British release, the Pretty Things' *Silk Torpedo*. In typical Zep fashion, this was a black Halloween with strippers dressed in nuns' habits posing on altars. In 1978, when Pere Ubu toured the United Kingdom with the Human League and the Soft Boys, they organized what they called the "Magical Mystery Ubu Tour," for which fans bought tickets on a bus trip to an unknown destination and found themselves watching the band play on an improvised stage in a hole in the chalk walls of the caves.

Chislehurst Caves

These days, fire authorities have limited the capacity to 100, meaning that the only events are jazz club nights and private parties. For £3 it's possible to take a tour of the caves (check for times), and you might just be able to spot some old graffiti relating to T Rex and the Troggs. *Caveside Close, off Old Hill, Chislehurst BR7, tel. 0181/467-3264.*

Dartford

Mick Jagger met Keith Richards properly for the first time on the Dartford-to-London train in 1960. Jagger, who was traveling to the London School of Economics, was carrying a stack of blues records under his arm—which attracted Richards's attention. Although they had attended the same Dartford primary school, Wentworth, they were in different classes and had had next to no contact. The town now has a Jagger Close, built in 1988 in a housing development for old people.

Dover

Many rivers to cross...as I travel along the white cliffs of Dover—Jimmy Cliff, "Many Rivers to Cross"

Cliff was living in England and recording for Island Records' burgeoning West Indian market in the mid-'60s when he wrote the mournful "Many Rivers to Cross," little heard until the release of the soundtrack for *The Harder They Come* in the early '70s. Cliff's song was later butchered by UB40 for their 1983 Top-20 hit single.

The white cliffs—towering chalk formations that rise out of the sea on the southeastern edge of Britain—have long been popular with songwriters and poets: Acker Bilk and the Righteous Brothers both had Top-30 hits with "The White Cliffs of Dover" in the '60s.

When rock stars want to prove they've joined the establishment, they move to upmarket Surrey, a stockbroker-belt county just south of London. First in were John Lennon and Ringo Starr, who bought expensive mock-Tudor boxes in a private estate in Weybridge. Today, Mick Jagger and Pete Townshend have big-money mansions in the suburb of Richmond. Spiritually, Surrey is about as far away as you can get from the blues cradle of the Mississippi Delta, but it's where Eric Clapton—oft cited as Britain's best blues guitarist—was born and where he spends much of his time when in Britain.

Croydon

Few suburbs south of London have grown quite so spectacularly over the last 30 years as Croydon. It now looks a bit like a typical American downtown, with a divided highway running between office blocks and malls sprouting on its outskirts. Clash bassist Paul Simonon was born in the Thornton Heath neighborhood on December 15, 1955. Others to come from here include smarm-school DJ Tony Blackburn; folk-rocker Kirsty McColl; St. Etienne's Bob Stanley; Pete Wiggs; the trippy, hardcore Loop, who

Suburban singer Kirsty McColl

formed here in 1986 and then split into Main and the Hair and Skin Trading Company some five years later; and the all-female U.K. chart-toppers, Eternal; plus rock partycrasher/supermodel Kate Moss.

EATINGDRINKINGDANCINGSHOPPINGPLAYINGSLEEPING

In the '60s and '70s Croydon had a healthy gigging scene, with the likes of Jimi Hendrix playing before a crowd of 100 at the long-gone **STAR** (296 London Rd.), and everyone on the touring circuit dropping in at the Greyhound (now the **BLUE ORCHID** disco), where ELO made their debut in 1972 and Bowie, Mott the Hoople, and other major bands also performed. The **GUN TAVERN** (83 Church St., tel. 0181/686–4684) is a smallish central pub that puts on local rock bands.

The record stores here make a visit worthwhile. Besides **BEANO'S** (*see below*), there's **101 RECORDS** (11 Keeley Rd., tel. 0181/681–8282), which has both new and used stock at reasonable prices. There are also big branches of **VIRGIN** and **HMV** on the pedestrian mall.

BEANO'S

Reckoning itself to be Europe's largest used-record store, Beano's has been going since 1975. The smart, bright premises is spread over three floors of an old warehouse. The stock—lots of vinyl and CDs—is immaculately organized and usually pretty clean.

Prices are generally good; they research the prices well, so you won't be ripped off, but you won't find incredible bargains, either. Beano's is particularly strong on '50s, '60s, and '70s rock & roll and pop, but all genres are covered well, and what's on display is only a fraction of their stock. The stage is also available for local bands to play every Saturday; Rocket from the Crypt did a mad show here in late '96. On the top floor is a diner-style café, lots of memorabilia, a tiny six-seat movie theater, a free pinball machine, and other entertainment. Owner David Lashmar says the philosophy behind Beano's is to "put on a good show for people who visit us. It's something that sets us apart from the chains." *Middle St., tel. 0181/680–*

David Lashmer at Beano's, 1997

1202; beanos@easynet.co.uk; http://easyweb.easynet.co.uk/~beanos/home.htm. East Croydon BR.

FAIRFIELD HALLS

A major touring venue for big-name bands over the years, Fairfield Halls also includes a theater and an art gallery. In October 1963 it hosted a U.S. blues package show with Muddy Waters, Big Joe Williams, and Sonny Boy Williamson II. The show had a major impact on the London-area R&B scene, out of which the Yardbirds, Rolling Stones, and the Who emerged. The Nice recorded the first side of their *Five Bridges* album in October 1969. A few years later, the toilets were being cleaned by one Ray Burns, who later became Captain Sensible when he joined the Damned on bass. *Park La. at Barclay Rd., tel. 0181/688 9291. East Croydon BR.*

Godalming

This small town is home to one of Britain's most expensive schools, **CHARTERHOUSE** (Hurtmore Rd. at Charterhouse Rd., tel. 01483/291500). Peter Gabriel, Tony Banks, Mike Rutherford, and Anthony Phillips, students at this prestigious public (private, in U.S. usage) school, formed Genesis in 1966. They sent a demo to school old boy Jonathan King, who signed them to Decca. Their first album, *From Genesis to Revelation*, released in 1969, barely sold 1,000 copies. They found success only after signing for the more sympathetic Charisma Records, where they became one of the holy trinity of '70s British prog-rock bands (with Yes and ELP). Despite Phil Collins's taking over the vocals after Peter Gabriel left in 1975, they continue to be one of the world's biggest-selling (if least hip) groups. During World War II, Charterhouse was used as a safe rural retreat for working-class boys from the bombed parts of inner London; one evacuee was the future Led Zeppelin manager and definitely not public school material, Peter Grant.

Guildford

There were six men in Birmingham/In Guildford there's four/That were picked up and tortured/And framed by the law—The Pogues, "Streets of Sorrow/Birmingham Six"

Surrey's county town is now best known for the 1974 IRA bomb that killed seven and led to four innocents'—"The Guildford Four"—being jailed for 15 years. Their tale was told in the movie *In the Name of the Father*. The Stranglers formed here in fall '74 as the Guildford Stranglers.

The town's annual **GUILDFORD FESTIVAL** (tel. 01483/454159) scored a big hit in summer 1996 with the first publicized appearance of Peter Green in decades. After years of mental illness, the former Fleetwood Mac guitarist was coaxed into fronting a new band called the Splinter Group (with Cozy Powell on drums), and festival organizers reckoned that (apart from a warm-up show in Buxton a few weeks prior) this was the first opportunity that most fans had had to hear him since the start of the '70s. He cut a rather sad figure but still showed some of the old skills; the gig was a good start for the outfit.

SURREY UNIVERSITY

Led Zeppelin's first gig under that name took place at the Surrey University students' union on October 15, 1968. The group had been playing as the New Yardbirds, a name that Keith Moon claimed would go down like a lead balloon. He was right. Promoters found the Yardbirds tag passé, and after a brief confab, Plant, Page, and co. tinkered with Moon's comments and came up with Led Zeppelin. For their next date, at London's Marquee, they dropped it and played as Jimmy Page with the New Yardbirds before becoming Led Zeppelin permanently. *East of Guildford Bypass, tel. 01483/300800.*

Hersham

Sham 69 took their name from a graffito on a wall in this nothing town that originally read "Hersham 69" but had been worn away to read "Sham 69." The "69" referred to the key year in the skinhead chronology.

Kew

A verdant splash on the south bank of the River Thames, swanky Kew is best known for its huge botanical gardens, where, as the story goes, Jimi Hendrix was refused admission in 1967 on the grounds that "we don't let anyone in wearing fancy dress."

CHANDLER GUITARS

High-profile customers of this internationally known store include members of Genesis and Pink Floyd, Eric Clapton, Gary Moore, and Kirk Hammett of Metallica. In addition to stocking top-of-the-line gear, they don't overlook equipment for amateur musicians. It is one of the few stores in the country that has a demo room where prospective buyers can thrash away. Chandler's also has a reputation for repairs—Prince comes here when he's in the United Kingdom, and when Jimmy Page needed repairs done on the acoustic guitar on which he first strummed out "Stairway to Heaven," he came here. *300 Sandycombe Rd., TW9, tel. 0181/940–5874. Kew Gardens tube.*

PHIL LYNOTT HOUSE CA. 1978–85

Around 1978, Thin Lizzy's Phil Lynott bought the Walled Cottage, a tasteful property on half an acre behind electrically controlled gates. Initially he moved in with his girlfriend, Caroline Crowther, whom he later married in Richmond. The couple had two children and spent much of their time at another property in Ireland. After Caroline left him in 1982, the singer spent more time here, apparently most of it in bed either with new girlfriends or recovering from drug binges. For Christmas 1985, he invited his mother to stay, along with some friends, including Lizzy guitarist Brian Robertson and Jimmy Bain of Rainbow. Lynott partied so much on drink, bad food, and hard drugs that he ended up being taken in a semi-comatose state to a drug clinic and then on to a hospital in Salisbury, where he died just over a week later (*see* Salisbury *in* the West). *184 Kew Rd., Kew Gardens tube.*

Kingston

Like Croydon, it is a south London suburb that has huge shopping centers (populated with branches of the HMV, Tower, Virgin, and Our Price chains) and traffic-clogged roads. Eric Clapton spent much of his youth gigging and going to college around here and in wealthy Kingston suburbs like Surbiton.

BELL'S MUSIC SHOP

Eric Clapton bought his first guitar, a Kay electric, here in 1958 when he was 13. Some of the Rolling Stones shopped here in the early days. Today it stocks guitars and other instruments, amps, and sheet music. *157 Ewell Rd., Surbiton, tel. 0181/399–1166.*

CINDERELLA'S (THE RITZY)

Pop revelers Dodgy started to make a name for themselves with their "Dodgy" club night, which they opened here in 1991. After two years they went on to other venues such as the Garage in north London. The club was designed as a hangout for fans of pure but eclectic pop. The trio would DJ a mix of soul and indie sounds and invite along guest acts that ranged from folkie Ralph McTell through the London Community Gospel Choir to bands like Oasis and Shed Seven. A steady following built up, Dodgy won a demo clash on Greater London Radio for several weeks in a row, and soon A&R sniffers were hanging 'round this wine bar. A&M won out. Around the time when Dodgy's debut album—*The Dodgy Album*—was released in 1993, they had to give up the weekly slot. The venue changed into The Ritzy, which leans toward handbag house music. *4 Bishop's Hall, tel. 0181/541–1515.*

Richmond

This highly affluent Thames-side suburb just outside southwest London looks like it's the perfect chocolate-box "heritage" town. Nevertheless, behind the teeming high street with its fancy tea shops and upmarket gift stores, Richmond is certainly a striking place full of spectacular hill views and great riverside stretches. In the late '50s and early '60s, Richmond had a bit of a bohemian feel thanks to the local R&B fans, who would hang around the town center cafés by day and go to see bands play local pubs at night.

HOMES OF THE RICH AND FAMOUS

Two old-timers of Britrock own property on exclusive Richmond Hill. Mick Jagger bought the Georgian Downe House, worth £3 million and with the best view in town, in 1991 to go along with properties in Hollywood and the Loire Valley and his estate on the Caribbean island of Mustique. In 1996 Pete Townshend paid £2.5 million for the Wick mansion, with its conservatory, billiard room, and swimming pool, on Richmond Hill at Queen's Road. Previous owners include the actor John Mills (grandfather of Kula Shaker's Crispin Mills), who sold it to Ronnie Wood in 1972. During Wood's tenure, Keith Richards lodged for a time in a small cottage in the grounds. Richards later told rock critic Nick Kent how he had kept a huge opium stash in kilo sacks in the outhouse, but when he returned to retrieve his stash a few years later, he found that the barn had been demolished and the opium was gone. Richards blamed birds for pecking it away.

CRAWDADDY CLUB/STATION HOTEL, FALL 1962–JUNE 1963 (BULL & BUSH)

Though short-lived, this nomadic club helped break the Yardbirds and the Rolling Stones in the early '60s. Named after the Bo Diddley song "Do the Crawdaddy," the club, run by Soviet émigré Giorgio Gomelsky, first met on Sundays in the back room of Richmond's Station Hotel pub (now the Bull & Bush). The first resident band was the Dave Hunt

Phil Lynott and Caroline Crowther's wedding, 1980

group, featuring Ray Davies, but when they couldn't make it one snowy January 1963 night, Gomelsky invited the just-formed Rolling Stones (then known as the Rollin' Stones) to take their place. The audience was so sparse Gomelsky had to go into the pub to round up more people. The set went down well, and after a few more appearances, the Stones were given a residency. During this time they met their first manager, Andrew Loog Oldham. A few days later, the Beatles popped by to see what all the fuss was about and met the Stones for the first time, as a plaque on the wall outside the pub explains. In June 1963 Gomelsky was told to quit, as the pub had no music license. He found a new location for the Crawdaddy at the clubhouse of the Richmond Athletic Ground (*see below*). *1 Kew Rd., tel 0181/940–6882. Richmond tube/BR.*

RICHMOND ATHLETIC GROUND

In 1960 the first National Jazz Festival (the forerunner of today's Reading Festival) was staged here. Everyone sat nicely in deck chairs and watched a fuddy-duddy jazz bill of Humphrey Lyttleton, Tubby Hayes, and Johnny Dankworth. Noisy R&B surfaced in 1962 with Cyril Davies's All Stars and Graham Bond, and the following year the Stones headlined. In 1965 the event became The Jazz and Blues Festival, and the Who and the Yardbirds topped the bill. After that, the festival went to the Plumpton and Kempton Park racecourses before settling in Reading in 1971.

The Crawdaddy Club (*see above*) moved to Richmond Athletic Club's clubhouse in June 1963. By that time, the Rolling Stones had quit their residency, but promoter Gomelsky came up trumps again, with an even more exciting act—the Yardbirds. Their more uncompromising R&B earned so much praise that Sonny Boy Williamson II dropped by to record a live album in December 1963. *Richmond Athletic Ground, southeast part of Old Deer Park, Twickenham Rd. entrance, close to Kew Foot Rd. Richmond tube/BR.*

ST. ELIZABETH OF PORTUGAL CHURCH

Thin Lizzy leader Phil Lynott married Caroline Crowther, daughter of the late TV personality Leslie Crowther, at this Catholic church on St. Valentine's Day, 1980. Just under six years later, on January 9, 1986, the church held a memorial service for the singer attended by members of Lizzy, Motörhead, the Boomtown Rats, and other bands, before his body was taken to his hometown of Dublin for burial. The church's crypt hosted a major folk club during the early '70s. *The Vineyard at Richmond Hill. Richmond tube/BR.*

Ripley

This village in the west of the county originated as a stagecoach stop. Surrey's greatest blues guitarist, Eric Clapton, was born at No. 1 The Green, the house of his grandparents, Rose and Jack Clapp, on March 30, 1945. As he was the result of a brief liaison his mother, Patricia, had had with a Canadian soldier before marrying a German and moving to Canada, her parents brought him up here in Ripley. He used the surname Clapton after being teased at school with jokes about "the clap."

Weybridge

Even in Surrey terms, Weybridge, just south of the Thames some 20 miles southwest of central London, is pretty exclusive, full of private estates where £2-million-plus mansions, secluded among trees, lie behind electronically locked gates. Besides two Beatles, Tom Jones and Engelbert Humperdinck lived in the area. Nowadays, the only resident with the slightest rock link is Cliff Richard.

JOHN LENNON RESIDENCE, 1964–68

John Lennon lived with his first wife, Cynthia, at the mock-Tudor Kenwood between 1964 and 1968. In 1965 the photos for the cover of *Rubber Soul* were shot in the grounds. Lennon moved out in 1968 after Cynthia, returning home from a stay at a friend's, found him and Yoko Ono (Yoko wearing Cynthia's robe) sitting at the kitchen table having breakfast. He and Yoko had sneakily recorded the *Two Virgins* album in Kenwood's studio while Cynthia was away. *Wood La. off Cavendish Rd.*

RINGO STARR RESIDENCE, 1965–68

In 1965 Ringo bought the Sunny Heights mansion (overlooking St. Georges Hill golf course), half a mile from Lennon's place, and lived here for three years. *St. Georges Rd.*

Long popular with Londoners, Sussex is a mix of London exurbs, smart little villages, and prime coastline. The major town and resort of Brighton is a great hangout. Thanks to the fights between their '60s predecessors and the rockers, as celebrated in the movie *Quadrophenia,* the county is a bit of a mod magnet. The Jam's "Saturday's Kids" mentions two beauty spots, the Selsey Bill promontory and Bracklesham Bay, both near Brighton.

Brighton

Brighton is Britain's best major beach resort. It's a mix of great views, ostentatious architecture, and grand hotels along with an alternative air, some scuzzy spots, and a very visible youth culture and gay presence. In the 1950s, teenage gangs from London (just over an hour away by train) started hanging here in the many coffee bars. By the early '60s, clubs were hosting soul and R&B all-nighters. The bloodiest and, thanks to the *Quadrophenia* movie, most-documented clash between mods and rockers spilled out onto the Grand Parade and beach in May 1964. These days, the beach is quieter. Brighton, surrounded by reactionary shire-towns, showed its quirky side by designating an area as Britain's first nude beach. On a similar theme, some brave entrepreneur in the early '90s tried to set up a spliff café à la Amsterdam but got closed down a few hours after opening its doors.

There's always been a healthy local music scene in Brighton, but few big names have emerged from here until recently. The outfit most associated with the town is undoubtedly the Levellers, the unwashed crusties (ragged types) whose output draws equally from punk and English folk. Formed in 1988, they named themselves after a radical section of Oliver Cromwell's followers who supported freedom of worship during English Civil War times, though there's also an area of countryside next to Brighton called the Level. Extensive touring, appearances, free festivals, and a firm political viewpoint helped them build up a

Courtesy of Essential Music Festival

Essential Music Festival from on high, 1996

strong fan base who follow them around the continent in a way similar to what Phish-heads do in the States. In 1995 they set up a studio and headquarters in town (*see below*) and released the single, "Hope Street," which has nothing to do with an actual thoroughfare but is rather a tale of alienation in 1980s and '90s Tory society.

In the early '80s a couple of post-punk bands made a slight dent in the charts. The Piranhas used brass to the full on punked-up adaptations of southern African traditional songs in "Tom Hark" and "Zambesi." The Lambrettas could also cut a tune but spoiled it all by taking up an overtly mod stance that could never last; still, they provided a little humor by adapting the Two-Tone logo to read 2-Stroke on one of their sleeves until the ska label objected. Other names associated with Brighton include Keith Emerson (*see below*), promoter Harvey Goldsmith, who started putting on bands while studying at the local Polytechnic (now Brighton University), and veteran DJ Annie Nightingale, who worked on the local paper.

Essential Music Festival

This three-day outdoor event, held over the Bank Holiday weekend at the end of May, has really grown in prominence in the mid-'90s. Each day of the Essential Music Festival (info: tel. 0891/230190) has a distinct flavor: there's an indie/Brit-pop day, followed by a dance day (1997's event had the Chemical Brothers and the Orb), rounded off by a helping of reggae on the Monday that brings legends like Lee "Scratch" Perry, Grandmaster Flash, and Gregory Isaacs to town. It's held in Stanmer Park next to the University of Sussex in the town of Falmer. The EMF forms the major contemporary music input to Brighton's annual interna-tional arts festival, which runs for several weeks and also covers classical music, film, theater, and dance.

EATINGDRINKINGDANCINGSHOPPINGPLAYINGSLEEPING

For decades, Brighton has attracted thousands of fun-seekers every weekend, many even from London. The first stop or phone call has to be **Flying Fish** (39A Sydney St., tel. 01273/6800077), a friendly promotion company and ticket agency with heaps of flyers for all the events in town, staffed by people who'll tell you the best places to go.

The **Freebutt** (26 Albion St., tel. 01273/603974), a tiny pub whose gig room holds the grand total of 35, still manages to wangle some good gigs; the noisy County Down band Backwater played in fall '96. The **Albert** (Trafalgar St., tel. 01273/730100) holds twice the capacity of the Freebutt, has a proper stage, and provides a good atmosphere to watch local and new bands. The **Richmond** (31 Richmond Place, tel. 01273/702333) has mostly young, touring bands playing most nights of the week. The seafront **Concorde** (Madeira Dr., tel. 01273/606460) is a live venue and club that puts on a wide range of dance sounds, from Hawaiian to techno, with no decent stage; it gets its fair share of touring bands. A bit bigger, and probably the most famous venue in town, the **Zap Club** (188–193 Kings Rd. Arches, tel. 01273/821588) built its reputation on live music in the '80s, but now has bands only infrequently and then ends the gig early so they can shunt people out and reel in more money for a club night later on. The Univer-sity of Sussex Students' Union has a reasonable program of live bands on the student circuit. The Dome (*see below*), the Event, and the acoustically poor Brighton Centre, where the Jam rounded off their final tour in 1982, have top-name acts.

Brighton is most famous for its club scene and its gay scene. One of the best clubs in town is the **Escape** (10 Marine Parade, tel. 01273/606906), with the latest house, garage, and funk tunes and some big-name guest DJs from the United States. The **Jazz Place** and **The Retreat** (10 Ship St., tel. 01273/328439) are two venues that share the same address; the former plays cool jazz, funk, and worldbeat in the sweaty basement; the latter has a more hip-hop edge. There are many, many more club nights; Flying Fish (*see above*) can tell you what's hot. If there's no live music on in Brighton itself, then consider the short drive to Worthing, where **THE CRYPT** (tel. 01424/444675) has the best new touring indie bands.

The **SUB CAFE** (166 Kings Rd. Arches, tel. 01273/777388) stays open 24 hours, has DJs on weekends, and is popular late at night with stragglers from the surrounding clubs and venues. For an offbeat photo opportunity, go to the **QUEEN'S HEAD** (10 Steine St., tel. 01273/602939), a pub whose sign bears a portrait of Freddie Mercury.

As for record stores, **BORDERLINE** (41 Gardner St., tel. 01273/677698) has a good stock of new alternative discs.

Courtesy of Zap Club

The Zap Club in Brighton

BRIGHTON BEACH

During a Daltrey family holiday in 1956, the young Roger made his public performing debut on the beach, singing contemporary rock & roll songs and accompanying himself on guitar.

THE DOME

The sizable Dome Complex embraces three theaters: the Dome Theatre, the Corn Exchange, and the Pavilion Theatre. It was originally the stables and riding school of the adjacent Royal Pavilion. The pavilion started off life as the seaside villa of the playboy Prince Regent (later King George IV), but in the 1820s he had it revamped into a bizarre palace with Chinese, Indian, and Gothic ideas clashing throughout in an exuberant fusion of minarets, wrought-iron details, and domes.

As a live music venue, the immaculately restored complex probably hasn't come close to generating the excitement that went on amid the hay of the stables, but it was at the 2,000-seat Dome Theatre that Pink Floyd premiered *Dark Side of the Moon* on January 20, 1972. They had to abandon the performance during "Money," when the power failed. Two years later, the Eurovision Song Contest was held here and Abba romped away with the prize, singing "Waterloo." The Dome rarely has rock events, and there are even fewer gigs in the smaller Corn Exchange: June 1996 saw its first gig in 10 years—a fund-raiser for the Festival of Freedom that had the Levellers and numerous unknown local bands playing. *New Rd., tel. 01273/709709.*

GRAND HOTEL

Brighton's landmark hotel—now fully restored after an IRA bomb killed a Tory politician and nearly got Margaret Thatcher, too—was where the mods and rockers clashed in *Quadrophenia.* The movie starred Phil Daniels, who later provided the horrible grating, laddish vocals for Blur's "Parklife" smash. The Angelic Upstarts' 1986 song "Brighton

Bomb" didn't mourn the bombing and caused some ripples in the press. *King's Rd., tel. 01273/202694.*

FANFARE TO THE COMMON MAN

Before joining the Nice, Keith Emerson worked in Brighton as a bank clerk. In the heady days of Emerson, Lake and Palmer, the ensemble played a hometown gig in 1971 with a model of Tarkus, the half-tank, half-armadillo creature that gave its name to the 1971 No. 1 album, on stage. Tarkus was supposed to spew polystyrene at the audience, but they aimed it in the wrong direction and the stuff went all over the grand piano, rendering Emerson's performance useless.

Crawley

In 1976 in this suburban town in the flight path of London's Gatwick International Airport, the Cure started out as Malice. They later became the Easy Cure and adopted their lasting name in 1978. The group first rehearsed in St. Edward's Church Hall and did early gigs at St. Wilfrid's Comprehensive School and a long-gone club called the Rocket.

Hartfield

COTCHFORD FARM

On July 2, 1969, Brian Jones—"the talented one in the Rolling Stones," according to Psychic TV's bitter and brilliant "Godstar" single—was found dead at the bottom of the swimming pool of his country mansion. He had been fired from the band in May of that year, and the story goes that he took too many pills and too much booze and decided to go swimming, though several books and articles devoted to the death suggest that it might have been murder. Death by misadventure was the official explanation.

The Queen Anne house, which Jones bought for £35,000 less than a year before his death, was no ordinary place. One previous owner was A. A. Milne, who invented Winnie the Pooh here. In the grounds are statues of Pooh and Christopher Robin. This likeable little Ashdown Forest village (pop. ca. 600) is a well-touristed spot, thanks to the Pooh connection. The friendly people at the **POOH CORNER** store (High St., tel. 01892/ 770453) are well versed in dealing with queries about Brian Jones as well as the fat bear, and provide a walking trail map that gives precise directions to the house on the edge of the village. There's no memorial to Jones, but the swimming pool is still there. *Cotchford La., Hartfield.*

West Wittering

REDLANDS

In the mid-'60s Keith Richards bought this moated, half-timbered country mansion in the well-to-do village of West Wittering. On February 12, 1967, he threw an acid party attended by, among others, Jagger, George Harrison, Patti Boyd, art dealer Robert Fraser, the so-called Acid King, David Schneidermann, and Marianne Faithfull. In the early evening they were paid a call by around 20 police officers, who had a warrant to search the joint for drugs.

The cops failed to arrest anyone and could find no acid—it was all in Schneidermann's attaché case in the middle of the room, and when they went to inspect it, he said that it was full of unexposed film. Cops did take away some white powder, which they'd found searching Fraser, and four amphetamine pills that belonged to Marianne Faithfull but that Jagger chivalrously claimed were his.

The case about the white powder was held at nearby Chichester at the West Sussex Quarter Sessions court on June 27–29, 1967. A crowd of fans turned up for one of the first rock-star court hearings. The Stones were defended by Michael Havers (later the Attorney General in Thatcher's cabinet). Jagger was convicted of possessing four tablets of amphetamine sulphate (speed) and methylamphetamine hydrochloride, even though a doctor testified that he had prescribed them for the Stone. Jagger received a £200 fine and three months in jail. He was sent to Brixton prison. Richards was found guilty of allowing his house to be used for drug taking and was given a year in jail, fined £500, and sent to Wormwood Scrubs prison. The sentences caused an outcry. Even the *Times* newspaper took the Stones' side and wrote a famous editorial on July 1, 1967, called "Who Breaks a Butterfly on a Wheel." The Who rush-released a single—with proceeds going to the defense fund—of two Stones songs: "The Last Time" and "Under My Thumb." The public pressure paid off, and the two rock stars only spent a couple of days in jail. The band later released a thank-you song, "We Love You."

In between times, Richards managed to work out most of his ideas for *Beggars Banquet* here, but later sold the house. Today, it's very hard to see anything from the road, thanks to a wall and thick foliage. *Redlands La., West Wittering.*

BRISTOL & AROUND

Bristol

If England has a funky city, then it's Bristol. A historic port with a wealth of normal tourist attractions, it's also one of Britain's most ethnically mixed cities, one of its major college towns (with an inordinate number of graduates staying on because they like the place), a key clubbing center, and an important date on any band's touring itinerary. This is Slacker City U.K., where skateboards and mountain bikes are forever cool, where cafés serve proper Continental coffee, and where every musical genre—from punk to trip-hop—seems to have a visible presence. New Age is big business here, too—probably something to do with the town's close proximity to Glastonbury (which also accounts for the number of crusties—unwashed traveler types—walking around with dogs on strings). Although the gorgeous Clifton neighborhood might be one of the United Kingdom's best urban spaces, the town is not entirely cutesy: Areas like St. Paul's, where there were major riots in the '80s, have an edge.

Many local bands always seem to have kicked around Bristol, but it wasn't until the late '70s that any garnered much attention. The most important band of that era was the intense, agit-prop Pop Group, whose brief time together produced the epic album, *For How Much Longer Do We Tolerate Mass Murder?* They split into four factions: Pigbag, Rip Rig + Panic (which featured a 15-year-old Neneh Cherry on vocals), Maximum Joy, and Mark Stewart and the Maffia, whose distorted, stripped-down electro-funk sound is crucial to the Bristol trip-hop sound of today.

Beezer

Several others emerged from Bristol in the '80s, of which the long-running Blue Aeroplanes are perhaps the best known. The resolutely pro-vinyl Sarah label set out in 1987 to produce dreamy Anglican pop music that became a favorite whipping post for critics. The most successful outfit on the label were the Field Mice (from Surrey); other bands included Another Sunny Day, the Sea Urchins, and Heavenly. The city also had a hand in the coming together of the quirky pop dreamers the Sundays, who met at Bristol Poly before moving to London and scoring success with *Reading, Writing and Arithmetic* in 1990.

By the start of the '90s, the music and style press were touting Bristol as the next hot scene even before the Madchester craze had died a natural death. The accolades were grounded in the dance-friendly rhythms coming out of the city's sound systems, heavily influenced by the reggae heritage of Afro-Caribbean neighborhoods like St. Paul's. A key sound system was the Wild Bunch, whose number included Nellee Hooper (who would later produce Soul II Soul, Björk, U2, and Madonna) as well as 3-D, Daddy-G, and Mushroom. This trio went

Tricky, né Adrian Thawes

on to be the core of Massive Attack, whose fusion of soul and reggae with added punk punch created Bristol's breakthrough album, 1991's *Blue Lines.*

One of the key vocalists on that album was Tricky, born Adrian Thawes in 1964, in the tough Knowle West district. He emerged as one of Bristol's most surreal rappers with his 1995 debut album, *Maxinquaye* (his mother, who died when he was five, was named Maxine Kaye). A young programmer on the *Blue Lines* album, Geoff Barrow, who had also worked with Tricky, teamed up with barroom vocalist Beth Gibbons to form Portishead, named after a local seaside town.

Locals also point to the sounds coming out of the extremely innovative dubby artists of the Cup of Tea label. DJ Crush, DJ Die, and a posse of others push the frontiers of drum & bass further, faster, forward. Meanwhile, the guitar-based side of things is in good hands with the Planet label, whose roster includes the local bands Movietone and Crescent, plus the experimental Glaswegians, Ganger.

EATINGDRINKINGDANCINGSHOPPINGPLAYINGSLEEPING

Venue magazine offers great gig listings fortnightly. It's available from all decent newsagents in the region. **BIERKELLER** (All Saints St., The Pithay, tel. 0117/926–8514), the second rung for bands on their way up, holds around 800 people and still functions as a Bavarian oompah-oompah beer hall on Saturday nights. **COLSTON HALL** (Colston St., tel. 0117/922 3686 or 0117/922 3682), the major large venue—AC/DC did their first U.K. gig here with Brian Johnson as lead singer in November 1980—may soon be superseded by a new development down by the harbor. **FLEECE AND FIRKIN** (*see below*) has live music six nights a week. **LOUISIANA** (Bathurst Terrace, Wapping Rd., tel. 0117/026 5978), a great, homey little room over a pub close to the city center, holds fewer than 100 people but usually gets good indie bands—Placebo, Super Furry Animals, Longpigs—on their first visits to Bristol. **NEW TRINITY COMMUNITY CENTRE** (Trinity Rd., tel. 0117/907–7119), as well as offering martial arts classes and club nights, books an eclectic range of midsize live acts most weeks. **UNIVERSITY OF BRISTOL STUDENT UNION** (Queens Rd., tel. 0117/973–8374), at the Anson Rooms venue, gets in some top bands: Zion Train, Dodgy, and the Cardigans have been recent visitors.

The month of July sees the city's two major festivals. The *St. Paul's Festival,* held in and around the predominantly Afro-Caribbean neighborhood of the same name, is like a scaled-down version of London's Notting Hill fest. The *Bristol Community Festival* presents dozens of local bands, DJs, sound systems, and poets on six stages in the gorgeous grounds of Ashton Court Estate on the outskirts of the city.

Recognized as one of the best clubbing cities in the United Kingdom, Bristol has top spots that change all the time. For established joints, head for **LAKOTA** (6 Upper York St., tel. 0117/942–6193), on the edge of St. Paul's and downtown, a major club where Daddy-G of Massive Attack still DJ'd in 1996. The **BLUE MOUNTAIN** (2 Stoke's Croft, tel. 0117/942–0341) is pretty basic but has a wider range of nights (everything from gothic rock to acid jazz), including some by the local Cup of Tea record label. **THEKLA** (The Grove, tel. 0117/929–3301) presents popular trip-hop and fusion nights on a boat. A popular pre-club spot, the **MUD DOCK** (40 The Grove, tel. 0117/929–2151) is a licensed café and mountain bike store during the day that spins cool jazzy tunes in the evening.

With so many students, ex-students, DJs, and prospective DJs, Bristol is a great source for records, especially vinyl—both new and used. As well as some wonderfully unusual little stores run by local enthusiasts, the city also has branches of all the main chains—HMV, Our Price, and Virgin. **ECLECTIC** (190 Cheltenham Rd., tel. 0117/942–8116), as the name suggests, is a good all-round little store, particularly on U.K. folk rock. **GARAGELAND** (BS8 Centre, 34 Park St., tel. 0117/940–2700) stocks predominantly techno and house vinyl but

Nellee Hooper and Milo, alias the Wild Bunch, spinning at the St. Paul's Festival

has a good selection of '60s, punk, and indie, some of it on CD. **NUBIAN RECORDS** (148 Lower Ashley Rd., tel. 0117/941–1998) is a popular, well-stocked reggae store. **PLASTIC WAX** (222 Cheltenham Rd., tel. 0117/942–7368) has some reasonably priced collectibles and a massive amount of used vinyl. **PURPLE PENGUIN** (70 Colston Rd., tel. 0117/ 929–0860) is one of the hippest dance/new music stores in town and the place to score discs on the local Cup of Tea label. **REPLAY** (9A Haymarket Walk, Horsefair, tel. 0117/ 926–5316) has a good range of new and used sounds. **REVOLVER** (1 The Triangle, Clifton, tel. 0117/949–3963) is Bristol's best-loved record store; the emphasis is on vinyl; knowledgeable staff can advise on all genres (except top 40); the Planet label has an office at the back of the store. **RUBBER SOUL** (83 West St., St. Philip's, tel. 0117/941–1790) offers a solid stock of '50s and '60s vinyl. **TONY'S** (58 Park St., tel. 0117/987–9700), with blues, jazz, and local trip-hop, is in the back of a clothing joint.

COACH HOUSE STUDIO

Portishead's Geoff Barrow got his first job here soon after the studio opened in 1989, as a tape operator. He was also asked to write backing tracks for Neneh Cherry's *Homebrew* album and did some mixing on singles by Depeche Mode, Primal Scream, Gabrielle, and Federation (a local band on the Mo Wax label). In 1991, while he was assisting on Massive Attack's breakthrough *Blue Lines* album, the band allowed him spare studio time to get his own ideas on tape. A few years later, when the Portishead project had been assembled, the group came here to record "Sour Times" (the Mission Impossible-ish big hit single from *Dummy*). Others to have worked at Coach House recently include Smith and Mighty and Neneh Cherry. *7 Richmond Hill Ave., Clifton, tel. 0117/923–8444.*

THE DUG OUT (THE THAI HOUSE)

The place often regarded as the formative nightclub in Bristol's recent musical history was a dark, basic space that the Wild Bunch sound system filled to the rafters with people on Wednesday nights in the late '80s. Among the ever-changing personnel of the Wild Bunch crew were virtually all of Massive Attack plus Nellee Hooper, now one of the world's most in-demand producers. The club had an insanely small dance floor and a

PJ Harvey and John Parish at the Fleece and Firkin, Bristol

video lounge upstairs. In addition to the Wild Bunch, the Dug Out put on a range of other nights; the alternative space was popular with punks and crusties, too. The Thai House restaurant now occupies the site. *52 Park Row, Clifton, tel. 0117/925-3079.*

FLEECE AND FIRKIN

Since the tail end of the '80s, this venue (originally a wool mill and later a pub) has been getting the best of the new bands coming through Bristol. Supergrass, Sleeper, and the Lightning Seeds all played here in the Britpop era. Prestigious names from the U.S. alternative circuit on their first U.K. tours (such as Jon Spencer and Rocket from the Crypt) played here. Some like the place so much they come back well after they have turned famous: John Parish and Polly Harvey (from the nearby nowhere town of Yeovil) played four nights here in October 1996 as a low-key promotion for their *Dance Hall at Louse Point* album. Currently it has live music six nights a week, mixing in roots and blues (Terry Allen, Albert Lee, Peter Green) with the newer bands. On weekends it's usually tribute acts. *12 St. Thomas St., tel. 0117/927-7150.*

PORTISHEAD STUDIO/OFFICE

After renting this studio to do samples for *Dummy,* Portishead bought the building in 1995 with the advance for their second album. The band's sound engineer, Dave McDonald, who counts as a full-time member of Portishead, furnished it with scores of machines and bits of things that make noise. With its trippy blend of jazz, funk, and samples influenced by spy movie scores, plus Beth Gibbon's haunting vocals, their 1994 debut album, *Dummy,* scored massive acclaim. *Unit 4, Lawnwood Business Park, Easton.*

Out from Bristol

Aust

Richey Edwards, guitarist with the Manic Street Preachers, was last seen alive leaving a Bayswater hotel (*see* West London *in* Outer London) at 7 AM on February 1, 1995. Management, family, and friends reported him missing the next day. His silver Vauxhall Cavalier auto was found 15 days later, parked at the windswept Severn Bridge Service Station (near a spot where suicides had been reported before). As of spring 1997, he hadn't turned up dead or alive, and various reports of sightings have been unsubstanti-ated. The service station is on the English side of the older and more northerly of the two bridges that cross the Severn between England and Wales.

Bath

Tourists descend in their multitudes on this ancient city, the main attractions being the Roman baths (which give the place its name and are worth checking out, though they're always very crowded) and the sweeping, well-preserved Georgian terraces. There's not much of rock & roll interest here: Even the 1970 Bath Festival took place in Shepton Mallett, some 20 miles southwest of town. Bands to come out of Bath in the '80s include Tears for Fears and the grebo types Eat, who described their sound as "Louisiana swamp mindfuck blues."

EATING DRINKING DANCING SHOPPING PLAYING SLEEPING

MOLES (*see below*) tends to get the best touring bands. **THE BELL/HUB INTERCAFE** (103 Walcot St., tel. 01225/460426; http://hub.co.uk/) is a reasonably priced hangout with internet access and local bands several nights of the week. **THE HUB** (The Paragon, tel. 01225/446288) puts on a mix of live bands and DJ'd sounds.

NASHER'S (72 Walcot St., tel. 01225/332298, www.nashers. demon.co.uk/) is a well-organized used records store that often gets in some real rarities. **10–15 RECORDS EXCHANGE** (21 Broad St., tel. 01225/339789) sells some musical instruments as well as a good stock of records.

MOLES CLUB AND STUDIO

One of the best clubs in the west of England opened in 1978 in this five-story Georgian sandstone building. Since then, virtually everyone on the way up on the touring circuit has played in its rather cramped performance room; recent appearances have included Radiohead, Oasis, PJ Harvey, Alabama 3, and Stereolab. Many of these have been recorded live here, for on the upper floors is a well-equipped studio. James did their *One Man Clapping* live LP here. Others to have used the studio are Por-tishead, who mixed *Dummy* here; Spiritualized, who recorded much of their output in these studios; Paul Oakenfold; and "Bart Simp-

Nigel M. Adams

Oasis's Liam Gallagher at Moles

son," who recorded tracks for the Simpsons' album. There's a chill-out bar upstairs; tech-nically you need to be a member to get in, but it's rarely a problem, especially if you phone ahead. *14 George St., tel. 01225/404445; http://www.moles.co.uk/moles/.*

REAL WORLD STUDIOS

In the small Wiltshire village of Box, about 8 miles northeast of Bath, Peter Gabriel converted a mill right next to the rail line into the Real World Studios in the '80s. He recorded *Passion, Us,* and other albums here. Many of his worldbeat music buddies come to hang out here when they're in England. Even reformed punks like Joe Strummer and Iggy Pop have been known to drop in to jam with Indonesian gamelan players and Armenian nose-flautists. The village of Box is halfway between Chippenham and Bath and is most famous for the rail tunnel built by Isambard Kingdom Brunel in 1841. Two miles in length, it was for a long time Europe's longest railroad tunnel, and legend goes that around Brunel's birthday in April of each year, the sun, as it's rising, shines straight through the tunnel. *Box Mill, Mill La., Box, tel. 01225/743188.*

King Waslu Ayinde Marshal and his band at Real World Studios

Stephen Lovell-Davis

SOLSBURY HILL

A site of great Iron Age archaeological interest, a couple of miles northeast of Bath town center, Solsbury Hill was introduced to rock fans through Peter Gabriel's memorable 1977 single of the same name. It was an allegory of how he left Genesis. The hill made the news in the mid-'90s when the government announced plans to extend the A46 highway through the site. Gabriel, who lives and records nearby and used to jog around the area, backed the unsuccessful protests calling for alternate routes. It's worth coming up here for great views of the city.

Beckington

WOOL HALL

Van Morrison has a financial interest in the Wool Hall studio. He has worked on many of his recent albums here, starting with 1987's *Poetic Champions Compose* and including *Avalon Sunset,* and *Days Like This.* Other albums recorded at the Wool Hall include 808 State's *Don Polaris,* the Pretenders' *Last of the Independents,* and Christy Moore's *King Puck.* The first band in when it opened in 1987 was the Cars, and a few months later the Smiths came here to do *Strangeways Here We Come,* despite its Mancunian title. *Castle Corner, tel. 01373/830731.*

Cheltenham

Brian Jones (born Lewis Brian Hopkins-Jones in this horse-racing town) attended Dean Close Public School and then Cheltenham Grammar School, where he was twice suspended. He left it when he made a girl pregnant. His funeral was held at Hatherley Road Parish Church on July 10, 1969.

BRIAN JONES GRAVE

The former Rolling Stone is buried under a simple headstone that reads "In Affectionate Remembrance of BRIAN JONES. Born 28th February 1942. Died 3rd July 1969 at Hartfield, Sussex." The grave is in section V in line with the back of the chapel right on the corner near the roadside. The cemetery office (open weekdays 9–1 and 2–5) can supply a map. A few fans usually show up on the anniversary of his death each year. *Bouncers La. (toward Prestbury), tel. 01242/244245.*

Chippenham

EDDIE COCHRAN CAR WRECK SITE

Only 21 and already a legend thanks to a string of chart-busting, generation-defining singles such as "Summertime Blues" and "C'mon Everybody," Eddie Cochran was involved in a fatal car wreck on Easter Sunday 1960. Cochran was just finishing a British tour at the Bristol Hippodrome and, in a hurry to get to London, where he was to take a plane back to the United States, he dropped plans to go by train and instead decided to travel by taxi. On the A4, just outside the market town of Chippenham, the driver braked suddenly and the car skidded into a concrete lamppost. Cochran was thrown out and suffered severe head injuries. He died soon afterward in a Bath hospital. Gene Vincent was also injured in the crash but survived.

Cochran's Gretsch guitar was rescued by a police cadet named Dave Harmon, who would later become Dave Dee of the chart-topping multinamed Dave Dee, Dozy, Beaky, Mick and Tich. Harmon/Dee played the guitar to fellow cops in the station until it had to be returned to Cochran's mother. Before he died, the singer had recorded "Three Steps to Heaven," which became a posthumous U.K. No. 1 in May 1960. Sometimes fans leave flowers at the site on his birthday. *Bottom of Rowden Hill (A4), Chippenham.*

Portishead

Portishead take their name from this sleepy little coastal community overlooking the mouth of the Severn about 12 miles west of Bristol. Geoff Barrow, who programs the Portishead sound, moved here with his mother from nearby Weston-super-Mare in 1984 when he was 13. Barrow soon joined what he called a number of "dodgy rock bands," including one called the Ralph McTell Official Fan Club, and DJ'd at the Youth Centre on Harbour Road.

Courtesy of Island Records

Beth Gibbons and Geoff Barrow of Portishead

The town's other rock link is that it's the base of the Rolling Stones Supporters Association (44a High St., BS20 9EL), run by a husband-and-wife team.

Sherston

Marvin Gaye hung out in this tiny village about 25 miles northeast of Bristol from fall 1980 to spring 1981, when he used to visit local aristocrat Lady Edith Foxwell. She had parties at her country pile, called Home Farm, inviting such celebrities from the arts world as dancer Wayne Sleep and actor Gareth Hunt. Gaye was trying to extricate himself from his Motown contract, had fallen out with Berry Gordy, and faced a huge tax bill.

CARPENTER'S ARMS

Marvin popped down to this whitewashed 16th-century pub with open hearth and low ceiling, where he would sample the local scrumpy cider. *Tel. 01666/840665.*

Weston-super-Mare

The cover of Oasis's "Roll With It" single has a picture of band members watching televisions on the beach of this well-preserved Victorian seaside resort about 20 miles southwest of Bristol. Oasis came here because they were playing Glastonbury the following day and this was the nearest beach.

Glastonbury

Steeped in religious lore, both pagan and Christian, Glastonbury is said to be the site of the Isle of Avalon, the Celtic dream world where King Arthur was buried. Van Morrison is particularly keen on the Avalon theme, calling his 1990 album *Avalon Sunset* and singing about how "The sun was setting over Avalon, the last time we stood in the west" on the track "When Will I Ever Learn to Live in God?" Tradition also says that under Glastonbury Tor, a sacred site for ancient Celts, Joseph of Arimathea buried the Holy Grail, the chalice used at the Last Supper, and also planted a staff that turned into a thorn tree that only flowers at Christmas. Just for good measure, the two main ley—ancient track—lines running through the country intersect by Glastonbury Abbey.

It's not a surprise, then, that in recent decades Glastonbury has become the spiritual center of hippie/New Age Britain. Head shops line the main drag, along with cafés selling vegan sausages. The buskers here seem to prefer harps to guitars. The place is a mix of big city escapees, rural Tories, New Age yuppies, hippie idealists, and the rock band Reef, whose Kravitz-style riffs must upset the more laid-back locals. Since 1970 it's also been home to the Glastonbury Festival, held over the summer solstice and now Britain's best-attended music festival. The site is actually some 5 miles east in Pilton.

GLASTONBURY FESTIVAL OF THE PERFORMING ARTS

Though archaeologists suggest that midsummer festivals took place in the area as far back as 500 BC, and in the '20s George Bernard Shaw and others were involved in a left-field arts fest here, the first modern Glastonbury Festival of the Performing Arts was held in September 1970. Local organic milk farmer Michael Eavis had been so impressed by the Bath Festival earlier on that summer that he decided to put on a show himself. He managed to book T Rex (whose singer Marc Bolan arrived in a crimson velvet-covered Buick) and several other bands. Fifteen hundred people paid a £1 entrance fee (that included free milk) for the weekend event. Due to an organizational glitch, David Bowie came on at 5 AM; the sun rose just as he was singing the line, "the sun machine is coming down and we're going to have a party," from "Memory of a Free Festival."

The following year, Eavis moved the date of the festival to the summer solstice weekend in honor of the history of the region. With the financial backing of some rich hippies, he was able to put on a free show. More than 7,000 turned up to see a bill that included David Bowie, Fairport Convention, the Pink Fairies, Traffic, and the perennial free festival types, Hawkwind and the Edgar Broughton Band, all of whom appeared on a stage shaped like a pyramid. The event was filmed, and the following year the artists who played at the festival contributed tracks to a 3-disc LP, *Glastonbury Fayre,* which also carried the Grateful Dead, who were supposed to play the 1971 festival but couldn't get it together.

That was it until 1978, when Eavis resurrected the fest as a low-key gathering after meeting some crusties in town. The following year was the first real attempt to get in lots of people, with Peter Gabriel, Steve Hillage, and the Alex Harvey Band playing, plus crowds of new-agey stalls and tents. The modern Glastonbury Festival really took off in

1981 with a Mancunian-flavored bill that included New Order, John Cooper Clarke, and Roy Harper, plus Hawkwind and Taj Mahal. The event was billed as a fund-raiser for the Campaign for Nuclear Disarmament. Anti-bomb speeches were sandwiched between acts, and Eavis was particularly proud of being able to raise £20,000 for the campaign at an event in this very conservative shire. He also built a new pyramid stage that doubled as a cowshed during the winter months.

S. J. Rumens

Petty violence marred the 1982 event, prompting an irate CND spokesman to leap on stage and announce: "How can we expect the world not to make war when we can't behave ourselves at a CND festival?" He was sent packing with a hail of beer cans and a volley of oaths from non-pacifist sections of the crowd. Van Morrison and Jackson Browne topped the bill that year after U2 pulled out at the last minute.

The Glastonbury Festival grew throughout the '80s and went pop in 1985 when the Smiths head-

Getting the best view at the Glastonbury Festival

lined and the hippies were joined by thousands of indie kids. The huge crowds at that event sparked some local residents to campaign against any further festivals and persuaded the local council to refuse a license for the 1986 festival. The opponents were mostly new arrivals in the area who didn't want to see their real estate prices fall, but Eavis and other old timers organized an appeal and magistrates overturned the council decision. More and more people started turning up, and Eavis declared he needed fallow fields in 1991. By the time Primal Scream stormed the show in 1992, the organizers had already had to put a limit of 100,000 on attendance. The re-formed Velvet Underground topped a bill in 1993 that included many new indie bands, as well as Robert Plant, Van Morrison, and the temporarily trendy Rolf Harris. Along with the Manic Street Preachers, Oasis was the hot act in 1994, but the following year they were eclipsed by Pulp.

It's a different festival from Britain's other big summer events. Some turn up for the music, and many others (including crusties who spend their time traveling between free festivals in clapped-out vans) come just for the vibe. For the vibe people, there are different zones, such as a healing field, a women's space, lots of aromatherapy tents, and whatever else fits into the Glasters ideal. There's even a replica stone circle here these days to complement the massive pyramid stage, which burned down prior to the 1994 festival and cost half a million pounds to replace. There was no festival in 1996, as Eavis took time out to concentrate on his role as a parliamentary candidate for the Labour Party in the May 1997 general election. The 1997 fest sold out months in advance even though no acts were officially announced ahead of time. Neil Young, Smashing Pumpkins, and the Prodigy were the rumored headliners. *Worthy Farm, Pilton, 5 mi east of Glastonbury; http://www.glastonbury.org/.*

SECOND COMING

The Stone Roses played their first gig after 1990 on the green at Pilton's village fete on September 1, 1995. They did the show free as a favor for Glastonbury Festival promoter Michael Eavis to make up for having pulled out of headlining that year's bash a few months earlier.

Eavis puts on this low-key event every year as a kind of thank-you to locals for putting up with the big crowds during festival time. Proceeds go to the local parish council, and headliners are usually kept hush-hush until a day or two before. In 1996, even though there was no festival, Supergrass played for free and for their generosity were rewarded with a headline spot at Glasters the following year.

Salisbury

A medieval city and regional capital, Salisbury is one of England's most delightful places. Its cathedral has the tallest spire in the country.

SALISBURY INFIRMARY
(SALISBURY DISTRICT HOSPITAL)

After he fell ill in his Richmond home (*see* Surrey *in* the Home Counties and the South) on Christmas Day 1985, Phil Lynott was taken to a drug clinic. When his condition worsened a few hours later, he was transferred to this hospital. He died here from a mix of liver, heart, and kidney failure on January 4, 1986, at the age of 36. Rumor had it that while he was in huge pain and discomfort, a nurse came and asked him if there was anything he wanted, to which the reply was, "A wank." *Odstock Rd., tel. 01722/336262.*

STONEHENGE

And did they dance the little people of Stonehenge—Spinal Tap

This circle of stone blocks on the vast Salisbury Plain, one of Britain's most heavily visited sights, remains mysterious. Even today, experts are divided over how ancient people dragged the huge blocks to the site, although what's for sure is that they did not make as embarrassing a mistake over dimensions as did Spinal Tap's management who, in the scene from the Rob Reiner *This Is Spinal Tap* movie, provided 18-inch rather than 18-foot styrofoam models as a stage prop for a tour.

Stonehenge

Many people feel that Stonehenge has special significance for them, not least the New Age types and the police, who have had regular run-ins since the first Stonehenge People's Festival, attended by a few hundred hippies and with no notable bands, on the summer solstice 1974. The event was organized by one Wally Hope, who was arrested later that year for possession of three tabs of acid. Whereas bail would have been the usual procedure, he was sent to a mental hospital, diagnosed as schizophrenic, and given some hard drugs to keep him under control. On his release the following fall, he committed suicide; his supporters scattered his ashes in the middle of the stone circle at the 1976 solstice festival. In 1982 members of '90s festival stalwarts Ozric Tentacles agreed, over a campfire next to the stones, to form a band. The festival carried on until 1984 with acts such as Crass. Then, on June 1, 1985, hundreds of cops attacked a convoy of vehicles on the way to the festival, dragging some 800 travelers, including women and children, from the vehicles into a nearby field and beating them with truncheons before smashing up the vehicles. Some 570 travelers were arrested, and the cost of preventing the annual hippie bash was £5 million. The heavy altercation inspired the Levellers' 1991 "Battle of the Beanfeast" song. Police kept a strong presence on the site for the rest of the '80s, but these days, there's not so much confrontation. Most people go to the Glastonbury Festival, even though it's as commercial as any other European festival and a far cry from the hippie jamboree Wally Hope had planned.

Other than at solstice time, the site has proven a popular rendezvous for spaced-out rock stars over the years. Gram Parsons, who was wont to get stoned in the mystic Joshua Tree park back in Cali, came out here with various Stones when the Byrds were touring Britain in 1968. It was over a spliff and a bottle of whiskey that Keith Richards persuaded him not to go with the rest of the Byrds on their naively ill-conceived tour of South Africa, and so Parsons left that band after working on just one album. *A360 at A303, 12 mi northwest of Salisbury.*

Oxford

Until the 1990s, the spired university city of Oxford provided virtually nothing to the world of rock, but this decade has seen a miniboom of bands, headed by Radiohead and Supergrass.

The first band from the city to get some headlines was Ride. Formed at art school in 1988, this four-piece group was signed soon after that by Creation Records. At one time Ride, with their particular brand of shoegazing indie music shot through with some interesting ideas, looked to be heading for the top, but their third album (released in 1994) was slashed by the press. Ride was leapfrogged by Blur, Oasis, and the rest, and called it a day in 1996.

Radiohead also formed around 1988 at a private all-boys' school in nearby Abingdon, where they called themselves On a Friday (the day they were allowed to rehearse). They put the band on hold while several of them went for degrees and got together again in Oxford in 1991. After a few gigs, they were signed to Capitol/Parlophone, but it fell to American college radio stations to break them by playing the anthemic "Creep" continuously. When it was re-released in the United Kingdom in 1993, it hit the Top 10. With their second album, 1995's *The Bends,* Radiohead was established internationally as one of the most important British bands of the mid-'90s.

Thom Yorke of Radiohead

Pat Loughnane

When he was just 14, Gaz Coombes's band, the Jennifers, released a single on Nude records. After that band split, he and drummer Danny Goffey formed Supergrass in 1993 with Mickey Quinn. Their energetic set built up a following in local pubs. In 1994 the tiny Backbeat label released 250 copies of "Caught by the Fuzz," which told the tale of how Coombes was busted for dope at 15. After the song received much radio play and release on a compilation album, Capitol/Parlophone signed them up. Two successful albums have generated top chart success in the United Kingdom and much acclaim in the States.

New bands to watch for are the Candyskins, Dustball, the moddish Thurman, the Mystics, the trancy, psychedelic, truly excellent The Egg, all-girl punkers Beaker, and The Bigger the God, who cut their first video for £44 and then went mad on the second one by doubling the budget.

EATINGDRINKINGDANCINGSHOPPINGPLAYINGSLEEPING

Oxford would be great if it weren't perpetually crowded by tourists and students, both of whom seem to place a low priority on live music. After struggling away for years, the city's promoters and club owners got a boost when Radio 1 FM announced that their annual weeklong Sound City jamboree of gigs would be held in Oxford in 1997.

Although it holds only around 400 people, Radiohead, Supergrass, Reef, and Space have recently played **THE ZODIAC** (190 Cowley Rd., tel. 01865/726336), which, formerly known as the Oxford Venue, managed to put on such names as Björk, the Bluetones, and Bis in 1996; all the Oxford bands have played here at one time or another. In July 1996 Radiohead previewed new material at two low-key shows at the Zodiac for under-18s only, and Supergrass has also done "secret" shows here. Mac gets the best new bands into **THE POINT** (upstairs at Pub Oxford, 1 Issley St., tel. 01865/790291). It has a capacity of 220 and is a great place to see the Cardiacs, Super Furry Animals, the 60ft Dolls, and others before they go onto larger venues. One of the more unusual venues in the country is the **MANOR CLUB** (Manor Ground, London Rd., tel. 01865/63063), which is actually part of the Oxford United Football Club's Supporter's Club. In the room that on match days is used as the hospitality suite for sponsors, there's a steady flow of touring indie, punk, and soul bands. They occasionally capture fair-sized names such as 60ft Dolls and Catatonia. A couple of smaller venues out on Cowley Road are worth looking for: The **BULLINGDON ARMS** (162 Cowley Rd., tel. 01865/244516) has mostly roots and jazz funk, while the **ELM TREE** (95 Cowley Rd., tel. 01865/244706) specializes in local bands. *Nightshift* is a great listings and music mag that's available from record stores, venues, and some bars and cafés.

HMV (43–46 Cornmarket., tel. 01865/728190) has some in-store appearances, such as the 1996 launch of The Bigger the God's geeky-punk debut album, *Variety.*

Pat Loughrane

Martin Rossiter of Gene at the Jericho Tavern

JERICHO TAVERN (PHILANDERER & FIRKIN)

Thom Yorke and company played their first gig here as On a Friday just a few days after their first rehearsal in the late '80s. Ride and Supergrass (as Theodore Supergrass, no less) had their first gigs at a proper venue here, as did basically all the Oxford bands.

This was Oxford's leading small venue from mid-1987 to early 1992, when the owners failed to renew the promoter's lease, ironically at a time when the Oxford scene was just grabbing some media attention. During that time, though, they managed to book the Cranberries four times, as well as Primal Scream, Carter U.S.M, and others that would go on to be big names. The Jericho, in the heart of student bedsit land, is now a Firkin theme pub. *56 Walton St., tel. 01865/54502.*

OXFORD UNIVERSITY

Oxford University has produced few students with rock connections and no major bands (the Radiohead guys went to Cambridge, Exeter, and other unis, and Supergrass didn't get the grades). Kris Kristofferson won a Rhodes scholarship to go to Oxford to read English literature in 1958. He performed locally as Kris Carson but failed to make an impact, though he did make the college boxing team. In the mid-'60s Bill Clinton also won a Rhodes scholarship and shared a room with Paul Gambaccini, until recently a long-serving Radio 1 FM DJ. Another leading politician with Oxford University rock roots is Prime Minister Tony Blair, who was in a student band, Ugly Rumours, in the early '70s.

Boy George, Billy Joel, and Mick Jagger are the only pop icons to have addressed Oxford University Union's self-important Debating Society. Radiohead's "Prove Yourself" alludes to the snobby attitudes of Oxford students.

Out from Oxford

Van Morrison's "Rolling Hills" (from the 1979 *Into the Music* album) was inspired by the lush riverscapes and pretty wooded hills of Oxfordshire; the county is rated as one of the most scenic landlocked counties in the country.

Aston Tirrold

TRAFFIC'S COTTAGE

Traffic came to this farm to escape swinging London in 1967 and unwittingly started a trend that led to hundreds of other bands' "getting it together in the country." Band members Stevie Winwood, Dave Mason, Chris Wood, and Jim Capaldi lived in the farm's wisteria-covered keeper's cottage, which they rented for a fiver a week from William Pigott-Brown, co-owner of Island records. They existed on a diet of peaches and cream and peanut butter. Here Traffic wrote and demoed the "Paper Sun" single and their heady debut album, *Mr. Fantasy,* a mix of Latin rhythms, jazz, and R&B. One track, "Berkshire Poppies," contrasted city life with their rural idyll, while Dave Mason's "House for Everyone" was a surreal Carrollian fantasy dedicated to the cottage. Pictures of the group hanging out here were liberally spread over the sleeves of early albums. *Keeper's Cottage, Sheepcott Farm, Aston Tirrold, 14 mi south of Oxford.*

Barford St. Michael

WOODWORM STUDIOS

Fairport Convention has colonized this tiny north Oxfordshire village. The folk rock veterans have set up their record label in an old Baptist chapel a few doors down from bassist Dave Pegg's thatched cottage. The weather vane is in the shape of a Fender. They prefer people to write or fax, rather than just drop in unannounced. *Box 37, Banbury, Oxon OX16 8YN, fax 01869/337142.*

Cropredy Festival's headquarters

GEORGE

The back room of the pub is plastered with folk-rock memorabilia, particularly framed cuttings and record sleeves of Fairport Convention, Jethro Tull, Richard Thompson, and their ilk. In the early '90s the landlord took down the pub sign of a King George and replaced it with a painting of Lowell George. Unfortunately, after a recent change of management, the late Little Feat guitarist has been replaced by a more conventional sign of the flag of St. George. *Lower St., 20 mi north of Oxford, near Banbury, tel. 01809/338220.*

Cropredy

Since 1979 the British folk-rock pioneers Fairport Convention and friends—including Richard Thompson, Dave Swarbrick, Jerry Donahue—have held an annual mid-August festival in a field just outside this quaint north Oxfordshire hamlet. Veteran fiddler Dave Swarbrick (who now occasionally guests with the band) moved here in the early '70s, and Fairport soon began doing benefits for the Village Hall and fetes in the garden of Prescote Manor by the Oxford Canal.

In 1979 Fairport Convention decided to call it a day and organized an emotional farewell bash in a Cropredy field. It went down so well they decided to stage an annual local reunion concert. By 1985 the band had officially reformed, but the

The re-formed Fairport Convention, plus instruments

Cropredy Festival (for details, fax 01869/337142), a gathering of the manifold Fairport clans, continues, supported by ex-members and their offshoot bands as well as guests, who have recently included acts as diverse as Procol Harum and Joe Brown.

BRASENOSE ARMS

This is the village pub where Fairport Convention's members and fans drink around festival time. The Brasenose is pictured on the band's *Nine* LP. *Station Rd., 28 mi north of Oxford, near Banbury, tel. 01295/750244.*

Shipton-on-Cherwell

MANOR STUDIOS

Virgin Records boss Richard Branson bought this 15th-century manor house near the Oxford canal from the Who in 1972 for £35,000. He converted it into the label's main studio. The Manor, popular with bands because of its rural setting, attracted nearly every major band on the Virgin label—the Sex Pistols, Mott the Hoople, Simple Minds, the Bonzo Dog Band, Mike Oldfield (*Tubular Bells*), Tangerine Dream (*Phaedra*), Van Morrison (*A Period of Transition*), the Cure (*Wish*), the Cranberries (*No Need to Argue*), and Radiohead (*The Bends*). Robert Wyatt recorded *Rock Bottom* in 1974 just after becoming paralyzed when he fell out a window while chasing a girl around a room at a party. The Manor closed in April 1995 when accountants from EMI, who had just bought Virgin, claimed the place wasn't making enough money. Last in were the Liverpudlians Cast, and as producer John Leckie (who did the Stone Roses' debut) was laying the finishing touches, EMI accountants came by to hurry him up. XTC shot their "Generals and Majors" video on the grounds. Plans are now afoot to turn it into a health farm. *¼ mi east of Banbury Rd., Shipton-on-Cherwell, 10 mi north of Oxford, tel. 01865/377551.*

Swindon

All the members of XTC grew up and still live around the Swindon area. The packaging that went with their 1978 *Go 2* album includes a poster containing a map of this former railroad center focusing on the Swindon New Town and Gorse Hill districts. The legend, drawn up by bassist Colin Moulding, covers such jocular locations as, "Place of Virginity-Loss" (half-mile east of junction of A361 and A420), "Place of Hallucination" (just off the A361 opposite Queens Park), and "Place of Self-Abuse" (just south of the Allotment Gardens in Gorse Hill). The pictures are typical laddish snapshots—the band pissing in a toilet, the band smoking, the band wearing embarrassing mid-'70s flares—plus one of a dog strolling past the public library, with the letter "l" in public missing off the sign. XTC later honored the town's role in Britain's railroad development by naming their 1984 album *The Big Express*. Its cover carried a picture of a locomotive wheel. The track, "Red Brick Dream," has a line about being under the rusting North Star, an early Swindon-made engine, while another song, "Train Running Low on Soul Coal," also contains railway imagery.

XTC, then called Star Park, had their first gig in 1973, supporting Thin Lizzy at Swindon College. The college still puts on gigs by outside promoters every now and then. During the mid-'70s XTC played several clubs in town, especially the Affair (still standing on Theatre Square, but now called the Theme Arena), where A&R scouts from several labels came to see them before the band signed with Virgin. Besides XTC, there have been few famous people from Swindon, save for Moody Blues singer Justin Hayward, crooner-pianist Gilbert O'Sullivan, and comic and radio DJ Mark Lamarr.

PLUM RECORDS (14 Curtis St., tel. 01793/511133) is a friendly used store with a large collection of vinyl and flyers for local gig information. **LEVEL 3** (73 Commercial Rd., tel. 01793/534238), one of the few clubs in town without a dress code, has been going since the late '70s and puts on local bands plus some (rare) touring acts.

OASIS LEISURE CENTRE

In the late '80s Noel Gallagher was doing roadie work for the Inspiral Carpets at a gig in this huge public fitness and entertainment center and, as he said during an interview on Radio 1 FM, thought that it would be a good name for a band. The center's main hall holds around 2,000 and tends to put on mainstream acts like Status Quo and comedians. *North Star Ave., tel. 01793/445400.*

THE MIDLANDS

Cambridge

Down pokey quaint streets in Cambridge—The Fall, "English Scheme"

The once-great university city, now looking a bit down-at-heel, is the unlikely spiritual home of Pink Floyd. Syd Barrett and Dave Gilmour were born and grew up here; Roger Waters, born in Surrey but raised in Cambridge, met Barrett at Cambridge High School for Boys. From the ashes of various mostly local groups—Geoff Mott and the Mottoes, the Hollering Blues, the Architectural Abdabs, and the T-Set—Pink Floyd formed (in London) in 1966.

Syd Barrett, the eccentric acid casualty who many feel still embodies the quintessential Floyd spirit, is the only past or present band member who now lives in the city (though they did use a photo taken at the medieval cathedral in nearby Ely for the cover of the 1994 album *The Division Bell*). Recently turned 50, Barrett spends much time at home painting (mainly on black canvases) and gardening. Devotees still come to Cambridge on the off chance that they might bump into him on one of his rare days out or discover his address: The TV Personalities even released a jokey single, "I Know Where Syd Barrett Lives." One such outing takes place every year on soccer's FA Cup Final day in early May.

Cambridge's only contribution to punk was the Dolly Mixtures. The studious, poppy country-rock outfit the Bible emerged in the mid-'80s, but sales did not match their crafted sound, and vocalist Boo Hewerdine now pursues a reasonably successful career as a singer-songwriter. In the '90s, while its great varsity rival Oxford has pumped out Radiohead and Supergrass, the homegrown Cambridge music scene has remained quiet.

EATING DRINKING DANCING SHOPPING PLAYING SLEEPING

Details of what's on are listed in the student *Varsity* magazine. Bands on the indie circuit play **THE JUNCTION** (Clifton Rd. near Cambridge rail station, tel. 01223/412600), which also has club nights offering a wider range of sounds. The Australian tribute band Pink Floyd made a homecoming of sorts here in late 1996. Smaller touring bands and those on the way up (like Oasis in 1994) play the **BOAT RACE** (East Rd. at Burleigh St., on the edge of the Grafton Centre, tel. 01223/570063), a center run by a workers' cooperative; do volunteer work for them for a couple of hours, get two free tickets to a gig. Name acts may turn up at the **CORN EXCHANGE** (*see below*). **THE CAMBRIDGE ARTS CINEMA** (Market Passage, tel. 01223/504444) is good, but clubbing is split between handbag house and Student Union discos. The annual late-July three-day **CAMBRIDGE FOLK FESTIVAL** (grounds of Cherry Hinton Hall on east side of city, tel. 01223/357851), running since 1962, has always had a healthy number of rock-folk crossover acts. Paul Simon, Jimmy Page, Paul Butterfield, and Bo Diddley have performed here. In the mid-'90s headliners included Elvis Costello, Ray Davies, and Billy Bragg.

THE ANCHOR

Roger Barrett renamed himself Syd Barrett at this riverside pub's folk club in 1962 in mock honor of Sid "The Beat" Barrett, who played bass in the resident group. The Anchor, in the heart of the city, is still one of Cambridge's most popular pubs, occasionally putting on live music. *Silver St. at River Cam, tel. 01223/353554.*

Cud hypnotizing fans at Cambridge's Junction

SYD BARRETT BIRTHPLACE

Pink Floyd's first songwriter, vocalist, and frontman was born in this gray-brick semi-detached house on January 6, 1946. *"Jesmond," 60 Glisson Rd.*

SYD BARRETT RESIDENCE, '50S

The Barretts moved here in 1950; by the end of the decade, the pre-Syd Roger was learning to play guitar despite the protests of his police pathologist father. *183 Hills Rd.*

CAMBRIDGE UNIVERSITY

The university is made up of a number of self-supporting colleges. The singer-songwriter and minor cult figure Nick Drake attended the Uni. While Jonathan King was a Trinity student in 1965, he cut the sentimental ballad, "Everyone's Gone to Moon," which soared to the top of the U.K. charts. Fred Frith and Tim Hodgkinson formed Henry Cow as students here in 1968 and made their debut supporting Pink Floyd at that year's May Ball. Two years later, they won John Peel's Rockertunity Knocks talent competition. Notable '70s alumni include Robyn Hitchcock (Trinity College) and Factory Records founder Anthony Wilson, who went to Jesus College and edited the student paper, *Varsity* (in 1972). Singer-songwriters Andy White and John Wesley Harding graduated from here in the '80s. Colin Greenwood of Radiohead, Entertainment Secretary at Peterhouse College in the late '80s, was able to give his mates, including Thom Yorke, some paying gigs.

CORN EXCHANGE

Syd Barrett's short-lived post-Floyd band Stars played their first gig here in February 1972, before an audience that barely numbered double figures, even though the MC5 were top of the bill. Stars' set ended prematurely owing to an injury to Barrett's finger. A few years later, the Corn Exchange was putting on bands like the Clash, Sex Pistols, and AC/DC. Since refurbishment in 1988, the Exchange has become an all-purpose arts center where "rock" usually comes in the shape of Chas & Dave or Mike and the Mechanics. My Bloody Valentine's super-loud December 1991 appearance, a week after *Loveless* was released, drew attention for its volume. *Wheeler St., tel. 01223/357851.*

DAVE GILMOUR BIRTHPLACE

Pink Floyd's guitarist was born in this large Gothic-style house on the southwest edge of town on March 6, 1946. Joker's Wild, the band he was in before joining Floyd, used to rehearse here in the mid-'60s (it also included Rick Wills, who went on to join Foreigner). Grantchester Meadows, the name of this smart but unmemorable street, is also the name of the fields that run down to the River Cam. Roger Waters wrote a song called "Grantchester Meadows" on the *Ummagumma* album. *109 Grantchester Meadows.*

"THE LUNATIC IS ON THE GRASS" LOCATION

Thousands of people line up each year to visit King's College Chapel, one of the city's main tourist attractions, but it is the lawn lying between here and the Old School administration building (on which visitors are warned not to walk) that Pink Floyd are referring to in the line "the lunatic is on the grass" on *Dark Side of the Moon*'s "Brain Damage." *Off King's Parade, outside King's College Chapel.*

Castle Donington

This otherwise peaceful little village, 12 miles southeast of Derby and 18 miles northwest of Leicester, is home to the green, undulating grounds of Donington Castle, which hosts international car and bike races as well as the nation's main heavy metal festival.

MONSTERS OF ROCK FESTIVAL

Staged annually since 1980 (except 1989 and 1993), the Monsters of Rock is Europe's biggest fest specializing in hard rock (and only hard rock). The first event was headlined by Rainbow, with support from Judas Priest, the Scorpions, and others. AC/DC have headlined on three occasions ('81, '84 and '91). The band that has made the most appearances is Metallica, who have played four times since making their debut halfway down the bill in 1985.

Ticket stub from an AC/DC concert

In true Spinal Tap fashion, the event has had its quirks. In 1981 Blue Oyster Cult's drummer left the band the night before the event and a roadie had to stand in. Prior to the 1983 festival, local police learned of the reputation of Twisted Sister vocalist Dee Snider and asked him to limit his F-word usage to 16 during the set. Snider appeared to take no notice, but when asked after the performance why he had exceeded the limit, he said he "hadn't realized that 'motherfuckers' would be included."

The highest-ever Monsters of Rock attendance was 97,800 in 1988, with Iron Maiden (who hold the decibel record for the loudest-ever band at the event) headlining above Kiss, David Lee Roth, Megadeth, Guns N' Roses, and Helloween. Tragedy struck earlier in the day when two teenagers died in a massive crush during the Guns N' Roses set.

When the outbreak of grunge rock dented the popularity of the festival, 1995's event looked in doubt until Metallica stepped in as late headliners. Therapy?, previously viewed as an indie band but having earned respect playing down the bill the previous year, provided able support. 1996 was a Kiss/Ozzy double headliner, but the event didn't happen in 1997. *Donington Park, Castle Donington.*

ST. EDWARD'S CHURCH

In 1995 the Rev. Brian Whitehead held a special pre-festival service here to ward off the "forces of the occult" that he felt would be unleashed on the local populace by the Monsters of Rock event, and in particular the band White Zombie. *St. Edward's Church, Castle Donington., tel. 01332/810364.*

Northampton

Uninspiring, workaday Northampton is the nation's boot-making capital, though the most famous grunge rock brand, Dr. Marten, is actually made a 15-minute drive away in Wellingborough. Art goths Bauhaus formed in Northampton in 1978 but never really surpassed their debut single, "Bela Lugosi's Dead." The quirky sounds of the veteran Jazz Butcher, formed here in 1982, have gone down better in Europe and even in the United States than in their home country.

ROADMENDERS

Northampton cannot command big touring names, but thanks to the well-run Roadmenders club, it is assured of all the best up-and-coming acts. Oasis, Blur, and the rest of the currently successful Brit bands have played here, as have Faith No More and Jesus Lizard (their singer David Yow lost his wedding band while crowdsurfing at a summer '96 gig here and the band stopped playing while fans helped to look for the ring, which was found). Open since February 1992, the Roadmenders also puts on theater, exhibitions, and club nights. *1 Lady's La., tel. 01604/604603.*

Norwich

The Higsons come from Norwich/They eat a lot of porridge Robyn Hitchcock, "Listening to the Higsons"

Norwich has always had a lot of bands, but few have broken out of the region. In the early '80s a trio of quirky pop bands, the Higsons, Serious Drinking (both formed at the university, *see below*), and the aptly named Farmers Boys, almost made it. Catherine Wheel, shoegazers with a bigger following across the Atlantic than in their native England, also has roots here.

EATINGDRINKINGDANCINGSHOPPINGPLAYINGSLEEPING

Apart from the **NORWICH ARTS CENTRE** (*see below*) and the **UEA STUDENTS UNION** (*see below*), the **WATERFRONT** (Music House La. on King St., tel. 01603/632717), a purple-fronted warehouse owned by the council and managed by the Student's Union, has indie bands and club nights covering everything from '80s retro through rock to dance.

NORWICH ARTS CENTRE

One of the incidents that hurtled the Manic Street Preachers onto acres of music press space happened here on May 15, 1991. Backstage

D. Russell-Price

Norwich's The Waterfront

after a gig, they were being interrogated as to how "punk" the band really was by Steve Lamacq for the *NME*. Guitarist Richey Edwards got a razor blade and carved "4 REAL" onto his forearm. The incisions required 15 stitches. *NME* wasn't sure what to do with the pic of Edward's bloody arm; the ensuing argument among the paper's editors found its way onto "Sleeping with the NME," on the Manic Street Preachers 1992 EP, "Theme from M*A*S*H (Suicide Is Painless)."

The Wilde Club has been the premier promoter of gigs at the NAC since 1988, when Baz McHat (a.k.a. Barry Newman) put on a gig by King of the Slums. Britain's love of all things Sub Pop got off to a start when Mudhoney's first headlining U.K. tour opened here in May 1989. Since then Nirvana, Oasis, the Stone Roses, Ash, and nearly everybody else has played here in their early days. At the core of the Wilde Club's ethos is to give local talent a place on the bills. Some local bands have also been released on the Wilde Club label, notably Catherine Wheel with its debut 1991 EP, *She's My Friend*. *Reeves Yard, St. Benedict's St., tel. 01603/660352.*

UEA—UNIVERSITY OF EAST ANGLIA

This was where the severely truncated Sex Pistols' *Anarchy in the U.K.* tour should have started. The university's Vice Chancellor took it upon himself to bar them from campus, an action that promoted punk-loving leftie students to stage a sit-in at the administration building. The LCR in the Union House gets in the biggest indie names; in late 1996 they had sell-out crowds for (London) Suede, Skunk Anansie, and the like. *LCR, Student Union, UEA campus, 4 mi from city center via Bus 12 or 14, tel. 01603/505401.*

Nottingham

This likeable but early-closing city is where that most derivative of loud-guitar long-hair bands, Ten Years After, formed in 1966. The late '80s band Asphalt Ribbons didn't achieve much success until some members left for London and reassembled as Tindersticks. For the most part, Nottingham has been preoccupied with the goth, metal, punk, and hardcore scenes, evident through the local Earache label (home of Godflesh, Napalm Death, Dub War, and Nottingham-based Fudge Tunnel), but this is countered by Midlands conservatism as mainstreamers from the surrounding towns come into the cattle market clubs on weekends.

EATING DRINKING DANCING SHOPPING PLAYING SLEEPING

The city's clubs attract people from all over Nottinghamshire. Unfortunately, Nottingham is famous for its head-in-the-sand magistrates; even by the end of 1996, clubs were forced to close at 2 AM. **ROCK CITY** (*see below*) is the premier place for live music in the city. The **OLD ANGEL** (Stoney St., tel. 0115/950–2303) has new local and touring bands in the upstairs room for a low cover. **SAM FAY'S** (Great Northern Close, London Rd., tel. 0115/953–8333) performs a similar function and has a late-ish license. Only two of the 92 league soccer clubs (the other is Oxford) have rock gigs in their supporters' club; the **MEADOW CLUB** (Meadow La., tel. 0115/986–3235) is a little out of the way down by the River Trent but has moddish bands and acts. It's worth checking to see what's on at the **MARCUS GARVEY CENTRE** (Lenton Blvd., tel. 0115/978–0300), just over 2 miles out of town toward Derby.

The Hockley area, a few blocks on the south side of the city center, is where most of the alt-culture—dance music stores, trendy cafés, techno parties—can be found. The **LIZARD LOUNGE** (St. Mary's Gate, tel. 0115/952–3264) plays a variety of tunes and plies flavored vodkas until 2 AM. **THE MARKET BAR** (Goose Gate, tel. 0115/924–1780) is another Hockley hangout bar that's popular with students. A few strides away in the Lace Market, the **BEAT ROOT** (6–8 Broadway, tel. 0115/924–0852) is a two-room club with indie downstairs and anything from soul to techno upstairs. A little to the west, the cave-like **TRIP TO JERUSALEM** (1 Castle Rd., tel. 0115/947–3171), popular with bikers, is hewn out of a wall of Nottingham Castle. Dating back to 1189, it claims to be England's oldest surviving pub. The **ALLEY CAFE** (Cannon Court, Long Row West, tel. 0115/955–1013), the chilled-out minimalist place to hang, serves veggie and vegan food.

SELECTADISC (*see below*) is the main place to look for records. If you're a fan of the local Earache label, then **WAY AHEAD** (18–20 St. James St., tel. 0115/233–0444) is the place to buy their product, along with underground U.S. punk metal releases.

NOTTINGHAM MAGISTRATES COURT

In November 1977, the Pistols were being prosecuted here under the 1899 Indecent Advertisements Act for use of the supposedly obscene word "bollocks" in the title of their debut album, *Never Mind the Bollocks, Here's the Sex Pistols,* many copies of which were on display in the window of Nottingham's Virgin Records store. The Pistols were represented by John Mortimer QC, champagne and hunting socialist and creator of TV lawyer Rumpole of the Bailey, who had acted for Virgin boss Richard Branson in the early '70s. Mortimer claimed the band was being victimized and called as a witness James Kingsley, professor of English at Nottingham University, who cited the word's Anglo-Saxon history and explained that it had been regularly used in the 19th century to describe clergymen. The Pistols won the case. *The Guildhall, tel. 0115/955–8111.*

ROCK CITY

One of the top rock venues in the country is a place where bands insist on playing even after they achieve stadium status. INXS played here after *Kick* was released, and the Cure came here even after their greatest hits compilation had come out. Several groups, including Poison, have played here to warm up for the Monsters of Rock fest in nearby Castle Donington.

In 1995 Ozzy Osbourne phoned on a Monday night to book a secret show for that Friday—his first U.K. gig in almost five years—to give his new guitarist some experience before going out on tour. No love is lost, though, between the venue and Ash and 60ft Dolls, both of whom were banned from here in June 1996 after one of the Dolls was nude on stage and then dived into the crowd while Ash set off fire extinguishers backstage.

Resolutely rocking Rock City (there's not much concession to trendy fads here) has been going since 1980. In October 1995 its management opened a smaller venue, The Rig, next door. *8 Talbot St., tel. 0115/941–2544.*

[SELECTADISC]

It's almost worth coming to Nottingham just for a sortie through the three Selectadisc stores on Market Street. At No. 3 are all the latest dance and indie singles; No. 19 stocks secondhand CDs and cassettes. The main three-floor store at No. 21 has used and deleted vinyl, new CDs, and a basement full of specialty music and T-shirts. These are also good places to pick up flyers and alternative music magazines (*AP, Maximum Rock n Roll,* and more). Although it started out in Nottingham some two decades ago, the Selectadisc name is best known for its more recently opened London branch in Berwick Street, featured on the cover of the Oasis *What's the Story? Morning Glory* album (*see* Soho–Around Berwick Street *in* Central London). *3, 19, and 21 Market St., tel. 0115/947–5913.*

Birmingham

Be sure that you write me if you're coming to Birmingham—The (English) Beat, "Jeanette"

Birmingham's stellar live music years were in the late '60s, when progressive clubs headed by Henry's Blueshouse and Mother's sat alongside larger spaces like Town Hall, Bingley Hall, and the Odeon. The vibrant scene proved a good breeding ground for bands as diverse as the Moody Blues and Black Sabbath, plus the Edgar Broughton Band and the Spencer Davis Group (in which Stevie Winwood started out), which played regularly at the Golden Eagle. The venue has now been replaced by the yuppie Henry's on Victoria Square. The Move also started out here in 1966 at the long-gone Cedar Club. Bands with ties in neighboring towns, like Slade and Led Zeppelin, also helped pep things up.

Spencer Davis Group reading the local music newspaper The Midland Beat

Though the city produced few major punk-era names, it was a popular stop on any band's touring itinerary, especially those big enough to play the legendary Barbarella's. More successful were the bands who tapped Birmingham's cosmopolitan heritage, principally the reggae lite of UB40 and ska revivalists the (English) Beat (which also spawned General Public as well as the Fine Young Cannibals). It was also a major center for the New Romantic scene, thanks to the presence of Duran Duran, who made the Rum Runner into a Romo shrine far and wide.

The '90s kicked off with Apache Indian's bhangra and hip-hop fusions taking him to international stardom. More recently there's been the retro sound of Ocean Colour Scene; emerging bands include indie guitar types Laxton's Superb and Broadcast, cast as a cross between Stereolab and Portishead.

Today, with most of the historic venues gone, Birmingham lacks variety and has been eclipsed on the circuit by grottier and smaller Wolverhampton. Part of the reason is that no midsize hall has picked up where the Hummingbird left off in the early '90s. The fortnightly *What's On* magazine (70p; free from tourist offices) gives a full rundown of gigs, club nights, and other cultural events.

The City Center

Over the past two decades, much of the center has been ripped up and massively revamped. In terms of bringing business and convention trade downtown, it's been a great success. If you want a decent place to go, however, you may be disappointed, as every bar seems to be themed, and bouncers stand at the doors. In among all the corporate joints are quirky landmarks of rock past and present. The well-worn Digbeth district around the bus station is a nice contrast to the glitz of the Convention Centre area.

EATINGDRINKINGDANCINGSHOPPINGPLAYINGSLEEPING

Indie bands play at the popular and central **FOUNDRY** (Beak St. off John Bright St., tel. 0121/643–6843). The canalside **FLAPPER AND FIRKIN** (Kingston Row, tel. 0121/236–2421) is part of a chain but does a decent job of getting new bands into its cozy basement bar. The **QUE CLUB** (Central Hall, Corporation St., tel. 0121/212–0550), a huge old converted church with lots of quaint corridors linking the rooms, is one of the leading dance clubs in the city. **XPOSURE ROCK CAFE** (Fletcher's Walk, Paradise Pl., tel. 0121/236–5701) mostly plays DJ-ed heavy metal sounds, though occasionally it has live sets by the likes of the Driven. The **CUSTARD FACTORY** (*see below*) usually has plenty going on.

Birmingham is pretty well served for record stores. It's all vinyl at **THE DISKERY** (99/102 Bromsgrove St., tel. 0121/622–2219), with a great supply of 7-inch singles. **HIGHWAY 61** (Unit 12, Fletcher's Walk, tel. 0121/212–1421) is good for American alternative sounds. The wonderful **PLASTIC FACTORY** (183 Corporation St., tel. 0121/233–2967) has new, used, bootleg, and rare stuff at decent prices. **REDDINGTON'S RARE RECORDS** (17 Cannon St., tel. 0121/643–2017) tends to have some good stuff but has few bargains. The always-crowded **SWORDFISH** (14 Temple St., tel. 0121/633–4859) stocks new and used CDs and vinyl and has lots of obscure and weird sounds. **TEMPEST** (The Bull Ring, Centre Court, tel. 0121/236–9170) veers toward metal and hardcore and also sells tickets for gigs. **DON CHRISTIE RECORDS** (10–12 Gloucester St., tel. 0121/622–5420) is good for reggae, ska, and soul.

BARBARELLA'S

In the toilets at Barbarella's—The Prefects, "Barbarella's"

One of the nation's key punk venues is now a parking lot for the city's massive Convention Centre. This former factory, which was able to squeeze in almost a thousand, was featured in the Clash movie *Rude Boy,* and by two local bands, the Prefects (in the repetitive "Barbarella's") and the Photos (in the angsty "They're Closing Down Barbarella's"). Another local outfit here in 1977 was Spizz.

The tradition of punk gigs started with a Sex Pistols show in August 1976, and the Ramones, Suicide (who got bottled offstage when they were supporting the Clash), and the Damned also played here. In the days when they were headed by Stephen "Tin Tin" Duffy, Duran Duran did their first shows here. The club closed in September 1979, officially because of the skinhead violence that had flared up at a Sham 69 gig. The building itself was ripped down around 1981. Before it was a punk paradise, Barbarella's was a vintage soul club where James Brown, Herbie Hancock, the Fatback Band, and the Ohio Players had all performed. *Cumberland St.*

THE BARREL ORGAN (THE DUBLINER)

The many styles that Dexy's Midnight Runners have adopted over the years could be crystallized in the ambience of this former rock pub, a favorite of head Dexy Kevin Rowland and a popular hangout for the band during the early '80s. It's at the back of the city's main intercity bus station. Rather fittingly, it's become the Dubliner, a much more overtly Irish affair—similar to the way Dexy's progressed, really. *Digbeth St., tel. 0121/ 622-4729.*

BIRMINGHAM TOWN HALL

This municipal venue with its now-faded grandeur attracted some major acts during the '60s and '70s. It was one of the first places in the country to stage all-night jazz raves. The Beatles, Bob Dylan, and the Rolling Stones all played here in the mid-'60s; in the progressive era, the people from Mother's Club (*see* Out from Birmingham City Center, *below*) booked a host of big names, including Love, whose 1970 gig is still hailed by critics. Also in 1970 at a Derek and the Dominos gig, Robert Plant tried to get on stage to jam but was turned away by a council employee who didn't know who he was.

In the mid-'90s Town Hall underwent extensive renovation. The council hopes to have the place open—and the horrible acoustics sorted out—by 2000. *Victoria Sq., tel. 0121/ 605-5007.*

THE CUSTARD FACTORY

Once a factory that made Bird's custard powder, this snazzy redevelopment is a mixed-media complex just out from the center past the bus station. Based here are Chapter 22, which released the first Pop Will Eat Itself, Ned's Atomic Dustbin, and the Mission U.K. recordings. They also put out a single by a local band called the Fanatics in 1989. The group transformed into Ocean Colour Scene and now has its management suite in this building as well. The center also contains art galleries, jewelry stores, the suitably trendy Medicine Bar, and the Cafe des Artistes. *Gibb St., tel. 0121/604-7777.*

DEP INTERNATIONAL

After falling out with their original label, Graduate, the many members of UB40 decided to form their own label, Dep International, in late 1980. They acquired this canalside for-

The first-ever Moody Blues photo session, 1965

mer abattoir near the main bus station, and the hits have kept coming. *92 Fazeley St., tel. 0121/633–4742.*

HENRY'S BLUESHOUSE

A key '60s venue was this room above the Crown Hotel, a big corner pub at the back of New Street rail station. Claiming to be the first progressive rock club outside London, it was opened around 1968 by Jim Simpson. Black Sabbath made their debut here in 1969 and instead of taking the usual £5 fee as support band, they made a deal with Simpson to take four "Henry's Blueshouse" T-shirts instead. They played support slots here for Jethro Tull and Rory Gallagher. Simpson kept the club going through the Sabbath heyday, but it wound up in 1974.

The Crown is owned by Mitchell and Butler, one of the two big regional brewers. For a short time in 1964, the Moody Blues were known as the M&B Five, a name, suggesting the name of the brewery, that no doubt helped them get bookings in pubs like this. *Crown Hotel, Hill and Station Sts.*

THE HUMMINGBIRD

This rock venue was called the Top Rank in the '60s and '70s, but adopted the Hummingbird as its name in 1981. It took over much of the new wave scene after Barbarella's closed, and later in the '80s was one of the main breaking venues for the Stourbridge grebo (slang for "greasy bastard") trio of Pop Will Eat Itself, the Wonderstuff, and Ned's Atomic Dustbin. It was also the place the Buzzcocks chose to start their U.K. Reunion tour on December 7, 1989. Sadly, the Hummingbird closed around 1993 and left a gap in the Birmingham gig scene that has yet to be filled. It's the vacant building next to the fake-Irish Scruffy Murphy's pub. *Dale End.*

THE MERCAT CROSS

This unattractive concrete pub, built in the '70s near the main bus depot, was an important ska venue for a time. The (English) Beat made their debut here in 1979, and most other major names on the circuit played here in their early days. It hardly ever puts on live music, bar the very occasional R&B or cover band, and has reverted to its role as a market pub, opening at 6 AM for traders. *25 Bradford St., tel. 0121/622–3281.*

THE ODEON

Eric Clapton made his speech supporting the ultra right-wing, then-Conservative Party MP Enoch Powell at a gig here on August 5, 1976. Apparently the man who made his fortune playing Chicago blues licks and had had a hit with Bob Marley's "I Shot the Sheriff" just two years earlier was upset at Arabs' buying up parts of Mayfair. Though he wasn't cheered for remarks that were clearly out of synch with the views of his fans, few, if any, of the audience protested or walked out. However, the backlash came soon afterward, when a political group called Rock Against Racism, set up in 1976 to counter fascist activity, attacked Clapton strongly in their publicity statements, which were widely covered in the music and left-wing presses. The building of the NEC (*see* Out from Birmingham City Center, *below*) spelled the end for the Odeon as far as gigs went. It's been converted to a multiscreen movie theater. *New St., tel. 0121/643–6103.*

THE RUM RUNNER

This dark club underneath a betting shop was the principal New Romantic shrine in England in the late '70s and early '80s. As well as offering a regular diet of Bowie and Roxy Music nights, the Rum Runner was also the home venue of Duran Duran (though they played their first gig in the now-gone Hosteria Wine Bar) just before they hit the big time. Fans of the band came from around the world to write messages on the wall even after the place closed early in 1983. The site of the club is now buried under a hotel next to the Convention Centre. *Hyatt Regency Birmingham, 2 Bridge St.*

TOWER RECORDS

The American transnational retailer got a bit of a shock at the opening celebrations for its big Birmingham branch on December 2, 1996. The management had booked the Glastonbury-based rockers Reef to play a live set, and the band's equipment caused a power failure that disabled the store's lighting and security devices. Spotting an opportunity to make himself popular, the band's singer, Gary Stringer, started taking CDs off the racks and distributing them to fans. Tank, the band's manager, was later cautioned by the cops. Tower also had the Spice Girls, My Life Story, Alisha's Attic, and Dina Carroll at the event, but none of them showed similar initiative. *5 Corporation St., tel. 0121/616–2677.*

Out from Birmingham
City Center

Although it has its rough spots, suburban Birmingham is surprisingly green, if a little dull. Studenty Moseley has some good small venues and other places to hang.

EATINGDRINKINGDANCINGSHOPPINGPLAYINGSLEEPING

On the main southeast drag out of town are two pub venues: **HARE AND HOUNDS** (High St., Kings Heath, tel. 0121/444–2081.), where UB40 debuted in February 1979, sometimes presents bands; the excellent **JUG OF ALE** (43 Alcester Rd., Moseley, tel. 0121/449–1082) is a big, studenty pub whose tiny upstairs has had Ash, Elastica, and others on the way up. **BIRMINGHAM UNIVERSITY** (*see below*) doesn't have many gigs these days, though the **UNIVERSITY OF CENTRAL ENGLAND STUDENTS' UNION** (Franchise St., Perry Barr, tel. 0121/356–8164) gets a reasonable program of indie and guitar bands. There's also the massive **NEC** (*see below*) and the slightly smaller **ASTON VILLA LEISURE CENTRE** (8 Aston Hall Rd., tel. 0121/328–5377), where Ocean Colour Scene did a massively oversold homecoming in late 1996.

MASTERS OF ASTON

After Birmingham was heavily bombed during World War II, the city set about supplying its citizens with ample motorways, rotaries, flyovers and high-rise

Black Sabbath

blocks in the process of rebuilding. In among all the concrete lies the district of Aston, mildly famous for a good soccer team (Aston Villa) and some remaining streets of row houses. All the original Black Sabbath members—Ozzy Osbourne, Tony Iommi, Bill Ward, and Geezer Butler—were born and raised here, just a mile and a half from the city center.

In late 1968, describing himself as Ozzy Zig, Osbourne placed an ad as a would-be vocalist; the others, who were in a band already, came to visit him at his parents' house at 14 Lodge Road. They were shocked to find he had short hair.

Sabbath didn't have to make up tales of working-class hardship. All came from solid blue-collar backgrounds and held down dead-end jobs before becoming professional musicians. Tony Iommi had the top of one of his fingers cut off in an industrial accident and, lacking the funds needed for plastic surgery, used the top of a dishwashing liquid bottle for years to help him play his guitar. For an early tour, Ozzy's metalworker dad cut the band four big aluminum cross pendants in his spare time at work.

BIRMINGHAM UNIVERSITY

On May 2, 1980, just 16 days before singer Ian Curtis committed suicide in his Macclesfield home, Joy Division played what was to be their last concert in the university's High Hall. The recorded concert was included on the part-live/part-studio double album, *Still*. R.E.M., UB40, and many others played here, though notable gigs are now rare. *Birmingham University campus, Bristol Rd., 2 mi west of downtown, tel. 0121/472–1841.*

THE FIGHTING COCK (FIELDMOUSE AND FIRKIN)

A much-loved new-wave venue in the early '80s, the Fighting Cock pub was where the Au Pairs played many early gigs, along with other Birmingham bands of the time like Fashion, Ausgang, and Mighty Mighty. It recently became part of the studenty Firkin chain, but such was the appeal of the old venue that the company has had to give the new pub the full title of the Fieldmouse and Firkin at the Fighting Cock. *1 St. Mary's Row, Moseley, tel. 0121/449–0811.*

BOB LAMB'S HOME STUDIO, 1978–82

In 1980 UB40 crammed into this house to record their debut hit album, *Signing Off*, on basic equipment. Duran Duran also cut demos here around that time. In 1982 Lamb moved to a bigger studio nearby, at 120A Highbury Road, where he has worked with dozens of artists, including Stephen "Tin Tin" Duffy, Slade, Ruby Turner, and, more recently, Ocean Colour Scene. *68 Cambridge Rd., Kings Heath.*

UB40

NATIONAL EXHIBITION CENTRE

Generally referred to as the NEC, this massive hangar of a place was the first major arena besides Wembley to be used for rock gigs. Without any significant competition, it managed to get all the big names for many years and generally still does. Rory Gallagher was first to play a gig in it after it opened in early 1976. He didn't fill it, as this was a dry run to gauge its suitability for rock gigs. The first full-blown show was a few months later, when Rod Stewart packed the place. The NEC also has the dubious honor of being the place where Prince Charles saw his first rock gig, in 1982, when he attended a Status Quo concert that was raising funds for his Prince's Trust charity.

In 1983 Black Sabbath rehearsed here for the tour to promote the *Born Again* album. They met with the Light and Sound Design (LSD) firm to talk about stage sets, and Geezer Butler volunteered Stonehenge. The chief stagehand thought it sounded interesting and asked the bassist for dimensions, to which the answer was "life-size, of course!" So, they constructed full-size models of a Stonehenge cross, but when they brought them down to the NEC, where the band was rehearsing, the models wouldn't fit through the doors and had to be taken apart and reassembled inside. *10 mi southeast of downtown; signposted off M6 and M42 motorways, tel. 0121/780–4133.*

TOWER BALLROOM AND BANQUETING SUITE

This gaudy '50s-style ballroom, complete with mirror balls, was where Apache Indian made his name at the start of the '90s, mixing rap and bhangra on his way to success at home and megastardom in the Indian sub-continent. It's a likeable venue but unfortunately underused for gigs. It's also where the (English) Beat had their farewell show in 1983. Soon after that, vocalist Dave Wakeling formed General Public with the band's toaster (reggae shouter), Ranking Roger, while the rhythm section, Andy Cox and David Steele, went on to even bigger success in the Fine Young Cannibals. *Reservoir Rd., Edgbaston, 1½ mi northwest of downtown, tel. 0121/454–0107.*

Coventry

This town is comin' like a ghost town—The Specials, "Ghost Town"

Jason Tilley

Duran Duran at the National Exhibition Centre

Coventry is a candidate for one of the country's ugliest major conurbations. After it was thoroughly bombed in 1940, not much thought was put into the new buildings, most of them concrete monstrosities. Musically, Coventry is best known for the Two-Tone bands, particularly the Special A.K.A. (usually referred to as the Specials) and Selecter. When these bands formed in the late '70s, the city had various prominent skinhead gangs, and the multiracial influences and line-ups of the Two-Tone acts undoubtedly did much to negate the effects of the right-wing elements.

EATINGDRINKINGDANCINGSHOPPINGPLAYINGSLEEPING

BROWN'S (Earl St., tel. 01203/221100), run by Ken Brown, who used to be at the General Wolfe (*see below*), is part café bar, part venue, with mostly local bands and club nights. **COVENTRY UNIVERSITY STUDENTS' UNION** gets the occasional name. **SPIN-A-DISC** (83–87 Lower Precinct, tel. 01203/632004) is part of a small regional chain that holds its own against the big names and is the best in town for new music.

THE BINLEY OAK

The cold, drafty rehearsal room in this pub was used regularly by the Specials. The day before they were booked to record "Gangsters," a fierce argument led their drummer, Silverton, to walk out. With studio time booked, they had to rope in Jerry Dammers's flatmate to play drums. The Binley Oak is also where Pauline Black successfully auditioned for Selecter. *Paynes La., tel. 01203/223361.*

Pauline Black of Selecter

JERRY DAMMERS'S FLAT

The Specials rehearsed here in their early days largely because Dammers had a bulky electronic organ that was too big to keep carrying around. Once the group set up the Two-Tone label in 1979, the fledgling company used the flat for office space. *52 Albany Rd.*

GENERAL WOLFE

From 1975 to early 1984, the big General Wolfe pub was the prime place for live music in the city. The Specials used the back room to rehearse, while the Selecter practiced in an upstairs room.

The short film, "Three Minute Hero," based on a Selecter song, was filmed around here; the last scene was done at the Wolfe, with the briefly popular Birmingham band, Fashion, on stage. The neighborhood was also featured in the Specials' video for "Ghost Town" (though most of the shooting was done in even bleaker Bermondsey, south London).

In addition to the local heroes, the pub put on a varied range of new and established rock. After an album and two singles, Talk Talk played their first live gig here; U2, the Eurythmics, and Jo Boxer have also taken this stage. More established performers included Eric Bell (ex-Thin Lizzy), Steve Gibbons, Bo Diddley, and Robert Plant and the Honeydrippers. The joint, just a bit north of the center, is still open, but there's been no live music for years. *551 Foleshill Rd., tel. 01203/688402.*

GLASSHOUSE PRODUCTIONS

Once the Two-Tone acts became big, Coventry learned the hard way that most of the time people have to go to London if they want to pursue a career. Two of the city's main ska scene movers, Amos Anderson of Hardtop 22 and Selecter's Charlie Anderson, determined that the city should develop its own music business, set about lobbying the council to help fund a studio and training programs for local people. They were able to move into these premises on the edge of downtown in 1982. Since then they have worked very closely with national bodies and local colleges to provide accredited courses in all areas of the music business. They also run a commercial studio space and the Democracy record label, whose most recent releases have been in the drum & bass field. *Upper York St., Earlsdon, tel. 01203/223892.*

HEATH HOTEL

The Specials, when they were still known as the Coventry Automatics, had a residency in this big, bleak pub. They decided to dispense with their vocalist after a few gigs on the grounds that he wasn't a good singer—and then got in Terry Hall. The new lineup with Hall made their first appearance here in 1978. The pub is now vacant and boarded up. *Foleshill Rd., tel. 01203/688412.*

HORIZON STUDIOS

This cheap studio with cheap equipment was where the first Two-Tone hits were recorded. The Specials ran out of money after cutting "Gangsters"; to speed up its release, they put "The Selecter" by Selecter on the B-side. Horizon was demolished long ago; the site is now a parking lot for a railway station. *Warwick Rd.*

MR. G'S

The Specials' 1978 residency at this club established them as a big name in their home-town. At that time live music was common at the club—the Sex Pistols played here once—but today it's just a city-center handbag disco. *102A The Precinct, tel. 01203/221353.*

THE LOCARNO

Chuck Berry is probably glad that they wiped this club off the map and built the Central Library on the site. It was here in 1972, at the Lanchester Arts Festival, that he inserted a throwaway ditty, "My Ding-A-Ling," into his set. It was then released as a single, and where "Memphis Tennessee," "Promised Land," and all his other great songs failed, this disaster reached No. 1 in the U.K. charts and seemed to stay around forever.

Later, for a short while, it was a Tiffany's club, a beer monster cattle market paradise where Pete Waterman occasionally DJ-ed. Specials singer Terry Hall met his wife here. Its closing in the late '70s was one of the things that prompted the writing of "Ghost Town." *Coventry Central Library, Smithford Way at The Precinct, tel. 01203/832314.*

TOO MUCH PRESSURE

Before becoming the guitarist for Selecter, Noel Davies worked at the Lucas Aerospace factory on Read Street. One day, after an argument with his wife and various cash problems, he came to work and told a colleague that everything was "too much pressure." The stressful events, however, gave him the idea for one of the British ska era's best-known songs.

Dudley

In this town just to the west of Birmingham is the Black Country Museum, dedicated to the region's manufacturing heritage, as well as the long-running JB's venue.

GRADUATE RECORDS

After a support slot on a Pretenders tour, the eight-piece soft reggae outfit UB40 were chased by various record companies. Instead, they signed with tiny Graduate Records, run by David and Susan Virr from a room above their record store. Success came immediately—the first three singles, all of them double A-sides ("King"/"Food For Thought", "My Way Of Thinking"/"I Think It's Going to Rain" and "The Earth Dies Screaming"/"Dream a Lie") all hit the U.K. Top 10. The debut album, *Signing Off,* did rather well, too. However, before 1980 was out, the band left Graduate, after accusing the company of omitting an antiapartheid track from the album. The band then formed their own label (*see* Birmingham, *above*). *1 Union St.*

Robert Plant at JB's, 1981

JB'S

After 25 years at its original King Street location, JB's moved to the present 1,000-capacity site in 1994. During its lifetime JB's has seen just about everyone come through. Robert Plant shot videos here; in the late '80s it was a center for the so-called Stourbridge bands, with Pop Will Eat Itself, the Wonderstuff, and Ned's Atomic Dustbin all doing important early shows here. Over the past few years, facing stiffer competition, it has been putting on more and more tribute bands. Nevertheless, its hard-rocking tradition led the Wildhearts to choose JB's for their final show on December 22, 1996. *15 Castle Hill, tel. 01384/253597.*

Stoke-on-Trent

The "Potteries" town of Stoke, in the northwest reaches of the Midlands, is notable for two things. The first is the view of hundreds upon hundreds of toilet bowls stacked up alongside the rail tracks in the yard of the Armitage Shanks plant (the name of a hard-gigging band who supported Thee Headcoats in the mid-'90s, as well as the Green Day track "Armatage Shanks" [sic]).

The second is that Slash was born here as Saul Hudson on July 23, 1965. Slash's mom, Ola, was a clothes designer who did Bowie's *Man Who Fell to Earth* garb; dad Tony was a graphic designer, responsible for the cover of Joni Mitchell's *Court and Spark* in 1974. Slash got out of here in 1976 when he left with his father to go to Los Angeles.

Stourbridge

A Black Country town, a little off the beaten track, that's famous for its lead crystal became the center of the grebo (greasy bastard) scene in the late '80s. The three key bands—Pop Will Eat Itself, the Wonderstuff, and Ned's Atomic Dustbin—all came from the area and made their debut gigs in town. Also from Stourbridge are Diamondhead, the hard metal band formed in the late '70s that both Metallica and Megadeth cite as a major influence.

THE BROADWAY

The roots of the grebo scene stretch as far back as July 1982, with the debut gig here of Eden, who would, less than four years later, split into Pop Will Eat Itself and the Wonderstuff. The pub no longer has live music. *The Broadway, tel. 01384/394267.*

THE MITRE

In the upstairs room of this pub, all three local grebo bands cut their teeth before going on to bigger venues such as JB's in Dudley and Birmingham's Hummingbird. The landlord, John, who has been putting on live music here since 1976, speaks particularly affectionately of Ned's, who attracted much interest when they did their debut here in 1987. Although they never played here, a couple of members of Diamondhead drank here regularly. The Mitre still puts on a varied program of live music every night but Tuesday, ranging from bluegrass to rock. *Lower High St., tel. 01384/395374.*

Stratford-Upon-Avon

[PHOENIX FESTIVAL]

When the London-based Mean Fiddler organization announced the first running of this festival in July 1993 outside Shakespeare's main town, few thought that it would grow to rival the Reading and Glastonbury festivals. The first event, a three-day affair, was headlined by Sonic Youth, Faith No More, and the Black Crowes. It had a shaky beginning, but when the Glastonbury festival opted not to produce a show in 1996, the Phoenix capitalized on the opportunity; it announced a four-day bash that offered the lineup of the summer. The stats alone were amazing: 250 acts appeared on eight stages before a sellout crowd of 35,000. The main acts for the big stage each day were Bowie, Prodigy, Neil Young and Crazy Horse, Alanis Morissette, Manic Street Preachers, Foo Fighters, Björk, Massive Attack, Sex Pistols, and Terrorvision. The Megadog Dance Stage had Leftfield, Prodigy (again), Goldie, and the Chemical Brothers; the jazz and acoustic stages both had lineups that would have made top-notch minifestivals themselves. The success of the

Beck relaxing at the Phoenix Festival

1996 event—broadcast live on the internet—could well eclipse the Mean Fiddler's other main festival, at Reading. Headliners in '97 were Black Grape, the Charlatans, Jamiroquai, and David Bowie. *Long Marston Airfield, tel. 0181/963–0940 (festival details).*

Streetly

THE MELLOTRON FACTORY

A Harp Lager plaque marks the spot of the factory that used to make the Mellotron, an instrument first manufactured here in 1963 that performed a function similar to today's sample playback machines. It works when pressure on a key sets a length of prerecorded tape in motion. Despite being bulky, unreliable, and expensive, the instrument soon found aficionados in the rock world: the Beatles, Led Zeppelin, Genesis, and King

Crimson were some of the more prominent users. The Moody Blues even recruited Mike Pinder, who worked at this factory as a keyboard player and Mellotron operator. The Mellotron machine, in its various guises, ceased to be manufactured in 1986. The building is now occupied by Streetly Windows, a double-glazing manufacturer. *338 Aldridge Rd., tel. 0121/353–5886.*

Wolverhampton

Hardly a tourist magnet, Wolverhampton has nevertheless beat out larger Midlands cities as a key stop on most bands' touring itineraries. The fact that one of the country's biggest promoters—MCP—is based nearby might have something to do with it. It also has a good range of venues designed for crowds of 200, 800, and 2,000. In the past, industrial Wolverhampton has been written off as redneck due to fascist activities, but, seeming finally to have realized that the millennium is around the corner, it is sharpening up its act. A downtown campus helps give a bit of a studenty feel.

EATING DRINKING DANCING SHOPPING PLAYING SLEEPING

The two biggest venues in town are the **CIVIC HALL** and the **WULFRUN HALL** (*see below* for both). The downtown **VARSITY** (Stafford St. at Wulfruna St., tel. 01902/711166) has been open since 1992 but began putting bands on in earnest in October 1995. Since then it has had Super Furry Animals, Red Kross, and Catatonia among the headliners. **MIKE LLOYD MUSIC** (25 Queen Sq., Mander Centre, tel. 01902/26876) sells new—including lots of alternative stuff—and used records as well as tickets for local gigs.

SLAID

One of the biggest-ever bands to come from the Midlands were Slade, who formed in Wolverhampton in 1965 as the N'Betweens after the four members had played in various other combos in the area. It took six years (that included a transitional name change to Ambrose Slade) for them to bring their noisy brand of rock and pop into the charts, scoring their first No. 1 with "Coz I Luv You" (covered in the United States by Quiet Riot 12 years later).

A couple of the old gigging haunts that they played when they were still known as the N'Betweens are still going. The **CONNAUGHT** (Tettenhall Rd., tel. 01902/24433) still has some acoustic nights. The **SHIP AND RAINBOW** (480 Dudley Rd., tel. 01902/351417), where Led Zeppelin also played, has since been converted into a microbrew pub called the **BREWERY TAP** and no longer has live music.

REVOLVER MUSIC AND RECORDING STUDIO

In January 1990 all four members of the Stone Roses staged a spectacular attack on the offices of their former record company, FM/Revolver. They were incensed that the company had re-released their 1987 single, "Sally Cinnamon," and made a video to go with it, without their consent. Their retribution took the form of pouring gallons of blue and white paint over three company cars, office walls, label owner Paul Birch, and, just for good measure, his girlfriend. The quartet was arrested at studios in Monmouth and bailed to appear at Wolverhampton Magistrates Court, where they were fined £3,000.

Revolver has been going since 1979. In that time, it has put out albums by as varied a bunch as Magnum, the Scorpions, and Sister Sledge, as well as having Ned's Atomic Dustbin and Terrorvision in the studios. *152 Goldthorn Hill, tel. 01902/345345.*

WOLVERHAMPTON CIVIC HALL

The city's municipal buildings have been putting on rock shows continuously since 1957. Over the past decade or so the complex has really come into its own as the top midsize venue in the Midlands. Morrissey made his solo debut here in December 1988, playing with all Smiths except Marr, two years after the last Smiths gig. Morrissey promised free admission to those wearing a Smiths T-shirt: 17,000 came to oblige, but nearly all of them failed to get in. This caused hysterical scenes and faintings after hundreds of fans had slept out overnight to get a place in line. The show formed most of the video, *Hulmerist.*

In the same building is the smaller Wulfrun Hall, a no-smoking venue that holds 800, where the Swedish popsters the Cardigans played a gig in November 1996. The Wulfrun also gets bands on the way up; one show in the not-too-distant past featured Oasis supported by Ocean Colour Scene. *North St., tel. 01902/312030.*

WOLVERHAMPTON WANDERERS (WOLVES) FOOTBALL CLUB

Pop Will Eat Itself, lifelong fans, sponsored the Wolves-versus-Grimsby Town game on October 15, 1994. The grebo band got the full corporate hospitality deal, meaning they received VIP treatment and had their photo taken with players and officials, including the very un-rock & roll manager at the time, Graham Taylor. Other vocal supporters of the club include Robert Plant and Bev Bevan. *Moulineux Ground, Waterloo Rd., tel. 01902/655000.*

Pop Will Eat Itself with Mark Venus, second from left, defender for the Wolverhampton Wanderers

Blackburn

4,000 holes in Blackburn, Lancashire—The Beatles, "A Day in the Life"

A story in the *Lancashire Evening Telegraph* about council officials going around town and counting the exact number of potholes in local roads ("4,000 in the roads of Blackburn, 1/25th per person") inspired Lennon and McCartney to write the line above on the *Sgt. Pepper* album's closing track. A scene in the movie *Yellow Submarine* depicts a land full of holes and a character who remarks, "This place reminds me of Blackburn, Lancashire." The Beatles played this mill town only once, at the King's Hall on Northgate in June 1963, sharing a bill with Roy Orbison.

Blackpool

I'm going up the 'pool, from down the Smoke below—Jethro Tull, "Going up the 'Pool"

Blackpool has been Britain's most popular seaside resort for more than a hundred years, despite having one of England's dirtiest beaches. In summer months crowds line the so-called Golden Mile of amusement arcades, greasy cafés, chip shops, and cotton-candy stalls; in fall Blackpool sees a round of political conventions. Throughout the year, the town is popular with (mostly gay) clubbers, who come for Blackpool's kitsch value, as did previous generations of northern soul fans.

Blackpool has spawned one major rock band, Jethro Tull, none of whose main members were born locally. The band moved to Luton and then London. Tull celebrated the place with tongue slightly in cheek on the "Life Is a Long Song" EP track, "Going up the 'Pool," in lines like "along the Golden Mile they'll be swigging cups of tea." The Kinks were more overtly sentimental on the 1967 single, "Autumn Almanac," reminiscing about "going to Blackpool for my holidays." The cultish '80s punk/DIY outfit the Membranes (from nearby Preston) recorded a track about the place called "Tatty Seaside Town," later covered by Therapy?.

WINTER GARDENS

The Stone Roses played their biggest gig up to then at the Winter Gardens Empress Ballroom in August 1989. The sold-out show was released as a video in 1991. The Levellers recorded a live album and video here, both called *Best Live: Headlights, White Lines, Black Tar Rivers* in February 1996. In August of that year, the ballroom hosted a festival to mark punk's 20th anniversary, with 50 bands from the late '70s. As well as the Buzzcocks, Sham 69, and other better-known names, many bands like the Drones, Slaughter and the Dogs, eater, and the Not Sensibles reunited especially for the three-day event. X-Ray Spex played for the first time in years but without Poly Styrene; they drafted Poly Filla instead.

The Who, when they were still the High Numbers, supported the Beatles here in the gardens' Opera House in the summer of 1964 and, as they were loading their equipment into a van, were mobbed by hordes of screaming fans. The teenies started ripping the clothes off their heroes until they realized that they were molesting Townshend and co. and not the Beatles. *Church St. at Leopold Grove, tel. 01253/27786.*

Bolton

The northern punk pioneers the Buzzcocks emerged in 1976 in this typical antiquated northern town surrounded by run-down mills and overwhelming hills. The group took their name from an article in London's *Time Out* magazine that ran "Get a buzz, cock." Originally, the Buzzcocks were led by Howard Devoto, who formed the group as an antidote to "having to endure boring music in pubs."

BOLTON INSTITUTE OF HIGHER EDUCATION STUDENTS' UNION

When student Howard Devoto (then Trafford) advertised on the college notice board in 1976 for people to form a group to perform a version of the Velvet Underground's "Sister Ray," Pete Shelley (then McNeish) answered the ad. They rehearsed some Eno and Iggy numbers, formed a band, the Buzzcocks, and played their first gig at the college on April 1, 1976. It lasted for three songs, one of which was a cover of David Bowie's "Diamond Dogs," before the events secretary pulled the plug. *Deane Rd. campus.*

WINTER HILL

A Certain Ratio named the closing track of their *To Each...* album after this windswept hill—at around 1,500 feet, the highest spot in the area. Popular with hikers, it has a huge television antenna at its crest. *Off A675, near Belmont.*

Burnley

An anachronistic mill town that looks as if it were frozen in 1921, Burnley does boast one excellent venue, the **MECHANICS ARTS AND ENTERTAINMENTS CENTRE** (Manchester Rd. at Yorke St., tel. 01282/430055), which puts on a wide range of performances and welcomes Fairport Convention every February. One of the few bands to make it out of here was the Not Sensibles, who had a punk-era novelty hit with "I'm in Love with Margaret Thatcher."

TURF MOOR

The Fall shot the video for 1983's "Kicker Conspiracy," a single about the problems then facing soccer, at this stadium, home of Burnley FC. Drummer Paul Hanley played the part of the club coach. *Turf Moor, Burnley, tel. 01282/427777.*

Oldham

Oldham, once a booming manufacturing center but now closed down like much of Lancashire, was also the birthplace of two classic bandwagon-jumping groups, soporific prog-rockers Barclay James Harvest and Inspiral Carpets, who played in local pubs before obtaining de rigeur pudding bowl haircuts and a Rick Wright organ sound circa 1967 and joining the Madchester scally boom. One of the few new local groups making a splash beyond town limits is Puressence, from the Failsworth suburb.

SADDLEWORTH MOOR

Over the moors, take me to the moors—The Smiths, "Suffer Little Children"

"Suffer Little Children," which closes the Smiths' 1984 debut album, was written as a requiem to Edward Evans, Lesley Ann Downey, and John Kilbride, the three children killed by the "Moors Murderers," Ian Brady and Myra Hindley, in the mid-'60s and buried in "a shallow grave" on the bleak moor. The unfolding story, which dominated the newspaper crime sections for years, gripped the young Morrissey, who imagined himself a potential victim. The moor is 10 miles northeast of central Manchester.

U2 joins the Greenpeace protest heading for the Sellafield nuclear reactor site, 1992

SELLAFIELD

Chernobyl, Harrisburg, Sellafield, Hiroshima; stop radioactivity—Kraftwerk, "Radioactivity"

U2 wanted to play a gig outside the Sellafield nuclear reactor, north of Lancashire, to demonstrate against the expansion of the plant and to leave barrels of contaminated mud collected from the Irish Sea. When British Nuclear Fuels slapped an injunction on them, they had to make do with a benefit gig in Manchester, where they were joined by Kraftwerk, Public Enemy, and B.A.D. II. Immediately after the Manchester concert, U2 made for a beach near Sellafield to board a Greenpeace dinghy headed for the restricted shore where the reactor was to be built. A picture of the band dressed in white boiler suits, using barrels with radioactive labels as props, was beamed round the planet's newsrooms. The power plant now has a visitor center and tour. *Off A595, Sellafield, tel. 019467/27027.*

Rochdale

One of Lancashire's more pleasant, if rather windswept, towns, Rochdale, some 10 miles north of Manchester on the edge of the Pennines, is home of the MOR-ish white soul singer Lisa Stansfield. Local comedian Mike Harding entered the U.K. charts in 1975 with an inane retort to Glen Campbell's "Rhinestone Cowboy" predictably entitled "Rochdale Cowboy."

The locally based Imaginary Records, an indie label run by ex-bookie Alan Duffy, specializes in tribute compilations to formative artists like Syd Barrett, Captain Beefheart, and the Byrds, with contributions from such key contemporary bands as the Shamen, Sonic Youth, and Dinosaur Jr. Imaginary also released work by a few locals, including the now-defunct Mock Turtles, who later signed to Sire and had a hit with "Can You Dig It?" in 1991.

CARGO STUDIOS (SUITE 16 STUDIOS)

New Order/Revenge's Peter Hook owns and records at this studio. What certainly attracted Hook to the place where Joy Division had recorded "Atmosphere" was the "live room," perfect for getting the raw, live, cracking sound that Hook's side project Revenge was after. Along with local musician Shan Hira, he bought the joint in 1985. Since then they have upgraded from 16 to 24 track, and the client list has included the Stone Roses, Happy Mondays, the Chameleons, and Therapy?. *16 Kenion St., off Drake St., tel. 01706/353789.*

TOWN MEADOWS

In February 1843 Pablo Fanques's circus arrived in town and performed on the now long-built-over Town Meadows for three nights. The poster printed for the show read: "The last night but three, being for the benefit of Mr. Kite." John Lennon found a copy in a junk shop in 1967 and adapted the message for the track, "Being for the Benefit of Mr. Kite," which closed the first side of the *Sgt. Pepper* album.

Wigan

A town best known for George Orwell's 1930s reportage work, *The Road to Wigan Pier,* Wigan claims it is trying to shake off its grime-encrusted image of be-shawled, clog-wearing residents keeping coal in the bath. Unfortunately, Wigan's biggest tourist attraction is a sprawling industrial museum called...Wigan Pier (the only body of water in the town is a canal), usually publicized with pictures of period workers dressed in shawls and clogs.

In the rock world, Wigan is best known as the spiritual home of "northern soul," the name club-goers in Lancashire gave to obscure '60s and '70s soul records made in the American deep south and imported to England to be played excessively at north England clubs. To keep the northern soul scene pure and have enough platters to play during all-nighters, ever-more obscure records had to be found, and so things that record buyers in Alabama and Georgia had rejected became hip items at clubs like the now-demolished Wigan Casino.

The 1972 Bickershawe Festival, held just outside town and featuring the Grateful Dead, Captain Beefheart, and others, was among the worst-organized events of its kind. Facilities were atrocious, most people sneaked in for free, and organizer Jeremy Beadle (the future prime-time TV host) was saddled with huge debts.

Wigan Casino advertisement

I'm going down to Liverpool to do nothing, all the days of my life—The Bangles, "Going Down to Liverpool"

Liverpool has the most fearsome reputation of any British city, derided as a violent, confrontational place full of uninhabitable housing projects, militant strikers, petty thieves, and football hooligans, all rotting next to a port no one wants to use in a part of the country few want to visit. That's the legend. The truth is that while parts of the city—such as Everton, Bootle, and Toxteth—are pretty squalid, downtown Liverpool is a vibrant, upbeat area well worth visiting—provided you're a Beatles fan.

Musicologists trace the reason for Liverpool spawning the world's most popular rock & roll group back to its role as a port. From the days of slavery on, the city had enjoyed closer links with the United States than had any other place in the United Kingdom, receiving cotton from the deep south to be spun in the surrounding Lancashire mill towns. By the end of the 19th century Liverpool was England's largest port and one of the empire's richest cities, with a highly cosmopolitan population of West Indians, Chinese, and Irish among the indigenous Liverpudlians.

When John Lennon, Paul McCartney, and co. were growing up here in the '40s and '50s, it was still the major port for American ships. Every week, hundreds of sailors and passengers would disembark at Pierhead, bringing with them the then seldom-seen luxuries of America such as Cuban-heeled boots, denim jeans, chewing gum, and, of course, rock & roll. It wasn't just the sound of Elvis Presley, Chuck Berry, and Gene Vincent that made hundreds of Liverpool kids form groups. In 1956 Lonnie Donegan from Glasgow had a huge hit with a version of Leadbelly's "Rock Island Line," using just guitar, rudimentary bass, and washboard, a style known as skiffle in the American south. Skiffle was easy to play, requiring minimal musical ability, and thousands of skiffle bands formed up and down the land, particularly in cities like Liverpool.

When the kids tired of skiffle (as did Donegan quickly), the better musicians kept the guitar-bass-drums line-up, ideal for covering Chuck Berry, Buddy Holly, and Eddie Cochrane numbers. Hundreds of budding beat bands began playing school gyms and church halls or forced their way onto the bill at clubs like the Cavern. Rory Storm and the Hurricanes (with Ringo on drums) were reckoned to be the best Liverpool group at the start of the decade, but by 1962 the Beatles, who had come of age in the sweaty Hamburg clubs, topped *Mersey Beat* magazine's poll and were Liverpool's hottest live band with their Cavern residency.

Local groups' access to the latest American sounds—music that was never played on U.K. radio, like very early Tamla/Motown records—gave Liverpool's Merseybeat scene a head start on other cities and led to a chart revolution in 1962 when Liverpool groups, led by the Beatles, began shifting huge quantities of records. Once groups started to write their own material, other cities, particularly London, with the Stones and the Kinks, overtook Liverpool, and the leading Merseybeat bands—Gerry and the Pacemakers, Billy J Kramer and the Dakotas, and the Searchers—soon became passé. Worse still for Liverpool, the Beatles moved to London, leaving a huge local vacuum.

There was a brief beat poetry boom around Brian Patton, Roger McGough, and Adrian Henri, but Liverpool had no part in late-'60s psychedelia or early-'70s prog-rock. It wasn't until punk that the city's music was revitalized. In Liverpool this was a twisted form of psychedelia dominated by groups formed around Liverpool's leading punk club, Eric's, such as the Zoo label pairing of Teardrop Explodes (named from a scene in a *Marvel* comic and led by the marvelously eccentric Julian Cope) and Echo and the Bunnymen.

By the mid-'80s there was a lull, only partly filled by the sexually outrageous but ultimately vacuous Frankie Goes to Hollywood, who, like Gerry and the Pacemakers 20 years previously, saw their first three singles reach No. 1. The best-received band of the period was the La's ("la" is how the word "lad" is spoken locally), whose only album, which finally came out in 1990, drew applause for their guitarist and singer Lee Mavers. Mavers couldn't stick the pace, and the La's broke up.

Julian Cope

Bands to emerge during the '90s are the poppy Lightning Seeds, the quirkier Boo Radleys, and the lightweight Space. Meanwhile, Liverpool prefers to dwell on its past, milking every last drop out of its Beatles heritage.

GEOGRAPHICAL NOTES

No British city has so dramatic a setting as Liverpool, by the wide Mersey estuary. Its center was built up during the late 18th–early 19th century and soon became one of the British Empire's leading ports. Decline has increased in this century, and parts of downtown are derelict and uninviting, but around the cathedrals, the streets have retained their elegant Georgian buildings. To the west are Seel and Slater streets, where Merseybeat bands, including the Beatles, played in the early '60s and punk acts in the '70s, and where the best clubs, like Cream/Nation, can be found now. The main street of musical interest is still Mathew Street, where the Cavern Club, rebuilt since the Beatles were house band, stands. Eric's, Liverpool's main punk venue, stood opposite the Cavern and is now one of a number of local Beatles theme bars. The annual Beatles Convention, held at the end of August, takes place in and around Mathew Street.

The tourist information office (Great Charlotte St. at Elliot St., tel. 0151/236–9091), in the Clayton Square shopping center near Lime Street station, overflows with leaflets and maps of Beatles sites. The Magical Mystery Tours (tel. 0151/236–9091) take Beatles fans around Penny Lane, Strawberry Field, and so on, in bright yellow coaches. The local rail network, part underground, doesn't seem to go anywhere that tourists would want to visit, so the best way to get around on public transport is by bus (70p from the center to Penny Lane).

Songs of Liverpool

Chuck Berry, "Liverpool Drive" (1964)
Gerry and the Pacemakers, "Ferry Cross the Mersey" (1964)
Delaney Bramlett, "Liverpool Lou" (1965)
Judy Collins, "Liverpool Lullaby" (1966)
Little Jimmy Osmond, "Long-Haired Lover from Liverpool" (1973)
The Teardrop Explodes, "Kirkby Workers Dream Fades" (1979)
The Bangles, "Going Down to Liverpool" (1985)
Teenage Filmstars, "There's a Cloud Over Liverpool" (1991)
Suzanne Vega, "In Liverpool" (1992)
Ian McNabb, "Merseybeat" (1996)

Downtown–Around Albert Dock

Until the '80s Liverpool's waterfront was lined with mile after mile of busy docks, and the Mersey teemed with cargo ships and transatlantic liners. Now, thanks to the city's unfavorable location for the European market, the only action on the river comes from a few pleasure craft and some sad-looking local ferries.

Liverpool's population was built on the many hundreds of thousands of immigrants who arrived, mainly from Ireland, in the 19th century. These included Paul McCartney's family and John Lennon's grandfather, Jack. Pete Best (the original Beatles drummer) and co. arrived here in the '40s from colonial India. George Harrison's father, Harry, worked on the transatlantic liners before World War II. The only Beatle employed nautically was Ringo, who worked as a steward on the St. Tudno pleasure steamer, which plied the sea lanes between Liverpool and Llandudno in north Wales. John Lennon tried to run away to sea in 1957 but got only as far as the seamen's office, where they phoned his Aunt Mimi, who ordered him to return home at once.

The major landmark on the city's shoreline is Pierhead. Just to the south is the revamped Albert Dock, a group of converted 1840s warehouses that now contains the northern branch of the modern art Tate Gallery, the Beatles Story, a couple of other civic museums, a TV studio, and shops, bars, and restaurants. It's hard to believe that this motley collection is Britain's most heavily visited tourist attraction.

THE BEATLES STORY

If you like the Beatles, avoid this tacky tourist trap. The city's only permanent Beatles exhibition, the basement display charts the rise of the world's best-known rock band with props from key moments in the group's development—the Reeperbahn, *Mersey Beat*'s office, the Cavern, the Yellow Submarine, Abbey Road, and so on. *Britannia Vaults, Albert Dock, tel. 0151/709–1963. Admission £5.45. Open daily 10–6.*

PIERHEAD

Ferries cross the Mersey—as in the Gerry and the Pacemakers song—from this riverside spot overlooked by three famous structures, the Royal Liver building, the Port of Liverpool Authority, and the Cunard building. Some vessels turn the trip into a 45-minute mini-cruise. Others just make the short trip to the Wirral peninsula, easily visible from the water's edge.

The Beatles performed in 1960 and 1961 on a ferry called the *Royal Iris,* which used to journey from here to the Wirral. It was by Pierhead that Yoko Ono promoted a poorly attended John Lennon memorial concert on May 5, 1990, with performances from Lou Reed, Randy Travis, and Cyndi Lauper. *Riverside at Water St.; ferries, tel. 0151/630–1030.*

Downtown–Around the Cathedrals

Religion used to be big business in Liverpool. The northern part of the city was Irish Catholic and the south, Protestant. Both denominations have cathedrals just south of the city center. By the 1950s, this area had declined but had taken on a Bohemian edge, teeming with junk shops, artists' studios, and West Indian drinking clubs, all popular with students from the nearby art school and Liverpool University.

EATING DRINKING DANCING SHOPPING PLAYING SLEEPING

YE CRACKE (*see below*), where Lennon met Stuart Sutcliffe, should not be missed. THE PHILHARMONIC (36 Hope St., tel. 0151/709–1163), built by shipwrights in crystal, mahogany, and marble, is absurdly overdecorated and requires a visit if only to see the bright purple marble toilets; Lennon and Sutcliffe were regular visitors here while attending art school. At SUNNYLAND SLIMS TAPAS BAR (45 Hardman St., tel. 0151/709–2322) you can eat as much as you want for £5 and listen to live blues and jazz on weekends. THE FLYING PICKET (Merseyside Trade Union Centre, 24 Hardman St., tel. 0151/709–3995) puts on decent regional bands several times a week.

BRIAN EPSTEIN RESIDENCE

While John Lennon was staying in Epstein's smart, two-story Georgian house in 1962, he wrote "Do You Want to Know a Secret?", inspired by the fact that the Beatles' manager brought his boyfriends here at a time when homosexuality was still illegal. Some Beatologists believe that Epstein and Lennon had a homosexual affair; Lennon beat up Cavern DJ Bob Wooler for suggesting it. *36 Falkner St.*

JOHN LENNON BIRTHPLACE

Beatles experts are divided over whether there was an air raid around 6:30 PM on October 9, 1940, when John Lennon was born. Some stories claim that the infant Beatle was put under a bed for safety while the bombs dropped around the hospital, but one archivist later discovered that there were no newspaper reports of bombing that week. *Oxford St. Maternity Hospital, 29 Oxford St.*

JOHN LENNON RESIDENCE, 1960–62

John Lennon's first address away from his Aunt Mimi was in this apartment that he shared with Stuart Sutcliffe in the early '60s, when they were both students at the local art school. From the outside, Gambier Terrace looks classy, but inside it had been left to rot. The apartment was even featured in the *People* tabloid as an example of a beatnik hovel in 1960. When Lennon moved out in 1962, he told the new tenant, Rod Murray, to keep anything he wanted. Murray threw away more or less everything, apart from one of Lennon's music exercise books, which he sold at Sotheby's in 1984 for £15,000. *3 Gambier Terr.*

LIVERPOOL CATHEDRAL (ANGLICAN)

When he was 12, in 1953, Paul McCartney failed an audition for the cathedral choir. Nearly 40 years later, in June 1991, McCartney, never one to bear a grudge, was happy to allow the world premiere of his classical collaboration with Carl Davies, *A Liverpool Oratorio,* to be performed here. The huge cathedral, the largest Anglican church in the world, hosted a memorial service (A Festival of Peace) for John Lennon on March 29, 1981, with Lennon-McCartney songs played on the organ. Three years later, Echo and the Bunnymen did a set here recording several songs— including "All You Need Is Love" and their own hit, "The Killing Moon." *St. James Rd.*

Liverpool Cathedral (Anglican)

LIVERPOOL COLLEGE OF ART (JOHN MOORES UNIVERSITY)

John Lennon attended this college from September 1957 to May 1960, beginning a long tradition of British rock & rollers at art school. He was lucky to win a place, having failed all his "O" levels, and did little in his first few months to suggest he deserved to be there. Tutors considered him a poor talent.

In the late '50s, students were heavily into Dixieland jazz and frowned on rock & roll. Lennon's love of rock and his Teddy Boy clothes did nothing for his popularity. Things started to improve when a tutor spotted one of his cartoons, was impressed, and encouraged him to do more. After a while, as Lennon became more accepted, the college authorities allowed the Quarry Men to play to students on Friday nights in the basement canteen. Lennon's tutor, Arthur Ballard, even let the band practice in his room, which was handy for Paul McCartney, who was still at the Liverpool Institute, based in the same block as the art college.

Lennon soon struck up serious relationships with two fellow students, Cynthia Powell, whom he later married, and Stuart Sutcliffe, who went on to play bass temporarily in the Beatles. After his mother, Julia, was killed in a road accident in July 1958, Lennon became unruly, cynical, and nihilistic. Lennon left the college in 1960 (just before he would have been thrown out) to tour Scotland with the Silver Beatles.

In 1984 Yoko and the Lennon-Ono offspring, Sean, turned up on a nostalgia trip. They donated John's Bag One lithographs to the college, but the works were later stolen. The college is now part of John Moores University, named for the local football pools/mail-order king, who was also a great patron of the arts. *Hope St. at Mount St.*

LIVERPOOL INSTITUTE (LIVERPOOL INSTITUTE FOR PERFORMING ARTS)

Paul McCartney and George Harrison's old school is now the Liverpool Institute for Performing Arts, specializing in degrees in rock & roll (composition, band management, production, and so on), acting, and design. When McCartney and Harrison began attending in the '50s, it was the Liverpool Institute (known locally as the "Inny"), one of Liverpool's top establishments. McCartney, the model student, passed five "O" levels; George Harrison, the rebel, passed none and was then best known for the daring canary-yellow waistcoat he wore under his school blazer. Other alumni include McCartney's brother, Mike (later of Scaffold), and Beatles roadie Neil Aspinall, who now runs Apple.

By the mid-'80s, the place had closed, and the building was in a bad state of disrepair. Up stepped McCartney, who wanted to do something "worthwhile" but discovered that the rules of the trust that owned the building meant it could be used only for educational purposes. McCartney then rounded up friends like Harrison, Ringo, David Hockney, and Jane Fonda to come up with some cash; the idea was to help budding songwriters learn the ropes so they would not be ripped off as McCartney and Lennon had been in the early days. The revamped Institute, with state-of-the-art recording and video facilities, opened in 1995; the Queen turned up to do the official honors in June 1996. There are places for only about 200 new students each year. Since opening, the institute has reportedly had problems with funding. *Mount St., L1 9HF, tel. 0151/330–3000.*

YE CRACKE

It may look a bit of a dive from the outside, but Ye (pronounced "the") Cracke is a superb back-street local full of tiny rooms and alcoves. John Lennon met Stuart Sutcliffe here in the late '50s. Theirs was an unlikely pairing: Sutcliffe was considered to be the brightest talent of that year's art school intake, Lennon the worst. Sutcliffe thought rock & roll crude and commercial; Lennon loved it. The only thing they had in common was a love of the beat poets. Sutcliffe, however, was into the James Dean look. Lennon

Courtesy of Old Hall Inns & Taverns Ltd

Ye Cracke

got Sutcliffe into rock & roll via performers like Gene Vincent, who borrowed elements of Dean's style. Before long, Sutcliffe took up the bass so that he could join Lennon's group, the Quarry Men. Although he was a great painter, Sutcliffe wasn't much of a musician and used to play with his back to the audience. The pub has been popular with art students and lecturers for decades. In Lennon's day tutors would often hold seminars in the back room. *13 Rice St., tel. 0151/709–4171.*

Downtown–Lime Street and South

Lime Street is Liverpool's best-known thoroughfare, famous for the station of the same name and home to the Empire Theatre and the grand St. George's Hall. Many of the city's most interesting streets and all the most useful stores can be found just south of Lime Street.

EATINGDRINKINGDANCINGSHOPPINGPLAYINGSLEEPING

Slater Street is nearly all bars, many of them fake Irish, such as **GUINAN'S** (No. 15, tel. 0151/707–0834). The magnificent **JACARANDA** (*see below*) is worth looking out for. The **BLUE ANGEL CLUB** (*see below*) is where the Beatles used to hang out; it's now a popular bar. **JAK'S** (40 Seel St., tel. 0151/709–2803) puts on club nights covering everything from indie to swingbeat. The **051 CENTRE** (1 Mt. Pleasant, tel. 0151/707–0257) is a decent arthouse cinema that also has a couple of bars; on Saturday night it hosts a Clear/Voodoo night that attracts all the top house and techno DJs. The **BAA BAR** (43–45 Fleet St., tel. 0151/708–0610), a popular pre-clubbing place and daytime café based in a former hemp warehouse, has two floors and three bars. Liverpool's best-known club is **CREAM/NATION** (Parr St., tel. 0151/709–1693), in an old ammunition store. Cream has issued platinum-selling albums, attracts the big-name DJs, and gets crowds of thousands on Saturday night.

Liverpool Palace (6–10 Slater St.) houses a number of alternative stalls in one building, selling punk gear, leather, comics, and records. **Probe Records** (9 Slater St., tel. 0151/708–8815) has moved from the site where Julian Cope worked in the late '70s (*see below*) and is now pricey. Seel Street, which crosses Slater, has a couple of rummagable used bookstores. There's a **Cream store** (32 Slater St.) near the club of the same name full of T-shirts and brand-name bags.

THE BLUE ANGEL

In May 1960 at this long-running club, the Silver Beatles failed an audition, organized by leading rock & roll impresario Larry Parnes, to back Billy Fury. Parnes, however, was impressed enough to offer them a slot backing Johnny Gentle in Scotland—the group's first tour.

In those days, the club was still known as the Wyvern. In 1961 then-Beatles manager Allan Williams took over the place, changed the name to the Blue Angel (after the Marlene Dietrich movie), and made it into one of the most popular late-night hangouts for local beat groups. Gerry and the Pacemakers, the Searchers, and Rory Storm and the Hurricanes came here to jam until the early hours. Brian Epstein discovered Cilla Black singing here one night and signed her to his NEMS organization. In the '80s the Blue Angel became the Razamataz, but in the '90s reverted to its previous name and is now a studenty bar. *108 Seel St., tel. 0151/709–1535.*

[JACARANDA]

Spread over three floors, the Jacaranda was a major Beatles hang-out and live music spot in the early '60s, when many of Liverpool's top beat bands would drop by after gigs to hang out until the early hours (even though it then had no alcohol license). It was opened in 1958 by Allan Williams, who went on to manage the Beatles before Brian Epstein. Early patrons included John Lennon and Stuart Sutcliffe, who would sit around for hours cadging cigs. Williams hired the pair to paint murals, which are still in the tiny basement next to the stage where local bands play. In 1960, when the Silver Beatles started playing the basement for £1, they were simply one of thousands of Mersey bands—Rory Storm and the Hurricanes and Cass and the Casanovas were top dogs—and not a very good one at that. In the same year, the Silver Beatles came here to cut some live recordings that helped the group secure gigs in Hamburg. It was from the Jacaranda that the group plus Williams and several hangers-on left for the German city on August 15, 1960.

In the '70s the bar became the Maxie San Suzie and was then briefly squatted by anarchists. In the early '80s it reopened under its original name. The Jacaranda now makes little of its Beatley past—an honorable thing in a city saturated with tenuous Fab links. *21–23 Slater St., tel. 0151/708–9424.*

PICKWICKS

Frankie Goes to Hollywood made their debut at this dive disco in 1983. Liverpool's first Beatles convention was held here in October 1977. *Fraser St., tel. 0151/207–4605.*

ROYAL COURT THEATRE

The late-'70s rock satire troupe Alberto Y Los Trios Paranoias premiered their rock opera *Sleak* at the Royal Court in 1977. Two years later Paul McCartney and Wings held a benefit gig here to raise money for McCartney's plans to turn the Liverpool Institute into a performing arts center.

In February 1986, Manchester's three top bands, the Fall, the Smiths, and New Order, staged a benefit for Liverpool councillors (who had been fined heavily for refusing to implement Tory government mandates) under the banner, "From Manchester with Love." A year later, the Beastie Boys' much-hyped May 30 gig was canceled after 10 minutes when the venue filled with tear gas. The show occurred in the light of press reports—that the Beasties have always denied—that the band had insulted child cancer patients a few days before. Some local would-be heroes apparently came purposely to wreck the event. In the riot that followed, some seats and the band's equipment were destroyed. Another benefit gig here, on April 29, 1989, saw the Mission headline, along with the locally based La's, for victims of the Hillsborough football stadium disaster. The Royal Court still puts on top bands; the Bluetones, Manic Street Preachers, and Julian Cope played in 1996. *Roe St. (opposite south face of St. George's Hall), tel. 0151/709-4321.*

Manic Street Preachers at the Royal Court Theatre

ST. GEORGE'S HALL

Outside this monstrous Hellenic Revival hall opposite Lime Street station around 30,000 Beatles fans gathered to sing "She Loves You," on December 14, 1980, a week after John Lennon's murder. Presumably, no one realized that Paul McCartney wrote the song. Once Liverpool's chief concert hall, it now hosts exhibitions and conferences. *Lime St.*

SHOW OF STRENGTH

One of Liverpool's strangest rock events, Echo and the Bunnymen's all-day May 1984 Bunnython, was organized to promote the band's *Ocean Rain* album. The program began with breakfast with the band at their favorite café (Brian's Diner, 27 Stanley St., near the Cavern, tel. 0151/236-1953). Bunnymen fans had been given an open invitation; while the band and the lucky few tucked in, a queue of nearly 1,500 waited outside. Breakfast was followed by a bike ride around Liverpool, an organ and choir recital at the Anglican cathedral, and a ferry trip across the Mersey, before the day ended with a gig at St. George's Hall.

WALKER ART GALLERY

Stuart Sutcliffe became the first Beatle to make a splash in the local news when one of his paintings was shown at the gallery's annual exhibition in 1959. Sponsor John Moores, the mail-order and soccer pools king, bought the work himself for £65; Sutcliffe spent the money on a bass guitar. A Sutcliffe retrospective was held at the Walker in 1964 at the height of Beatlemania, two years after he had died of a brain hemorrhage in Hamburg. His Hamburg Painting No. 2 is stored in the basement and can be viewed on request. An Art of the Beatles exhibition in 1984 opened by Cynthia Lennon was accompanied by nonstop Beatles records; it included Lennon's Bag One drawings, some of his childhood belongings and drawings, and a pile of bricks from the Cavern. The exhibition drew 50,000 visitors. *William Brown St., tel. 0151/207–0001.*

Downtown–Mathew Street and Around

Mathew Street, a small but lively strip halfway between Lime Street Station and the river, is home to the Cavern, the underground club that made the Beatles' reputation in the early '60s. The street is also, unsurprisingly, the center of Liverpool's Beatles industry, with a banner at one end proclaiming, "Welcome to Mathew St., birthplace of the Beatles," and orange pennants everywhere advertising the Cavern Initiative Quarter. Various events linked with the annual Beatles convention take place here at the end of August, when around 150 bands play in the street or in its clubs and pubs. Mathew Street is also home to a handful of Beatley tourist traps, the Beatles Shop, and a number of predictably named bars (*see below*).

EATING DRINKING DANCING SHOPPING PLAYING SLEEPING

The city's premier venue for touring indie and alternative acts since mid-1993 is the split-level **LOMAX** (34 Cumberland St., tel. 0151/236–0329). The upstairs gig hall was instrumental in the rise of Cast, while Oasis, Supergrass, and Mansun (from nearby Chester) have played here.

BEATLES FOR ALE

There's no shortage of pubs named for Beatles songs or even with authentic Beatles connections on Mathew Street.

ABBEY ROAD PUB (inside Cavern Walks Mall, 8 Mathew St., tel. 0151/236–4554). With strange displays of '70s food packets and loads of London street signs, it's not worth visiting.

JOHN LENNON BAR (23 Mathew St., no phone). The trendiest-looking of the Beatles cash-in bars, it has lots of Lennon photos and is always crowded.

RUBBER SOUL OYSTER BAR (19 Mathew St., no phone). Occupying some of the space that was Eric's, Liverpool's leading punk venue, Rubber Soul contains two huge rooms on either side of a covered passageway. There is plenty of French decor but no Beatles stuff.

CAVERN PUB (Mathew St., opposite the Cavern, tel. 0151/236–1957). The best of the bunch, the Cavern pub opened in 1994. It sells food and drink with hilarious, contrived Beatley names like Octopus's Garden (seafood salad), Yellow Submarine (ploughman's lunch), and Give Peas a Chance. Rocktails include a Maxwell's Silver Slammer, Chilla Black, Black in the USSR, and most ridiculous of all, an Eric (Coffee with Cream and a shot of Jack topped with cinnamon and a hint of Ginger). There are memorabilia and framed photos of everyone famous who played at the Cavern.

BEATLES SHOP

If it's Beatles memorabilia you want, there are few outlets with more ephemera. The Beatles Shop, which predictably claims to be open eight days a week, stocks the entire range of mid-'60s Beatles goods—wigs, models, calendars, clocks, combs, and coke tins, plus the usual range of mags and posters. Avoid the vinyl, which can be bought cheaper elsewhere. Above the awning are four bronze busts of you know who. *31 Mathew St., tel. 0151/236–8066.*

BEATLES STATUE

The Beatles tend to attract tasteless tributes, none more so than Arthur Dooley's 1974 statue, which is set high in the wall opposite the Cavern Walks entrance. Dooley's tribute is a shrouded Madonna bearing three cheap toy dolls representing the individual Beatles. Behind her on the wall are the letters J, P, G, R; Paul McCartney's doll, tragically, has been stolen, and where it should be there is a sign reading "Paul has taken wings and flown." On the other side of the Madonna is a Lennon cherub, added after Lennon died, which carries a guitar and sports a halo reading "Lennon Lives." Underneath is a verse from "Imagine" and an extract from the Bible. *31 Mathew St.*

[THE CAVERN]

One of the world's most famous rock venues, this basement club put on the Beatles no less than 292 times in the early '60s and became the leading northern venue for the Merseybeat sound. The Cavern, based on a Parisian nightspot, Le Caveau Français,

opened on January 16, 1957, in a moldy cellar—all low brick arches and alcoves—that had been a wine bar, and before that an egg-packing warehouse. The only furnishings were tiny, uncomfortable wooden chairs just dumped by the stage. In those days it was a jazz venue; the resident group was the Merseyssippi Jazz Band. Rock & roll was frowned upon, as the pre-Beatles Quarry Men found when they played (without Paul, who was at scout camp) on August 7, 1957, and remained so until May 1960 when new owners took over and relaunched the club with Cass and the Cassanovas and Rory Storm and the Hurricanes (including Ringo on drums).

Lennon, McCartney, and co., by now calling themselves the Beatles, returned early in 1961 and started attracting rave notices. Huge lines began to form to hear a band who went beyond covering the usual R&B standards, who swore and fought with each other on stage, but who still maintained a tight and exhilarating sound.

Brian Epstein went to see them—and his first rock & roll gig at a lunchtime show in November 1961.

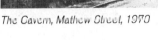

The Cavern, Mathew Street, 1970

Epstein was ten years older than most of the others there, his pricey suit and briefcase set him apart, and he generally stood out like a sore thumb in this damp, noisy, smelly environment. It took Epstein a few additional visits to convince the Beatles that he was the man to be their manager. One of the first moves under his management was the drafting of Ringo Starr to replace Pete Best. When Ringo appeared on stage with the Beatles here for the first time in fall '62, he drew boos from many in the crowd who idolized Best. Over the next few days, fights broke out in the lines outside the club between Starr and Best fans.

The Beatles' last Cavern gig was on August 3, 1963, the day they entered the U.S. chart for the first time with "From Me to You." Hundreds of other Merseybeat groups played here around that time, including Gerry and the Pacemakers, the Searchers, Billy J Kramer and the Dakotas, the Fourmost, and the Big Three, who presented Cavern cloakroom attendant Priscilla White as guest vocalist. White soon changed her name to Black and joined the Beatles management to become one of Britain's most successful '60s singers. She went on to become ubiquitous on British TV.

As Merseybeat declined in the mid-'60s, so did the Cavern. It went bust in February 1966, with fans barricading themselves inside in protest. Although it reopened that summer, it was never the same. When Londoners like Eric Clapton and Rod Stewart or visiting Americans like Stevie Wonder came, the only locals available to front for them were obscure acts like the Hideaways.

The Cavern closed again in March 1973 to make way for a ventilation shaft for Liverpool's small subway system. The land above the club was leveled for a parking lot, which was festooned with flowers and mementoes for days after John Lennon was killed in 1980. Around that time architect David Backhouse began plans to revive the Cavern as part of the Cavern Walks shopping mall. While the mall was being built, excavators found the original Cavern Club intact amid the rubble but filled with water; the water table had risen and swamped the cellar club. Some of the original bricks were sold for charity and the rest were used to recreate the club with the same dimensions close to the site of the original. Cavern Walks opened in 1984. Parts of the facade were designed by Cynthia Lennon. Nowadays the Cavern puts on local bands and studenty discos at night and is highlighted in the Beatles Magical Mystery coach tour by day. *10 Mathew St., tel. 0151/236-1964 or 0151/236-1965.*

ELEANOR RIGBY BENCH

This grotesque seated female figure on a marble bench was sculpted by, of all people, Tommy Steele, who made some of Britain's first rock & roll-ish records in the '50s. Steele donated the statue, which was unveiled on December 3, 1982, for "half a sixpence" (the title of one of his ludicrous records). Inside he placed a four-leaf clover, a pair of soccer shoes, a page from the Bible, an adventure book, and a Shakespearean sonnet. *Stanley St.*

Eleanor Rigby bench

[ERIC'S]

Liverpool's leading punk club opened in fall 1976 as the New Cavern—it was directly opposite the site of the old club—but soon changed its name to Eric's. The club was run by Roger Eagle, a northwest DJ who had started the region's first-ever all-nighters at Manchester's Twisted Wheel in the mid-'60s. As soon as Eagle opened Eric's, he installed a jukebox full of garage records like "96 Tears" and "Louie Louie" and began booking all sorts of punk bands—the Clash, Sham 69, the Fall, and Warsaw (Joy Division).

Soon the place was hangout central for a crowd of local punk wanna-bes—Julian Cope, Ian McCulloch, Pete Burns, Pete Wylie—whom Eagle encouraged to form bands. When Cope's devilish dancing at a Clash gig in May 1977 blocked Pete Wylie's view, the two began arguing but made up and a few days later set up a group, Arthur Hostile and the Crucial Three, with another Eric's regular, Pete Burns. They soon changed their name to the Mystery Girls and played their only gig at Eric's in November 1977, supporting Sham 69, during which Wylie wore a toilet seat on his back. Cope went on to launch the Teardrop Explodes (who made their debut here in November 15, 1978, supporting Echo and the Bunnymen); Wylie formed Wah! Heat; and Burns assembled Dead or Alive. Other club regulars who went on to form major bands were Jayne Casey, Holly Johnson, and Ian Broudie, who formed Big in Japan, with Johnson later going on to form Frankie Goes to Hollywood, Broudie the Lightning Seeds, and Casey Pink Military.

Eric's was closed down by cops on March 14, 1980, on the day that Wah! Heat made their live debut with Cope on organ. A club called Brady's, where an up-and-coming U2 played, ran for a while, but the building has now been taken over by one of Mathew Street's Beatles bars, Rubber Soul. *9 Mathew St.*

MERSEY TUNNEL

Making love to the Mersey tunnel, with a sausage; have you ever been to Liverpool?— The Stranglers, "London Lady"

The Stranglers' colorful song, the B-side of their debut "Grip" single from 1977, was dedicated to a female London-based rock writer who had a reputation for bedding young rock stars. The quoted line bore no connection with the rest of the song and, in fact, there are two tunnels from Liverpool city center to the Wirral—Kingsway and Queensway.

NEMS

It was in the early '60s, while running this record store, one of several branches of the Epstein family's North End Music Stores business, that Brian Epstein first heard about the Beatles and became their manager. Epstein, a classical music buff, had only a commercial interest in rock & roll. When some customers began asking for a copy of a record cut in Hamburg by a group named the Beatles, he looked it up in the catalog but couldn't find any mention of the disc, which had been credited to Tony Sheridan and the Beat Brothers. After making some inquiries, Epstein was amazed to discover that the Beatles were part of a growing new music movement in Liverpool and appearing regularly at the Cavern (*see above*), a club near the store.

Epstein signed the Beatles to his fledgling management company at this store on January 24, 1962. It was also here on August 16 that year, just as Parlophone had agreed to record the Beatles, that Epstein told Pete Best he was out of the group. The shocked Best immediately told his best pal, Neil Aspinall, the Beatles' driver, who quit in sympathy. Best insisted Aspinall stay on, which was just as well because the latter eventually became managing director of Apple Corp.

After Best left, Epstein began molding the Beatles' new cutesy, cuddly, clean-cut, loveable mop-top image—no leathers, no cursing, no cigs or beer (on stage), no chatting with fans—which Lennon hated, McCartney loved, and the group gradually accepted. By 1963 Epstein's NEMS management wing was taking up all his time; he had also signed Gerry and the Pacemakers and Billy J Kramer and the Dakotas, the Big Three, the Fourmost, and Tommy Quickley. He eventually moved the company to London, leaving Pete Brown in charge of the store. Brown, like Aspinall, also later became an Apple executive and was best man at Lennon and Yoko Ono's wedding. The building is now a hi-fi store. *12–14 Whitechapel.*

PROBE RECORDS

Pete Wylie and Julian Cope worked here when it was the Probe record store, at the height of punk in the late '70s. Probe's policy was to refuse to sell (but not refuse to stock) what the owner deemed crap records. When a metal fan wandered in asking for the new Rush album, he was ushered out with a "No, you fucking can't have it." It is now a Ted Baker clothes store. *Rainford Gardens at Button St.*

ZOO LABEL

Bill Drummond and Dave Balfe formed Zoo, Liverpool's major punk-era indie label, in 1978 and moved into this huge Victorian office block near Eric's. Zoo signed the city's two best punk-era bands, the Teardrop Explodes (whom Drummond also managed) and Echo and the Bunnymen. In an attempt to create a mystique around the label, they ensured that early releases were uncollectible or of little interest to Teardrops/Bunnymen fans. Zoo 1 was the then-unreleased Teardrop Explodes album, *Everybody Wants to Shag the Teardrop Explodes,* which stayed in the vaults until 1990, when it appeared as a compilation; Zoo 2 was Julian Cope's Scott Walker compilation, *Fire Escape in the Sky—The Godlike Genius of Scott Walker;* and Zoo 3 a still-unreleased Teardrop Explodes album, *The Great Dominions.* Less unusual releases, like early Teardrops and Bunnymen singles, quickly became cult favorites and propelled the groups to stardom. But Zoo became a vehicle for Drummond to launch his maverick and bizarre career, which would take in the Justified Ancients of Mu Mu and the KLF, then a long-term label. When the Teardrops signed to Mercury and the Bunnymen to WEA, Zoo folded. *1 Chicago Buildings, Whitechapel.*

The Justified Ancients of Mu Mu

East Liverpool

Liverpool's east side is dull, dominated by faceless suburbs like Wavertree and Childwall.

GEORGE HARRISON BIRTHPLACE

The youngest Beatle was born in this tiny two-up, two-down redbrick terrace (with no indoor toilet) on February 25, 1943. The Harrisons moved away on January 2, 1950, when they were eventually rehoused by the council in better accommodation. *12 Arnold Grove, Wavertree.*

KENSINGTON RECORDING STUDIO

The Quarry Men made their one and only recording in this tiny studio in a friend's house in summer 1958. The band, which then comprised John Lennon, Paul McCartney, George Harrison, Colin Hanton, and John Lowe, didn't have too much confidence in their own compositions and plumped for Buddy Holly's "That'll Be the Day" as the A side, although they did include a rare Harrison-McCartney composition, "In Spite of All the Danger," on the flip.

Only one copy was pressed; it was kept by pianist John Lowe, who in 1981 announced his intention to auction it at Sotheby's. McCartney was not too happy about this and offered him £5,000, but Lowe refused to sell. McCartney's solicitors then obtained a court order preventing sales on the grounds that the ex-Beatle owned the copyright to Holly's work. An arrangement was made that McCartney would buy it for the £5,000 offered. He then had it recut for friends as a Christmas present. The building, in one of Liverpool's most run-down districts, was long ago demolished and replaced by apartments. *53 Kensington.*

KENSINGTON FIELDS FOREVER

After much pressure from Beatles fans, Liverpool council agreed by a slim majority in the late '70s to name a new public housing development after the group. The estate, Kensington Fields, officially opened in November 1981, is a collection of bland, rabbit hutch–like houses and bungalows a couple of miles east of the city center. It originally contained Ringo Starr Drive, John Lennon Drive, Paul McCartney Way, and George Harrison Close; a few years later, Epstein Mews, Apple Court, and Cavern Court were added. Some residents have predictably named their houses "Imagine" or "The Cavern."

North Liverpool

The northern suburbs nearest downtown Liverpool contain some of the city's most depressing neighborhoods—run-down terraces and housing projects, boarded-up buildings, weed-strewn lots, and an ever-present menacing atmosphere near Everton and Anfield (home of the city's two famous football clubs, Everton and Liverpool). Farther north are some better suburbs, such as West Derby, where the cult soap opera Brookside—on which Morrisey appeared briefly as himself in 1987—is shot behind closed doors.

[CASBAH CLUB]

In this unlikely setting, a makeshift rock venue-cum-coffee bar in the basement of a huge secluded Victorian house, the Beatles played their first U.K. gig under that name just after returning to Liverpool from Hamburg in December 1960. The idea of rigging out the huge basement area as a teenage hang-out came from Mona Best in 1958. She named it the Casbah after the line, "Come with me to the Casbah," in her favorite movie, *Algiers*, and opened it in August. The Quarry Men—John Lennon, Paul McCartney, George Harrison, John Lowe (piano), and Colin Hanton (drums)—even though they had barely played for months and were on the point of folding, performed opening night before a crowd of 250. They so impressed Mona's son, Pete Best, who lived upstairs, that he took up the drums. He made quick progress and within two years was asked to join the Quarry Men, by then calling themselves the Silver Beatles, shortly before they went to Hamburg. Another resident in those days was Neil Aspinall, who became the Beatles' road manager and eventually managing director of Apple. The Beatles played here regularly in 1961 and 1962 and continued to use the place as a daytime refuge until Best was sacked in August 1962, just before they made their first record. The house, under different ownership, now has no Beatles connections. *8 Hayman's Green, West Derby.*

LIVERPOOL FOOTBALL CLUB

Pink Floyd sampled crowd noises at this stadium, the home of England's most successful soccer club, on the track, "Fearless," from 1971's *Meddle* album. In the early '90s the demolition of the terrace behind the goal, the "Kop," was marked by a "Last Night of the Kop" concert, featuring Ian McCulloch, Pete Wylie, the Farm, and Gerry Marsden of Gerry and the Pacemakers, who had enjoyed a 1964 No. 1 with what became the club anthem, "You'll Never Walk Alone." In 1979 the club's erstwhile star player, the ridiculously permed Kevin Keegan, hit the dizzy heights of No. 31 in the charts with the sugary "Head Over Heels in Love." *Anfield Rd., Anfield.*

PAUL MCCARTNEY ADDRESS, 1942

In the shadow of Liverpool Football Club, this cramped, furnished terrace house, into which the McCartneys moved when they married in spring 1941, was Paul's first home. They didn't stay long, moving across the Mersey to Wallasey for a brief spell. *10 Sunbury Rd., Anfield.*

PAUL MCCARTNEY BIRTHPLACE

The Beatles' bassist was born James Paul McCartney on June 18, 1942, in this hospital. Because his mother had once worked in the maternity ward, she was given five-star treatment. *Aintree Hospitals, 107 Rice La., Walton.*

South Liverpool—The Dingle, Toxteth

Nothing can prepare the first-time visitor for the bleakness, emptiness, and desperation that is Toxteth. Here, grand houses with steps and pillars, built for merchants made wealthy by the local shipping industry, were left to rot when the port and docks died and are now in a state of collapse. In the early '80s local youths rioted and burnt down buildings like the Rialto Ballroom. In the mid-'90s the district experienced a series of drug-related murders. The eeriest thing about this area is its emptiness—the lack of people, cars, and buildings.

Dingle (or the Dingle), to the south of Toxteth, is stacked with tiny terrace housing and retains a community feel, but not a very welcoming one. Here Ringo and Billy Fury were raised. Fury (real name Ronald Wycherley) was a river tugboat man until he got a break with Larry Parnes's stable of teen idols and became Britain's greatest pre-beat rock & roller. On the river bank near the Dingle was Liverpool's beach, the Cast Iron Shore (as mentioned in the Beatles' "Glass Onion"), which the council uprooted for the 1984 Garden Festival.

Billy Fury

RINGO *SENTIMENTAL JOURNEY* COVER

Ringo used a picture of this grotty pub (with his image superimposed) on the cover of his debut solo album, *Sentimental Journey*. The pub wasn't really a place where he used to hang; he just happened to have been brought up nearby and fancied a trip back to his roots to kick off his solo career. *The Empress, High Park St., Dingle.*

RINGO STARR ADDRESS, 1946–63

When Ringo (then plain Richie) was six, his mother swapped her Madryn Street address for this two-up, two-down house. Ringo, who lived here through his childhood, left school at 15 and, like many of his contemporaries, joined a skiffle band in the mid-'50s. In 1960 he joined Liverpool's top beat band, Rory Storm and the Hurricanes, and went off to Butlin's holiday camp in north Wales for the summer season. There he changed his name to Ringo Starr. Despite the tiny space, he held his 21st birthday party here in 1961, the guest list including Cilla Black (then Priscilla White) and Gerry and the Pacemakers. He was still living at this address when the Beatles began their rise, but after Ringo moved to London, his mother decided the hassle from fans was too much, and she moved out in 1965. *10 Admiral Grove, Toxteth.*

RINGO STARR BIRTHPLACE

The eldest of the Beatles was born Richard Starkey in this now-boarded-up terraced house on July 7, 1940. His parents split up when he was three, and he spent much time with his paternal grandparents at No. 59. He left the street in 1946 when his mother got a new home in Toxteth. Nearby is the Empress pub (*see* Ringo *Sentimental Journey* Cover, *above*). *9 Madryn St., Dingle.*

South Liverpool—Garston, Allerton, Speke

Speke is a soulless, post-war council estate (public housing development), purpose-built 10 miles southeast of downtown Liverpool around an auto plant and airport. It was also home to both George Harrison and Paul McCartney at various times in the '50s. Garston, just north of Speke, has traditionally been one of Liverpool's rougher districts. In the '50s when the Beatles started playing local (and now demolished) venues, it was patrolled by vicious gangs of Teddy Boys, who would often set about beat groups whom they deemed to have come from the "wrong" part of town or who played covers of songs by out-of-favor artists.

GEORGE HARRISON ADDRESS, 1950–62

The Harrisons moved into this cul-de-sac on January 2, 1950. While living here, George Harrison first took up the guitar. Traveling to school in central Liverpool on the 86 bus, he met neighbor Paul McCartney for the first time. In 1958, just after Harrison joined Lennon and McCartney in the Quarry Men, the group played a gig here, the wedding reception for Harrison's brother Harry. *25 Upton Green, Speke.*

GEORGE HARRISON ADDRESS, 1962–65

The Harrisons moved here from Speke just before the Beatles became household names. As Beatlemania raged, crowds began to gather outside the house continually, much to the annoyance of George's father, who quit his bus driver's job in 1965. He and his wife left the city for Warrington and some peace. *174 Mackets La., Hunts Cross.*

JULIA LENNON ADDRESS, 1949–58

When John Lennon hit his teens, he began spending more time with Julia, his real mother, in this quiet suburban semidetached stucco house. In 1945, when Julia's marriage to Freddie Lennon floundered, she had handed five-year-old John over to her sister Mimi. Lennon liked staying here because Julia was a bit barmy (she used to wear woolen knickers on her head while doing the housework), played the piano and banjo, and, unlike nearly everybody else's parents in those days, was into rock & roll. She regularly invited the Quarry Men in to rehearse, and she was happy to let Lennon come here just to change into his Teddy Boy clothes after he left Aunt Mimi's in school uniform. It was while Lennon was staying here in July 1958 that a policeman knocked and told him that Julia had been knocked down in a road accident. He rushed off to Sefton General Hospital only to find that she was dead. Lennon later dedicated a number of songs to her, including "Julia," off the so-called *White Album*, and "Mother," from the first Plastic Ono Band album. *1 Blomfield Rd., Garston.*

PAUL MCCARTNEY ADDRESS, 1947–53

The McCartneys moved here from Everton when Paul was four. His mother, Mary, worked as a district midwife and was so popular that people used to leave gifts outside the front door. Their road, in the middle of the Speke housing estate, is now a busy divided highway. *72 Western Ave., Speke.*

PAUL MCCARTNEY ADDRESS, 1953–55

In 1953 the McCartneys were on the move again, to this council house in what is now a very run-down stretch of boarded-up houses. While living here, Paul McCartney met George Harrison on the bus they took to school. *12 Ardwick Rd., Speke.*

PAUL MCCARTNEY ADDRESS, 1955–64

The McCartneys' last Liverpool address, in Allerton, recently bought by the National Trust, was a massive improvement on Speke, but still a bit of a dump. A year after the

McCartneys moved in, Paul's dad bought him his first guitar, a £15 "'cello," but he made little progress until he realized that being left-handed, he'd be better off trying it "upside down" with all the strings rearranged.

In 1956 Paul McCartney's mom Mary died. A year later, McCartney met John Lennon for the first time at St. Peter's church in Woolton (*see below*), and before long the Quarry Men were rehearsing here, encouraged by Paul's dad. Over the years, Lennon and McCartney wrote a number of major Beatles songs in this house, including "I Saw Her Standing There," "I'll Follow the Sun," "Love Me Do," and "When I'm Sixty-four."

By 1964, with the Beatles' millions racking up, Paul McCartney bought his pop a large detached house in the posh bit of the Wirrall, over the Mersey in Cheshire, and the whole family moved out of Liverpool. When the house was bought by the National Trust in 1995, McCartney said: "Our mam would be dead chuffed to think that our little house would end up with the National Trust." *20 Forthlin Rd., Allerton.*

South Liverpool—Strawberry Fields, Penny Lane, and Around

Strawberry Fields and Penny Lane, the two most famous Beatles suburban Liverpool landmarks, are major disappointments. Strawberry Fields is a children's home that has been completely rebuilt since the young John Lennon hung out in the grounds, while Penny Lane is an insignificant street leading to a traffic junction (not even called Penny Lane).

EATINGDRINKINGDANCINGSHOPPINGPLAYINGSLEEPING

Since the song was written, a number of local stores have adopted sympathetic names like Penny Lane wine bar and Penny's fashions. There used to be a Penny Lane Records, but it is now, ironically, named after a Led Zeppelin song, **No Quarter** (114 Penny La., tel. 0151/734-0438).

DOVEDALE ROAD PRIMARY SCHOOL

John Lennon (1945–52), George Harrison (1948–54), and the unfunny TV comic Jimmy Tarbuck all attended here. Lennon was referring to this school when he sang, "then you decide to take a walk by the old school," on "Good Morning Good Morning" from the *Sgt. Pepper* album. A painting of a soccer scene that Lennon did when he was a student here in 1952 was used on the front cover of his 1974 solo *Walls and Bridges* album. *Dovedale Rd., Mossley Hill.*

John Lennon, Walls and Bridges, *1974*

JOHN LENNON ADDRESS, 1940–45

It was to this small Wavertree house near Penny Lane that Julia Lennon brought new-born John in October 1940. Its address was No. 9—a favorite Lennon number, revisited in the Beatles' "Revolution No. 9" and his solo 1974 single "No. 9 Dream." With her husband Freddie at sea, Julia struggled to look after John and occasionally left him alone at night while she went out. When Julia found herself a new boyfriend, John Dykins, in 1945 and announced that they were all moving into his one-bedroom apartment, her sister Mimi stepped in and took young John with her to her home in Menlove Avenue (*see below*). *9 Newcastle Rd., Mossley Hill.*

JOHN LENNON ADDRESS, 1945–63/"LIVE FOREVER" COVER

Lennon moved into this smart '30s suburban semi in a middle-class area when he was five. The young Lennon was obnoxious and criminally minded; as legend has it, he placed objects on tram lines to try and derail the trams, smashed street lamps, and regularly went on shoplifting sprees. But in 1956 things changed when he formed his first group, a skiffle outfit, with just him on guitar and his pal Pete Shotton on washboard. At first they were called the Black Jacks, but within days they became the Quarry Men after the local Woolton quarries where they played and in mock honor of their school, Quarry Bank (*see below*).

Aunt Mimi was the least tolerant of all the Beatles' parents, and rehearsals rarely took place here. Even when Lennon was just strumming his guitar, he was banished to the porch, but he did come up with a couple of songs later recorded by the Beatles, including "Please Please Me" and "The One After 909," plus scores of others that never made it, like "Thinking of Linking" and "Winston's Walk." (A 1986 compilation album of outtakes from Lennon's 1974 *Walls and Bridges* album was called *Menlove Avenue*).

It was outside the house on July 15, 1958, that Julia was killed by a car as she crossed the divided highway. A couple of years later, Lennon moved out to live nearer the art school he was attending, and in 1965 Aunt Mimi moved off after being hassled by fans, who used to dig up the front lawn. The new owners had little time for the Beatles and refused to let anyone look around, including Yoko Ono. The house has since changed hands, and plans are now afoot to turn it into a Lennon museum.

The house recently resurfaced in rock mythology when a photo, taken from a Beatles tour bus as it passed the house, was used on the sleeve of Oasis's "Live Forever" single, issued on the 25th anniversary of the release of *Abbey Road*. *"Mendips," 251 Menlove Ave., Woolton.*

PENNY LANE

This legendary Beatles setting is a quiet residential street about a mile west of where John Lennon was raised, leading to a traffic junction (Smithdown Place), where the barber, banker, and "shelter in the middle of a roundabout" mentioned in the song can be found. The barber's, Tony Slavin (11 Smithdown Pl., tel. 0151/733–7171), stands on the curve of Cronton Road and Church Road. The bank is a branch of the TSB at the east of the junction of Heathfield Road and Smithdown Road. As for the "shelter in the middle of the roundabout," it is now a grotty café with an as-expected

Tony Slavin barbershop, 1997

Beatley name—Sgt. Pepper's (36 Smithdown Pl., tel. 0151/733–1818).

The John Lennon song, "In My Life," from *Rubber Soul* begins, "There are places I remember, all my life," but then fails to mention a single landmark. Lennon's original, unrecorded version did, however, mention many local places.

"Penny Lane is one I'm missing" refers to the traffic junction where Penny Lane meets the main Smithdown Road (see above).

"Up Church Road to the clock tower" refers to the 1884 clock tower at the junction of Church Road North and High Street, about a mile north of the Penny Lane roundabout.

"In the circle of the Abbey" is about the upper seats of the Abbey cinema (corner of Church Rd. North and High St. and now a Somerfield supermarket, opposite the Picton Clock Tower), where Lennon spent many hours watching the westerns on Saturday afternoons in the late '40s and early '50s.

"Past the Dutch and St. Columbus" is in memory of the Old Dutch Café (316 Smithdown Rd.) near the Penny Lane junction, an all-night café where Merseybeat bands used to meet. It is now a plumber's, but the windmill sign remains above the awning. St. Columbus, a late Victorian church, is really St. Columba (Smithdown Rd. near Gorsebank Rd.).

"Past the tramsheds with no trams." These were opposite the Old Dutch—now an empty lot.

"To the Dockers' Umbrella that they pulled down" is dedicated to the Docker's Umbrella, an overhead railway with a shelter that looked like an umbrella. It ran the full length of the shore until 1957, when the authorities unfortunately decided that the docks needed a more modern image.

QUARRY BANK GRAMMAR SCHOOL (CALDERSTONES COMMUNITY COMPREHENSIVE SCHOOL)

John Lennon started attending this secondary school in 1952. Quarry Bank was a pretty good school. Two former pupils, Peter Shore and Bill Rogers, went on to become Labour cabinet ministers, but Lennon was no scholar. He was caned for fighting, smoking, and disrupting lessons and labeled a "clown" in reports, with the rider, "this boy is bound to fail." He did, however, spend some of his time constructively, producing a scurrilous rag called *The Daily Howl,* which included caricatures of his teachers and, very unchristianly, of people who were crippled. Lennon left school in July 1957, the month that the Quarry Men played a 6th-form disco. The budding genius somehow managed to fail all his "O" levels, even art, for which he was asked to provide an illustration on the theme of travel and drew a wart-infested hunchback. Nevertheless, headmaster William Pobjoy, who had encouraged his painting, managed to wangle him a place at art school. *Harthill Rd., Calderstones.*

[STRAWBERRY FIELD]

"Strawberry Fields Forever" was named for a children's home, Strawberry Field, which still stands beside this tree-lined road near semirural Woolton Village. John Lennon used to play in the grounds of the home and attend the annual summer fete when he was a kid, and the song tried to capture a feel of hazy summer days. The original Gothic Victorian building has been demolished; only the wrought iron gates bearing the name remain. A Lennon Court wing now exists, and in January 1984 Yoko Ono and son Sean visited. Ono later sent the home a check for £100,000. *Beaconsfield Rd., Woolton, tel. 0151/428–1647.*

[ST. PETER'S CHURCH AND CHURCH HALL]

This lovely Victorian sandstone church played a significant role in the development of the Beatles. In 1956 the Quarry Men played their first gig in the hall opposite the church.

A year later, in July 1957, Lennon first met Paul McCartney, when the Quarry Men played twice at the church summer fete, once in the afternoon in a field by the church, and a few hours later in the hall. For both gigs, the lineup was Lennon, Pete Shotton, Eric Griffiths, Colin Hanton, Rod Davis, and Len Garry. They played skiffle numbers like "Cumberland Gap" and the traditional "Maggie Mae."

After the Quarry Men's second appearance, a lad called Ivan Vaughan, who occasionally played tea-chest bass for them, took his friend Paul McCartney to meet the group, including Lennon, who was impressed that McCartney knew the words to Eddie Cochran's "Twenty Flight Rock" and how to tune a guitar. They got on so well that within weeks Lennon invited McCartney to join the Quarry Men, who returned here to play many times over the next few years.

In 1984 the grave of a local woman named Eleanor Rigby, who died on October 10, 1939, was discovered among the many in the churchyard. McCartney had thought he'd made the name up when he wrote the song. *Church Rd., Woolton.*

Out from Liverpool
Birkenhead

It took a tattooed boy from Birkenhead to really really open her eyes—The Smiths, "What She Said"

Birkenhead is the major neighborhood on the Wirral, an oblong peninsula between the Mersey and the Welsh border. The area is home to the humorous '80s post-punks Half Man Half Biscuit, who plugged into the local obsession with the welfare state by naming their 1985 LP, *Back in the DHSS* (DHSS = Department of Health and Social Security). The best thing about the band was their witty song titles: "Outbreak of Vitas Gerulaitis," "I Love You Because (You Look Like Jim Reeves)." The soccer-mad band once turned down a spot on *The Tube* TV program to watch their local team.

PAUL MCCARTNEY ADDRESS, 1942–43

The McCartneys lived in this stucco semidetached house for a year during World War II, when McCartney senior was making aircraft parts in Knowsley. They soon moved back to Liverpool to escape the air raids, which were worse here than in the city. *92 Broadway Ave., Wallasey.*

TOWER BALLROOM

When it was built at the beginning of the century, the 620-foot New Brighton tower was the highest structure of its kind in

Courtesy of Liverpool Libraries and Information Services, Liverpool Record Office

The New Brighton Tower and Ballroom, circa 1900

Britain and the second highest in Europe after the Eiffel. The tower was demolished in 1921, but the 3,000-capacity ballroom thrived and began putting on rock in the early '60s. In November 1961, the leading Merseybeat groups of the day came together for a mega gig starring the Beatles, Gerry and the Pacemakers, Rory Storm and the Hurricanes, the Remo Four, and many others. The Beatles returned in October 1962 to support Little Richard. In 1969 the ballroom was destroyed in a huge fire and had to be demolished. The site, now an empty lot, affords a great view of Liverpool and the pier head. *Promenade at Victoria Rd., New Brighton.*

Widnes

An industrial town on the Mersey near Liverpool, Widnes is best known in rock terms for its railway station, where Paul Simon supposedly wrote "Homeward Bound."

SPIKE ISLAND

Stone Roses played before 28,000 people at a 1990 gig described as a Woodstock for the baggy generation on this narrow stretch of land between the river and a canal. The event was dogged by organizational and sound problems. Fans had food confiscated at the gate by security men in league with food stallholders. Lots of drugs were available; according to a Jarvis Cocker fan, a couple of guys were walking around asking, "Everybody sorted for E's and whizz?" Hence the name of Pulp's 1995 single, "Sorted for E's and whizz."

WIDNES RAILWAY STATION

A plaque commemorates the fact that Paul Simon began writing "Homeward Bound" while waiting for the milk train at this small station in 1964 after a gig at Liverpool's Windsor Rooms. He finished writing the song a few months later in a grotty apartment in London's East End and then tried unsuccessfully to sell it and the rest of his song catalog to publishers in London's Denmark Street.

Oh Manchester, so much to answer for—The Smiths, "Suffer Little Children"

In contrast to other major European second cities, such as Barcelona, Munich, and Milan, Manchester is a mess. Nevertheless, the city has a youthful air, provided by the nation's highest concentration of students, as well as a healthy nightlife scene. It has contributed more to British rock than any other city apart from London, having spawned such bands as the Buzzcocks, Magazine, the Fall, Joy Division, New Order, the Smiths, James, the Stone Roses, Happy Mondays, and Oasis.

Although most of its glory rests in the post-punk era, Manchester had a lively local scene as far back as the early '60s, when skiffle mutated into beat and Manchester had more actively gigging groups than Liverpool. When the Beatles emerged, Liverpool overtook Manchester as the hippest city in the North, but there was plenty of noise from this part of Lancashire. The Hollies racked up 24 Top-30 entries over the next 10 years, more than any other band. Following in their commercial wake were Herman's Hermits, Freddie and the Dreamers, and Wayne Fontana and the Mindbenders.

In the early '70s a lively local club scene was flattened by developers who organized the destruction of much of downtown, replacing it with an awful mall, the Arndale Centre. Punk revitalized the dormant Manchester rock scene in the mid-'70s. An early and much-celebrated summer 1976 gig by the Sex Pistols in the Free Trade Hall inspired the formation of scores of guitar-thrash punk bands, all with suitably in-your-face names like Slaughter and the Dogs, Ed Banger and the Nosebleeds, the Drones, and the Worst. They were quickly eclipsed by a handful of interesting new acts—the Buzzcocks, the Fall, and Warsaw (later Joy Division).

Around these bands a thriving cottage industry of fanzines, promoters, agents, and record labels grew up. The labels included New Hormones, which released the Buzzcocks' "Spiral Scratch" EP, punk's biggest-selling 7-inch by the end of the decade; Rabid, which gave the world John Cooper Clarke; and most successful of all, Factory, which released Joy Division.

Along with New Order, the mid-'80s belonged to the Smiths, who in their five-year career captured the gloominess of living in Manchester better and more sympathetically than anyone else. Soon after the Smiths' split in 1987, the rock press discovered a new sound and dubbed it Madchester. The scene was led by the psychedelic-influenced guitar sounds of the Stone Roses and Happy Mondays (whose 1988 "Madchester Rave On" EP supplied the movement with its name) and owed a debt to dance music, warehouse raves, and Ecstasy. When the hub of the Madchester scene, the Hacienda Club, was temporarily closed down in early 1991 after a series of gun- and drug-related incidents, the boom ended.

The early '90s saw Manchester acts dominate the international charts, but not in rock. The rock & roll sound re-emerged with Oasis, who spotted a niche in the market for a band with coarse northern accents playing good old-fashioned guitar rock. From 1993 to 1995 they rose from the obscurity of a boring south Manchester suburb to stadium status.

The latest wave of Manchester hopefuls—the teenage Northern Uproar, who are having problems shaking off Oasis-clone accusations; the trashy rockabilly punkers Gold

221

The Smiths' Morrissey

Coen Rees

Blade; Island Signings; Puressence; and the bands signed to ex-New Order manager Rob Gretton's Manchester Records—may or may not come up with a more inspired legacy. The future could lie more in the hands of the dance crossover outfits, led by Lamb and Audioweb.

GEOGRAPHICAL NOTES

The center of surprisingly small downtown Manchester is hard to pinpoint. Albert Square is dominated by the Town Hall, from near where Oxford Street runs south toward the universities; just off Oxford Street, the biggest cluster of clubs and café-bars in the city lines Whitworth Street West. Spanning out from Piccadilly Gardens, little more than a big open-plan bus stop, is Bohemia central, Oldham Street, and the main shopping strip of Market Street. On the northeast edge of downtown stands the dilapidated district around Victoria station, notable for its empty lots, enlarged by a June 1996 IRA bomb.

For current events try the fortnightly *City Life* listings magazine. Places such as Cornerhouse Cinema, the stalls in Afflecks Palace, and record stores are usually awash with posters and flyers.

Albert Square and Oxford Street

I put your statue up in Albert Square—The Distractions, "Time Goes By So Slow"

The area around Albert Square, the civic heart of Manchester, is dominated by the Town Hall, Britain's largest but certainly not best public library, and an art gallery full of pre-Raphaelite paintings created elsewhere. On the south side is Oxford Street, which after a few blocks of theaters, fast-food joints, and bars becomes Oxford Road (*see below*), which cuts through the two main university campuses.

EATINGDRINKINGDANCINGSHOPPINGPLAYINGSLEEPING

In late 1996 a branch of Bill Wyman's restaurant, **STICKY FINGERS** (2 St. Mary's St., tel. 0161/835–4141), opened, decked out with some 300 items of predominantly Stones memorabilia. The best club around here is **42ND ST.** (2 Bootle St., tel. 0161/831–7108), which plays lots of indie, psychedelic, and retro. At Oxford Road station you can find the **PALACE THEATRE** (Oxford St. at Whitworth St., tel. 0161/242–2503), whose program is mostly lowbrow productions, though it does have occasional MOR concerts. Diagonally opposite is **CORNERHOUSE** (70 Oxford St., tel. 0161/228–2463), a worthy arts center with three screens, galleries, a café, plus a bar. The packed **LASS O' GOWRIE** pub (36 Charles St., tel. 0161/273–6932) serves beer brewed downstairs. The only long-running nightclub along this strip, Rockworld (*see* Rafters, *below*) has been playing metal for the past two decades.

POWERCUTS (3 Chepstow St., tel. 0161/228–0473), where Morrissey used to work, has bin after bin of discounted new vinyl and CDs.

A1 MUSIC CENTRE

One day in 1977 Barry Adamson wandered into this music store to buy a string for a bass guitar he had never played. He met Howard Devoto and joined Magazine the next day. Adamson made rapid progress on the instrument and when Magazine broke up in 1981, he went on to play with the Birthday Party and then with Nick Cave and the Bad Seeds until he was offered a solo deal by Mute in 1987. Since then he has released a handful of albums and has worked on several movie scores, including *Gas Food Lodging*, a collaboration with J Mascis of Dinosaur Jr. *1 New Wakefield St., tel. 0161/236–0340.*

BBC

The BBC's northern outpost churns out few programs. Its best-remembered contemporary music offering was The Oxford Roadshow, broadcast in the '80s as a more teen-oriented version of ITV's The Tube (an influential early-'80s rock TV program).

When a then-unknown Oasis turned up to make their debut radio appearance here in 1994, Liam Gallagher cockily made fun of guest host New Order bassist Peter Hook's leather trousers. He so annoyed Hook that he was banned from New Order's nightclub, the Hacienda. *Oxford Rd. at Charles St., tel. 0161/200–2020.*

[FREE TRADE HALL]

Built as a tribute to the free trade system that gave Manchester its 19th-century wealth, the hall was the setting for the two Sex Pistols gigs in July 1976 that practically reinvented Manchester's music scene. Both gigs took place in the tiny Lesser Free Trade Hall above the main auditorium. The Pistols' first northern outing was billed in the local listings magazine with the warning "Eat your heart out on a plastic tray if you miss them." At the Pistols' second gig, they debuted "Anarchy in the U.K." Although barely a hundred people watched these two shows, many more later claimed attendance. Those who formed bands following the shows include Ian Curtis, Peter Hook, Bernard Sumner, Mick Hucknall, and Morrissey (*see* Virgin, *below*).

Both Pistols gigs were organized by Buzzcocks Pete Shelley and Howard Devoto, whose band was meant to open for the Pistols at the first gig but had to pull out when they couldn't find a drummer. Instead, Shelley staffed the door for the night and met the group's next bassist, Steve Diggle, who turned up to meet another band and was mistakenly introduced to him. The Buzzcocks did, however, get their act together for the second Pistols gig, as did Slaughter and the Dogs.

The Free Trade Hall had been putting on non-classical concerts in the main auditorium since 1958, when Muddy Waters brought over a raucous electric blues backing band.

The anachronistic Manchester audience, wanting the solo acoustic stuff, booed. Eight years later, on May 17, 1966, an FTH audience booed again, this time at Bob Dylan, who was also accompanied by a rock band. Dylan was heckled throughout. One fan shouted "Go play with the Rolling Stones...we don't need you, we've got the Animals"; another bellowed "Judas" during a quiet moment, as eerily captured on the bootleg, *In 1966 There Was*. One of Dylan's songs that night, a rocked-up "I Don't Believe You," was introduced with the explanation, "It used to go like that, now it goes like this." Even those who admired Dylan's new direction gave him grief on account of the awful sound—all that could be heard were the vocals and organ.

The hall continued to put on rock spasmodically until the '90s. Tyrannosaurus Rex began their first tour here on February 22, 1969, David Bowie opening the show with a one-man mime about a Tibetan priest. Genesis recorded part of their 1973 *Genesis Live* album at the FTH, and the north Manchester band the Chameleons recorded a live album, *Free Trade Rehearsal,* here 20 years later.

For more than a hundred years the hall was home to Manchester's Hallé orchestra, for whom the Passage's Dick Witts played percussion in the '70s. These days the orchestra is conducted by Kent Nagano, who in the past has conducted orchestral work by Frank Zappa. The Free Trade Hall is currently being converted into a hotel. *Peter St. at Southmill St., tel. 0161/834–1712.*

G - M E X

In 1986 the cavernous glass-roofed G-Mex, built as a railway terminus and now used as an exhibition hall, staged The 10th Summer festival, a celebration of punk's explosion in 1976. It featured Pete Shelley, A Certain Ratio, the Fall, New Order, and the Smiths, who used a photo of the crowd taken from the stage for the gatefold sleeve of their live album, *Rank.*

At the height of the Madchester phase, hometown gigs by 808 State, New Order, James, and Happy Mondays turned the place into heaving parties. The Wonderstuff recorded their 1991 *Live in Manchester* album here. U2, Public Enemy, Big Audio Dynamite II, and Kraftwerk (making a rare stage appearance) played a Greenpeace benefit in 1992 originally scheduled for the beach next to the Sellafield nuclear plant (*see* Lancashire Towns, *above*).

For Morrissey, G-Mex has macabre connotations: It was by the station milk bar in 1965 that moors murderer Ian Brady picked up his last victim, part of a killing spree that inspired the Smiths' requiem for the victims, "Suffer Little Children." Another Smiths song, "William It Was Really Nothing," was based on the John Schlesinger movie *Billy Liar,* the closing scene of which was shot here. Now that the Nynex Arena has opened on the other side of town, bands no longer have to put up with the hall and its terrible acoustics. *Windmill St., tel. 0161/832–9000.*

OASIS CLUB

The Oasis claimed to be "the North's top teenage rendezvous" when it reopened after a stint as the 2Js Jazz Club in 1961. Along with the Twisted Wheel, it was Manchester's leading early-'60s beat club. When the Beatles played their second Manchester gig here in February 1962, they were optimistically described as "Polydor recording stars." The following night, the Hollies played their first gig under that name, having changed it from the Deltas in honor of the club's Christmas decorations. The Oasis closed a few years later and the building was later demolished to make way for new council offices. *45–47 Lloyd St.*

RAFTERS (JILLY'S ROCKWORLD)

Joy Division (when they were still known as Warsaw) played their second-ever gig in this basement club in 1977, supporting the now-forgotten punk outfit Fast Breeder. The headliners allowed Warsaw to go on last—at one in the morning—when nearly everyone had gone home. Ian Curtis, never too happy at the best of times, began picking fights with the handful of remaining punters. In April 1978 when two London indies looking to sign the best of the new wave Manchester bands put on the "Stiff/Chiswick Challenge," Warsaw returned as Joy Division but bombed after going on at 3 AM. Nevertheless, that night Curtis introduced himself to Granada TV's Tony Wilson. His unusual chat-up line was, "You're a bastard. You're a cunt."—Curtis was annoyed with Wilson for not putting Joy Division on his *So It Goes* TV show. Wilson promptly booked them for a show and soon after signed them to his new Factory label. The club is now a metal haven, Jilly's Rockworld. *65 A Oxford Rd., tel. 0161/236–9971.*

THE TWISTED WHEEL

The main rival to the Oasis Club as Manchester's leading beat-era venue, the Twisted Wheel took over the premises of the beatniky Left Wing Coffee Bar, whose house band, Dean West and the Hellions, became Herman's Hermits. On the Twisted Wheel's opening night, the Graham Bond Quartet and the Spencer Davis Group played from midnight till dawn. Others who played included the Yardbirds, Rod Stuart (sic), and John Mayall. Tony Hicks landed the job as lead guitarist of the Hollies after an audition here. Cream made their world debut here on July 2, 1966, the night before their "official" debut in Windsor. They deliberately chose Manchester to get away from London's hype, but it backfired when the audience booed the band's long jams and heavy sound.

Cops, stationed just round the corner from the club, used to like turning up to flex their muscles and make the line stand in the gutter. In 1967 they busted the place for letting in nonmembers—like Jimi Hendrix, who dropped in one night after playing a gig elsewhere in the city. The whole operation was set up to find drugs; as Hendrix left to get into a car, plainclothes cops threw him against the railings of Bootle Street Police Station (known locally as Brutal Street) and searched him.

The Twisted Wheel was one of the first clubs in the United Kingdom to regularly put on all-nighters and became a leading northern soul spot in the early '70s. The building was demolished shortly thereafter to create a drab piazza with a statue of Abraham Lincoln in it. *26 Brazennose St.*

YANKS (POWERCUTS)

Morrissey's short but unhappy stint working in this discount record store in February 1979 inspired the line, "I was looking for a job and then I found a job," in "Heaven Knows I'm Miserable Now." Yanks, which has since expanded and changed its name to Powercuts, occupies a large and very cold warehouse basement area. It's an excellent place for bargains, especially in the metal/thrash racks. *3 Chepstow St., tel. 0161/228–0473.*

Whitworth Street West and Castlefield

Whitworth Street West has been Manchester's main nightlife neighborhood since the Hacienda set up shop in 1982. Running parallel to Whitworth Street West on the Hacienda side of the street is the Rochdale Canal. Just beyond the junction of Whitworth Street West and Deansgate, the canal empties into the Castlefield Basin, one of Britain's first industrial estates. The area has now been gentrified and turned into expensive waterside apartments, offices, and bars. One local resident is former Take That member Jason Orange, accounting for the posse of teenage girls on permanent guard outside one of the blocks.

EATING DRINKING DANCING SHOPPING PLAYING SLEEPING

Manchester's highest concentration of clubs inhabits the once-awful Whitworth Street West, jutting off from Oxford Street at the Cornerhouse complex (*see* Albert Square and Oxford Street, *above*). **THE GREEN ROOM** (54 Whitworth St. W, tel. 0161/236–1677) puts on fringe theater and has a decent hangout café. The **RITZ** (Whitworth St. W. opposite Station Approach, tel. 0161/236–4355) is an old ballroom that mostly has awful mainstream discos, but the same people have been running its Monday alternative night since the late '70s. The sweaty **BRICKHOUSE** (66 Whitworth St. W, tel. 0161/236–4418) is one of the few Manchester clubs that play guitar-based sounds. The **VENUE** (15 Whitworth St. W, tel. 0161/236–0026) used to put on Smiths-only discos after the annual band convention and has a fluctuating program. The big place here is the **HACIENDA** (*see below*), which more or less created the Madchester/rave scene of the late '80s and still pulls the crowds.

The area is dotted with hip bars, some of which put on live music. The **CANAL CAFE BAR** (19 Whitworth St. W, tel. 0161/237–1819) and **ATLAS** (376 Deansgate, tel. 0161/834–2124), built into a former auto showroom and always packed with a pre-club crowd, are the best.

Castlefield has two great bars: **DUKE'S 92** (end of Castle St., tel. 0161/839–8646) is utterly relaxing; and **BARCA** (Catalan Sq., tel. 0161/839–7099), owned by Simply Red's Mick Hucknall, is nicely designed and has decent tapas. The best place to eat around here is the Mediterranean-flavored **DIMITRI'S** (corner Tonman St. and Campfield Ave. Arcade, tel. 0161/839–3319), where there are always heaps of flyers advertising what's on.

[BOARDWALK]

Manchester's best small venue—a former school building turned rehearsal rooms where Joy Division practiced in the late '70s—opened for gigs in 1986 and has helped break James, the Happy Mondays, the Charlatans, Inspiral Carpets, and Oasis, who played their first gig under that name on August 18, 1991, going on stage here between the Catchmen and Sweet Jesus. Oasis played several times over the next few months, but Noel Gallagher, then a roadie for Inspiral Carpets, wasn't in the group. After one gig, the band asked Noel what he thought about the show. When he replied that it was the worst gig he'd ever seen, Oasis suggested he manage them. But Noel chose a more hands-on role: lead guitarist and band leader. To prove his worth, he strummed and sang a song he'd written, "Live Forever." The rest of the band agreed to his demands immediately.

Rob Carter

Tim Burgess of the Charlatans, 1992

The new Oasis lineup, with Noel alongside brother Liam, made its debut at the Board-walk on October 19, 1992, for an audience barely numbering 20. The group played four songs, including what became "Columbia" and the wishful "Rock & Roll Star," which brought a few laughs. Oasis rehearsed in the basement almost daily in 1992 and 1993.

Others who have used the venue's popular rehearsal rooms include James, Swing Out Sis-ter, and the Railway Children. Although the club's capacity is only 440, the Boardwalk has attracted many big indie names, including (London) Suede, Sonic Youth, Big Black, Dodgy, the Bluetones, the Afghan Whigs, and Green Day. *Little Peter St., tel. 0161/228–3555.*

TONIGHT I'M A GAS BOARD FITTER

When Noel Gallagher played with Oasis for the first time, in 1992, he was still working for British Gas on the same street as the club. A year earlier, a steel cap had fallen off a pipe and landed on his foot. Gallagher was out on disability for weeks; when he came back, he was given a less demanding job handing out equipment to the other workers, allowing him time to practice guitar skills.

FACTORY TOO

After the Factory label went into bankruptcy in 1992, the revamped Factory Too was set up in 1994. Early signings included Durutti Column (veterans of the old label) and indie guitar hopefuls Hopper, from London. The cataloging policy is still willfully bizarre, with hats and rucksacks being given catalog numbers alongside records. *2–4 Little Peter St., tel. 0161/834–4440.*

GRANADA STUDIOS AND CORONATION STREET

Britain's major independent TV company has put on one or two watchable rock shows, particularly *So It Goes* in the late '70s, presented by Granada reporter Tony Wilson, who went on to found Factory Records. *So It Goes* gave many punk bands, including Joy Division, their first northern TV exposure. After Wilson put on a few punks in bondage gear, Granada executives told him, "If one more bloke comes on with a horse's tail coming out of his arse, you're fired." When the Pistols came on set sporting swastikas, the company's Jewish founder and chairman Sidney Bernstein, watching on in-house monitors, went apoplectic and sent an order for the group to take them off, which they did.

Photos for two important record sleeves were shot on the Granada studios lot. After Iggy Pop performed in 1977, he was photographed for a session used on the cover of *Lust for Life*; 12 years later, a shot of the Stone Roses playing here turned up on the back cover of their debut album. *Quay St. at Atherton St., tel. 0161/832–7211.*

[HACIENDA]

The Hacienda, now owned by New Order, revolutionized nightclubbing in Britain. It was at the center of the late-'80s Madchester/rave scene that broke bands like Happy Mondays and the Stone Roses. Founded by Factory Records, the Hacienda opened in May 1982. The building, which had been a yachting showroom, was redesigned by Ben Kelly, who rammed home the "Factory" message by covering the I-beams with yellow-and-black safety stripes. Outside, the only clue to its identity was a Fac 51 name plate.

At first the club put on bland indie stuff, with Aztec Camera and ABC dominating the turntable. Thanks to the influence of local funk clubs, particularly Legend, it switched in 1983 when Mike Pickering (now of M People) began spinning electro-funk, like the Peech Boys and Afrika Bambaataa, back-to-back with early Pink Floyd and Can. They booked the Smiths for their third-ever gig in February 1983, a barely-known Madonna in 1984, and a rare show by Grandmaster Flash the same year.

Jon Shard/Courtesy of The Hacienda

The Hacienda

By the end of the decade, it was the most hyped nightclub on the planet—even featured on the cover of *Newsweek*—and "Madchester" bands like Factory's own Happy Mondays claimed the club as inspiration. In January 1991 police closed the club when a 16-year-old died after taking Ecstasy and a patron pulled a machine gun when told to remove drugs from the premises. The closure lost Factory £250,000, but, though the label soon went bust, the club reopened, albeit with airport-style security. Since then, it has become virtually indistinguishable from the other Manchester clubs playing house, techno, and garage. *11–13 Whitworth St. W, tel. 0161/236–5051.*

"THE HACIENDA MUST BE BUILT"

Factory Records took the club's name from the line, "the Hacienda must be built," in the obscure left-wing tome, *The Situationist International Handbook.* The club wasn't too popular with all Factory workers. Joy Division producer Martin Hannett, who was in dispute with Factory at the time, tried unsuccessfully to sue to prevent the company from running the club only a few days before it was due to open. The place has its own Factory Records label catalog number, Fac 51. Other nondisc Factory output was numbered in this way to stop buffs' owning the entire catalog. Fans got their own back by ripping off the name plate. When the Hacienda opened in 1982, New Order wanted it to be a club "where you could get in dressed as you liked," as at the time Manchester was full of dives that required "smart dress only." By the end of the '80s, though, everyone turned up in identical baggy jeans, smiley T-shirts, and hooded tops.

The Smiths played a triumphant gig in 1984, a few hours after making their Top of the Pops debut, traveling up from London by train to find 1,000 fans inside the club and 2,000 locked outside. "Handsome Devil," the B-side of their debut single "Hand in Glove" was recorded live at an earlier Smiths gig when the band filled the place with flowers "to warm up the architecture."

Happy Mondays played in aid of victims of the Hillsborough stadium disaster in May 1989. Also at a 1989 gig, Primal Scream revealed their new line-up, the one that recorded the *Screamedelica* album, *NME*'s album of 1991. Evan Dando joined first-wave U.K. psychedelic band the Creation on stage in August 1994.

Videos shot here include the Fall's *Tempo House* and Gun Club's *Live at the Hacienda* (both 1983).

THE RITZ

I could hear them playing all the hits at that mecca of modern dance, the Ritz—John Cooper Clarke, "Salome Maloney"

The Smiths made their live debut at this ballroom in October 1982, supporting Blue Rondo à la Turk with a set that featured, "The Hand That Rocks the Cradle," "Suffer Little Children," "Handsome Devil," and the unrecorded cover, "I Want a Boyfriend for My Birthday." The gig was promoted by hairdresser Andrew Berry, lead singer of the Weeds and later the subject of the Morrissey song, "Hairdresser on Fire." On stage with the Smiths was James Maker (later of Raymonde), whom a nervous Morrissey had invited up to take the spotlight away from him. Maker spent the gig dancing around in stilettoes alongside the singer. Morrissey had performed here previously with the nerdy Manchester punk band the Nosebleeds, who supported Magazine in May 1978.

The Ritz is one of Manchester's few surviving pre-war ballrooms, complete with polished floor, chandeliers, and tasteless wallpaper. It used to be dominated by the big-haired, matching miniskirt and handbag crowd but now has indie and student nights. John Cooper Clarke sent up the place as the "Mecca of the modern dance" on his uproarious 1978 number "Salome Maloney." *Whitworth St. W, opposite Station Approach, tel. 0161/236–4355.*

PETE WATERMAN'S STUDIO/ THE CHURCH

Veteran northern soul DJ and Kylie Minogue mentor Pete Waterman, the man behind the PWL label, has built a studio in this former church. Here he cranks out chart fodder like Loveland's "Let the Music Lift You Up," *Music Week*'s top dance number of 1994, as well as club sounds for the Waterman-owned Eastern Bloc record label. *380 Deansgate, tel. 0161/834–2791.*

Piccadilly and Oldham Street

Queen Victoria is a large black slug in Piccadilly, Manchester—The Fall, "City Hobgoblins"

Pete Waterman's studio

Piccadilly is the name of the city's main rail terminus, its main bus station, and the area around Piccadilly Gardens, a huge square enclosing a few lawns and flower beds. Although it's one of Manchester's two main centers (along with Albert Square), it is not a pretty part of town.

Two very different kinds of shopping streets run off Piccadilly: pedestrianized Market Street has all the chains; scruffy Oldham Street, which became the retail and hangout center of the Madchester period, is still the place to pick up alternative items and secondhand records.

Over on the west side of Piccadilly is the Village, whose gay scene rivals that of London's Soho. Although there are plenty of bars and clubs, it is still Manchester's major, and very seedy, red-light district. Nearby, Chinatown has sprung up since the early 1980s along George and Faulkner streets, where there are scores of restaurants.

EATINGDRINKINGDANCINGSHOPPINGPLAYINGSLEEPING

At the eastern edge of Piccadilly Gardens on Newton Street is the **ROADHOUSE** (*see below*), a small venue where the Fall like to play. Underneath Piccadilly rail station, the hulking, gloomy **STAR AND GARTER PUB** (18 Fairfield St., tel. 0161/273–6726) presents up-and-coming bands and hosts a tri-monthly Smiths/Morrissey night packed out with quiffed, Levi'd Mozzer clones. The smart and fashionable **HOME** (Ducie House, Ducie St., tel. 0161/237–3495), based in a former clothing warehouse, plays mostly house. A former Oasis hangout, **TEN** (10 Tariff St., tel. 0161/229–2238) doubles as a trendy daytime café and nighttime club, with a wide range of different sounds from rock to Latin. On the south side of the Village, the **PARADISE FACTORY** (114–116 Princess St., tel. 0161/228–2966) was Factory Records' last resting place; it's now a predominantly gay club pumping out hi-NRG sounds.

DRY 201 (*see below*) is the place that kicked off the designer-bar fetish in Manchester. Next door, the Continental-style **NIGHT AND DAY CAFÉ** (26 Oldham St., tel. 0161/236–4597) stays open till 2 AM and puts on a cool mix of rock bands, jazz, ambient, and spoken word. Another popular joint is the dark and minimalist **ISOBAR** (Afflecks Arcade off Oldham St., tel. 0161/839–1989). **AFFLECKS PALACE** (*see below*) has several cafés; the best one is on the top floor. In the Village area, **MANTO'S** (46 Canal St., tel. 0161/236–2667), a stylish café with a post-industrial mood, blasts dance music and displays works by local artists and photographers. In the basement of the **COLISEUM** (*see below*) is the inevitable **OASIS CAFE,** where for certain of their low-standard meals (called Digsy's Dinners) "you get a roll with it." In Chinatown, try the no-frills **WONG CHU** (63 Faulkner St., tel. 0161/236–2346).

The **COLISEUM** (Church St. at Joiner St.) is the home of stalls where the range of goods for sale is similar to what you might find at Afflecks (see Afflecks Palace, below), but veers more toward New Age ideals with a proliferation of head shops and tarot readers. Among Manchester's best record stores is **EASTERN BLOC** (66 Oldham St., tel. 0161/236–4300), once owned by 808 State, which sells mainly dance albums. **VINYL EXCHANGE** (18 Oldham St., tel. 0161/228–1122) is the city's biggest used-records dealer. **M1 MUSIC** (16 Oldham St., tel. 0161/236–5585) is a smaller secondhand outlet. Just off Market Street is the indie specialist **PICCADILLY RECORDS** (5–7 Brown St., tel. 0161/839–8008), which has good rarities, fanzines, and T-shirts. Two big chains, **HMV** and **OUR PRICE** both have sizable branches on Market Street itself. Fifty yards farther along, **GOLDMINE RECORDS** (8 Shambles Sq., tel. 0161/839–3616) has a major collection of oldie 45s, including a huge selection of Northern Soul.

[AFFLECKS PALACE]

This enormous covered clothes bazaar, which takes up every inch of a four-story Victorian warehouse, has been at the center of the city's alternative scene for more than 10 years. Afflecks stalls sell pretty funky gear; you can also get vinyl obscurities, jewelry, or an absurdly fashionable haircut. *52 Church St., tel. 0161/834–2039.*

[DRY 201]

Manchester's longest-running designer bar was the first in the North to challenge the traditional heads-down-no-nonsense-mindless-drinking attitude. It paved the way for the scores of well-appointed continental-style drinking places that can now be found all around the city serving food from the rest of Europe. Based in a former furniture store, Dry was opened by Factory Records in July 1989 as a daytime outlet for the Hacienda crowd—it even has its own Factory Records catalog number, 201—and was designed by Ben Kelly, who had given the Hacienda its industrial look. Kelly gave it a decor that is part '50s school dining hall (with Formica-topped tables and bottom-breaking chairs) and part '80s high-tech, with lots of tasty wood, marble, and steel and a 25-yard bar, the longest in town.

Following Factory's early-'90s demise, the label's top band, New Order, bought Dry. In 1992 Happy Mondays singer Shaun Ryder smashed up the place after reading a newspaper article that alleged he had been a rent boy. Oasis's Liam Gallagher was thrown out as early as 7 PM one night in 1995 when, after downing some double gin-and-tonics, he went supersonic and insulted a woman, whose boyfriend then decked him. Liam and friends threw some ashtrays and things around and were bundled out. The Oasis camp later denied the incident had happened and claimed Liam had been elsewhere.

Dry has inevitably suffered from the competition—so many places have ripped off its look, it's hard to believe how revolutionary it was back in '89. The crowd is pretty mixed, with plenty of suntans and yobbish types among the students and posers. During the day, decent tapas are served in the eating area; at night, hard techno blasts out over the speakers. *28 Oldham St., tel. 0161/236–5920.*

EASTERN BLOC, 1990–PRESENT

808 State started in this store when it was Earwig, a cooperatively owned specialist dance/techno record store within Afflecks Palace market, directly opposite where it now stands. One of the store's partners, Martin Price, shop regular Graham Massey, a recording engineer, and the local hip-hop duo the Spinmasters (Darren Partington and Andrew Barker), discovered that they shared a mutual admiration of one another's hi-fi equipment. They named the band 808 State after a drum machine. In 1986 the store, by then called Eastern Bloc, was taken to court for displaying the cover of Flux of Pink Indians' *The Fucking Cunts Treat Us Like Pricks,* but this only gave the place more kudos. In 1990 the store moved out of Afflecks Palace. Pop impresario Pete Waterman, who introduced a more cosmopolitan stocking policy, bought the place in 1993; for years, the store had sold nothing on a major label. There is also now an Eastern Bloc record label, which has scored chart hits with dance numbers from Atlantic Ocean and Loveland. *66 Oldham St., tel. 0161/236–4300.*

FACTORY RECORDS HEADQUARTERS (PARADISE FACTORY)

Now one of Manchester's swishest nightclubs, this building was Factory Records' headquarters in the early '90s. Ben Kelly, who designed the Hacienda and Dry 201, was again brought in to make the place look chic. One of his embellishments was a boardroom table that hung from the ceiling—until Happy Mondays sat on it. But the cost of buying the building, a former warehouse, only hastened Factory's £2 million bankruptcy in 1992. Other factors in the label's demise included the spiraling costs and late release of the Happy Mondays *Yes Please!* album and the temporary closure of the Hacienda club the previous year. Once Factory was declared bankrupt, the staff threw a massive party and wrecked much of Kelly's expensive work. Soon after, the people who own the nearby Manto's bought the building and turned it into the Paradise Factory nightclub. The place has a mainly gay clientele, and there's also now a Paradise Factory (gay) record label called Out on Vinyl. *112–116 Princess St., tel. 0161/273–5422.*

Courtesy of The Paradise Factory

Crowd control at the Paradise Factory

MANCHESTER COLLEGE OF COMMERCE
(MANCHESTER METROPOLITAN UNIVERSITY)

Pink Floyd recorded parts of the *Ummagumma* album here in May 1969. The LP's strange name is wartime Cambridgeshire slang for sex. *Aytoun St., tel. 0161/247–2000.*

PICCADILLY GARDENS

In what was Manchester's first rock news story, "high-spirited rhythm-crazed young-sters," as *Melody Maker* put it, ran amok and trampled flower beds after seeing the *Rock Around the Clock* movie in 1955. The Gardens' multitudinous pigeons, whose droppings are omnipresent, inspired James's 1988 single, "What For." Three years later the group played a triumphant gig on the roof of Piccadilly Radio overlooking the place.

ROADHOUSE

This recently opened small venue gave the local teenager band Northern Uproar a res-idency in September 1995. The place drew A&R men, and the band signed to Heavenly Records. The Fall launched their *Light User Syndrome* album here in June 1996. As well as local acts, the Roadhouse also pulls in some good touring bands, including some Americans on their first tour of the United Kingdom. *8 Newton St., tel. 0161/237–9789.*

"SPIRAL SCRATCH" COVER

The Buzzcocks are pictured stand-ing by the Duke of Wellington's statue on Piccadilly on the cover of their debut recording, 1977's "Spiral Scratch" EP. *Piccadilly Gardens opposite Lever St.*

The Buzzcocks' Spiral Scratch EP, 1976

STONE ROSES DEBUT

In summer 1984 the Stone Roses made their U.K. debut in one of the many disused railway arches on Fairfield Street in the shadow of Piccadilly station. They had been known as English Rose—after the Jam song—but renamed them-selves the Stone Roses (for Sarah Gainham's 1959 cold-war spy thriller). Over the next few years, railway arches all over Manchester were graffiti'd with the band's name as they became one of the city's staple giggers. Their big breakthrough in 1988–89 coin-cided with the Hacienda/rave/Madchester boom; the Roses, who were then indie and music press darlings, quickly added funky wah-wah guitar to their psychedelic sound. The band then signed a multimillion dollar deal with Geffen Records but took six years to record their second album, by which time no one was interested. *Fairfield St.*

VIRGIN RECORDS, 1975–79

When Peter Hook and Bernard Sumner posted an ad in Manchester's first Virgin branch store in 1977, looking for a singer for their group Warsaw, they were answered by Ian Curtis. Hook and Sumner vaguely knew Curtis from local punk gigs and gave him the job. Warsaw soon became Joy Division. It was also at the Lever Street branch in 1977 that fellow New York Dolls fan Phil Fletcher approached Morrissey, setting off a train of events that led to the formation of the Smiths. The store moved in 1979 and a stationery shop currently occupies the site. *9 Lever St.*

VIRGIN RECORDS STORE (OUR PRICE RECORDS)

In 1979 Virgin moved to this much bigger two-floor space on pedestrianized Market Street. The Freshies immortalized the place the same year with the power-poppy, "I'm in Love With the Girl on the Manchester Virgin Megastore Checkout Desk." Soon after, the Freshies' Chris Sievey re-emerged as Manchester's village idiot comic pop star Frank Sidebottom. It became Our Price Records in the late '80s. The site was near the center of a massive IRA bomb explosion in summer 1996. *Market St. at Cross St.*

Victoria Station and Around

Victoria Station, a sorry-looking but once-grand railway terminus, has two ugly neighbors. On one side stands the Nynex Arena (9 St. James Sq., tel. 0161/930–8000), a hideous monstrosity that is also Europe's largest indoor arena. Its track record of concerts seems more concerned with acts like Take That and Neil Diamond than rock. A couple of hundred yards to the other side of Victoria is a corner of the even larger and more awful-looking Arndale Centre, until recently Europe's largest mall, partly destroyed by an IRA bomb in 1996. Locals call it "Europe's biggest toilet" on account of its tiny yellow tiles.

EATINGDRINKINGDANCINGSHOPPINGPLAYINGSLEEPING

One of the few small clubs that survived Arndalization was **BAND ON THE WALL** (25 Swan St., tel. 0161/832–6625), a steamy, sweltering venue based in an old pub that's been promoting live music since 1975. It's best known for jazz, blues, and roots, with occasional biggish names—Mica Paris, Dirty Dozen Brass Band—passing through.

One notable business that survived the bomb is **JOE BLOGGS** (18–24 Bury New Rd.), a clothing firm that made its name in the Madchester era supplying flared pants and baggy clothing to music-minded Mancunians.

THE BEACH CLUB/OOZIT'S

New Order made their debut at this club in July 1980, supporting A Certain Ratio. The now-demolished venue was known as Oozit's but was called the Beach Club on Wednesday nights when *Eraserhead* and other avant-garde movies would also be shown. On their first full British tour, U2 played here in June 1980 supporting Fashion. New Order sang about the place on their breakthrough single, 1083's "Blue Monday," the B-side of which they called "The Beach." The site, on a small, flattened street, is now an empty lot, and the area, one of the most vicious in Manchester when the streets had buildings on them, has now largely disappeared. *Newgate St.*

STRANGEWAYS PRISON

The Smiths named what became their farewell album, *Strangeways Here We Come,* for this imposing and overcrowded Victorian jail, although no Smiths members had any connection with the place. In August 1964 John Walby, alias Gwynne Evans, became the last person to be hanged in Britain (at the same time as Peter Allen was hanged at Liverpool's Walton prison). Walby was the uncle of Martin Hannett, who went on to produce Joy Division's early stuff. *Sherborne St.*

STEPHEN STREET

The Smiths' decision to use Stephen Street as producer for *Strangeways Here We Come* was carefully made. In the shadow of the prison, between Lord Street and Carnarvon Street, is a turning called . . . Stephen Street.

The Smiths featured a road sign pointing to various local less-than-exotic destinations on the back cover of *Strangeways Here We Come*. The original sign used in the photo was stolen soon after, but an identical one is now in place; it's just a half-mile away from the prison. *Corporation St. at Munster St.*

East Manchester

Ancoats, the first community east of the city center, is being touted as a coming area where artists are colonizing old warehouses, but it's still considered a dangerous place.

EATING DRINKING DANCING SHOPPING PLAYING SLEEPING

This is probably one part of Manchester that you don't want to wander. Many people take taxis to the pricey **SANKEY'S SOAP** (Jersey St., tel. 0161/950–4230), which deals out fusion and souly house and has some live crossover acts on at weekends.

ELECTRIC CIRCUS

This former cinema was Manchester's leading punk venue, putting on the biggest names of the day: the Sex Pistols, the Clash, the Buzzcocks, XTC, John Cooper Clarke, Penetration, and Johnny Thunder's Heartbreakers. The Pistols, Clash, and Buzzcocks played on the same bill on December 9, 1976, at the height of a nationwide council boycott on the Pistols, following their encounter with Bill Grundy on the Today TV program (*see* Thames TV *in* Central London, King's Cross). That night Ian Curtis met Bernard Sumner (a.k.a Bernard Dicken and occasionally Barney Albrecht) for the first time. Curtis soon joined Sumner's group, Warsaw, whose first gig was also here (May 1977). Their reception was such that it was surprising they ever played a second gig, let alone became Joy Division.

Warsaw became regular Electric Circus giggers, alongside the Buzzcocks, who signed to United Artists after a gig here, plus some Manchester punk bands that failed to outlive the scene—the Prefects, the Drones, and the Worst. They all played the night the venue closed, October 2, 1977 (as captured on the live 10-inch album, *Short Circuit— Live at the Electric Circus*), as did Big in Japan, the Fall, and Magazine (who made their live debut).

The Electric Circus was a hole. Sumner described it as "a dump—damp, freezing and dead scruffy"; the building stood alone among bomb sites in a slummy, dangerous area. When the Pistols played a December 1976 gig, fans queuing to get in were pelted with bottles by local youth. The building has since been demolished and replaced with new houses. *Collyhurst St.*

North Manchester–Salford

I can't get back to Salford the cops have got me marked. Enter the dragon, exit Johnny Clarke—John Cooper Clarke, "Kung-Fu International"

Locally born punk poet John Cooper Clarke (often described in the music press as the Bard of Salford) cheekily proclaims this miserable centerless city, north of the river Irwell, as the "capital of Manchester." But for folk-music poet Ewan MacColl, who settled here in the '20s, Salford was "Dirty Old Town," its most romantic image that of the "gas works...by the old canal." The song was later covered by the Pogues (who have worked with MacColl's daughter Kirsty) on their *Rum, Sodomy and the Lash* album.

The breakup of the old Salford communities, captured in movies like *A Taste of Honey,* obsessed Morrissey in the early days of the Smiths. *A Taste of Honey,* originally a play, was written by Shelagh Delaney, a local who is pictured on the cover of both the compilation *Louder Than Bombs* and the single "Girlfriend in a Coma." The Smiths showed a Salford road sign on the back cover of *Strangeways Here We Come* and posed outside Salford Lads' Club for the inner sleeve of *The Queen Is Dead*.

HIGHER BROUGHTON ASSEMBLY ROOMS

Jimmy Savile began what he claims was the world's first disco in the building's Whiskey A Go Go Ballroom in 1955 simply by doing away with a live band and playing records for dancers. The discos were advertised as "top pops and fun games on the stage with Jimmy Savile, how about that then?" and the ridiculously coiffured Savile (who once presented the Top of the Pops show with his hair dyed tartan) has since made the phrase "how about that, then?" his trademark. The venue, then part of the Rialto cinema and dance hall, is now a pool hall. *300 Great Cheetham St. W, at Bury New Rd., Higher Broughton.*

Courtesy of New Departures

John Cooper Clarke

SALFORD DOCKS

For much of the 20th century the area now known as Salford Quays, 35 miles from the sea, was Britain's third-busiest port, thanks to the Manchester Ship Canal, which linked the city with Liverpool. The Docks closed in the early '80s, shortly after the Fall's Mark E. Smith had worked as a customs clerk for Hoffman La Roche. The group's 1979 "Rowche Rumble" single tells of suburban wives downing pills imported by the company (they had to misspell Roche as Rowche to avoid litigation). A later Fall single, "Cruisers Creek," is about an office party held in the Docks, at the end of which no one is sure whether anyone is still alive. *Off Trafford Rd., Ordsall.*

[SALFORD LADS' CLUB]

The Smiths posed outside this club, at the end of a depressing stretch of terraced houses by the motorway, for the inner sleeve of 1986's album, *The Queen Is Dead*. The club was chosen for two reasons: its address is Coronation Street (though not *the* Coronation Street of TV soap fame), and it was the teenage haunt of actor Albert Finney, a Morrissey icon who, ironically, had recently upset the Smiths by refusing to allow his photo on the cover of the band's "Heaven Knows I'm Miserable Now" single.

Following the release of the album, Smiths devotees started visiting the club to re-enact the photo or daub Smithsonian graffiti on the wall, much to the annoyance of the janitor and the working-class youth who used the dive. The Smiths themselves returned to shoot the video of their "I Started Something I Couldn't Finish" single, in which Morrissey and some bespectacled, bequiffed lookalikes rode bikes through the streets around the club.

Two of the Hollies' founding members, Graham Nash and Allan Clarke, were regular performers at the club's beat nights in the late '50s under the names Ricky and Dane Young. *Coronation St., tel. 0161/767-7946.*

West Manchester–Altrincham

As south Manchester becomes ever shabbier and more studenty, the middle classes cross the Mersey into Altrincham, a pleasant enough place but with next to no cultural amenities. It is where the Vegetarian Society was founded in the 19th century. The organization claimed that membership doubled to 20,000 after the release of the Smiths' *Meat Is Murder* album in 1985, a time when Morrissey lived locally. Morrissey moved out when Smiths fans started camping in his garden.

West Manchester–Stretford

The most famous rock & roll star from this dull stretch of suburbia and industrial estates is Steven Patrick Morrissey, born May 22, 1959, in Park Hospital, Davyhulme. The hospital receives a credit for his stomach scar on the back cover of *Your Arsenal.*

Courtesy of The Vegetarian Society (UK)

> **MORRISSEY**
>
> **ADDRESS 1969–84**

In this ordary-looking semidetached council house, Morrissey—after writing a series of hilarious wannabe-rock-critic letters to the *NME* from here in the mid-70s—formed the

"Parkdale," Vegetarian Society headquarters

Smiths in 1982. The Morrissey family moved here in 1969 when their street in nearby Hulme was demolished. When Morrissey announced to friends in 1982 that he wanted to form a group, Billy Duffy (later to join the Cult) told him of a south Manchester guitarist, Johnny Marr, who was looking to team up with a competent songwriter. Marr was so impressed when Morrissey showed him "Suffer Little Children," an elegy to the victims of the '60s local moors murders that Morrissey had written in the form of a play, that he immediately agreed to form a band—the Smiths, named for the couple who turned in the murderers. *384 Kings Rd., Stretford.*

MORRISSEY'S "IRON BRIDGE"

Above the Metrolink rail line near the house where Morrissey lived is the bridge referred to in the line "under the iron bridge we kissed" from the Smiths' "Still Ill." *Off King's Rd. at Metrolink.*

MORRISSEY'S SCHOOL

The Smiths song, "The Headmaster Ritual," opens with the line, "Belligerent ghouls run Manchester schools," and explains how teachers used a variety of brutal techniques to subjugate their charges. Less than a mile away on Edge Lane are the Turn Moss Playing Fields, where Morrissey was "thwacked on the knees" by gym teachers as described in the same song. *St. Mary's Roman Catholic Secondary School, Renton Rd.*

South Manchester–Around the Universities

South of downtown, Oxford Road cuts through the main campuses of the University of Manchester and the Manchester Metropolitan University, each with an enrollment of more than 12,000. Add the Royal Northern College of Music and the nearby University of Manchester Institute of Science and Technology (UMIST) and you get a very high concentration of students. The campus buildings are clustered virtually on top of one another, there's little open space, and stores have been crammed into minimalls.

EATINGDRINKINGDANCINGSHOPPINGPLAYINGSLEEPING

The city's premier midsize venue, the **ACADEMY** (Oxford Rd. at Spa St., tel. 0161/275–2930), run by the University of Manchester Students Union, has seen performances by such bands as Nirvana, Sonic Youth, and Oasis. University of Manchester students control two other venues in the **UM UNION BUILDING** (tel. 0161/275–2930) next door to the Academy: the main hall and the smaller Hop and Grape room, which puts on mostly local acts. Manchester Metropolitan University students tend to have more club nights than live acts at their **MMU UNION BUILDING** (Mandela House, Oxford Rd. at Sidney St., tel. 0161/273–1162). The largest venue in the area is the **LABATT'S APOLLO** (see below), a converted cinema that usually hosts more mainstream rock and soul acts.

Just about the only old pub left, the **SALUTATION** (Chatham St. at Boundary St. W, tel. 0161/273–1416) is full of character and patronized by a mix of Irish laborers and students. Of the new drinking places, the best is **JABEZ CLEGG** (2 Portsmouth St., tel. 0161/272–8612), a former church hall, though it is very studenty.

LABATT'S APOLLO

Until the Academy and the Nynex Arena were built in the '90s, the Apollo was Manchester's only large venue. Since the late '60s, the Apollo has presented the likes of David Bowie, Iggy Pop, Bob Dylan, and Bruce Springsteen. Joy Division's *Here Are the Young Men* video was filmed here in October 1979.

In January 1986, the first-ever Red Wedge gig was held here. This collective of musicians who got together to support the Labour Party started a nationwide tour with Billy Bragg, Junior Giscombe, Jimmy Somerville, and Jerry Dammers. A big jam at the end included Johnny Marr and Gary Kemp. Kraftwerk's 1991 gig to promote *The Mix*, a compilation album of the group's best-known tracks, attracted just about every major rock star on the Manchester scene. Bob Dylan played to only lukewarm applause in 1995. In 1996 it booked Patti Smith, Prodigy, and Jackson Browne. *Ardwick Green, Ardwick, tel. 0161/242–2560.*

MANCHESTER HIPPODROME

The Beatles played their first gig outside Liverpool at this long gone venue on November 15, 1959, at the semifinal auditions for a local TV show. Just before the gig, they changed their name from the Quarry Men to Johnny and the Moondogs. Audience reaction determined the winner, and the not-so-fabulous four missed out. They were too poor to stay overnight and left early for the last bus. The venue was demolished years ago, and the site is part of an empty lot next to the Labatt's Apollo (see above). *Hyde Rd. at Ardwick Green, Ardwick.*

MANCHESTER POLYTECHNIC STUDENTS UNION (EARLY '70S–1984)

At the end of the '70s this former department store was the best new-wave venue in town. All the important breaking bands of the era, from Adam and the Ants through Dexy's Midnight Runners to the Plasmatics played here. The Buzzcocks played at least one farewell show here in the early '80s. Another memorable gig of that time was U2 playing third on a bill (behind Wah and Pink Military), not long before their debut album came out. Morrissey, singing with the Nosebleeds, made his debut here in 1978.

The old Poly union is now used by the college's art school, which recently became the Manchester Metropolitan University.

Former students include Mick Hucknall, later of Simply Red, who studied fine arts here in the early '80s and DJed in the new students' union; Linder, who designed early singles covers for the Buzzcocks, formed the local art-punks Ludus, and recently published a book of Morrissey photos called *Morrissey Shot*; and Carmel, who fronted the jazzy combo of the same name. *Cavendish St. at Higher Ormond St, All Saints.*

UNIVERSITY OF MANCHESTER STUDENTS UNION

The wild dancing of drama student Tim Booth in the union's Cellar Disco in the early '80s attracted the attention of the band Model Team, which invited him to join. Booth woke up the next morning hung over but with the group's phone number written on his hand. Model Team soon renamed themselves James (after bassist Jim Glennie) and made their debut in the Union's cramped Solem Bar (now the Hop and Grape).

The main gig room, the Main Debating Hall (MDH for short, or main hall for less confusion), has seen performances of all the top names since the late '60s, when the likes of Led Zeppelin and Pink Floyd would play before the student masses, who parted with a shilling (5p) for the pleasure. After the fire chiefs cut the capacity to 600, the big names could no longer play. The Union erected the larger purpose-built Academy next door in the early '90s to attract the top names. The main hall still manages to get some great bookings, such as a Rollins Band–Beastie Boys double bill in 1992 just before the former hit the big time and the Beasties hit the top form of their career. Groups that formed after hanging around the union building include prog rockers Van Der Graaf Generator (in the late '60s), James (in the early '80s) and the Chemical Brothers and Sleeper (in the '90s). *Oxford Rd. at Lime Grove, Chorlton-on-Medlock, tel. 0161/275–2930.*

South Manchester–Hulme and Moss Side

Recently razed, Hulme was one of England's worst and largest '60s housing projects, built of awkward-looking low-rise slabs of concrete dumped on an area that the council had entirely cleared of traditional roads, houses, and stores. One of the streets wiped out was Harper Street, where Morrissey was brought up, at No. 17.

With college expansion in the late '70s, students moved in, stayed here, and became ex-students. The area soon became a haven of bohemia where no one got up before tea time and nearly everyone was in a band. Hulme's biggest hit was the acid house anthem "Voodoo Ray," recorded in 1988 in a Robert Adam Crescent bedroom by the mysteriously named A Guy Called Gerald. Around this time Manchester's first "warehouse" parties were held here, with DJs playing acid house all night to an Ecstasy-fueled crowd. In the '90s, with everyone having fun and hardly anyone paying rent, the council got their own back by declaring the place unfit for human habitation and knocking it down.

Steve Gullick/courtesy of Mute Records

Moss Side, less than a mile south, has been for decades Manchester's main black neighborhood, achieving notoriety in 1981 for riots and in the '90s for vicious drug wars. Moss Side's most famous musician is Barry Adamson, who played bass for Magazine and Nick Cave before writing film scores. The council has now more or less solved Moss Side's long-running crime problem by flattening most of the area.

Barry Adamson

In an area full of weirdness, Hulme's biggest eccentric was songwriter and video director Edward Barton, who rented two adjacent flats in Charles Barry Crescent, knocked down the wall between them, and refurbished the room with wooden railway sleepers. He also planted a tree in the middle and decorated the branches with pacifiers and shoes. Here Barton wrote "It's a Fine Day" (a hit for Opus III, it was also the first ever nonround CD, serrated like a saw) and various things for Kylie Minogue, the Ruthless Rap Assassins, 808 State, Fatima Mansions, and Inspiral Carpets. Barton also directed James's *Sit Down* video and performed his own ridiculous song, "I've Got No Chicken But I've Got Five Wooden Chairs" on *The Tube* TV show. (*See* Afflecks Palace, *above.*)

[FACTORY CLUB (THE LIGHTHOUSE)]

A long-standing West Indian nightspot and one of the few local buildings more than two years old, the club—very dark, very gloomy, very cold; typically Mancunian, really—was a major draw in the '70s, when it was known as the Russell. Around this time Granada TV's Tony Wilson ran a weekend club here called the Factory. It opened with a May 19, 1978, show headlining Joy Division, Big in Japan, and Durutti Column (their debut). The poster advertising the gig was given a Fac 1 catalog number by the newly formed Factory record label, and thereby became instantly collectible (and nearly impossible to find).

At an autumn 1979 gig, bassist Peter Hook chased a heckler through the crowd and refused to go back on stage, so Ian Curtis had to stand in for him. Other Factory nights involved Wire, Cabaret Voltaire, Ludus, Big in Japan, the Tiller Boys, and an amazing double bill of Pere Ubu and the Pop Group. In the '80s the place was taken over by bus drivers and renamed the PSV (Public Service Vehicles) club. It is now the reggae-playing Lighthouse. *Royce Rd. at Clayburn Rd.*

South Manchester–Beyond the Universities

In contrast to the rugged north side of the city, much of south Manchester is a bit posh—which in Mancunian terms means that there's a wine bar and an antiques store—and a lot of it has been taken over by students.

Just south of the University of Manchester is Rusholme, birthplace of intense folk rocker Roy Harper (June 12, 1941). This is Manchester's big Asian area; a half-mile stretch of Wilmslow Road (the continuation of Oxford Road) teems with neon-signed curry restaurants, all of which serve a similar menu of reasonably priced food. East of here is scummy Burnage, once a pioneering garden village, but now a suburb that has been declining since the early '70s, when the brothers Gallagher were growing up in one of its many run-down council houses. The Oasis boys no longer live in this godforsaken place, but their mom Peggy does, refusing all attempts to invest some of her sons' millions in a new pad. It was also nearby that the ex-Durutti Column guitarist Dave Rowbotham—the subject of the Happy Mondays' "Cowboy Dave"—was murdered with an axe in his home in November 1991.

On the southern end of South Manchester is Didsbury, the most desirable residence within the city of Manchester. On one of its most sought-after streets, Factory Records founder Anthony Wilson was a neighbor of Happy Mondays' singer Shaun Ryder, who has since decamped for London. Another resident of the area is Oasis's Bonehead, whose flat was used for the cover of the band's debut album, *Definitely Maybe*. Over on the west side, semi-bohemian Chorlton, where the Stone Roses lived prior to the Geffen advance, is more interesting.

THE BAR (533 Wilbraham Rd., Chorlton, tel. 0161/861–7576) is a top hangout with really well-priced and unusual import beers. Didsbury's brasher O'NEILL's (6655 Wilmslow Rd., Didsbury, tel. 0161/434–0054), a fake Irish bar, occupies what was until recently Times Square, which put on local bands, including Rain, the group that later became Oasis. KING BEE RECORDS (519 Wilbraham Rd., Chorlton, tel. 0161/860–4762) is a small new-and-used store that sometimes turns up bargains. SIFTERS RECORDS, mentioned in song by Oasis, is always worth a trawl for cheap goodies.

BEE GEES ADDRESS

The toothsome singing brothers had to sleep three to a bed when they lived here in the mid-'50s before leaving for Australia. They attended the nearby Oswald Road Primary School. Keppel Road, near the center of Chorlton, is now part of student bedsit land. *51 Keppel Rd., Chorlton.*

CHORLTON STATION/SAFEWAY

Now a Safeway supermarket (where during the late '80s the Stone Roses and Mick Hucknall occasionally shopped), this was the site of Chorlton-cum-Hardy railway station. Just before it shut for good in 1966, the station was decked out for a Granada TV blues show as Chorltonville, a mock-Southern States' rail stop, with bales of straw, woodcut lettering, and a goat to welcome Muddy Waters, Sister Rosetta Tharpe, and Big Bill Broonzy off the steam train from Manchester. The three blues stars played in their rocking chairs on the platform while students gaped open-mouthed from the other side of the tracks. *Albany Rd. at Wilbraham Rd., Chorlton.*

CLIFTON GRANGE HOTEL

In the '70s and '80s this hotel was run by Phil Lynott's mom, Philomena. Temporary home for many actors and bands, it earned the title "The Showbiz" from many clients. When her son's band, Thin Lizzy, played Manchester, they staged wild nightlong parties here, with Phil inviting all his favorite sporting stars from Manchester United. The joint also prompted the track, "Clifton Grange," on Lizzy's first album. It's now flats called Carlton Grange. *17 Wellington Rd.*

[FACTORY RECORDS (1979–90)]

Manchester's top indie label was founded by Granada TV presenter Tony Wilson in 1979 and based in this large, Gothic-style house until 1990. Wilson set up the label to release material by the band he managed, Durutti Column, a quirky, Muzak-y combo named for a cartoon strip in the left-wing *Situationist International.* He soon signed other acts, particularly Joy Division, but also A Certain Ratio, Biting Tongues, Crispy Ambulance, the Distractions, and Orchestral Manouevres in the Dark. The Fall wouldn't join because the label was based on the "other side" of Manchester—the university side.

To stop fans from collecting everything on the label, Wilson cataloged the releases among other Factory output: Fac 1 was the poster advertising the opening night at the Factory club in Hulme; Fac 15 was the Leigh Valley summer 1979 festival, a bit difficult to "collect," as was Fac 51, the Hacienda nightclub.

Factory soon began to produce remarkable records like A Certain Ratio's "Shack Up," the Distractions' "Time Goes by So Slow," and the first Joy Division album, *Unknown Pleasures,* but found it hard to get hits until Joy Division's Ian Curtis committed suicide and the posthumous "Love Will Tear Us Apart" single reached the dizzy heights of No. 13. In 1992, just after the label brought out a four-disc retrospective compilation, *Palatine,* Factory Records went bust with debts of £2 million. This building is now a reflexology practice. *86 Palatine Rd., Withington.*

MANCHESTER CITY FOOTBALL CLUB

Manchester's only professional football club (United is based outside the city bound-aries in Trafford) has long attracted the cooler members of the local rock scene. Johnny Marr had an unsuccessful trial for the club in 1977, while other supporters include ex-Hacienda DJ and current M person Mike Pickering, plus Radio 1FM show hosts Mark Radcliffe and Mark Riley. Nowadays it's Oasis who milk their City links, modeling club gear in the Man City catalog.

The stadium has also been an important gig site. Oasis played a couple of triumphant shows in April 1996 that sold out in eight hours; fans even had their tickets ripped out of their hands by local kids. Other gigs at the stadium, some of which have involved Prince, David Bowie, Bon Jovi, Guns N' Roses, and Fleetwood Mac, have passed off peacefully. *Maine Rd., Moss Side, tel. 0161/224–5000.*

SIFTERS RECORDS

The only decent record store in this part of Manchester was where the Gallagher broth-ers spent many hours sifting through the bargain bins in the early '80s. They honored the place in "Shakermaker" with the lines, "Mr. Sifter sold me songs when I was just 16. Now he stops at traffic lights but only when they're green." *177 Fog La., Burnage, tel. 0161/445 8697.*

SOUTHERN CEMETERY

The Smiths' song "Cemetry Gates" (sic) describes the late-'70s days when Morrissey and Linder (from Ludus) used to go walking in this massive cemetery—"a dreaded sunny day so I meet you at the cemetry gates"—built next to what is now Europe's biggest traf-fic junction. *Barlow Moor Rd. at Princess Rd., West Didsbury.*

TOP OF THE POPS STUDIO (1964–67)

The first episode of Britain's longest-running pop show was filmed in this former BBC studio on New Year's Day 1964. It was set up to compete with ITV's *Ready Steady Go.* Jimmy Savile emceed a bill that had a studio lineup of the Rolling Stones (performing "I Wanna Be Your Man"), the Hollies ("Stay"), Dusty Springfield ("I Only Want to Be With You"), the Dave Clark Five ("Glad All Over"), and the Swinging Blue Jeans ("Hippy Hippy Shake"). It was only supposed to run for six weeks, but the idea caught on; it has been running ever since. The show moved to London in mid 1967 after it became hard to get the stars of the day to journey up to Manchester. Meanwhile, the original studio (built as a Wesleyan chapel and, in the '40s, home to Manchester's only sizable movie company, Mancunian Films) has since been demolished and replaced by a telephone exchange. *Dickenson Rd. at Hythe Close, Rusholme.*

South of Manchester
Macclesfield

It was in Macclesfield that Joy Division singer Ian Curtis hanged himself at home in 1980. The band reformed soon after as New Order and did most of their work in a remote farmhouse in the hills near the town.

This cold, windy, culturally vapid settlement was responsible for rearing the gruesome Macc Lads, described by the local paper as "the most disgusting, nastiest, ugliest, rudest, crudest band in the world." John Mayall, Britain's oldest rocker, was born here on Novem-ber 29, 1933, while the latest band to break from the town is the youthful Marion.

The Macc Lads

Jason Tilley

IAN CURTIS DEATH SITE

Joy Division's Ian Curtis committed suicide in this two-up, two-down house on May 18, 1980. An epileptic and depressive obsessed with death imagery and the Third Reich, Curtis decided to take his own life when the pressures of increased touring, amplified by the band's imminent U.S. tour and cheating on his wife, became too great. Out of tragedy Joy Division gained their biggest chart success, the single, "Love Will Tear Us Apart," and then reformed as New Order, becoming one of England's biggest-selling '80s bands. *77 Barton St.*

IAN CURTIS GRAVE

The Joy Division singer was cremated, and a stone has been laid on one of the lots on the edge of the adjoining cemetery. The Crematorium office—which reports many visitors from Europe each year—is always happy to offer directions. *Macclesfield Crematorium, Prestbury Rd. at West Park, tel. 01625/422330.*

Stockport

A contender for the title of shabbiest town in England, Stockport, 5 miles south of Manchester, is where two rivers meet to form that most romantic of British rock & roll waterways, the Mersey. Unfortunately, the first mile or so of the river stinks like an open sewer. Stockport's main contribution to rock, 10cc, formed around ex-Mindbenders Eric Stewart and Graham Gouldman in the early '70s. More recent names include IntaStella, who just missed the Madchester bandwagon; metallists Dearly Beheaded on the Music for Nations label; and teenagers Northern Uproar, who come from the soulless Heald Green area. Crooner Frankie Vaughan once lost a bet and had to cut "Stockport, Stockport," a joke version of Frank Sinatra's "New York, New York."

EATINGDRINKINGDANCINGSHOPPINGPLAYINGSLEEPING

A half-mile east across town is an excellent record store, **DOUBLE FOUR** (45 Lower Hillgate, tel. 0161/477–1335), with bin after bin of bargain vinyl and loads of posters.

BIRTHPLACE OF KARAOKE

Local inventor Roy Brooke didn't realize what he'd set off when he created Roy's Sing-along Machine at his workshop in this canalside mill in 1975. His invention, which allowed singers to read song lyrics while an instrumental version of the track plays, was taken up by a Japanese company that renamed it karaoke—"empty orchestra." Though the fad has died out a bit, during the early '90s no blue-collar British pub was complete without a karaoke night. In 1993 Brooke unveiled his latest invention, a CD compatible with Sega computer games hardware that enables games players to sing along to favorite tracks. *Goyt Mill, Upper Hibbert La., Marple.*

[STRAWBERRY STUDIOS]

One of the North's most sought-after studios during the '70s and '80s, Strawberry was where Joy Division recorded *Unknown Pleasures* in April 1979 (at a cost of £8,500, label owner Tony Wilson's life savings). The Smiths cut their first two singles, "Hand in Glove" and "This Charming Man," here a few years later. Until then Strawberry was best known as the base for 10cc, whose Eric Stewart and Graham Gouldman founded the place in 1968. On their excellent run of '70s singles, including "The Dean and I" and "Rubber Bullets," the band made increasing use of the studio's technology, culminating in their Todd Rundgren-ish 1975 No. 1, "I'm Not in Love."

Others who have recorded here include the Sisters of Mercy, A Certain Ratio, the Stone Roses, Happy Mondays, and Paul McCartney. In 1991 studio owner Nick Turnbull, completely misreading the music scene, closed down the recording facility to concentrate on producing videos. He thereby missed the chance to record new bands from nearby Manchester—like Oasis. *3 Waterloo Rd.*

Kingston-Upon-Hull, to give the place its rarely used full name, has an edge-of-the-world feel about it. It's flat and far from anywhere else of note. A drizzle seems to fall all the time and the town smells of its cocoa-refining plants. Few people come here except to catch ferries to Rotterdam and Zeebrugge. It does, however, boast a reasonable-size university; both students and locals try to make up as much as they can for their enforced geographic isolation by partying. One longtime resident was the angst-ridden poet Philip Larkin, who defined the arrival of the permissive age in his 1967 "Annus Mirabilis," which famously opened: "Sexual intercourse began/In nineteen sixty-three...Between the end of the Chatterley ban/And the Beatles' first LP."

Hull's most successful exports have been the *Thriller*-writing Rod Temperton and Mick Ronson, guitarist with the Spiders from Mars, as well as that band's drummer, Mick "Woody" Woodmansey, whose surname comes from a village 5 miles north of the city. Though born elsewhere, Roland Gift of the Fine Young Cannibals and the wacky new wave-era singer Lene Lovich grew up here. Former students here include the Scaffold's Roger McGough (ex-University) and Wreckless Eric (who went to Hull College of Art), but the most famous academic union is Tracey Thorn and Ben Watts of Everything But the Girl duo. They got together in 1982 and took their name from a long-gone used furniture store show window ad.

Everything But the Girl

Nigel M. Adams

In 1984 the Housemartins, who peddled cheesy pop (though often with an ironic twist), called their debut album *London 0 Hull 4*. With sophomoric tunes like their mega-hit "Happy Hour," they put forward a nerdy image evoking an English Weezer. Their original drummer, Hughie Whittaker, showed another side in the early '90s when he was sentenced to six years in the nearby Everthorpe prison for attacking a local car dealer with an axe. After the band split, Norman Cook went home to Brighton to form Beats International and then become Fatboy Slim, but Paul Heaton and Dave Hemingway stayed in Hull and came up with Beautiful South. More recently, the woozy Spacemaid, who had a single produced by Joey Ramone, have gained national attention, as has the genre-busting Pork Recordings label roster.

EATINGDRINKINGDANCINGSHOPPINGPLAYINGSLEEPING

Apart from the **ADELPHI** (*see below*), the main place to catch up-and-coming bands is **THE ROOM** (George St., tel. 01482/323154), which also has a reputation for its happy hardcore and drum & bass nights. **OFFBEAT RECORDS** (24 Anlaby Rd., tel. 01482/324879) sells new and used indie, hardcore, dance sounds, fanzines, and whatever else is breaking. The other independent source of sounds is **SYDNEY SCARBOROUGH RECORDS** ("under the City Hall," tel. 01482/320515), which has lots of vinyl.

THE ADELPHI

Hull's best-known small venue has been putting on "quality pop" since opening in October 1984. As well as giving Hull-based bands early gigs, booker Paul Jackson is proud of having Pulp and the La's (who did their second-ever show here) play on this stage several times before they were noticed by the A&R men of major labels. Others to play here well before they made it include Radiohead, Primal Scream, the Happy Mondays, and Oasis.

Besides indie rock, the club books U.S. roots stars (e.g., the late Townes Van Zandt) and lots of African and other worldbeat acts. The funky dance/cross-genre "Pork" night run by the local label, Pork Recordings, has highlighted local names such as the touted

Courtesy of Mach 9 Ltd.

The Adelphi, Hull

Fela Brazilia as well as Baby Mammoth, Bullitnuts, and Solid Doctor. The club, whose front bar is constructed out of a bus, is a regular spot for the hard-drinking Daves (Rotheray and Hemingway) of the Beautiful South, whose love of gin and tonics apparently caused the ice-making machine to break. It's open 7–11 each night; the cover ranges from nothing to £6. *89 De Grey St., tel. 01482/348216.*

FAIRVIEW STUDIOS

Def Leppard cut their first demos, including "Getcha Rocks Off," at this eight-track studio, the first multitrack facility in Yorkshire, in 1978. Rod Temperton was here in the early '70s, when he was playing keyboards in Roger Bloom's Hammer, a local poppy soul combo. He hooked up with the disco soul band Heatwave in 1975 and later pursued a lucrative career as producer and writer for such zillion-dollar figures as Michael Jackson and Quincy Jones, writing the title track of *Thriller.*

Both the Housemartins and the Beautiful South have used Fairview for demos and B sides; other local and regional acts who have used the space include the Red Guitars, Kingmaker, Shed Seven, and Soda. Over the years Bill Nelson has been a regular visitor, as both artist and producer; in 1996 he produced an album for the top Russian outfit Nautilus Pompilius. The studio is in Willerby on the western edge of the city, just off the A164. *Great Gutter La. W, Willerby, tel. 01482/653116.*

QUEEN'S GARDENS

Before joining up with David Bowie in 1970, Spiders from Mars guitarist Mick Ronson (born in Hull in 1947) played with the local band the Rats and worked for the city council as a gardener in this park. Ronson later worked with Ian Hunter, toured with Dylan, and produced some work for Morrissey, as well as putting out some solo albums. After Ronson died from cancer in 1993, some former collaborators played a gig at London's Hammersmith Odeon to raise money for a memorial stage in his former workplace. A posthumous album by Ronson—*Heaven and Hull*—was released the following year. The council planned to unveil the stage in the city center park with a gala concert in the summer of 1997. *Access at Queen's Dock Ave. or Wilberforce Dr., tel. 01482/615623.*

Out from Hull
Bridlington

This windswept little seaside town some 30 miles northeast of Hull was the unlikely relocation for the raspy-voiced Texan singer Ted Hawkins in the mid-'80s. He rode around the coast on a mountain bike decorated with mink. Hawkins, whose material evocatively mixed rootsy blues and country, had previously spent the best part of a decade in California, busking on the Venice Beach boardwalk. He developed a loyal fanbase in Europe—at the end of 1986, *NME* critics voted two of his albums (*Out on the Boardwalk* and *Watch Your Step*) into their list of the year's best. Landing a record deal with Geffen, he moved back to the United States in the early '90s but died in LA from a stroke on January 1, 1995, just when he was being accepted in his native country.

Courtesy of Geffen Records Inc.

The late Ted Hawkins

BRIDLINGTON SPA

The town's seashore pavilion sees a dozen or more top name acts playing its boards every year. Few gigs caused as much fuss as the Stone Roses' first publicly announced U.K. gig in five years on November 28, 1995 (they had done a fund raiser a few weeks earlier in Pilton, near Glastonbury). Fans journeyed from all over the country to this out-of-the way place; scalpers got around £60 a ticket and the band played for two hours. The "second coming" seemed to be working out just fine, but within a year Ian Brown was left as the sole founding member and the Stone Roses were declared defunct. *South Marine Dr., tel. 01262/678258.*

LEEDS

Lord have mercy on me, keep me away from Leeds—Dexy's Midnight Runners, "Thankfully Not Living in Yorkshire It Doesn't Apply"

Yorkshire's biggest city, the renascent economic powerhouse of the north, is reputed to have the best club scene outside of London. A succession of stimulating bands emerged out of next-wave punk, many of them formed at the city's colleges, of a left-wing view, and with intriguing names. However, with the lack of a music industry in Leeds, groups have always had to look elsewhere: At the end of the '70s, Gang of Four and the Mekons (now based in Chicago) both signed to Edinburgh-based indie Fast Product; as soon as art-school students Scritti Politti got their ideas together in 1977, they moved to London. Leeds didn't even have that many venues receptive to new wave: Left-wing post-punkers Delta 5 did many Rock Against Racism gigs with Gang of Four and for their efforts got some beatings from a short-lived Rock Against Communism faction that had emerged in Leeds.

Out of the Polytechnic (now Leeds Metropolitan University) came the synth-pop sound of Soft Cell, led by Marc Almond, while another '80s success, Sisters of Mercy, was formed by Andrew Eldridge in his hometown after he had packed in his studies at Oxford University. They made their name at the Futurama festivals held at various Leeds locations in the early '80s.

The Wedding Present, Leeds's most successful band over the past decade, named their 1987 album after Irish soccer legend George Best. The fact that he played for Manchester United rather than the home team of Leeds United badly affected sales of the

Courtesy of RCA

The Wedding Present, 1989

album in these parts. A 1989 LP, *Ukrainski Vistipu V Johna Peela,* was simply the band's John Peel sessions sung in Ukrainian (guitarist Peter Solowka then left to form the Ukrainians, whose output included an EP of Smiths covers—again, in Ukrainian).

Other bands include the gothy Red Lorry Yellow Lorry and March Violet; the anarchic Chumbawumba; indie bands the Parachute Men and Pale Saints; the Cassandra Complex, a hard electro-pop outfit; Cud, popular locally thanks to their usage of Leeds United colors on merchandising; and Age of Chance, temporarily cultish at the end of the '80s after recording several talked-about singles including a shouting version of Prince's "Kiss." More recently, rappers Credit to the Nation and the Black Star Liner trio (named for the '40s company Marcus Garvey set up to offer African Americans free passage back to their home continent) have received some critical acclaim for their mix of dub, rock, and bhangra.

EATINGDRINKINGDANCINGSHOPPINGPLAYINGSLEEPING

Leeds's reputation with bands was secured in 1970 when the Who recorded their *Live at Leeds* LP (its title parodied by the Mace Lads in their 1988 riposte, *Live at Leeds—The Who?*). Bands still play **LEEDS UNIVERSITY STUDENTS' UNION,** where the Who cut their live album in 1970 (*see below*). The **LEEDS METROPOLITAN UNIVERSITY UNION** (tel. 0113/243–0171), which used to be called the Polytechnic, has lately had the better booking policy. The city's main venue, the **TOWN AND COUNTRY CLUB** (Cookridge St. at Woodhouse La., tel. 0113/280–0100), was built in 1885 as a music hall. It hosted movies and bingo before being renovated in October 1992. At the rear is the **UNDER-GROUND** (55 Cookridge St., tel. 0113/254–0540), which has a late license and puts on blues, Latin, and indie nights. Every band on the way up since 1985, from Nirvana to Oasis, has played **THE DUCHESS OF YORK** (71 Vicar La., tel. 0113/245–3929); the only venue to put on live music seven nights a week. The **COCKPIT** (Bridge House, Swinegate, tel. 0113/244–3446), has space for 300 for gigs by mostly indie and alternative bands; it opens up into a maze of darkened rooms for indie/trip hop club nights. The upstairs room of the whitewashed **FENTON** pub (161 Woodhouse La., tel. 0113/245–3908), next to Leeds Metropolitan Uni, puts on local bands in sweaty surrounds. A little farther out, the **FEAST & FIRKIN** (229 Woodhouse La., tel. 0113/245–0539) hosts local and small touring bands in the room above the main bar every Tuesday and Thursday. Occasionally, **ROUNDHAY PARK,** 5 miles north of the city center, puts on open-air gigs. Bruce Springsteen ended his 1985 European tour here, and Pulp played the Heineken festival in 1995.

Leeds's shopping escalation stretched into the record market when **VIRGIN** (Leeds Shopping Plaza, Albion St., tel. 0113/243–8117) opened their largest store outside of London here in November 1996; Shed Seven and MN8 played live and (London) Suede turned up for a signing session. It's unlikely to affect the business of Leeds's specialist collector stores, headed by the five-story **VINYL TAP** (27 Call La., tel. 0113/245–1110; http://www.vinyltap.co.uk/). **CRASH** (35 The Headrow, tel. 0113/243–6743) stocks all kinds of current dance sounds. There's also a branch of **EASTERN BLOC** (24 Central Rd., tel. 0113/242–7797) a leading techno/dance/electro record store.

Back in the '80s, a night out in Leeds was synonymous with having to avoid soccer hooligans and beermonsters, but a reaction came from ground level that saw the city become home to several gender-busting club nights in the late '80s. Now Leeds is the nation's main clubbing center outside London; the local council wants to promote the place as a 24-hour city. The most famous club has been the popular techno/house nights of "Up 'Yer Ronson" and "Back to Basics," which mix all types of dance music and have live sets from crossover bands like the Alabama 3. As club nights become more and more lucrative, these big promotions have a habit of shifting around to the best-paying venues. Both UYR and BTB started out at the three-room **MUSIC FACTORY** (174 Call

La., tel. 0113/247–0480) and then moved onto a more recent arrival, the **PLEASURE ROOMS** (9 Lower Merrion St., tel. 0113/245–0923), with its suspended shark and huge fish tanks, until the Ronson crew moved on to the **EUROPA** (New Brigate, tel. 0113/242–2224). A safe bet for a night out is the **WAREHOUSE** (*see below*), which started out with goth nights in the early '80s and went through all the dance crazes to the highly successful Vague mixed gay night in 1996. **MEX** (2A Call La., tel. 0113/242–8522), has top DJs spinning tunes for the pre-club crowd. Other possibilities are **ALL BAR ONE** (27 East Parade, tel. 0113/243–445) or the **ARTS CAFÉ** (42 Call La., tel. 0113/243–8243). If you're still going by 4 AM, then **MONTEZUMA** (1 Church Walk, Kirkgate, tel. 0113/242–7121) is the café to look for.

LEEDS UNIVERSITY

The Who's revered live album, *The Who Live at Leeds,* was recorded at Leeds University Students' Union on Valentine's Day 1970. The band had wanted to use tapes from their 1969 U.S. tour for a live album, but when they got back home, Pete Townshend balked at the idea of listening to hours of material and decided to record a couple of shows in Yorkshire—in Hull and Leeds—well away from their London home patch. The tapes from the Hull gig got spoiled, and so the record turned out to be *The Who Live at Leeds* rather than *The Who Live at Hull.* It showcased the raunchy heavy metal side of the band at a time when they were being feted for the sensitivity and restraint of *Tommy.*

A few months later, the Rolling Stones cut the version of "Let It Rock" that was used on the B side of "Brown Sugar" here. In the late '70s, the union film society was run by Gang of Four's Andy Gill and Jon King. The loud, left-wing Three Johns met at Leeds University and played their first gig at a Fuck the Royal Wedding party in 1981. *Woodhouse La. opposite Blenheim Walk, tel. 0113/243–1751.*

THE WAREHOUSE

The Stone Roses appeared at this venue on May 9, 1989, amid fears of clashes between rival Leeds and Manchester factions. When the aggressive footballish chant of "We Are Leeds! We Are Leeds!" went up in an attempt to goad the cross-Pennine invaders, Roses singer Ian Brown merely shrugged his shoulders and matter-of-factly replied "This is Leeds." The band launched into "I Wanna Be Adored" and the bad vibes were dismissed. Since the opening of several rock venues in the '90s, the Warehouse has gone back to concentrating on dance. *19 Somers St., tel. 0113/246–8287.*

QUEENS HALL

John Keenan, who ran Leeds's F Club in the late '70s, organized the first Futurama, described as the "world's first science fiction music festival," in this now-demolished, freezing old tram shed on September 8 and 9, 1979. A strong bill included PiL, Cabaret Voltaire, Joy Division, Orchestral Manoeuvres in the Dark, and, bizarrely, Hawkwind. In the audience was Andrew Eldritch, yet to form the Sisters of Mercy (who would perform at subsequent Futurama festivals in the '80s). The event is now seen as crucial in helping establish a northern post-punk scene just as London was going stale. *Opposite the Hilton, Neville St. by Leeds station.*

THE YORKSHIRE DELTA—HOME OF THE BLUES?

Plans are underway to build Britain's first blues museum in this unrootsy city. The museum, the concept of Blues Band singer Paul Jones (ex-Manfred Mann) and drummer Rob Townsend (ex-Family), is targeted to be open before the end of the millennium. Although it will have artifacts and memorabilia from the Mississippi Delta, Memphis, and Chicago and will show how traditional blues sounds have been utilized by acts from the Rolling Stones to Ocean Colour Scene, the focus will be very much on live performances, broadcasts, and music workshops. The centerpiece will be a cozy juke-joint venue that can be arranged

to accommodate anywhere between 100 and 400. The hope is to get in top U.S. acts. The museum is based in Leeds because the business head behind it all, Nick Wayne, a former studio and tour manager, simply wanted it to be in his home city. It is to be built on Quarry Hill, behind the West Yorkshire Playhouse in the city's council-assigned cultural quarter. *For more details, contact Blues Museum Ltd., CDW, Castleton Mill, Armley Rd., Leeds, LS12 2DS (e-mail: blues@cdw.gdes.demon.co.uk).*

Out from Leeds
Bradford

Somewhat in the shadow of neighboring Leeds (the respective downtowns are less than 10 miles apart), the city of Bradford—a mix of industrial decay and posh suburbs—has produced a trio of noteworthy bands in the last two decades. The crusty, clog-wearing New Model Army, led by vocalist Slade the Leveller (a.k.a. Justin Sullivan), formed in 1980 and have been bringing their anti-Tory-flavored folk rock/punk to festivals ever since.

In 1982 Ian Astbury (who was at that time using his mother's maiden name of Lindsay) assembled the Southern Death Cult, which lasted a year until a major shift in personnel (notably the recruitment of ex-Theatre of Hate guitarist Billy Duffy), a relocation to London, and a truncation of the name to Death Cult. The Death prefix was in turn dropped within a year, as too many people thought they were goths. After years of trawling their heavy indie sound around stadia, they folded in 1995. One of the original members of the Southern Death Cult, drummer Haq Qureshi, resurfaced in the mid-'90s as Propa Gandhi in the hip-hop worldbeat Fun-Da-Mental.

Although they came to most people's attention with their second album, *How to Make Friends and Influence People*, in 1994, the wacky lite metallurgists Terrorvision had formed here as the Spoilt Bratz eight years earlier, playing local pubs for years before being noticed.

EATINGDRINKINGDANCINGSHOPPINGPLAYINGSLEEPING

Bradford is a relatively small, unpretentious, and likeable city with a big emphasis on beer-drinking. Nightlife can sometimes be spoiled—as in other similar cities—by the rural types who come into town from the surrounding countryside. Leeds gets a greater share of live acts, though Bradford doesn't do badly. Touring bands have been playing downtown at **ST. GEORGE'S HALL** (Bridge St. at Hallings, tel. 01274/757575) since the '60s. The Student Union's Commie or **COMMUNAL BUILDING** of the University of Bradford (whose alumni include Jean Jacques Burnel of the Stranglers) also attracts a fair number of top touring names—Nirvana, Belly, and Stereolab have played here in the past. **RIO** (Thorn House, Woodhead Rd., tel. 01274/735549) is an uncompromised, beer-swilling, smelly rock club with the best metal bands—from Cathedral to Downset—several times a week. The scruffy **WESTLEIGH** pub (Laisteridge La. at Easly Rd., tel. 01274/727089) boasts a pool table, a decent jukebox, and clientele that include members of Terrorvision and New Model Army.

Ultimately, Bradford is more famous for its curry houses than for its rock venues. There are dozens to choose from. The **KASHMIR** (27 Morley St., tel. 0114/272-3478) is cheap, cheerful, and very central, but everyone seems to have their own particular favorite and will wax on about it at length. The other reason for visiting the place is the thoroughly enjoyable **NATIONAL MUSEUM OF PHOTOGRAPHY, FILM AND TELEVISION** (Princes View, tel. 01274/727488; open Tues.–Sun. 10:30–6), which is free (its IMAX theater charges admission).

NEWCASTLE

The Northeast's major city, once the home of British shipbuilding and synonymous until recently with coal-mining, is the birthplace of one pioneering '60s R&B band, the Animals (named after a tough-guy friend, Animal Hogg). It was where two mega-selling superstars (Sting and Mark Knopfler) were raised. The early '70s produced a heavy pop/mild rock band called Geordie (the common nickname for locals) whose short career produced four U.K. Top-40 hits. By 1980 their former singer, the flat-topped Brian Johnson, was scraping by doing radio commercials when he got a surprise call from AC/DC to be the replacement for the late Bon Scott. Two noteworthy punk-era bands came from the district: Penetration, from the mining village of Ferryhill, 30 miles south of the city, and the leftist Angelic Upstarts, from South Shields. The theatrical Devo-type band Punishment of Luxury was also based in Newcastle.

Sting

The '80s saw the advent of Newcastle's only successful record label, Kitchenware (now owned by Sony). Kitchenware specialized in classy sophisticated pop from Prefab Sprout (who hailed from neighboring Durham) to Martin Stephenson and the Daintees and the Kane Gang. Prefab Sprout has been quiet for most of the '90s, but their main songwriter, Paddy McAloon, has composed hits for Jimmy Nail, the Geordie actor turned country "singer."

Considering its size, Newcastle has produced relatively few bands in either the '80s or the '90s. It's always had a fixation with heavy metal sounds and fashion. The Quireboys formed locally as the Queerboys in 1987, and '80s metallists Venom, started here. Although the rocking, drinking Wildhearts formed in London at the end of the '80s, vocalist Ginger makes much of his local roots on tracks like "Alice in Geordieland." Dubstar, who got together in 1994, are a more contrived affair, mixing pop dance and social awareness, as in their "Not So Manic Now" U.K. hit.

EATING DRINKING DANCING SHOPPING **PLAYING** SLEEPING

The Geordie answer to years of recession and industrial decimation has been to adopt a cheerfully hedonistic approach to life and spend whatever money there is on drinking, clubbing, and buying the latest fashions. Much of this conspicuous consumption goes on around Bigg Market just north of the railway station, packed with pubs serving the local brews and thumping to the sound of house and techno.

The city's best-known live music club is the **RIVERSIDE** (*see below*), and bands still play at the **CITY HALL** (*see below*). The **MAYFAIR** (Newgate House, Newgate St., tel. 0191/232–3109) is mostly a clubbing space (including some legendary metal nights), though some promoters still place bands here; when Nirvana played in January 1992, Kurt

Cobain opened proceedings by yelling, "I'm a homosexual, I'm a drug taker, and I fuck pot-bellied pigs." There aren't that many good rock music pubs, but the **CUMBERLAND ARMS** (Byker Buildings, tel. 0191/265–6151), in the Byker district, does get some breaking bands on the way up. The **BRIDGE HOTEL** (Castle Sq., St. Nicholas St., tel. 0191/232–7780) has live folk, blues, and jazz in the downstairs room.

CITY HALL

It was at the 2,000-seat City Hall that Eric Burdon disbanded the Animals after a December 22, 1968 gig. His excuse was that he was about to embark on a Hollywood film career; the world is still waiting for the results. Just over two years later, on March 26, 1971, Emerson, Lake and Palmer recorded their ambitious if exceptionally boring version of Mussorgsky's *Pictures at an Exhibition* at City Hall. In December 1976, Newcastle councillors banned the Sex Pistols' Anarchy tour (following the Thames TV debacle; *see* King's Cross *in* London) "in the interests of protecting our children," even though it was unlikely that any children would have wanted to go. The northeastern punk band Penetration announced their breakup at an October 1979 gig here. Bruce Springsteen came here to launch his 1981 U.K. tour, his first British dates since his 1975 *Born to Run* outing. It's still a fairly busy live venue, but its acoustics draw complaints. *Northumberland Rd. at John Dobson St., tel. 0191/222–1778.*

THE RIVERSIDE

Nirvana played their first-ever U.K. show at this converted warehouse on October 20, 1989, opening for TAD. Five years later, Oasis's Noel Gallagher was emphatically thumped by a fan who climbed onstage during "Bring It Down." The gig was called off, and 200 angry fans outside threw stones at the band's bus amidst cries of "Man City, wank, wank, wank," a not-so-reverential reference to the Gallagher brothers' favorite soccer team. The Riverside presents bands—everything from Girls Against Boys to the Aphex Twin—most nights of the week and has club nights on Fridays (indie) and Saturdays (house/garage). *57–59 Melbourne St, tel. 0191/261–4386*

The Riverside, Newcastle

Nick Murray/courtesy of The Riverside

SOON WE'LL BE STINGBUILDING

The city's vanished shipbuilding industry has occasionally captured the imagination of local rockers. Sting, who grew up on now-demolished Gerald Street in Wallsend near the fabled and defunct Swan Hunter shipyard, sings of a character called Billy, "born within the sight of the shipyard," in "Island of Souls," from the 1991 album *The Soul Cages*. On the following track, "All This Time," a Top-10 U.S. single, he refers to Newcastle as, "a city in the fog," that the Romans built. Sting played a nightclub owner in the movie *Stormy Monday,* which was filmed on Newcastle's quayside. Animal bassist and Jimi Hendrix manager Chas Chandler worked at the Swan Hunter shipyard in the early '60s.

RIVER TYNE

Every single time I roll across the rolling River Tyne—Dire Straits, "Southbound Again"

Newcastle's chief river, like its shipbuilding past, has been another major source of inspiration for Newcastle-bred rock stars. Mark Knopfler, born in Glasgow but raised here, told *Mojo* magazine in April 1996: "My idea of heaven is a place where the Tyne meets the Mississippi Delta." On "Down to the Waterline," the first song on Dire Straits' debut album, Knopfler reminisces about being 15 and crossing the Tyne on the train back from London, where he had been appearing in *Julius Caesar* for the National Youth Theatre. "Southbound Again," from the same album, also mentions the river.

When the Newcastle Arts Festival commissioned the Nice to write a piece of music in 1969, bassist Lee Jackson used the bridges over the Tyne as his main theme. The album that arose from the commission was *Five Bridges*, (*see* Croydon *in* the Home Counties and the South). Nice keyboard maestro Keith Emerson gained various ideas for the piece from the sounds of the trains and cars on the bridge that carries the main East Coast railway.

A better-known Tyne tribute is "Fog on the Tyne," the title track of the group Lindisfarne's 1971 No. 1 U.K. album. In 1990 local soccer star Paul Gascoigne, backed by Lindisfarne, brought the song to No. 2 in the U.K. singles chart.

TYNE TEES STUDIOS

The Tube, Britain's best '80s contemporary music program, named for the covered walkway that links the studio to the street, was recorded at Tyne Tees. The November 11, 1983, show, hosted by Squeeze pianist Jools Holland and Bob Geldof's then-wife, Paula Yates, is where R.E.M. made their first live European appearance, performing "So. Central Rain" and "Talk About the Passion." Despite *The Tube*'s popularity and high credibility rating, the show was doomed once Jools Holland used the line "groovy fuckers" in a 1987 show and was suspended for six weeks.

These TV studios also witnessed the last public performance of Thin Lizzy's Phil Lynott, who came up here a few months before his death in January 1986 to tape a special for the *Razzmatazz* pop program. *City Rd. by Gibson St., tel. 0191/261–0181.*

Out from Newcastle

Lindisfarne

English Christianity is believed to have started around AD 635 in the tiny North Sea island of Lindisfarne, or Holy Island, just south of the Scottish border. Lindisfarne was also the name of the crossover '70s folk/pop band that hit the charts with "Meet Me on the Corner" and "Lady Eleanor." When the band tried to go more progressive, they bombed but reunited for a special Christmas show in 1976 and have been staging yuletide reunions ever since. The island, site of Lindisfarne Castle, the ruins of the Lindisfarne Priory, and a small village with a pub, stands a couple of miles over coastal flats and is inaccessible at high tide. *Off the A1 at Beal, 12 mi south of Berwick-upon-Tweed; 50 mi north of Newcastle.*

Whitley Bay

Ten miles from downtown Newcastle, the most popular seaside resort on the unpopular coldwater northeast coast seemed an appropriate place for '70s and '80s metallurgists the Tygers of Pan Tang to be based.

SPANISH CITY

The Knopfler brothers used to play the slot machines at this fairground, which inspired "Tunnel of Love" on Dire Straits' 1980 *Making Movies* LP. Dave Knopfler would make the 5-mile journey from Newcastle city center hiding in the train toilets to avoid paying the fare. *Park Rd. at Marine Ave.*

SHEFFIELD

Oh the city is a woman/Bigger than any other—Pulp, "Sheffield Sex City"

A few years back, Americans were laughing about backwoods Cleveland getting the honor of hosting the Rock and Roll Hall of Fame. That's not quite how Brits treated the 1995 announcement that Sheffield would be home to the National Museum of Popular Culture, but for many the question "why?" did spring to mind. Nevertheless, it's as a good a place as any to have the country's first national music museum.

Outside of the capital, Sheffield, England's fifth-largest city, has consistently produced more quality rock acts since the early '60s than any other metropolis bar Manchester. First to hit it big was gangly Dave Berry (born David Grundy), who took his stage name from his hero Chuck Berry. Through residencies at unlicensed clubs like the Esquire, he built up a huge beat-era following in Europe. His first hit was in 1963 with "Memphis Tennessee," followed by "The Crying Game," "Little Things," and "Mama," which all went Top 5. Supporting Berry at gigs throughout the region for a time was a band called Vance Arnold and the Avengers, led by the gravel-voiced gas fitter Joe Cocker. Cocker went solo and reached No. 1 singing "With a Little Help from My Friends" in 1968 and stormed the Woodstock festival the following year.

By the early '70s, Cocker was disillusioned with the business and spent a legendary rocker's "lost week-end" in the city that brought him through to the middle of the decade. Otherwise, the early '70s were a quiet time in Sheffield, except for kids going headbanging at gigs in the City Hall, no doubt inspiring Sheffield's biggest-selling export, Def Leppard. While Joe Elliott and company were introducing the world to their brand of garage metal, other things happening in late-'70s Sheffield made this period the hottest time in the city's musical history. The Human League, Cabaret Voltaire, Clock DVA, Comsat Angels, ABC, and other bands saw the post-punk future and declared that it should be electronic. They all played basic venues like the Broad-field, Marples, and the Limit, while touring bands lined up to play the Top Rank (now the cheesy Roxy club), the Lyceum (now reverted to stage plays), the City Hall, and the Poly.

Human League, 1995

The city's once again on a pop culture high, thanks to landing the National Museum of Popular Culture, receiving the *NME* reader's favorite live music venue award for the Leadmill, and opening some of the country's most innovative dance clubs. Promoting it all with some zeal is the local council. In the mid-'80s, they opened a fully equipped studio that kickstarted the Cultural Industries Quarter, and the councillors have even produced the financing for a glossy booklet—*The Dirty Stop-Out's Guide*—that details the city's nightlife charms.

It also helps to have one of the mid-'90s' best-selling bands from the town in Pulp (though it took them 15 years to make it big), and BabyBird bursting onto the scene with some sweet pop in 1996 didn't do any harm, either. A leading dance label, Warp records (Aphex Twin, Red Snapper, and Jimi Tenor), is also based here. Add to that the dreamy synthpop of Moloko, spunky popsters the Longpigs and Speedy, who have both had chart success in 1996, and Blameless (deemed good enough to be flown to Boston and record at Fort Apache), and once more there's talk of a Sheffield scene. Above all, this is proof that, unlike other cities, whose stars flee to London at the first hint of success, Sheffield has the studios and facilities to keep bands in the area.

EATINGDRINKINGDANCINGSHOPPINGPLAYINGSLEEPING

The **LEADMILL** (*see below*) is undoubtedly the best place in the city to see live music. The **CITY HALL** (*see below*) and **SHEFFIELD UNIVERSITY STUDENTS UNION** (Western Bank, tel. 0114/275–3300) both put on lots of touring bands. When it was plain old Sheffield Poly-technic, the **SHEFFIELD HALLAM UNIVERSITY UNION OF STUDENTS** (Nelson Mandela Bldg., Pond St., tel. 0114/ 253–4122) got in all the big names for its great gig room right next to the railway station. Sadly, its booking policy now deals almost exclusively with disco nights.

Wolfgang Mustain

There are also a couple of small venues downtown. The **HALLAMSHIRE HOTEL** (182 West St., tel. 0114/272–9787) is a basic pub that has music in the upstairs room most nights, including ska bands and raves from the grave like the UK Subs. For metal music, try the **WAPEN-TAKE** (*see below*). Just over a mile from the city center, the **SPEAKEASY** (383 Abbeydale Rd., tel. 0114/258–0414) is a relatively new small venue that holds 200 and has mostly local bands, such as noisy, rocking Etiquette, but is also becoming a stop on the indie-band touring circuit.

Richard James of Aphex Twin

The Devonshire Quarter is the best place for bars and cafés. The walls of the **CAFE MONDO** (119 Devonshire St., tel. 0114/275–9254) sport a permanent collection of rock & roll memorabilia by Sheffield artists from the '50s to the present day, as well as some general rock history items. **THE FORUM CAFE BAR** (127 Devonshire St., tel. 0114/276–6544) is a good, modern bar with decent food during the day and a pre-club and gig set at night; in summer you can drink outside on **DEVONSHIRE GREEN,** where occasionally there are rock music festivals. There's decent acoustic music most nights at the comfortable **BISTRO CASABLANCA** (150 Devonshire St., tel. 0114/249–0720). Also in the area is the **WASHINGTON** (79 Fitzwilliam St., tel. 0114/276–5268), a trendy bar with loud sounds that's part-owned and enthusiastically patronized by Pulp drummer Nick Banks.

With 50,000 students in the city, Sheffield has always had a ready audience for clubs, but now it is invaded by Londoners and others on weekends. Among the best places to go are **THE ARCHES** (9 Walker St., tel. 0114/272–2900), a recently converted railroad arch that plays hard house; people come for the underground vibe rather than big-name players. The **MUSIC FACTORY** (33 London Rd., tel. 0114/279–9022) gets in coaches of clubbers from other cities for its "Love to Be…" house night. The **REPUBLIC** (112 Arundel St., tel. 0114/249–2210) is a big, beautiful club and daytime café-bar and gallery that was opened in late 1995 in an old steelworks in the Cultural Industries Quarter. A postmodern facade conceals an exciting industrial interior.

Sheffield's record stores are not huge in size or number, but they're friendly and well worth a trawl. The trendy downtown Devonshire Quarter is the place to start searching. **JACK'S RECORDS** (102 Devonshire St., tel. 0114/276–6356), a great, friendly little store, has well-priced rock vinyl and CDs; it's the place to get early Cabaret Voltaire singles. **FOPP RECORDS** (40 Division St., tel. 0114/275–7585) stocks the latest alternative, dance, and hip-hop and is good for picking up flyers. **RARE & RACY** (166 Devonshire St., tel. 0114/270–1916) sells select secondhand books and some roots music CDs. Boasting some interesting pop memorabilia, the **FORUM POSTER SHOP** (127 Devonshire St., tel. 0114/272–0569) is in a trendy shopping center alongside head shops, clothing, record, and comic stalls. Hippyish **CAMBRIDGE MARKET** (Cambridge St. at Barkers Pool) has a good alternative record stall plus other vendors selling clothing. On the other side of town, **KENNY'S RECORDS** (32 The Wicker, tel. 0114/272–7857) specializes in used '50s and '60s rock & roll. **RECORD COLLECTOR** (233 Fulwood Rd., tel. 0114/266–0114), out near the Sheffield University campus, has a great reputation for reselling unwanted student vinyl at great prices, though their CD prices are not so keen.

The City Center

Sheffield's hilly downtown has been hit in recent years by the opening of a huge suburban mall. By far the most vibrant area is the Devonshire Quarter (a fancy name for Devonshire Street and the surrounding bits), where there are bars, cafés, record stores, and a couple of small venues.

BLACK SWAN (MUCKY DUCK)

The Clash played their first-ever public gig here, supporting the Sex Pistols on Sunday, July 4, 1976. The lineup of ex-101er Joe Strummer and ex-London SS Mick Jones, Paul Simonon, Keith Levene, and Terry Chimes had played a show for a handful of journalists in London a few days before, but this time the only coverage they got was a letter in *Sounds* from someone who was at the gig who described them as a barrage of noise. Joe Cocker used to jam onstage here with another Yorkshire artist, Robert Palmer. Now called the Mucky Duck, this is an interesting-looking semicircular corner pub that's been recently refurbished with comfy leather seats. It puts on a good range of local bands on weekends. *Black Swan House, Snig Hill, tel. 0114/272–8061.*

CITY HALL

When the big Art Deco structure was built on a downtown hillock for civic functions in 1932, it's unlikely the city fathers contemplated that their creation would be used for something as common as rock & roll. Buddy Holly was the first one in, in 1958. While the Beatles and other beat-era bands played here, its fame as a venue came in the '70s and '80s, when the City Hall became a revered stop on any heavy metal band's tour itinerary. This council-run venue has seen them all—Def Leppard, Judas Priest, AC/DC, and many more—and reeked with the smell of patchouli oil and Newcastle Brown Ale for days after. Actually, there was a strict policy of no drinks in the 2,300-seat main hall, enforced by council-paid security in bow-ties. These days, the metal bands are few and far between, but the City Hall still draws major rock acts, such as the Manic Street Preachers.

Also in the building is the smaller and shabbier **MEMORIAL THEATRE,** plus a basement ballroom where The Drop, a superb alt-rock disco, has been cramming kids in since the mid-'90s. The indie kids faced formidable enemies in the fifty-something ballroom dancers who colonized this space before the council decided that the foxtrotters were not a commercially viable set and looked for other promoters to pack people into the building. "They've ruined our dance floor and they're all on drugs," was how one of the disgruntled tango ladies was quoted in the *Sheffield Telegraph. Barkers Pool, tel. 0114/273–5295.*

JARVIS COCKER ACCIDENT SITE

For a period in the late '80s, Pulp caused a stir when they were fronted by a wheelchair-bound Jarvis Cocker (who incidentally is not related to Sheffield's other famous Cocker, Joe). The reason he ended up in a wheelchair was that at a get-together one night in a flat two floors above the Sven adult bookstore, he was trying to impress a girl and for some reason decided jumping out the window was the best way to do it. The gangly Cocker landed badly and broke his legs. He was still determined to keep Pulp on the road. A&R hunters invited to the city to see this locally heralded band didn't know Cocker couldn't walk and thought the singer-in-wheelchair deal was all too sick. Nevertheless it seems that Cocker got attached to his wheelchair and gigged in it for a while after his injuries had healed. *Division St., Devonshire Quarter.*

CRAZY DAISY

When Ian Craig-Marsh and Martin Ware left the Human League in 1980 to form the British Electric Foundation (which evolved into Heaven 17), the remaining Leaguers, Phil Oakey and Adrian Wright, were on the lookout for new ideas. One night at this sleazy old basement disco, they spotted two underage girls—Susan Sulley and Joanne Catherall—and got them into the band as vocalists. By early 1981 the new Human League emerged, saying good-bye to the experimental electronics of their early catalog and presenting a string of very catchy synthpop singles that topped charts worldwide, as well as the mega-selling *Dare* album.

In the '60s, the place was known as the Mojo club, run for a time by Peter Stringfellow and a major stop on the R&B circuit. A branch of the Bradford & Bingley Building Society now occupies the spot. *11 High St.*

THE LIMIT

An (un)employment office now stands on the site of downtown Sheffield's most happening rock club during the city's golden era of electronic bands. The Human League, Cabaret Voltaire, and Vice-Versa played here, along with other, lesser, local lights. Touring bands included U2, Ultravox, and Simple Minds. It kept going for most of the '80s, providing Pulp with a gigging space, until the bulldozers moved in. A peripheral local band, The Naughtiest Girl Was a Monitor, celebrated the place on their single "West Street." *55 West St.*

SHEFFIELD UNITED FOOTBALL CLUB

Def Leppard's Joe Elliott was offered a role in the movie *When Saturday Comes,* to be cast alongside Sean Bean as a Sheffield United player on his hallowed Bramhall Lane ground. He couldn't take up the offer, as he was working on *Slang,* the group's sixth studio album. Although Elliott has been living as a tax exile in Dublin since the early '80s, he takes in as many games as touring schedules permit, flying into Manchester, renting a car to Sheffield, and then having a cup of tea with mom after the game before going "home." Rick Savage, the Def Leppard bass player, was an apprentice professional at the club before the band was rapidly propelled into the big time. The band's first rehearsal room was in a now-demolished building in the shade of the stadium: They rented it for £5 a week.

Before the Don Valley Stadium was built, the Bramhall Lane ground put on several big summertime concerts: the video for Bruce Springsteen's "Spare Parts" live single was shot and recorded here in July 1988. The town's other, and slightly more successful, soccer team is Sheffield Wednesday, the subject of a song called "Steel City," recorded by the Hillsborough Crew (a.k.a. local band and club fans Heaven 17). *Bramall La., tel. 0114/273–8955.*

Chris Callow

Def Leppard at the Wapentake Bar

WAPENTAKE BAR

A stop on the 1995 Def Leppard homecoming and plaque dedicating day (*see* Crookes Workingmen's Club *in* Beyond the City Center, *below*), this basement rock club with a lingering smell of beer and disinfectant (the toilets are a problem here) was where the band did a short acoustic set before an audience of 300 journalists and chums. The last time they had played here was some 17 years earlier, when they made £15 for their efforts. Meanwhile the place rocks on in the old-fashioned heavy metal way each night and sometimes has live bands. Olga Marshall, who ran the club for decades, retired at the end of 1996, and there are plans afoot to kick the place into the '90s by catering to more alternative rock sounds. *13 Charles St., tel. 0114/272–0041.*

SEX AND GOD AND ROCK & ROLL—THE NINE O'CLOCK SERVICE

Sheffield's Reverend Chris Brain, a fully ordained Church of England minister, held some of his "raves for Jesus"—complete with dance music, dry ice, and psychedelic lighting—in the massive Rotunda Room underneath the Ponds Forge International Sports Centre. Known as the Nine O'Clock Service, it was originally thought by Church of England senior figures to be a good way of attracting young people to the way of God. However, Brain's raves, which started in 1985 and lasted for 10 years before collapsing, were not just about praising the Lord—they became a cult. Around 100 former members of the Service have had to seek counseling, and several women alleged sexual abuse by Brain, who surrounded himself with "nuns" dressed in black Lycra. The reverend has emigrated to the United States.

If the Nine O'Clock Service can be said to have done any good to anyone, then it was by demonstrating the viability of the Rotunda Room as a nightclub. The council originally had plans to use it as an exhibition space, but in fall 1996, after half a million pounds were spent on the interior, the place was re-opened as the **ROUNDHOUSE**, a 1,200-capacity nightclub that puts on '70s and '80s retro club nights. *Sheaf St. at Park Square roundabout, tel. 0114/275–0757.*

The Cultural Industries Quarter

Over the past decade, this district of old mills and warehouses directly south of the city center has been transformed from industrial aftermath to a thriving architecturally enhanced neighborhood that's home to more than 100 media-related businesses, including recording studios and the new National Centre for Popular Music. It also has an art-house cinema, several cafés, and pubs. At night it has two of the city's very best places in the Leadmill (for gigs) and the Republic (for the latest dance sounds).

THE AVEC

The Audio Visual Enterprise Centre, sensibly referred to by locals as the AVEC, has been home to the city's major studios for the past few years. **Axis** (tel. 0114/275–0283) is the chief fully equipped commercial studio in Sheffield. Set up by Kev Bacon of the Comsat Angels, it has done recent albums for Audioweb and locals the Longpigs as well as a client list that encompasses Danni Minogue and Robert Wyatt. The building also houses the imaginatively named **H. L. Studio** (tel. 0114/275–4959), which is owned and used exclusively by the Human League. Up until fall 1996, AVEC was also home to the much-loved **FON Studios**, started up by a collective of musicians known as the Manifesto; the name is an acronym for Fuck Off Nazis. Before they failed to pay the bills and were locked out, FON, over the past 10 years (and at various locations), recorded many Sheffield bands, plus Take That and PWEI. One of the last projects they were involved with was BabyBird's *Ugly Beautiful*; apparently the master tapes of this hit album were taken out of the studio just before the locks were put on. Stephen Jones, a.k.a. BabyBird, had written some 400 songs and recorded them here and at his Sheffield home studio in the '90s. He released five limited-edition albums in 1995, each of which contained a voting card asking listeners to vote for a "Best of." He then gathered a band, and the "Best of" album became the successful *Ugly Beautiful. 3–5 Brown St.*

Chris Callow

The Leadmill

THE LEADMILL/ ESQUIRE CLUB

Voted best venue in the country in the 1995 *NME* readers' poll, the Leadmill is a tasteful and functional conversion of an old flourmill that deserves every accolade it gets. The main room holds 900 for bands and club nights, and a cozier room holds about 300. The canteen has decent food, and there's a bar area. In the early

1980s, management allowed bus drivers from the big bus depot across the street to come in free for a drink after their shift finished. Jarvis Cocker and Russell Senior of then-struggling Pulp went out and bought themselves bus drivers' uniforms so they could also get into gigs without paying.

In the past 15 years the Leadmill has seen an A to Z of top bands passing through its doors. This building also housed one of Sheffield's best '60s venues, Esquire. The club was right at the top of the building, up many flights of narrow mill stairs, in what's now the management suite. It had a stage made from two grand pianos pushed together. There was also a pillar in the way; it's said that early Sheffield rocker Dave Berry developed his strange stage antics of ducking and diving here when he was swiveling round this pillar to get the crowd's attention. Vance Arnold (a.k.a. Joe Cocker) and the Avengers were resident band for a while, and touring acts that played here included the Rolling Stones, the Jimi Hendrix Experience, and Cream. *6 Leadmill Rd., tel. 0114/275–4500.*

NATIONAL CENTRE FOR POPULAR MUSIC

After four years of planning, work began on the construction of the £15 million National Centre for Popular Music in 1997. The striking, metal-clad building (this is steel city, after all) is scheduled to open sometime in late 1998.

Rock won't be isolated in this high-tech facility. It will be much more than just a static museum of gold discs, stage outfits, or guitars once used by rock behemoths. Instead, music will, through laser sound and video banks, be put in context, whether it be the familiar chain of influences from Africa to the Delta through Chicago blues to the Rolling Stones and the Britpop bands of today, or from classical composers like Stockhausen through Can and Kraftwerk and other Krautrockers to more recent bands like Public Enemy or Stereolab. In short, visitors will explore in a hands-on way what they want to know rather than being faced with a display of captioned artifacts and memorabilia.

Bringing the program together will be special exhibits (an early one is planned on African music) and workshops, seminars, and film series on every aspect of music and all the technological aspects of

Model for the National Centre for Popular Music, 1997

music-making. As well as attracting half a million visitors a year, the center—as opposed to a museum—will help focus attention on Sheffield's music industry and live venues.

The reason why such a prestigious center landed in the deserving yet unlikely home of Sheffield was simply, according to Tim Strickland, the Creative Director, "We thought of the idea first." *Paternoster Row at Charles St., tel. 0114/279–8941; http://www.fdgroup.co.uk.*

RED TAPE STUDIOS

Some of the London-based media laughed when Sheffield's left-wing council set up a recording and rehearsal room in 1986—the first time municipal bureaucrats had embarked on such an extensive venture. In broad terms it has been tremendously successful, forming a cornerstone of the now-thriving Cultural Industries Quarter and offering Sheffield musicians and technicians a reason to stay and work in their home city rather than trail off to London. Pulp, BabyBird, and the Longpigs are just some of the bands who have used the facilities. They include rehearsal rooms, 4-, 8-, and 12-track studios, and a programming suite.

Red Tape also runs comprehensive sound engineer and other technical training courses and has a library stocked with trade magazines, music manuals, and reference books. It's only open weekdays (9–9). *50 Shoreham St, tel. 0114/276–1151.*

Beyond the City Center

RICK ALLEN CAR WRECK SITE

On New Year's Eve 1984, Def Leppard drummer Rick Allen and his girlfriend were driving back from Manchester over the twisting Snake Pass (A57) in his new Corvette. They had planned to celebrate the New Year with friends and family in Sheffield, but started racing another souped-up sportster not far from the suburb of Hillsborough and went off the road into a field. The actual crash site was about 6 miles out of Sheffield on the A57, on a rugged hilltop called Moscar Top, on the Manchester side of a turning called Long Lane, some 80 yards before a small hospital building. Allen was rushed to the **ROYAL HALLAMSHIRE HOSPITAL** (Glossop Rd. at Hill Rd., tel. 0114/271–1900), but it was too late to save his left arm, and doctors had to amputate it. Allen persevered and rejoined the band playing a specially adapted drum kit.

BROADFIELD PUB

Although this big, lively student pub 2 miles south of the city center no longer puts on live music, it was the best place for local bands to start out in the late '70s. One incredible week in 1978 saw no less a line-up of future local stars than Clock DVA, the Thompson Twins, Vice-Versa, Def Leppard, the Human League, and Cabaret Voltaire. The Comsat Angels (formed in 1978 as Radio Earth), might well have been there, too, but in their early days they changed their name all the time to try to get as many gigs as possible. *452 Abbeydale Rd., tel. 0114/255–0200.*

JOE COCKER "LOST WEEKEND"

After Woodstock and the success of the "Delta Lady" single, Cocker was one of the biggest names in the business. His producer, Leon Russell, concocted a grueling and ill-conceived U.S. tour schedule designed to cash in on Cocker's success. However, the Mad Dogs and Englishmen tour in early 1970, with a massive 21-person backing ensemble that played 65 dates in under three months, almost ruined Cocker financially, physically, and mentally, even though it produced a double album and a feature-length movie. Disillusioned by the business, Cocker holed up in Los Angeles to get away from it all, but this didn't work. Much the worse for drink and drugs, he made his way back to Sheffield to stay at his mom's house on Tasker Road in the Crookes neighborhood. Apart from slouching around the house, Cocker, as the story goes, would nip down to the local **MASON'S ARMS** and drown his sorrows for hours. The following years saw unsuccessful concerts and very few recordings. It wasn't until 1975 that his career got temporarily back on track when his version of Billy Preston's "You Are So Beautiful" went Top 5 in the United States. Cocker still returns to this ordinary little northern pub when he's in town. *2 Carson Rd., Crookes, tel. 0114/268–1108.*

CITY COMPREHENSIVE SCHOOL

Jarvis Cocker formed Pulp (then known as Arabacus Pulp) while studying at this huge school. The group played their first gig—a lunchtime spot in the school cafeteria—in 1981, as a four-piece unit of which only Cocker remains. By the end of that year they had recorded a session for John Peel's radio show. Red Rhino released the *It* mini album in 1983, but Cocker had to wait more than a decade before the *His 'N' Hers* LP rocketed the band into the big time. *Stradbroke Rd., tel. 0114/239–2571.*

STEVE CLARK GRAVE

Def Leppard guitarist Steve Clark, a chronic alcoholic and addict who OD'd in a Chelsea flat in 1991, is buried under a headstone etched with the band's logo and a portrait of Clark. Fans from around the world come out and attach notes and mementoes to the grave, which is in a small burial ground on the west side of the city, just beyond Hillsborough and close to where drummer Rick Allen lost his arm in a car wreck. *Loxley Cemetery, Long La. off Loxley Rd.*

THE JOE COCKER TREE

During the 1994/95 academic year, the city's best-known solo artist, Joe Cocker, was given an honorary doctorate by Sheffield Hallam University (formerly the Polytechnic). One of the civic ceremonies organized to celebrate the success of the hometown guy was the planting of a commemorative tree at a prime downtown site at the top of Howard Street (at Arundel Gate, just up from the Students' Union). Unfortunately, the tree couldn't hack the icy winds of Sheffield and is no longer here. It's been moved to a more sheltered location at the college's Collegiate Crescent site, near the Royal Hallamshire Hospital, but there's no plaque to set it apart.

Joe Cocker planting the commemorative tree, 1994

CROOKES WORKING MEN'S CLUB

On October 5, 1995, Def Leppard made their first stop here on their much-hyped homecoming trip. They called in at this cozy, redbrick club with a bowling green out front to unveil a Sheffield heritage plaque dedicated to them. A couple of teenage fans had asked the city's lord mayor to honor the band in some way, and this is what the council came up with. The club was chosen because the band had a short residency here in 1979 (playing before four dozen people who had paid 50p to get in, with Joe Elliott's gran in the next room sipping milk stout), just before they signed up with Vertigo. Apparently, they hadn't been back since. The blue-collar Crookes neighborhood, close to the university campus, is a couple of miles out from downtown. Joe Elliott was born at 61 Crookes Road in 1959. In recent years, Crookes WMC has been home to the JuJu Club, the city's premier worldbeat showcase. *Mulehouse Rd., Crookes, tel. 0114/266–0114.*

DON VALLEY VENUES

Def Leppard have another plaque dedicated to them in the foyer of the gorgeous, new, slightly futuristic **DON VALLEY STADIUM** (Worksop Rd., tel. 0114/256–0607), proclaiming that in June 1993 they were "the first band to play and sell out." The undercard at this hometown gig, which drew some 40,000 fans, was Thunder, Ugly Kid Joe, and Ter-rorvision. There are big color photos of the headliners displayed next to the plaque. Others to sell out here have been Bon Jovi and the Rolling Stones. The stadium is 2 miles north of downtown just beyond the sleazy Attercliffe neighborhood (live strip shows in the pubs every Sunday).

Right next door, the **Don Valley Bowl** amphitheater hosts the weekend Music in the Sun Festival in July. Started in the late '80s, it's a mix of all types of sounds from Longpigs rock to reggae heroes the Mighty Diamonds; it also has some wicked dance tents.

The **Don Valley Arena** (Broughton La., tel. 0114/256–5656), right beside the Don Valley Bowl, is home to the city's hockey team and has put on Prince, Metallica, and Sting. Oasis played its first arena show in this huge brown bunker of a building on April 22, 1995, supported by Pulp, who went on to steal the more-fancied Mancunians' thun-der at that year's Glastonbury fest.

KING EDWARD VII SCHOOL

The Yorkshire nomination for Rock & Roll High School belongs to this former boy's gram-mar that's now a mixed comprehensive, known locally as King Ted's. Among those who call it their alma mater are Iron Maiden's Bruce Dickinson, Paul Heaton of the Housemartins, and BBC radio top dog Matthew Bannister, who made his name getting rid of the old-school DJs on Radio 1FM. A head boy (top honors student) in the mid-'70s was one Gra-ham Fellowes, who went on to study drama at Manchester and adopt the Jilted John persona, with which he had a novelty post-punk hit. *Glossop Rd., tel. 0114/236–2518.*

SHEFFIELD UNIVERSITY

Sheffield's electronic kings, Cabaret Voltaire, got their 1975 debut gig in the Upper Refectory by conning their way onto the bill saying they could play mainstream rock. They took the stage and played crude electronic stuff with guitars fed through synthe-sizers at a time when no one else in the rock world was doing that in Britain. The set caused unrest among the good-time, beer-drinking students and, according to the band's Richard Kirk, "a fight broke out and we won."

Although they weren't students, Cabaret Voltaire have a couple of other associations with the University. They were involved with the Now Society, a student club of the late '70s dedicated to electronic music that managed to raise enough interest to get Kraftwerk to come and play here. In 1982 under the pseudonym the Pressure Company, they did a benefit gig for the Polish trade union Solidarity, and the live recording is still available through Mute. They also had their famous Western Works studio here in the late '70s and early '80s—to which New Order came after Ian Curtis died to demo new work and see which of the remaining three was the best singer. The place was knocked down in the mid-'80s to be replaced by a new university building.

In the late '70s, Martin Fry was studying English literature at the college. He ran the *Modern Drugs* fanzine and interviewed local electronic rockers Vice-Versa; eventually he joined that band. They started playing more commercial, soul-based sounds, changed their name to ABC, and had a string of hits in the early '80s.

The campus is in leafy Broomhill, a couple of miles east of downtown. Today the Students' Union manages to book quality touring bands. *Western Bank, tel. 0114/272–4076.*

WESTON PARK

To accompany their 1994 single, "Do You Remember the First Time?," Pulp's Jarvis Cocker and Steve Mackey did a 26-minute video of the same name in which they asked celebri-ties, including John Peel, Ralph Steadman, and Vivian Stanshall, when and where was the first time that they had sex. Most of the interviews took place in studios, but there was footage from Sheffield, including this leafy park, where, Cocker admitted, he had it for the first time. In previous years Pulp was among the bands that played at Dole-busters benefit gigs in the park, which is just behind the university buildings and across the road from a boating lake. *Mushroom La. at Western Bank, Broomhill.*

Steve Gillett

Jarvis Cocker of Pulp

Out from Sheffield

Fans of Kid Creole and the Coconuts might want to know that August Darnell hitched up with a member of his U.K. fan club and now lives outside the city in the mining village of Dinnington, 15 miles west of Sheffield.

Cromford

In 1771 Richard Arkwright opened England's first factory (to spin cotton) in this stone-built Derbyshire village about 25 miles south of Sheffield. Some 223 years later, Oasis sent their design team to the local railway station, a tiny halt near the end of a dead-end line from Derby, to pose for the cover of "Some Might Say."

OASIS'S "SOME MIGHT SAY" COVER

Standing in the station, in need of education—Oasis, "Some Might Say"

The busy railway scene on the cover of Oasis's "Some Might Say" single was shot at tiny Cromford station. Rather than including pictures of the band, designer Brian Cannon used members of his own family: the man with the wheelbarrow is his father; the woman with the mop his mom. The dog is a proper actor and has starred in movies with Kevin Costner. The station is still in use, though the tracks were airbrushed out of the Oasis cover photo.

OASIS'S "WHATEVER" COVER

Oasis used another unlikely image—just moorland, heather, and sky—for the cover of the Christmas 1994 single, "Whatever." They took the photo in Eastmoor, off the A619, about 10 miles north of Cromford on the way to Sheffield.

Go to Scotland, no obligation—Gang of Four, "Return the Gift"

For a country with such a powerful cultural history and strong folk music tradition, Scotland's contribution to rock & roll is surprisingly small. The two large cities of Glasgow and Edinburgh have produced the bulk of Scottish acts, though Dundee (through the Average White Band and the Associates) and Aberdeen have also had a slight say in affairs. In the early '60s most of these places had a lively youth club and coffee bar scene, but unlike Liverpool, Belfast, Newcastle, or London, they produced no great '60s groups. Since then it's mostly been quantity over quality, especially in the '80s, with legions of slushy pop bands trying to graft a Caledonian angle onto American rock and soul. Only since the later '80s, with the likes of the Jesus and Mary Chain, Primal Scream, and Teenage Fanclub, have Scottish bands emerged with a fresh sound. This has led to an explosion of band-forming and the establishment of an exciting live scene based around Glasgow, Scotland's main rock & roll city, which has produced literally dozens of new bands in recent years.

EDINBURGH

Edinburgh, with its carefully preserved Georgian and Victorian architecture, romantic castle, wild city center park, extinct volcano, sweeping views, winding hilly streets, and foreboding-looking churches, may be the most beautiful city in Britain, and probably in Europe, but in the grand scheme of rock & roll it means diddly-squat. The fact that the Bay City Rollers—who got their name by sticking a pin into a map of the United States and pricking Bay City, Michigan—formed here in the early '70s is a blow from which the local scene is still recovering. It wasn't until punk that the city could cite any bands worth talking about and even then the Rezillos (later the Revillos), despite two great guitar-frenzy singles in "Can't Stand My Baby" and "My Baby Does Good Sculptures," weren't exactly first division material. Nor were the Valves, who sang "Ain't No Surf in Portobello" about a nearby sewage plant.

In the immediate post-punk years, there was some interest in the indie Fast Records and the jangly Josef K (signed to Postcard), but critical acclaim did not carve a big niche in many record collections. The late '70s also saw the recording debut of Waterboys' vocalist Mike Scott in a band called Another Pretty Face and the emergence of Marillion's Fish from nearby Dalkeith, 10 miles southeast of the city.

Since then, Edinburgh has come up with the gothy Goodbye Mr. Mackenzie, spotlighting Shirley Manson (now of Garbage), and the Proclaimers. Finitribe released "Animal Farm" with samples of the "Old MacDonald" nursery rhyme and got a few headlines with a "Fuck Off McDonalds" poster campaign. Other Edinburgh outfits of the past decade include Jesse Garon and the Desperadoes (named for Elvis Presley's brother); the

The Proclaimer twins hooting it up

Steve Gillett

267

dance indie outfit the Apples; Nectarine No. 9, formed in 1993, who have recorded for Postcard; the Nirvana-ish Flood; and dance acts like Blackanized 360°.

Every August, tens of thousands of tourists hit town for the **EDINBURGH FESTIVAL,** Britain's largest. The fest's growth has meant that the main (straight arts) events have been overshadowed by the various generic minifests—on movies, TV, literature, fringe theater, and so on—that take place simultaneously. Little of musical interest ever seems to happen, although there are loads of gigs every night in pubs, bars, and the city's various concert halls, which are all collected under the festival umbrella. At the 1996 event, Michael Stipe introduced the first-ever screening of *Road Movie,* the movie of the *Monster* world tour.

EATINGDRINKING**DANCING**SHOPPING**PLAYING**SLEEPING

Edinburgh is just about the only city in Britain that ranks with London when it comes to wandering around finding unplanned excitement, and visitors new to the city usually start off on Princes Street (depicted in the opening shots of *Trainspotting*), which runs east–west through the center of town.

Until the '90s, Edinburgh's nighttime delights were largely middle-of-the-road, but the city has now caught up with the designer bar/nightclubbing culture revolution of London and Manchester. Compared to Glasgow, Edinburgh doesn't have that many decent live music venues. Those worth checking out include a couple on Rutland Street, at the far western end of Princes Street: **L'ATTACHE** (Rutland St., tel. 0131/229–3402), a cellar bar that gets crowded early on, and **PLATFORM ONE** (Rutland St., tel. 0131/225–2433). The biker-frequented **CAS ROCK CAFÉ** near Grassmarket (*see below*) is the top small venue in Edinburgh these days. **QUEEN'S HALL** (S. Clerk St., tel. 0131/668–2019) is a converted church that holds 800, the seating in pews, and tends to have jazz (the late Don Cherry, Neneh's dad has played) and less noisy rock.

On cobbled Victoria Street, which climbs uphill from the Grassmarket, in the same building as the Byzantium flea market, is the **LIQUID ROOM** (9c Victoria St., tel. 0131/225–2564), broader than it is long, thereby enabling the audience to get up close to the stage for a great view of the bands. As the Music Box, it put on acts like Rocket From the Crypt and the Jon Spencer Blues Explosion in 1996 before being refurbished and extended to hold 1,000 revelers. Victoria Street was also where the city's best '60s beat clubs were based (*see below*). Below Victoria Street (literally) to the south is Cowgate, a gloomy, dirty road around which ramshackle venues and bars are always springing up. Longest-running is **LA BELLE ANGELE** (Hastie's Close, off Cowgate, tel. 0131/225–2774), a club venue that

Queen's Hall, once a church

puts on mainly new names but did recently have Jonathan Richman. The **ATTIC** (Dyer's Close, off Cowgate, tel. 0131/478–0093) bar hosts a variety of nights, including the techno "Lift" on Thursdays.

To the east, between the extinct volcano, Arthur's Seat, and Calton Hill (on which the Proclaimers stand for the cover of *Sunshine on Leith*), is **THE VENUE** (Calton Rd., tel. 0131/557–3073), a major stop for up-and-coming bands hoping to break out of the indie circuit. It also hosts visiting U.S. alternative acts and the celebrated Friday club night, "Pure." The Venue, so hot and small that sweat drips down from the ceiling, has also been putting on the club night "Misery," in which the worst sounds from every genre are mercilessly aired, and the fortnightly "LIS:EN" hard house/techno night.

Zion Train at La Belle Angele

Glasgow's **Fopp** (55 Coburn St., tel. 0131/220–0133) record store has a branch in Edinburgh. The entire bottom floor is devoted to vinyl and there are lots of cheap CD singles as well. **Record Shack** (69 S. Clerk St., tel. 0131/667–7144) has loads of attractively priced used records. Give yourself a few hours. Details of everything happening can be found in *The List,* Edinburgh's and Glasgow's excellent fortnightly listings guide.

CAS ROCK CAFÉ

During the 1996 Edinburgh Festival Teenage Fanclub played this biker-frequented dive—not their usual sort of venue—at the base of an ugly concrete office block just west of the Old Town. They were part of the infinitely smaller Planet Pop festival, which may become a regular event. *West Port, tel. 0131/229–4341.*

FAST PRODUCT

Bob Last ran his pioneering indie label from this office in Abbeyhill, just north of Arthur's Seat, at the turn of the '70s. The label made its name not from local bands but from signing three remarkable Yorkshire groups—Gang of Four, Human League, and the Mekons, all of whom first recorded for Fast in 1978. Although the Human League achieved the greatest success and the Gang of Four had the most influence, the Mekons came up with the most impressive Fast releases—the brutal "Never Been in a Riot" and the only slightly less barbed "Where Were You?" Fast's later *Earcom 2: Contradiction* compilation included exclusive Joy Division takeouts from the *Unknown Pleasures* sessions in "Auto-Suggestion" and "From Safety to Where." Fast did manage to find one decent Edinburgh band, the Scars, whose "Adultery/Horrorshow" single (1980) promised great things that, alas, never happened. Around the same time, the rock press went crazy for Edinburgh's Fire Engines, signed to another Fast label, Pop Aural. The public wasn't fooled, though, and studiously failed to buy their over-hyped records. *3 East Norton Pl., Abbeyhill.*

LEITH

The Proclaimers, formed north of the city in Auchtermuchty, gave Edinburgh's grotty port a surprise romantic slant with the song "Sunshine on Leith" on the album of the same name. On the cover, the Reid twins stand on Calton Hill gazing over Leith's chimneys, cranes, and tower blocks. Since the album came out (in 1988) Leith's semiderelict waterfront has been ever so slightly gentrified. The long walk to Leith from Princes Street up Leith Walk offers a glimpse of Edinburgh's less-genteel side.

VICTORIA STREET

Now full of expensive gift stores catering to tourists, this cobbled street is where Edinburgh's best early beat clubs, the Gamp and the Place, stood. The subterranean Place (4 Victoria St.), known as Jazz at the Place when it was a trad venue in the late '50s, later put on such local beat bands as the Premiers and such well-known international artists as Memphis Slim and Joan Baez in the mid-'60s. In the psychedelic era, it became Middle Earth North (the name lifted from London Covent Garden's similar cash-in flower-power-era venue), where Moby Grape staged a rare U.K. gig. As the **ROCKING HORSE** (tel. 0131/225–3326) the joint has now been expanded into a studenty nightclub with four bars ranged over several floors open every night except Mondays. Just opposite the Place was another early '60s beat club, the Gamp (1–2 Victoria Terrace, now replaced by council offices) whose house band, the Athenians, were the first Scottish outfit to release a single ("You Tell Me" in 1964).

GLASGOW

The frame is out of Glasgow/The tech is Balinese—Donald Fagen, "Trans-Island Sky-way"

This great industrial giant, the world shipbuilding capital for much of the past 200 years and one of the most powerful cities in the British Empire for much of the 19th century, dominates the Scottish rock scene. Almost every major Scottish band or performer has origins in or around Glasgow—from Alex Harvey and the Incredible String Band in the '60s through to the more recent Primal Scream and Teenage Fanclub.

Primal Scream's Bobby Gillespie in Glasgow

Harvey, Glasgow's first rock star, cut enthusiastic versions of R&B standards like "I've Got My Mojo Working" and "Bo Diddley is a Gunslinger" on his 1964 album, *Alex Harvey and His Soul Band*, now considered to be Scotland's first "rock" LP. Although Harvey's outfit wasn't able to make the transition from dance-hall covers to chart-topping self-penned hits like, say, the Beatles in Liverpool or the Rolling Stones in London, his legacy endures, as much for his galvanizing effect on the local scene as for his records, and these days artists like Nick Cave try to do an A.H. cover in their set whenever they play the city.

Many of Harvey's contemporaries took the folk route paved by Bob Dylan, whose own mentor, Woody Guthrie, spent part of World War II in Glasgow as a merchant seaman. At the forefront of the early '60s Scottish folk scene were the duo Robin Williamson and Mike Heron, guitar virtuoso Bert Jansch, and the singers John Martyn and Donovan. In 1966 Williamson and Heron formed the Incredible String Band, a major force behind the emerging psychedelic scene and often cited by Led Zeppelin as their favorite band. A year later Jansch formed Pentangle with John Renbourn (Johnny Marr's favorite guitarist) and Danny Thompson (now Richard Thompson's bassist).

As long as acts like these felt they needed to move to London to gain a wider audience, there was little chance of Glasgow's becoming a major music center. Punk changed things slightly as indie labels like Postcard (Orange Juice) began to form in Glasgow. By the mid-'80s, no fewer than 40 bands from Glasgow and around had been signed to various labels, but, the Blue Nile and Pastels apart, there was hardly a decent one among them.

Since then, with some help from Alan McGee and his (London-based) indie giant Creation, things have improved massively. Glasgow bands have gone from being terminally unhip to being frighteningly cool. McGee's first inspired signing was Jesus and Mary Chain (from East Kilbride, just outside Glasgow) in 1984. Their drummer, Bobby Gillespie, was also leader of another Creation band, Primal Scream. A third Creation signing, the tuneful lo-fi Teenage Fanclub, are a key link in the Scottish revival, along with the Vaselines/Captain America/Eugenius family tree that was plugged by Kurt Cobain, and the various bands associated with the Pastels, whose Stephen Pastel (né McRobbie) formed the 53rd and 3rd indie label (named after the Ramones song) and signed up the BMX Bandits and the Soup Dragons.

All this has meant that Glasgow now occupies an elevated position with lots of young bands. Glasgow for the most part spurned the crass commercialism of Britpop and instead started a scene that seemed genuinely into making fresh, slightly experimental sound influenced by Slint and Sebadoh. Among the key bands were the Delgados, whose Chemikal Underground label also featured the eclectic Arab Strap; the bubblegum pop trio Bis, who made history in early 1996 when they became the first band without a record label to appear on Top of the Pops and were soon signed to the Beastie Boys' Grand Royale label; Thrum, who have worked in San Francisco with Grant Phillips of Grant Lee Buffalo; Urusei Yatsura, doing well in the indie charts with a Pavementy sound; the exciting Krautrockish Ganger; and the largely instrumental Mogwai.

EATINGDRINKINGDANCINGSHOPPINGPLAYINGSLEEPING

Glasgow is working hard to improve an image that for years had it down as an uncouth city with a tendency for alcohol-fueled casual violence.

As a nightlife center for clubbing and gigging, Glasgow now ranks with the best in Britain outside London, helped by later bar-closing times than England. The best-known venue is **KING TUT'S WAH WAH HUT** (*see below*), a welcoming cellar bar about half a mile west of Central Station, where Creation Records boss Alan McGee first spotted Oasis. Over on the shabbier eastern side of town stands **BARROWLAND** (*see below*), a former ballroom that gets in big names. **THE ARCHES** (Midland St., off Jamaica St., tel. 0141/221–9736) under Central Station used to be La Cave, which, in the '60s, was Scotland's first rock & roll club and a regular gigging venue for the Alex Harvey Soul Band. After scores of name-changes and renovations, it now includes a theater, exhibition space, a dance floor, and gigging space and on Fridays puts on the raved-about Slam club as well as occasional gigs on other nights.

THE GLASGOW SCHOOL OF ART (167 Renfrew St., tel. 0141/332–0691), the city's most spectacular building, also puts on some gigs and club nights—with lots of rap and dance. Names like Mary Chapin Carpenter and Squeeze play the classy **ROYAL CONCERT HALL** (2 Sauchiehall St., tel. 0141/227–5511), Glasgow's main orchestral music venue, which stands at the eastern end of Sauchiehall Street, the city's most famous thoroughfare. It is along Sauchiehall Street that some of Glasgow's best clubs can be found. The **VENUE** (474 Sauchiehall St., tel. 0141/353–1927) is where Primal Scream made their debut in 1985. It's been the home of the Friday-night retro-indie "Helter Skelter" since 1988.

Some of the clubs, like **ROOFTOPS** (92 Sauchiehall St., tel. 0141/332–5883), where the Jesus and Mary Chain played their first gig (when it was known as Nightmoves) and **REDS** (375 Sauchiehall St., tel. 0141/331–1635), are little more than tacky discos.

Some of the music venues, like **LAUDER'S** (Sauchiehall St. at Renfield St., tel. 0141/332-1290), which has midweek blues nights, are just rough pubs done up with tacky Victorian motifs. But there are some excellent café bars along Sauchiehall now, particularly **NICO'S** (379 Sauchiehall St., tel. 0141/332-5736), with its exquisite Art Nouveau design. **NICE 'N' SLEAZY** (421 Sauchiehall St., tel. 0141/333-9637), named for the Stranglers song, a studenty haunt with posters for wallpaper, is the sort of place where new bands learn the ropes. **THE GARAGE** (490 Sauchiehall St., tel. 0141/332-1120) draws customers in with the shock effect of the front of a truck embedded in the awning.

Closer to the center of town, **BAR 10** (10 Mitchell La., off Buchanan St., tel. 0141/221-8353) is a classy and unpretentious joint with lots of gorgeous tile and marble work. A wooden door embedded with plastic "horns" leads down to the **TUNNEL** (84 Mitchell St., tel. 0141/204-1000), just east of Central Station, the city's first designer club. Just south of it, next to an amusement arcade, is the hot, sweaty **SUB CLUB** (22 Jamaica St., tel. 0141/248-4600), a weekend joint that stays open till 3 AM and has replaced Tunnel as *the* place where you're likely to hear exciting current dance sounds. A bit farther east is the **13TH NOTE** (80 Glassford St., tel. 0141/553-1638), a lively bar that is probably the best place in Glasgow to see up-and-coming bands (usually free).

The other great lively (student) area is the West End, overlooked by the imposing Gothic mass of Glasgow University, set high on a hill near the River Kelvin. Bustling, friendly Byres Road, running more or less north-south through the heart of the West End, is the center of student activity; **CURLER'S** (256 Byres Rd., tel. 0141/334-1284) is a huge hangar of a place next to Hillhead underground station; it attracts a serious, hard core drinking crowd and has some live music, particularly rootsy Scottish sounds. The most popular club in this area is the **VOLCANO** (15 Benalder St., tel. 0141/337-1100), just south of Byres Road, opened in the mid-'90s by the people who run the Tunnel; it's decorated like a tropical paradise. Some of the *Trainspotting* movie was shot here.

Glasgow is a great festival city. The annual calendar starts every spring with the **MAYFEST**, which incorporates a bit of everything and sees loads of bands play city venues. Glasgow put on the first Sound City festival in 1994 and now hosts the **TEN-DAY WEEKEND** every October, when the students return, in scores of venues across the city. Another annual event is **T IN THE PARK**, at Lanark Racecourse.

Details of everything happening can be found in *The List*, Edinburgh's and Glasgow's excellent fortnightly listings guide. Record stores and hip cafés are also awash with excellent flyers. Most useful is the free *Live Scene*.

Glasgow is well served for record stores. **FOPP RECORDS** (358 Byres Rd., tel. 0141/357-0774) in the West End is probably the best all-round record store in Glasgow with inexpensive CDs and vinyl and a friendly atmosphere. In the center of town, **RECORD FAYRE** (17 Chisholm St., tel. 0141/552-5696) stocks very cheap vinyl and loads of T-shirts. **23RD PRECINCT** (23 Bath St., tel. 0141/332-4806 or 0141/332-9740), just north of Central Station, specializes in dance records. **MISSING** (54 Oswald St., tel. 0141/248-2495; 82 Oswald St., tel. 0141/221-4239) has two branches in city center on Oswald Street, one with loads of cheap used stuff at No. 54 and a larger new record branch at No. 82. **JOHN SMITH'S BOOKSHOP** (Byres Rd., tel. 0141/334-2769), in the University area, has a likeable coffee bar and a record section where Stephen Pastel (né McRobbie and formerly the leader of the mid-'80s shambling rockers the Pastels) can often be found behind the counter.

BARROWLAND

Simple Minds reopened this 1,900-capacity ballroom just east of the city center, now one of Glasgow's top venues, with three gigs in 1982, at which their "Waterfront" video was shot. Barrowland was a major light entertainment and ballroom dancing venue in the '60s but closed after the so-called Bible John murders, in which a dapper, Bible-spouting lunatic picked up a number of women at the venue, took them home, and murdered them. In 1994 the place again attracted trouble when a fan was stabbed to death at an Ice Cube gig. The same year, Liam Gallagher walked off stage in the middle of an Oasis show claiming his voice was going. Noel did the rest of the set. The following year during a Hole gig, Courtney Love got a bit stroppy (annoyed) when she spotted a fan wearing a dreaded Pearl

Neon madness at Barrowland

Jam T-shirt. He refused to accept twice what he paid for it to take it off, and so Love offered to swap her knickers for the shirt. That did the trick, and when she threw her Victoria's Secrets into the crowd, the guy passed said T-shirt. Love told the crowd, "Giving up Pearl Jam is like accepting Jesus into your life." Garbage, during their first U.K. tour (1995), came back for an encore after a well-received gig in kilts. More recently Skunk Anansie, the Lightning Seeds, Runrig, Sepultura, the Beautiful South, and Kula Shaker have played. In sympathy with its history as a meat-market, Barrowland retains the old-fashioned disco orbs inside and a host of tacky stars and neon strips on the sign outside. *244 Gallowgate, tel. 0141/552-4601.*

THE CATHOUSE (THE RAT TRAP)

Oasis recorded a live version of "I Am the Walrus" at this 300-capacity club in June 1994 and used it as the B-side of "Cigarettes and Alcohol." Now known as the Rat Trap, and based in the former Seamen's Institute in a dismal southwest section of the city center near the Clyde, it puts on dance music club nights midweek and tends toward indie on weekends. The Cathouse, meanwhile, has moved nearer the center of town to 15 Union St. *9 Brown St., tel. 0141/221-7233.*

CELTIC FC

Gil Scott Heron's dad, Giles Heron, a.k.a. "The Black Flash," played for Glasgow's Irish-Catholic soccer team in the '50s. He was the first American, and just about the only African-American, to play for a British soccer club. Rod Stewart name-dropped the club on his 1977 "You're in My Heart" single. *95 Kerrydale St., Bridgeton, tel. 0141/556-2611.*

GLASGOW GREEN

In this long finger of a park at the southeast end of the city near the River Clyde, the original Stone Roses lineup played their last gig (1990). The setting for many gangland battles in the '50s and '60s, Glasgow Green was the place where in 1765 James Watt first envisaged the steam engine, a brainstorm that led to the industrial revolution, during which Glasgow made its name.

ALEX HARVEY MEMORIAL PLAQUE

There is a Harp Rock Plaque dedicated to Scotland's first rock & roll star on a wall inside Govan Town Hall, a performance arts center. The plan had been to stick the plaque on the house where Harvey was born, but that had long since been bulldozed. They then thought about putting it on the nearest building to the house but realized it would be "collected" by a fan or chiseled off by local kids, so that's why the memorial is a mile away from where it should have been. *Govan Town Hall, Summertown Rd., Govan, tel. 0141/445-1610.*

KELVIN HALL

The Kinks recorded their 1967 album *Live at Kelvin Hall,* one of rock's first live LPs, inside this ornate Moorish-looking sandstone building. The Hall, next to the Kelvin, Glasgow's second-largest river, was built as an exhibition hall in 1927 and converted into a home for the Museum of Transport as well as an international athletics sports arena in 1984. *Argyle St. at Bunhouse Rd.*

[KING TUT'S WAH WAH HUT]

There's been much written about events at this club on the night of May 31, 1993. That was when Creation records boss Alan McGhee saw Oasis live for the first time and signed them up immediately. Much rock legend and many lies center around how Oasis got on the bill. The usual hype goes that the Mancunians heard that McGhee would be at a gig by 18 Wheeler (the Creation-label band named after a gay truckers mag) that night and drove up here and muscled their way onto the bill with various outrageous threats to venue staff and management. In fact, there were some arguments and tensions, but nothing like the hard-man image that Oasis tried to project.

Set incongruously to the west of the city center in a row of smart stone Georgian houses converted into offices for solicitors and other professionals, King Tut's, a 300-capacity basement club, is still one of Glasgow's premier venues. In 1996 it presented acts such as Elastica, Placebo, Cast, the Aloof, the Real People, Shawn Colvin, and Ben Folds Five. By day it is a well-patronized bar, crowded at lunchtime and serving Tex-Mex food. *272a St. Vincent St., tel. 0141/248-5158.*

POSTCARD

Alan Horne was studying botany at Glasgow University when he started Postcard, one of Scotland's best-known indie labels, in his Kelvinbridge apartment just east of the University. The label forsook both the noisy guitar sound of punk and the popular synths of the day and concentrated instead on simple melodies, lush production, and a hint of '70s pop soul under the banner "The Sound of Young Scotland," nicked from Motown's Sound of Young America slogan. The label was dominated by one act, Orange Juice, but other bands included Josef K and, for a couple of records, Australia's Go-Betweens. The label wound down in the mid-'80s but recently restarted as a home for unreconstructed '80s Scotpoppers like Paul Quinn. *185 W. Princes St.*

RANGERS FC

I've never been asked and never replied if I supported Glasgow Rangers—The Pogues, "Down All the Days"

In 1986 the aptly named Celtic fans Simple Minds played at the Ibrox Park, home of the Rangers, Glasgow's strictly Protestant club. Despite having staged the gig in a bid to unify sectarianly split kids through rock & roll, they proceeded to sprinkle holy water in the goalmouth. *Ibrox Park, Edmiston Dr. at Broomloan Rd., Govan, tel. 0141/427-8500.*

STRATHCLYDE UNIVERSITY

The Student Union has made Dr. Alex Paterson (his prefix comes from his first two names, Duncan Robert) of the Orb honorary president. *George St. at John St., tel. 0141/552-4400.*

THE VENUE

Primal Scream played their first-ever gig at this pokey joint in October 1984 supporting the Jesus and Mary Chain. Their vocalist, Bobby Gillespie, had a busy night. He was roped in to play drums with JAMC after they fired their drummer, Murray Dalglish, but enjoyed it so much he carried on doing so for about a year. The Venue is now a nightclub (rock, indie) and doesn't put on gigs. *474 Sauchiehall St., tel. 0141/353-1927.*

Out from Glasgow

Belshill

This former mining village 10 miles east of Glasgow has reared a number of key Scottish '80s/'90s bands—Madchester bandwagon-jumpers the Soup Dragons, indie stalwarts BMX Bandits, and cult faves Teenage Fanclub. The Bandits, named after a humorous cult movie, cut their first sounds for the indie label 53rd and 3rd (named for the Ramones' song) and are now on Creation, as are Teenage Fanclub, with whom BMX Bandits have shared band members. TFC's influences number the Byrds (they named a 1993 song "Gene Clark" in honor of that group's late singer), Neil Young (a 1995 single was wittily titled "Neil Jung"), and Alex Chilton, who worked with them in 1992.

Easterhouse

The short-lived revolutionary communist indie band who named themselves after this notorious facilities-free '60s council housing project 5 miles east of Glasgow city center hailed not from here but from the Hulme estate, a similar social disaster area in central Manchester (*see* Manchester *in* the Northwest). Shortly after the estate was first built in the '60s, crooner Frankie Vaughan helped organize a knives amnesty in a highly publicized attempt to quell the local razor gangs, but the area is still plagued by gangs. Many sport exotic names like the Bartoi or the Torrantoi, just as they did in the '60s as depicted in the 1996 Glasgow-shot *Small Faces* movie, which was originally meant to be called *Easterhouse*.

East Kilbride

This grim, hilly new town is the home of the Jesus and Mary Chain, whose inspired mix of cool "surfing" harmonies and Velvet Underground-style feedback made them into a sort of Beach Boys from hell, or East Kilbride, which is pretty similar. The perfect antidote to Glasgow's sensitive Scotpop boys, JAMC quickly became the indie darlings of 1985, helped by a series of violent gigs and a marvelous debut album, *Psychocandy*, which they have never come anywhere near to matching since (nor have many others, for that matter).

East Kilbride spawned Roddy Frame, who recorded some appetizing pop for Rough Trade when he was still in his teens in the early '80s but whose career has faltered since. Also from here are the foul-mouthed McOi standard-bearers, the Exploited, who were responsible for such crusading nihilist anthems as "Fuck the Mods," "Punk's Not Dead," "I Believe in Anarchy," and "Sid Vicious Was Innocent."

Irvine Beach

In July 1995, Oasis shipped over one of the world's largest marquees (open-sided tent) from China so that 6,000 people could watch them play two gigs here. Irvine Beach, just southwest of Britain's only seaside New Town (public housing village), is 20 miles southwest of Glasgow. From the band's mailing list and an ad in a Scottish newspaper, the gigs sold out before they had even been announced in the music press. The following August, the On the Beach '96 event closed the festival season with Björk, Underworld, Supergrass, and others playing in an 8,500-capacity marquee on loan from Disney.

Mull of Kintyre

Paul McCartney's overplayed mega-selling 1977 single is named for this promontory, known for its sunsets, at the southwest tip of the Kintyre peninsula. At first glance on the map, Kintyre looks like an island, but it is in fact a long finger of land just barely connected to the Scottish mainland 80 miles southwest of Glasgow.

Elvis greets fans at Prestwick Airport, 1960

Prestwick International Airport

Elvis Presley's sole visit to Britain took place at Prestwick airport, 30 miles southwest of Glasgow, on March 2, 1960, when he flew in as U.S. Army serviceman Sgt. E.A. Presley 53310761. Presley's DC-7 plane landed at Gannett Airfield, next to Prestwick International, for refueling before returning to the States. The king got out, stretched his legs on British soil for the only time, and met a few fans at the perimeter fence. In October 1993 Elvis's long-standing sidemen, drummer DJ Fontana and guitarist Scotty Moore, revisited the site to unveil a Harp Rock plaque in the airport's Graceland Bar. The bar is open to the public but you can't follow the footsteps of Elvis, as that area is still part of a naval base and therefore out of bounds.

Less celebrated was a visit in 1975 by Who drummer Keith Moon, whose flight to a gig in Leicester was diverted here. Frustrated at not being able to get a drink, he smashed up a ticket turnstile and was arrested. After being fined in court, Moon offered to buy one of the airline's aircraft to make it up to them. *Off A77, Monkton, tel. 01292/79822.*

Aberdeen

Aberdeen's an old place—The Associates, "White Car in Germany"

Britain's oil capital, also known as the Granite City, has been party to some mysterious rock walk-outs. In September 1979 Siouxsie and the Banshees' drummer Kenny Morris and guitarist John McKay suddenly quit the band before a gig, claiming they could no longer cope with the "pressure."

Three years later, the Clash were due to begin their Know Your Rights tour when it was revealed that Joe Strummer had gone AWOL. He and a girlfriend had fled to Paris by boat train, also muttering something about pressure.

Nanci Griffith's "Road to Aberdeen" was written while she traveled here on a bus from Glasgow. Most of the chart-topping techno trancers the Shamen, apart from Cockney rapper Mr C, originate from Aberdeen. Also from Aberdeen are Nude signings Geneva and the long-running

Neo-Gothic decor at the Ministry of Sin, Aberdeen

Lorelei. The latter were big Peel faves and played rocky funk, supporting James Brown.
THE MINISTRY OF SIN (15 Gordon St., tel. 01224/211661) plays general dancey sounds.

Dunfermline

On the north bank of the Forth opposite Edinburgh, this former Scottish capital is home to the tuneful hard-rockers Nazareth. Also from here are the Skids, who formed in 1977 and had a couple of exciting punk-style singles in "Into the Valley" and "Masquerade." They named their retrospective compilation album *Dunfermline*. Stuart Adamson left the Skids to form Big Country, whose 1984 LP, *Steel City*, was also a reference to his home town.

BELVILLE HOTEL (JOHNSON'S)

Nazareth was called the Shadettes until one day in 1969 when they met up in the foyer of the Belville Hotel. The Band's "The Weight" was playing on the jukebox, and when the line "I pulled into Nazareth" came on, they had a flash of inspiration and decided to name themselves after the Pennsylvania town instead. The Bellville, which occupies two stone houses, was built in 1912 with Carnegie Trust money. Orange Juice, King, Silvester, and Fat Larry's Band played here in the '80s. The building is now home to Johnson's, a weekend disco that plays house sounds. *6a Pilmuir St., tel. 01383/721076.*

Compared to its Celtic cousins Scotland and Ireland, the land of the male voice choir has had a less-than-illustrious rock music history. Some credibility is derived from John Cale having been born in tiny Garnant, north of Swansea, but other than that, its most illustrious musical names have been Tom Jones and Shirley Bassey. A list of more typical rock & rollers headed by Amen Corner, Man, Budgie, Dave Edmunds, Andy Fairweather Low, the Alarm, cult punks Anhrefn, Bonnie Tyler, and Gene Loves Jezebel hardly adds up to a world-beating back catalog.

But things really took off in the mid-'90s. In the wake of the Manic Street Preachers' breakthrough at the start of the decade, A&R scouts discovered that there was indeed life west of Bristol. When they got here, they found that the industrial centers and valley towns of south Wales have been churning out dozens of new bands. The proliferation of loud bands coming out of gritty no-nonsense Newport has inspired comparisons with circa 1001 Seattle. The capital city of Cardiff has made its name through a more style-conscious set of poppier bands who are equally at ease singing in Welsh. Meanwhile, the seaside and mountain towns of the more beautiful and sparsely populated north Wales have had less say in rock history, though Led Zeppelin, Ringo Starr, and the Super Furry Animals have all done something to make their mark up here.

Bangor

UNIVERSITY COLLEGE (UNIVERSITY OF WALES)

It was here that the Beatles (accompanied by Mick Jagger and Marianne Faithfull) attended the Maharishi Mahesh Yogi's "spiritual regeneration" lecture on August 26, 1967. At a press conference, journalists annoyed the band by questioning their sincerity and the Beatles' claims that from then on they would be drug free. The following day, the four band members were brought down to earth when they learned that their manager, Brian Epstein, had committed suicide. The Yogi's tactless response was that death, being part of the physical world, was "not important." The Beatles got their own back by doing him down on the *White Album*'s "Sexy Sadie": "Sexy Sadie what have you done?/You made a fool of everyone." *College Rd. campus, tel. 01248/351151.*

Buckley

Buckley, basically a single main street between Chester and Wrexham, is the unlikely home of the chief live venue in north Wales.

THE TIVOLI

Since the start of the '90s, this former theater and cheesy disco has been putting on plenty of top names, filling the place to its 650-person limit. Blur, Elastica, Pulp, and many others have played on the way up. Because it is so out of the way but guarantees an enthusiastic crowd, the Tivoli gets names such as the Lightning Seeds and Gene to do pre-tour warm-up shows.

Welsh dragons greet punters at the Tivoli, 1997

An Oasis gig here on August 31, 1994 was massively oversold, and fans who couldn't get in were serenaded by Evan Dando (who had latched onto the band that summer) from the roof of the dressing room. Former Stone Roses guitarist John Squires chose the Tivoli to unveil his new band, the Seahorses, in November 1996, just three months after his former colleagues had put in an appalling, career-ending show at the Reading Festival. *Brunswick Rd., tel. 01244/550782.*

Llanfaelog

O.F.N. PRODUCTIONS

Producer Gorwel Owen's base is a compact bungalow that contains an even more compact studio on the southwest coast of the island of Angelsey. It's been used by two of the biggest new Welsh-language bands: the Super Furry Animals crammed in here to do their first two EPs, and Gorky's Zygotic Mynci have also recorded here. Owen and the SFA both have a background in techno, and the pair got together again to do that band's debut album in the more hi-tech surrounds of Rockfield (*see* below). *Ein Hoff Le, Llanfaelog, Ty Croes, Gwenyth, tel. 01407/810742.*

Llanfairpwllgwyngyllgogerychwyndrobwllantysiliogogogochynygofod

The Super Furry Animals' well-received 1995 debut EP—"Llanfairpwllgwyngyllgogerychwyndrobwllantysiliogogogochynygofod (In Space)"—recorded down the rail route in Llanfaelog, is named after the town with the longest railway station name in Britain (the world?). These days the village itself, just over the Menai Strait on the island of Anglesey, appears on maps as the more manageable Llanfairpwllgwyngyll; to make things really simple, just ask for Llanfair P.G., like most people do. Look out for it on the train route to Holyhead (for ferries to Ireland) or on the A5, the main road through the island.

Machynlleth

The small market town of Machynlleth lies in the southern reaches of the Snowdonia range.

[BRON YR AUR]

Led Zeppelin moved into this mountainside retreat a couple of miles north of town in 1970. Plant had visited the place as a child, as a friend of his father's was a previous owner. In contrast to the plush hotels that Zeppelin had refitted on their recent U.S. tours, this slate cottage near the banks of the River Dovey didn't even have electricity or running water. It was a time to take stock and go back to nature in an area rich in Celtic mythology. The group spent much time trekking through the hills with a tape recorder, which they used for taking in new ideas for songs. In this way they wrote many of the tracks for their folk-derived third album and the more bombastic fourth, which contained "Stairway to Heaven." Those who hung round the cottage with the band included Incredible String Band vocalist Rose Simpson (later mayor of nearby Aberystwyth and still an independent councillor). She and Plant would discuss how the Zep singer could add more folkiness to his voice at the expense of the macho yells. She gave him the address and phone number of someone in London who taught Bulgarian singing. He used the paper as a filter for his spliff.

Led Zeppelin's secluded cottage, Bron Yr Aur, 1997

The name Bron Yr Aur means "golden breast," a reference to the fall colors in this valley. The place was honored in two Zep songs: "Bron-Y-Aur Stomp" on *Led Zeppelin III* and "Bron-Yr-Aur" on *Physical Graffiti,* which reflect the fact that the placename can be spelled in two ways. A few years later Plant spent some of his royalties on a sheep farm just up the road in the Llyfnant Valley, where he got further into Welsh culture. The cottage, clearly marked on Ordnance Survey maps, is off a steep, narrow road that branches off the A493 just outside Machynlleth, which is 18 miles northeast of Aberystwyth. The current owner reports some dedicated Zeppelin trekkers turning up here from time to time.

To find out what's happening at venues throughout south Wales, grab a copy of the free monthly *finetime* magazine, available from all good venues and hangouts. They also have a page on the web (http://info.cf.ac.uk/ccin/main/ents/whatson/finetime/) that's comprehensive and up to date. *Discord,* another freebie, comes out bi-monthly. It deals specifically with music and is full of reviews, gossip, and gig news.

Blackwood

If you built a museum to represent Blackwood, all you could put in it would be shit—
Nicky Wire of the Manic Street Preachers (interview with *VOX* magazine)

There's no mistaking that Blackwood, in the high valleys about 12 miles northwest of Newport, is bleak. The population, which barely tops 1,000, like most other small south Wales communities, has had to cope with the closure of the coal mines and put up with lower-paying jobs in small high-tech factories or retail outlets. It has, however, two reasons to be placed on the rock & roll map: It's the hometown of the Manic Street Preachers, and it has a decent venue in the **BLACKWOOD MINERS' INSTITUTE** (High St., tel. 01495/227206). As well as attracting touring bands such as Ash and Gene, it provided early live experience for Ether, another Blackwood band who have recently been signed to EMI, and the Stereophonics, from nearby Aberdare, the first new act on Richard Branson's V2 label.

LITTLE THEATRE

While they were still called Betty Blue, three-quarters of the Manic Street Preachers played a less-than-successful early hometown gig here in 1988. They got jeered off amidst cries of "Simple Minds! Simple Minds!" Soon afterward, they fired the rhythm guitarist, replaced him with Richey Edwards, and changed their name. They didn't stick around south Wales for long; by the start of the '90s they were in London, firing off Situationist slogans and stirring up press interest prior to their debut album, *Generation Terrorists.*

This converted Methodist chapel has been used primarily by the local dramatics society since the '30s. During the '80s it had some folk rock, with names such as the Battlefield Band and June Tabor, as well as the local outfit, the Chartists, whose *Cause for Complaint* album focused on the 1984–85 miners' strike and its effects on this area. *Woodbine Rd., tel. 01495/223485.*

Cardiff

The Welsh capital likes to think of itself as a more cultured entity than the surrounding south Wales towns. They in turn like to remind Cardiff that it is the hometown of Shakin' Stevens, one of those "it could only happen in Britain" acts who was never out of the charts in the '80s with naff (tacky but funny) rockabilly revival numbers. Though it has a few points of historic and tourist interest, it's one of the least attractive capitals in Europe.

Until recently Cardiff has had little to do with rock music save for pub rocker Dave Edmunds; first-wave punks the Table, who made one great noisy record, "Do the Standing Still"; and art-house minimalists Young Marble Giants. Currently it's trying to wrest the honor of Wales's rock city from Newport, and although it has a way to go on the live scene, it does boast a couple of small record labels. The Ankst label has done much to promote bands who sing in both Welsh and English; its catalog includes Gorky's Zygotic Mynci, Super Furry Animals, Catatonia, Rheinallt H. Rowlands, Topper, and several others. Townhill records, run by former Pooh Stick Hue Williams, did the first releases by the Newport bands 60ft Dolls and Novocaine.

EATINGDRINKINGDANCINGSHOPPINGPLAYINGSLEEPING

Although it's about three times larger, Cardiff doesn't have as active a live scene as neighboring Newport. The **CARDIFF INTERNATIONAL ARENA** (Mary Ann St., tel. 01222/234500), known locally as the C.I.A., puts on anything from the Cure to Tom Jones to classical music. The **CARDIFF UNIVERSITY STUDENTS' UNION** (Park Pl., tel. 01222/396421) has bands on the college circuit play its 1,500-capacity Great Hall. The **HIPPO CLUB** (3–7 Penarth Rd., tel. 01222/341463) is primarily a dance club, though it does have some medium-size alternative bands occasionally. The city is really in need of a good permanent club venue and the **XPLOSURE** (tel. 01222/232673) people have been plugging away promoting bands from locals like the Stereophonics and Gouge to Pavement. Most of their gigs have taken place at **CLWB IFOR BACH** (11 Stryd Womanby Stwydda, tel. 01222/232199), also known as the Welsh Club. As well as Xplosure nights they have indie discos, acoustic nights, and other types of music.

SPILLERS RECORDS

This store has been running from its present site since 1927, but has in fact been trading since 1894, way before records were even invented, in the days of sheet music. The people from the Guinness Book of Records have confirmed it as the oldest store of its kind in the world. Spillers celebrates this fact on every bag, as well as broadcasting it further with a plaque outside the store. At just 960 square feet, it's small but carries a big stock of music, including a decent new music section. *36 The Hayes, tel. 01222/224905.*

Monmouth

Although it's just over the border from England, Monmouth is an out-of-the-way place that has proved popular with musicians who want to record away from the big city. The famous Rockfield Studios is in the town, and the Monnow Valley Studio (Old Mill House, tel. 01600/713338) is in the adjacent hamlet of Rockfield, where Oasis did most of their debut album, *Definitely Maybe.* The cover of the "Supersonic" single was shot in this studio.

ROCKFIELD STUDIOS

Now one of Britain's most famous studios, these converted pig barns have spilled out hit after hit since Dave Edmunds did "I Hear You Knocking" in 1970. Iggy Pop did *Soldier* here in 1980, and Queen inflicted "Bohemian Rhapsody" on the world from here, but it's probably seen its most successful action in recent years, with Oasis coming to record *(What's the Story) Morning Glory?* and Gorwel Owen producing the critically acclaimed *Fuzzy Logic* debut album by Super Furry Animals. The Stone Roses blew much of David Geffen's spare change by booking the place for 14 months to doodle over the *Second Coming* album.

While they were recording here on July 23, 1996, the Charlatans UK's keyboard player, Rob Collins, decided to drive down the country roads to a local pub in his BMW. On the way back to the studio, the car spun off the road and Collins was propelled through the

The Boo Radleys take a break from recording at Rockfield Studios

sunroof and died from a fractured skull. The postmortem report showed that he had more than twice the legal limit of alcohol in his body and had not been wearing a seat belt. *Amberley Court, Rockfield Rd., tel. 01600/712449.*

Newport

In 1996 some music journalists were calling Newport the "new Seattle." Both places are by the coast; Newport, after being ravaged by the fall of heavy industry, is now trying to go high tech like Seattle; and both have produced dozens of loud rock bands. Furthermore, just like Seattle, the "Newport scene" didn't happen overnight. In the mid-'80s it was largely a rock & roll desert, but the appearance of a top venue in TJ's and an infrastructure of rehearsal rooms, small studios, and other facilities built up by dedicated locals helped bands get to where they are today. Several Newport acts are worth watching out for: the rap metal-attacking sound of Dub War; the noisemongers Fly-screen, who recently signed to MCA; Novocaine; the raucous, heavy-drinking 60ft Dolls; and the wonderfully named industrial goths Distortious. Music really is just about the only conceivable reason to visit the city, but if you like your rock in your face, this spot needs checking out.

60ft Dolls at a Newport local

The Stone Roses' comeback single, "Love Spreads," carried on its cover an image of a stone cherub's head flanked by wings. It didn't take long for some fans to figure out that this was Newport's emblem, which can be found in many of the city's parks and on municipal buildings. Within a few days of the single's release in late 1994, some Roses fans had "collected" these vital pieces of memorabilia with the aid of hammers and chisels.

EATINGDRINKINGDANCINGSHOPPINGPLAYINGSLEEPING

Although its population isn't much over 100,000, Newport has managed to compete with larger entities like Bristol and Cardiff for live gigs. Besides the excellent **TJ's** (*see below*), Newport has a couple of other venues. The recently built **NEWPORT CENTRE** (Kingsway, tel. 01633/662662) is a larger affair and gets Terrorvision, (London) Suede, and other Top-40 guitar bands. **LE PUB** (1 Caxton Pl., tel. 01633/221477) puts on mainly local groups.

The place to pick up news, flyers, gig tickets, and alternative and collectable sounds is the long-established **ROCKAWAY RECORDS** (3 Newport Provision Market, tel. 01633/257244). **DIVERSE MUSIC** (12 Upper Dock St., tel. 01633/259661) also has a decent stock of new sounds. For cutting-edge dance sounds and details of clubs, try the informative **NU-VIBEZ** (13 Market Arcade, tel. 01633/243825).

KING'S HOTEL

The King's would be a normal, boring town-center hotel if it weren't for its great, old-fashioned ballroom upstairs and a booking agent who knows how to attract some of the biggest names in R&B and soul. Although the room holds only around 400, it's seen gigs by legends such as Dr. John and Jerry Lee Lewis (when his U.K. fan club held their convention here one year, the man himself played three consecutive nights).

It's said to be one of Van Morrison's very favorite venues. He's played here several times and has turned up at so many gigs that his appearance is no longer an item of gossip among Newport music fans. Some still do recall a 1993 gig in which Morrison was rambling on with an overlong intro when someone in the crowd shouted out a request for "Brown Eyed Girl." This didn't please Morrison, who went into a rant, transcribed at length in the 1996 Van Morrison biography by John Collis. The gist of it was, "I'm a soul singer. I'm more a motherfucking soul singer than some motherfucking motherfucker.... I don't want to play 'Brown Eyed Girl.' " *High St., Newport, tel. 01633/ 842020.*

STOWAWAY CLUB (HEIGHTS 2000)

The Police made their debut here on March 1, 1977, supporting Cherry Vanilla, an ex-Warhol hanger-on and ex-Bowie press officer. Then featuring Corsican guitarist Henry Padovani, the group played their own set and had to come back as Vanilla's backing band. The Stowaway managed to bring in many of the big punk and new-wave names; nowadays it is called Heights 2000, a hi-tech nightclub that occasionally attracts some of the top drum & bass DJs. *40 Stow Hill, tel. 01633/250978.*

[TJ'S]

The most famous venue in Wales started life as an American-style restaurant in 1970; after a wine bar was added, it hosted many national and international artists when the Newport Folk Club was based here. Then in 1985, both were transformed by owner John Sicolo and his late partner Trilby into a live-music venue with a new name.

Local gossip has it that this is where Kurt Cobain proposed to Courtney Love after a Hole gig. The night wasn't without its ups and downs. First, the pair and their agent drove up from London in a battered old Skoda; just 200 yards from the venue, they had a wreck on Newport Bridge. The car was a write-off, but they escaped unharmed and walked to the venue. Love and her agent strolled straight in, but a disheveled Cobain was stopped and asked for £3.50. He mumbled something about being with the band, and another member of the door crew came and asked him to cough up the cash. Only when he wiped his hair away from his face did they recognize who he was and let him in.

Justifiably popular with American acts—NOFX, Girls Against Boys, Rocket from the Crypt, and many other buzz names have played here—it's where both Green Day and the Lemonheads made their U.K. debuts. The stage is 6 inches high, there's no barrier, and at sold-out gigs, stewards have had to pluck fans out of the drum kit. Therapy? did some of their earliest gigs here and keep coming back to do shows, as it's conveniently en route from London to the Irish ferry. In addition, TJ's has had Oasis, the Cranberries, and all the "MOR indie" bands that swept Britain during the mid-'90s. The venue's eclecticism is further revealed in shows by such circuit veterans as Steve Marriott, Wilko Johnson, Steve Gibbons, and even Status Quo, who played here after a show at the Newport Centre until one of the owners, who was sleeping upstairs, came down and told them to "shut the fuck up." Another band who did a post-gig show here was the Black Crowes.

Each visiting band gets a full meal associated with its home region cooked by ex-restaurateur Sicolo. He's also printed out the menus and had the bands sign them and pose for photos. Whereas other venues bring out compilation CDs, he hopes to be the first venue to bring out a cookbook. In any case, TJ's already has a label up and running with a local roster that includes Disco, the Choke Teens, the Cowboy Killers, and Mumbo Jet. *14/16 Clarence Pl., tel. 01633/216608 or 01633/220984.*

THE GREEN, GREEN GRASS OF HOME

Tom Jones was born Thomas John Woodward on June 7, 1940, at **57 KINGSLAND TERRACE** in Treforest, a small hillside mining community just outside Pontypridd. His first paying gig was at **TREFOREST NON POLITICAL CLUB** (71 Wood Rd., tel. 01443/402625), and they have a plaque behind the bar to prove it.

From there, as a singer with bands including the De Avalons and the Senators, Jones toured around all the regional pubs and working men's clubs. After some 10 years of performing, he made it big with the U.K. No. 1 (U.S. No. 10) "It's Not Unusual," still one of the most perfect pop discs ever, which had a guitar break by Jimmy Page. His next U.K. chart topper came at the end of 1966 with "The Green, Green Grass of Home," taken by many to evoke a return to Wales; it was in fact an American song that had previously been done by both Porter Wagoner and Jerry Lee Lewis. Jones then concentrated on the American cabaret circuit, singing slushy songs night after night while female fans ritually whipped their knickers off and threw them onstage hoping Jones would wipe his brow with them before throwing them back. Finally, he was so successful he became a tax exile.

In the '80s he learned that the old red phone box on Tower Street in Treforest that he had used so often in his teenage years was being replaced with a new model. He paid £250 for it and had it shipped to his Beverly Hills house (said by some to rival Graceland in its excess), where it was installed poolside.

In the late '80s he started working again in Britain, appearing as the featured vocalist on the Art of Noise's 1988 version of the Prince song "Kiss." On Jones's 1991 album, *Carrying a Torch*, he collaborated with Van Morrison. He also moved back to Wales, buying a house outside Cowbridge in the Vale of Glamorgan, a few miles south of Treforest. He is known to enjoy a quiet pint at the **RICKARDS ARMS HOTEL** (Park St., Pontypridd, tel. 01443/402305), where he is matey with the landlord.

Raglan

The small village of Raglan is just off the A40 ten miles west of Monmouth.

RAGLAN CASTLE

Led Zeppelin was filmed acting out Robert Plant's medieval warrior fantasy scene in the grounds of the castle, one of the largest and most exciting-looking fortresses in Wales, for the "Rain Song" section of *The Song Remains the Same* movie. *Raglan St., tel. 01291/690228.*

Rhymney

Rhymney is the name of a deep valley, a river that runs into the sea just west of Cardiff, and an unremarkable little town between Merthyr Tydfil and Ebbw Vale. It's best known in rock terms for the song, "Bells of Rhymney," which was adapted from the words of Welsh poet Idris Davies by the American folk revivalist Pete Seeger. As well as mentioning Rhymney, the song tours other south Wales coal towns, including Merthyr and Blaenau, and was most famously covered on the Byrds' 1965 *Mr. Tambourine Man* album. Nineteen years later, the Alarm, formed in the north Wales seaside town of Rhyl and best known, perhaps, for supporting U2, did a cover of the song as a fund-raiser for striking miners.

NORTHERN IRELAND

Caught between the mainland British and the southern Irish music scenes, the province of Northern Ireland has always found it hard to establish itself in the rock world. Despite being the home of Van Morrison and a string of current bands headed by Therapy? and Ash, this predominantly rural region with a population of 1.5 million has only had sporadic success at rock & roll fame.

Them, with Van Morrison on lead vocals, was the first band to break big, in 1964. Although other acts, like the Wheels, Eire Apparent, and Fruup, got deals, Morrison alone kept the province on the rock map for well over a decade. Fourteen years after Them had a hit, the Undertones became cult figures throughout the world. They, along with Rudi and the other punk and new-wave bands on the Good Vibrations label, had managed to create a vibrant punk scene despite overzealous security forces and paramilitary distrust of anything

Cuckoo

that united kids from opposite sides of Northern Ireland's sectarian divide. It was almost as long again until the heavy pop riffs of Therapy?, from the pallid port town of Larne, started to pep up A&R interest. Record company staffers picked up the teenagers, Ash, whose brand of pop-punk-grunge brought platinum back to the province. Several Northern Irish bands—who have always been able to combine noise and melody much better than their equivalents in Dublin or the rather tuneless Britpop brigade—are currently poised to break from indie circles into the big time: There's the eclectic, quirky, and prolific pop of Tunic from Belfast; the cheeky Portadown rockers Joyrider; and the 4AD-signings Scheer (with a style that combines Cocteau Twins ambience with the brute force of Pantera), who come from the armpit towns of Maghera and Magherafelt. Derry, the home of the Undertones, has been knocking out good new bands like Cuckoo and Rare. DJ and remixer David Holmes is a big name in the techno world, and singer-songwriter Brian Kennedy (a longtime fixture of Van Morrison's live shows) is already a household name throughout Ireland. Morrison himself trundles on and on, keeping up an output of an album almost every year.

The capital, Belfast, has some key rock sites but a patchy live scene. On the other hand, there are few nicer rock & roll road trips than spending a day touring splendid County Down as chronicled and raved about by Van Morrison.

The most remarkable Belfast rock story is not about the the city's most famous son, Van Morrison, but of a certain character named Terri Hooley and the bands on his Good Vibrations punk label: While the mohawked punks of London were rebelling in proper Soho venues and the like, the Belfast chapter of the movement had to contend with a much-bombed city center that became a ghost town at the end of the working day. Only a handful of bars in this part of town stayed open in the evening, and punks—keen to get both Protestant and Catholic kids to gigs—played sleazy, downtown dives like the Harp and the Pound to keep away from the sectarian and paramilitary-controlled areas. The classic and still highly collectible Good Vibrations label grew out of this scene, introducing bands like Rudi, the Outcasts, and Ruefrex. Except for the Derry-based Undertones, none of the Good Vibes bands made it big, in part because, isolated due to the Troubles, they were inordinately naive about the workings of the music business.

Living in a society where shootings and bombings were commonplace, the last thing Belfast punks wanted to sing about was the civil unrest. However, Stiff Little Fingers—always more popular among English college kids than they were back home—milked their background with songs like "Alternative Ulster" and "Suspect Device." At least they spoke from first-hand experience, unlike many others who tried to give the musician's angle on the Troubles. Locals still speak with disdain of Simple Minds, who flew in to shoot the video to "Belfast Child" in Belfast's shipyards in 1989, allegedly flying back home the same night.

Though some bands, like Tiberius Minnow, Big Self, Colenso Parade, and Death of an American Airman, got deals and threatened to be famous, the '80s were a sad comedown from the euphoric pop-punk Good Vibrations years. Though that label kept trying to provide a platform for local talent, what small business acumen founder Terri Hooley had evaporated, and Belfast was a once again a rock & roll backwater.

Gigs by Therapy?, from nearby Larne, got interest going again at the start of the '90s. Venues like the Penny Farthing and the (now defunct) Warehouse kicked off hardcore and singer-songwriter nights respectively, and the Empire opened, a great midsize venue that provided a good place for prominent new bands to play. The club scene, thanks to DJs like David Holmes, started pulling people to Belfast from all over the island and beyond. Once again, the region's music is getting the exposure it deserves, and small labels like Project Rype, Immortal, and the sporadically exhumed Good Vibrations are at last giving local acts a better-organized first rung on the rock & roll ladder.

EATINGDRINKINGDANCINGSHOPPINGPLAYINGSLEEPING

Ever since the Troubles started at the end of the '60s, the live music scene in Belfast has been dire. Today, after a period of relative calm, the place has many fewer venues than Dublin; promoters have to battle to attract touring acts to the city. Belfast has also been dogged by bands pulling out or politics getting in the way. On the Sex Pistols' comeback tour in 1996, their gig at the Maysfield Leisure Centre was canceled due to fear that "Anarchy in the U.K.," "God Save the Queen," and other such songs would raise emotions too high during the week that the resolutely pro-monarchist Orangemen had their annual July 12 parade. Generally, however, the bands that do make the effort to play here are rewarded with a crowd that goes wilder than those in most other cities.

291

Empire Music Hall, Belfast

The **EMPIRE MUSIC HALL** (40/42 Botanic Ave., tel. 01232/328110) has quickly established itself as the best place to play in the city. With a decent big hangout bar down below, the gig hall has a good stage, acoustics, and sight lines. All the best of the current Irish hopefuls have played here, and the venue has also released the *Live at the Belfast Empire* (Empire Records), featuring Watercress, Disraeli Gears, and 15 other locals. The cramped **DUKE OF YORK** (11 Commercial Ct., tel. 01232/241062) is one of the few downtown bars that willingly promotes good new original rock and pop bands, especially on weekends. In 1990, after a gig in the city, Van Morrison made a surprise appearance at the large neighborhood pub and venue, the **ERRIGLE INN** (312/320 Ormeau Rd., tel. 01232/641410 or 01232/644596). **ROBINSON'S** (38 Great Victoria St., tel. 01232/247470) was recently upgraded from a dive to a designer Irish pub but has a good booking policy that allows local bands to play before they headline at the Empire. **LIMELIGHT** (17 Ormeau Ave., tel. 01232/665771) holds 500 and concentrates more on touring bands—Blur, Cast, Oasis, and the rest of the Britpop bands have all played here. **PENNY FARTHING** (96 Donegall Sq., tel. 01232/249423) has been quiet of late, but in the early '90s had Snuff and other cult English hardcore bands over. This inspired the underage Ash (who mention the place on the sleeve of their *Trailer* mini-album) to get gigs here along with Backwater, Indecision, Aquabucket, and other like-minded locals. The **ULSTER HALL** (*see below*), which holds around 1,200, still gets some touring bands in. The **STUDENT UNION** (*see below*) at Queen's University concentrates more on DJs than live music these days.

Most music fans arriving in the city head for the **GOOD VIBRATIONS** store (*see below*) for a slice of nostalgia and an eclectic range of discs. **VINTAGE RECORDS** (54 Howard St., tel. 01232/314888) is a chaotically racked store selling everything from cheapo Irish traditional compilations to the latest alternative releases. The pricing policy is even more disordered; some decent singles go for a few pence and copies of the same album may bear different prices. It's also where you'll find Terri Hooley working these days. **DR. ROBERTS** (15 Church La., tel. 01232/313130), the best-stocked indie shop in town, has lots of dance sounds and a bulletin board plastered with details of upcoming local gigs. **DOUGIE KNIGHT'S** (*see below*) has some good deals among its student-oriented racks of used CDs and vinyl.

City Center

Downtown Belfast is relatively small. The big gray City Hall is the hub from which streets radiate. Donegall Place is the main shopping drag (with big branches of HMV and Virgin). In between Donegall Place and the docks to the east is a maze of alleys and side streets with great old-fashioned bars. Three key venues—the Maritime, the Harp, and the Pound—were once in the area, but all have been redeveloped. Just to the west of City Hall is the start of the Golden Mile (*see below*).

BELFAST CITY HALL

The grounds of City Hall were the site of a massive reception for U.S. president Bill Clinton, who made a much-heralded visit to Belfast during the cease-fire period in December 1995. The authorities had organized a support act in the form of Van Morrison, who played a set that included "Days Like These," with the crowd of 60,000 singing along; this particular song had evolved into an unofficial peace anthem during the cease-fire of 1994–96. Clinton had been slated to play sax with Morrison and his band, but he turned up late,

By kind permission of Belfast City Council

Belfast City Hall

at least earning himself the distinction of being about the only person able to muck around with Morrison's timetable. *Donegall Sq. N.*

HARP BAR

In the late '70s nearly all the pubs in downtown Belfast were closed by 7 PM, as even the lushes didn't want to get caught up in potential bomb situations. The few bars that stayed open into the evening were sleazy, and the Harp, in among redbrick warehouses near the docks, was one of those places. Its stage was no stranger to strippers, but it was willing to put on the new punk bands.

Most of the early Good Vibrations bands played here and recorded a few yards away at Wizard Studios, which occupied part of an old clothing warehouse on Exchange Place. Gigs by Rudi, the Outcasts, and others were captured on film in John Davis's *Shell Shock Rock*, perhaps the best documentary movie of the punk era. At Terri Hooley's 30th birthday bash, the Good Vibes label boss got onstage, backed by members of Protex and the Outcasts, and ran through a barely rehearsed version of Sonny Bono's "Laugh at Me." A 7-inch version was soon released; although it got slagged as one of the worst records ever made, because of the Good Vibes association, it topped the U.K. indie chart in 1980.

In 1977 the Clash came here for a photo shoot that involved their posing next to barbed wire barriers and army trucks. According to eyewitness accounts, they were terrified. The Clash were too big to ever play here, but many English bands did, thinking that the danger element would add to their credibility. The first to make the journey were the Nipple Erectors, who counted the future Pogue Shane MacGowan in their lineup.

The smelly old Harp was pulled down long ago and is now a parking lot. Some of the pub's tilework and walls are still standing, though they may not last long, as the area is being turned into designer offices and coffee shops. *Hill St. at Gordon St.*

Although he played many other gigs in the city, it was at the Maritime Club where Van Morrison mastered his stage act, with Them. The Maritime was a charitable home run by the British Sailors' Society Seaman's Residential Club, who rented the building's stark, unfancy ballroom to outside promoters. Most of the nights had been trad jazz, but in April 1964 R&B nights were started, and Them was the first band to get a residency. At first they got strange looks because, while most of the showbands that dominated the live circuit wore matching suits and hair gel, Them came onstage with scruffy locks and tatty clothes. Morrison's manic saxophone solos were also in marked contrast to the slick, smarmy presentation of the showbands' syrup-laden set of covers. Within a few months, though, Them were getting in crowds of 400 (way beyond the safety limit), and by the end of the year had a Top 10 hit with "Baby Please Don't Go." Their experiences of the joint were recounted on the track, "The Story of Them," which also mentioned the nearby Spanish Rooms (now an empty lot on Divis Street between Millfield and the Westlink), another good gigging spot at the time. As the Spanish Rooms had a liquor license, the practice was to buy a gallon of (hard) cider for £1 and bring it to the Maritime, which did not have a bar.

After Them scored successes in both the U.K. and U.S. charts, the hunt was on for another Belfast band that could shift product. The Mad Lads took over Them's residency, and despite their record company's changing the band's name to Moses K and the Prophets, they had little following outside Belfast. Their singer, Kenny McDowell, would take Morrison's place in Them after he left in 1966. A more successful outfit was Taste, with future Irish guitar legend Rory Gallagher, who relocated from Dublin.

The building was sold in 1973, became a sports club for a time, and had its final gig with the bulldozer in 1991. The memory now lives on with a 26-track Ace records compilation called *Belfast Beat—Maritime Blues*, which was released in 1997 as a retrospective look at the Belfast R&B scene between '64 and '66. Them, the Mad Lads, the Wheels (briefly touted as the hometown rivals to Them), and the People (a Portadown band who later became Eire Apparent and toured the United States with Hendrix in 1967) are among those with tracks. The site is now part of RBAI school. Where the Maritime facade once stood is a tall, redbrick wall with steel spikes on top. *College Sq. N.*

THE POUND

A basic club down a cul-de-sac, the Pound had started as a jazz joint and later put on rock acts. By the late '70s, it was well and truly the preserve of the punks. Every punker in the United Kingdom knew about the place from the opening line of Stiff Little Fingers' "Alternative Ulster" single from 1978.

More important than the reference by SLF (who were never an integral part of the local scene in any case) was the night in 1978 when record store owner Terri Hooley came here to see Rudi and the Outcasts, two local punk bands who had been playing around town for some time. The Rudi set moved him so much that he started the Good Vibrations label. As Hooley later revealed on the liner notes of the excellent *Good Vibrations Story* retrospective CD (Dojo CD180) "I got so excited I went to the ladies loo twice! The second time some girl said 'Who is that?' and the other girl said, 'Oh that's your man, the mad flasher.' Well I wasn't a mad flasher, I was really excited by the music." The other band on the bill that night was the Outcasts, a rowdier bunch of shaven-headed punks whom Hooley thought were "the worst band I had ever seen." However, he soon changed his mind, signed them to his new label, and oversaw their rise to being the most popular live band in Northern Ireland by the end of the decade.

The gig that night ended in fights; police officers of RUC (the Royal Ulster Constabulary) came in in their usual heavy-handed way. They were met with the standard Belfast punk chant of "SS RUC." Just to help stir up the atmosphere, Rudi pumped out their song, "Cops," It started with a repeated shout of "SS RUC" and had a chorus line of "We hate the cops."

Like many buildings in the city center, the Pound is long gone. The site, rather ironically, now forms part of an extension to the Musgrove Street Police Station. *Townhall St.*

ULSTER HALL

Since the hostilities started at the end of the '60s, the number of visiting bands at the main downtown venue has been paltry compared to the number that come to cities of a similar size. Quite often those bands that came were from faraway places, like Focus (the Netherlands) and AC/DC (Australia), as English bands feared that they would become IRA targets. Nevertheless, Led Zeppelin, in a rare gig by a big English group, played here in March 1971, at the height of the Troubles, on a day when a gasoline tanker was blown up nearby, one person was fatally shot, and various bombs exploded around the province. The world stage debut of "Stairway to Heaven" provided a suitably bizarre contrast to the mayhem outside. It also marked the first appearance of Page's now-trademark double-necked guitar. After the gig, John Bonham's limo driver took a wrong turn and ended up driving down the Falls Road, the center of the battleground between Republicans and British troops.

An October 1977 Clash gig was pulled at the last moment after insurance cover was refused. Some punks smashed windows and lay down in the street; the police, well versed in antiriot maneuvers, got heavy and arrested five fans. Punks from both sides of the sectarian divide started up a chant of "SS RUC." After the skirmishes outside the venue died down, a hundred or so fans moved on to the Clash's hotel to congregate noisily outside. The Clash, of course, weren't staying in any old joint. These punks at the vanguard of social change chose to stay in the Europa Hotel (Great Victoria St. at Glengall St., tel. 01232/327000), the city's premier hostelry—and also the most-bombed hotel in Europe: The lofty tower block of the Europa has been a target for the IRA since the early '70s. These days it would cost around £150 a night to stay in the style to which members of the '77-era Clash were accustomed. *Bedford St. between Franklin and Clarence Sts., tel. 01232/323900.*

The Golden Mile

This mile-long stretch that starts just west of the City Hall, at the north end of Great Victoria Street, and travels south to the Queen's University Belfast (QUB) campus, is the city's cultural zone. Though it's a bit tatty in parts, there's a good range of pubs along the way, as well as the Good Vibrations store and some Van Morrison landmarks.

[GOOD VIBRATIONS RECORDS, 1978–90]

In 1978 local character and music enthusiast Terri Hooley was running a record stall in St. George's Market. A friend then persuaded him to become a co-tenant in a tattered old building that housed a community printing press and whole food store. Hooley took the space directly above the vegetarian emporium and opened his Good Vibrations Records store, specializing in garage and punk discs. A few weeks after he opened the store, someone told him he should check out a pair of local punk bands playing at the Pound (*see above*). Hooley was blown away by headliners Rudi and asked them if they were interested in recording a flexidisc that could be given away with a fanzine to publicize the Belfast punk scene. The band didn't even know what a flexidisc was, and Hooley hadn't a clue how much they cost. When they got around to doing the calculations, they found it was more feasible to bring out a proper vinyl 7-inch single. They quickly went into a cheap little studio and cut "Big Time" (one of *the* great punk singles). In April 1978 the first release on the Good Vibrations label (catalog number GOT 1) hit the streets. Rudi gigged relentlessly to promote the single, and it sold by the boxload. Hooley started to fancy himself an indie record mogul. Within a year about a dozen punk pop and new wave singles were churned out by the label based in a pantry-sized office in this building.

The other key Belfast band on the roster were the Outcasts, a more loutish bunch with great grinding tunes and infantile lyrics. Hooley hated them at first, but they were the first band to do an album for Good Vibes and built a massive following in their hometown. The most famous band on the label was the Derry-based Undertones, whose *Teenage Kicks* EP is still lauded by John Peel as the best pop disc ever. The Undertones became hot property, sought after by many other labels. Hooley virtually gave the Undertones away to Sire, getting £500 to release them from their Good Vibes contract.

Hooley put the £500 toward getting more bands into the studio. Some of these other late-'70s acts, like the Tearjerkers, Protex, Ruefrex, and the Moondogs, showed promise, but their careers were dogged not so much by bad luck as by bad decisions.

By the early '80s, the little label was in financial trouble, and Good Vibrations went bankrupt. Hooley and everyone else were too much into the music to bother with little things like bill collection. Since then Hooley has revived the label several times but has never come close to matching those perfect slices of punk-pop from the late '70s.

Not that much larger than the label's tiny office was the Good Vibrations store. Saturdays in particular would see the place crammed to over-capacity with local punks and members of bands on the Good Vibes list. Many bands who visited the city made a beeline for the store; the Monochrome Set managed to play here, while the Fall was among those to use it as a crash pad. The building was condemned at the start of the '90s, and Good Vibes moved across the road (*see below*). The site has since been redeveloped into offices. *102 Great Victoria St.*

[GOOD VIBRATIONS RECORDS, 1990–PRESENT]

After the first building practically fell down, the Good Vibrations shop moved across the street to a building that's in only slightly better shape. The store is eclectic rather than trendy, stocking a mix of everything from local bands, indie releases, dance, some chart stuff, and alternative country (the preferred listening material of Colin and Paddy, who run the joint), as well as *The Weedbus* and other good local fanzines. The artwork from the Undertones' *Teenage Kicks* EP (in a cheap frame) is the

Good Vibrations record store, 1997

only effort made to cash in on Good Vibrations' illustrious name. From time to time they unearth boxes of the original Good Vibrations punk singles, which sell out quickly to nostalgic collectors from all over the world.

For groups from overseas, it's one of the first points to seek out in the city. As Terri Hooley says, "The Beastie Boys and others have come here to pose outside and get their pictures taken. We couldn't be bothered telling them it wasn't the original store." *121 Great Victoria St., tel. 01232/233156.*

GRAND OPERA HOUSE

As with the neighboring Europa Hotel, this landmark theater built in 1894 has been closed down several times after bomb blasts. Each refurbishment has retained its warm Victorian decor. Although it offers mostly classical music or stage musicals, it's famous as the venue of Van Morrison's 1984 album *Live at the Grand Opera House, Belfast. Great Victoria St. at Glengall St., tel. 01232/240411.*

KNIGHT'S CYCLES AND ACCESSORIES

In operation since 1922, this family business diversified into stocking jazz and blues discs in 1957. Dougie Knight, the grandson of the company founder, could only get some of his required stock from Dublin and had to smuggle it across the border. On the various floors above the shop, Knight rented out rooms to bands for rehearsal space. The biggest and best rooms were taken by the showbands. Van Morrison's band, Them, was left with the cheapest room, an attic space that cost 7/6– a week (37.5 pence). Another tenant was a small religious sect called the Exclusive Brethren, who held gospel meetings here and had a big notice proclaiming, "There Is But One Step Between Ye and God" on their door. It became a bit of a joke among the stoned-out members of Them to purposely miss the step out. Them (named after a '50s sci-fi movie) asked Knight to be their manager, but he declined, though he did help them out by playing them John Lee Hooker's version of the Big Joe Williams song, "Baby Please Don't Go."

The store has long since gone, and the site has been eaten up by a road-widening scheme and a parking lot, just down from the current Good Vibrations store. *77 Great Victoria St.*

KNIGHT'S RECORDS

Dougie Knight moved to his current premises in 1967 and concentrated exclusively on records. In those early days the store was a popular hangout for beatnik types, especially for Sunday night jam sessions. The store had a counter on wheels that could be pushed out of the way; big cushions were strewn around, and everyone would get wasted. Among those who Knight (who has been promoting jazz and blues artists in the city since the late '50s) attracted to jam and play on the shop's piano were Champion Jack Dupree and Curtis Jones. Van Morrison was a regular visitor right up until he went to New York to record *Astral Weeks*, while a teenage Terri Hooley staffed the kitchen on sandwich duty.

The store today, with its understated sign and window displays, gives little hint of its glorious past. Dougie still pops in, and the mostly used selection is well priced and attracts a steady stream of Queen's University students. *33 Botanic Ave., tel. 01232/322925.*

QUEEN'S UNIVERSITY STUDENT UNION

Northern Ireland's major college union, dependent as it is on the makeup of the annually elected student executive, provides erratic support to the local live music scene. The '60s saw gigs by Them and visiting American blues greats, but after the bombings and shootings started at the end of that decade, fewer and fewer bands wanted to visit the city. A group of local enthusiasts, most of them nonstudents, set up the Esoteric Music Society (EMS) to try to get top names over. EMS booker Roger Armstrong (now a director of London-based Ace records) claims that Hawkwind made one of the lamest excuses for withdrawal ever when they said that their lead guitarist's mom wouldn't let him come. Groups willing to come here in the '70s were the pub rock bands like Brinsley Schwarz and Bees Make Honey, who played to bigger and more enthusiastic houses than they were used to in London.

A 1974 gig here marred the career prospects of Belfast-born Eric Bell, guitarist with Thin Lizzy. In a city known for being mean with riders, especially for local bands, there's usually a beer or two at least on offer at the Union. This proved all too much for Bell, who saw a table piled with food and drink and helped himself to it all—before the gig started. He was unable to hit any right notes, and that was the last straw for band leader Phil Lynott, who fired him and drafted a new lineup that went on to platinum worldwide sales.

June 1978 saw the first major punk gig in the city by local bands. Headlined by Rudi, it had six other sets of punks all on the Good Vibrations label: Protex, Victim, the Outcasts,

Ruefrex, and the Idiots, plus the Undertones, who were playing their first gig outside Derry and shocked the crowd by doing a cover of a Gary Glitter song. Label boss Terri Hooley had booked the hall with a fake name, and when Union officers found out about the scam, they tried to stop the gig. Good Vibes, however, had made an alliance with the Chosen Few biker gang to provide security, and they negotiated a settlement with the uppity student hacks. Currently the Union gives a lot more emphasis to techno and other dance nights than to live gigs. *University Rd. at Elmwood Ave., tel. 01232/324803.*

Bloomfield

Bloomfield, some 2 miles east of the city center, is a working-class Protestant neighborhood dominated by small row houses. Its streets and turnings are documented in the lyrics of Van Morrison, who grew up in the area.

CYPRUS AVENUE

Down Cyprus Avenue/With the childlike vision slipping into view—Van Morrison, "Madame George"

Less than half a mile from where Van Morrison grew up (*see below*) is this impressive, tree-lined residential street where the houses have huge lawns and there are few parked cars because everyone has garage space for at least one car. The lines, "I'm conquered in a car seat/nothing I can do," in the song "Cyprus Avenue," off *Astral Weeks,* might give a clue about what he was up to in the neighborhood. Then again it might not. The avenue runs parallel to the busy Newtownards Road, the main artery east out of the center; to get here, turn off at Beersbridge Road and Cyprus is the first left.

VAN MORRISON BIRTHPLACE

An only child, Van Morrison was born George Ivan Morrison on August 31, 1945, and grew up at 125 Hyndford Street, a small two-bedroom row house with an outside toilet. He had a head start musically on his Belfast contemporaries, as his father (George Sr.), an electrician at the shipyards, was an enthusiastic fan of American blues, gospel, and folk. Having spent some time working in Detroit, he accumulated a record collection that included such names as Mahalia Jackson, Leadbelly, Muddy Waters, Sonny Terry, Brownie McGhee, and other names that would crop up in his son's lyrics.

Van formed his first proper band—the Javelins—around 1957 with three other kids from the nearby streets. They got gigs playing before their contemporaries at cinema matinees. By 1959, when he was 14, the guitar- and sax-playing junior bluesman got a place in the semipro Monarchs showband and toured with them in Scotland and Germany. To bring in some money, he set himself up in a small window-cleaning business around Bloomfield, an occupation recounted in "Cleaning Windows," off 1982's *Beautiful Vision.* It was this album that saw Morrison's lyrics start to focus on his neighborhood. On

Plaque at Van Morrison's childhood home

1991's *Hymns to the Silence* he was in reminiscence overdrive, writing the track "On Hyndford Street" and featuring photos of his old neighborhood on the sleeve.

Although "Van the Man" (as he's invariably and repetitively called in his hometown) seemed exuberantly proud of his roots, an incident in 1991 proved that his thinking is never straightforward. The Belfast Blues Appreciation Society put up a plaque outside No. 125 proclaiming "Singer-songwriter Van Morrison lived here 1945–61." The guy who lived in the house had just bought it and didn't know that it was the Morrison home-stead, and when asked about permission to put a plaque up by his front door, he saw no reason to object. Other neighbors (some of whom, if you happen to ask, will gladly chat away about Van as a lad) thought it was a nice touch of boosterism for the area. How-ever, the man himself tried to get it taken down. He construed it as an invasion of pri-vacy and refused to attend the ceremony. It was left to Buddy Guy to unveil it.

ORANGEFIELD SCHOOL FOR BOYS
(ORANGEFIELD HIGH SCHOOL)

Van Morrison enrolled at his neighborhood high school in 1956 but didn't participate much in school life, preferring to concentrate on forming bands with friends. As he put it on "Got to Go Back," off *No Guru, No Method, No Teacher,* he would "gaze out my classroom window and dream." He left at age 15 without graduating. After a couple of jobs that lasted a few weeks, he became a window cleaner.

Morrison has also sung about the district, naming one of the tracks off *Avalon Sunset,* "Orangefield." As well as the School, the word Orangefield precedes a Lane, a Park, Gar-dens, an Avenue, a Parade, a Road, and a Drive that are all, confusingly, right next to one another. In Morrison's time the school was all male, but it's now coed. *Access at Cameronian Dr. or Clarawood Park.*

AROUND NORTHERN IRELAND

STAR OF THE COUNTY DOWN

The southeastern reaches of Down, with the sweeping Mountains of Mourne and a coastline dotted with small ports and inlets is among the most beautiful districts in Ireland. Van Morrison keeps an Ulster home in the village of Crawfordsburn, between Belfast and Bangor. Images and place names from Down have popped up in Morrison's massive body of work, but on the track "Coney Island," off *Avalon Sunset,* he waxes nostalgic about the place. The song is a mini road trip through the east of the county where Van and a companion have good crack watching birds at remote St. John's Point and passing through Shrigley, Killyleagh, and the Lecale district before going to the little fishing port of Ardglass, which is pretty without being cutesy. He stops here for some cholesterol-loading in the form of "a couple of jars of mussels and some potted herrings [in butter and cream], in case we get famished before dinner." From Ardglass it's a short ride to the hamlet of Coney Island itself, best approached from the east, to get a good view of its curved bay and beach. It's a small and insignificant place, and while it's pretty enough, it might come as a letdown after Morrison's poetic build-up. To follow his route, you will need a very good map, as the villages are tiny; Coney Island should not be confused with the place of the same name in the southwest corner of Lough Neagh.

Van Morrison

AND IT STONED ME

One of Van Morrison's greatest songs—"And It Stoned Me," the opening track of *Moondance*—recalls the times when, at around the age of 12, he and some friends would go fishing at Ballystockert Lake. On one occasion they stopped at a house and asked the old man who lived there for some water. The old man gave them a bottle and claimed it came from a nearby stream. Only after the young Morrison drank it did he realize it wasn't water; he got stoned.

Bangor

One of the most well-to-do towns in the British Isles, Bangor is where Derek Bell, harpist for the Chieftains, lives; his group's collaborative *Irish Heartbeat* album with Van Morrison included the traditional song "Star of the County Down."

THE TRIDENT (WOLSEY'S BAR)

OK so there's the Trident in Bangor, and then you walk back to the city—Stiff Little Fingers, "Alternative Ulster"

When SLF complained that there was nothing to do at night in late '70s Belfast, they mentioned this bar in Bangor, 10 miles east, as somewhere to go; due to the vagaries of public transport in the area, the only way to get home was to walk. The bar has since gone through a few name changes and is currently called Wolsey's, a youthful place that sometimes has live music. *24–26 High St., tel. 01247/460495.*

Downpatrick

The town where St. Patrick (yes, the St. Patrick responsible for green lager every March 17) is supposed to be buried has also produced a couple of '90s bands: Ash are well on their way to international success, while the noisier Backwater have a name that aptly describes their hometown.

DOWN HIGH SCHOOL

The three members of Ash, to date the most successful Northern Irish band of the '90s, made a splash in the music press when they turned down the support slot on Pearl Jam's 1994–95 Asian tour, as two of them preferred to sit their final-year examinations at this coed school. Ash cut their first demo, featuring the great "Jack Names the Planets" when they were around 14 years of age. They immediately attracted record company interest. Their first vinyl release came about from a school project in which bass player Mark Hamilton was involved. At Down High, teachers encouraged participation in Young Enterprise Groups, in which senior students had to attract investors and set up a small business. While others set up a firm to make jewelry and such, Hamilton's bunch decided to set up a record label. It was named Raptor Records at the insistence of Hamilton, and the Ash contribution was a grungey little number called "Season." The other groups featured were Marrowbone, fat, and Buttlip. This 1993 12-incher now changes hands for close on £100.

Ash did one gig at the school, but stagediving was frowned upon by the teaching staff, and the event was never repeated. To get gigging experience, they had to go to the Penny Farthing in Belfast. Despite all the touring and recording, drummer Rick McMurray (who was a school year ahead of colleagues Hamilton, the bassist, and Tim Wheeler, the vocalist, guitarist, and songwriter) managed to get straight A's in his A-Level (matriculation) exams in 1994. *Mount Crescent, tel. 01396/612103.*

Long Kesh Prison

It breaks your new dreams daily (H Block Long Kesh)—Gang of Four, "Ether"

One of the major chapters in Northern Ireland's Troubles was the 1981 hunger strike by IRA prisoners in this high-security prison designed in separate H-shaped buildings so that any potential flashpoint incidents could easily be cordoned off. Although the Undertones had written "You're Welcome" on the *Positive Touch* album about an H-Block prisoner unable to cope with the strain, it was the Dublin-based protesting singer-songwriter Christy Moore who became the major artist to be associated with the place. In the late '70s he managed to get a meeting in prison with an IRA leader. His first song about the prison was "90 Miles from Dublin," with an opening line of, "I'm 90 miles from Dublin town, I'm in an H-Block Cell." The IRA prisoners initiated the hunger strike in an effort to keep their political prisoner status; 10 of them died. Not long after their deaths, Moore released an album called *The Spirit of Freedom,* which included two songs written by Bobby Sands, the hunger strikers' leader and the first to die, who was a keen fan of Moore's previous traditional music band, Planxty. The album, which, because of its overt political stance, is not stocked by any stores in Ireland, also has a tribute to Sands, in "People's Own MP." Meanwhile, in America, the summer Sands died, the Grateful Dead at at least one concert dedicated "He's Gone" to the hunger striker.

The 15th anniversary of the H-Block hunger strike was marked by Black 47's including "Bobby Sands MP" on their *Green Suede Shoes* album, while Bill Whelan's soundtrack to the movie *Some Mother's Son* included a track called "Meeting Bobby Sands".

The prison is a bleak pile visible from the M1 motorway between junctions 7 and 9 just west of Lisburn.

Londonderry

Although the official name of Northern Ireland's second city is Londonderry, most people call it Derry, especially republicans, who're keen to lose the British association in the name. The best-known traditional song connected with the city, "Danny Boy" (with words set to an old tune called "The Londonderry Air"), provided the stage name for one of the Irish-obsessed rappers House of Pain and a track on their 1992 debut album. Thin Lizzy also had a "Danny Boy" track on their '79 LP, *Black Rose (A Rock Legend)*.

The events of Bloody Sunday, January 30, 1972, when British troops killed 14 unarmed civilian demonstrators, spurred protest songs from two ex-Beatles. First off the mark was Paul McCartney, who wrote the Wings song "Give Ireland Back to the Irish," which, to the consternation of BBC radio chiefs, made the United Kingdom charts in February 1972 despite being banned from the playlist. John Lennon followed suit with a brace of songs, "Sunday Bloody Sunday" and "Luck of the Irish," on the John and Yoko *Plastic Ono Band* album from the same year.

U2's "Sunday Bloody Sunday," off their 1983 *War* album, was very much a nonsectarian plea to stop violence. The band did get lots of criticism for the smug way Bono always introduced it on stage with the words, "This is not a rebel song." It was misinterpreted especially by American audiences, who saw it as being supportive of the hunger-strikers in Long Kesh.

The Derry incident was in fact the second bloodletting given the Bloody Sunday tag; the first was in 1921 in Croke Park (*see* Dublin *in* Republic of Ireland), when 12 were killed and some 60 others badly wounded.

Up until the punk years, the only music success story to come out of the city was squeaky-clean Dana, who won the Eurovision Song Contest for the Republic of Ireland in 1970. Things pepped up in 1978, when Belfast-based Good Vibrations records released the *Teenage Kicks* EP by the youthful local five-piece, the Undertones. This classic slab of punk-pop was championed by John Peel and other radio DJs, and the band soon signed to Sire, producing a couple of classic and two so-so albums before folding

The Undertones

in 1983. Their lead singer, the gargling-voiced Feargal Sharkey, had some short-lived solo success, while two other members of the band—the brothers John and Damian O'Neill—went into That Petrol Emotion. Sales fell far short of their critical reception. After shunting from label to label for 10 years, That Petrol Emotion folded in 1994. The Undertones family tree is still alive in the form of John O'Neill, who plays guitars and programs samples in Rare, a critically touted Derry-based band with a more experimental edge than either of his two previous outfits.

The two bands with Derry connections who have sold loads of records in the '90s are more mainstream pop outfits. D:Ream is basically Peter Cunnah, who was in an indie band called Tie the Boy and then went to London and had a string of catchy dance tunes in the upper reaches of the charts. Neil Hannon, who, like Cunnah, is basically his own man in the Divine Comedy, produces songs that could possibly be compared to Scott Walker (in the way that Little Leagues are compared to the World Series) but is nonetheless seen as OK by some merely because he did the theme song for the Irish cult TV comedy *Father Ted.*

THE NERVE CENTRE

Considering it is the home of the Undertones and a batch of current-day alternative bands, Derry has never had many places for bands to play live. Back in the late '70s one of the few places that the Under-

tones could play was a long-gone temporary "Portacabin" bar called the Casbah. At the end of '96, the Gweedore Bar (59 Waterloo St., tel. 01504/267295) where the likes of Rare, Cuckoo, and Schtum played shows, ripped out its stage and implanted a DJ booth. The sad state of affairs got to the point where bands couldn't find a venue in their hometown to launch their CDs or gain gigging experience.

The situation was saved in summer 1997 when the long-running Nerve Centre finally stopped moving from

Nerve Centre

one set of cheap rent premises to another and took over this purpose built downtown space that has a properly designed live music area. Run along the lines of the Temple Bar Music Centre in Dublin, the Nerve's new home gives them the space to carry on the good work they have been doing in providing rehearsal rooms, courses on sound engineering and new multimedia technology (Rare guitarist and ex-Undertone, John O'Neill is one of the lecturers), as well as resource information for the local music industry. Also connected with the Nerve Centre is Blast Furnace Studios (Foyle Arts Centre, Lawrence Hill, tel. 01504/377870), where the recent batch of Derry bands have recorded. *Magazine St., halfway up hill, tel. 01504/260562.*

REPUBLIC OF IRELAND

REPUBLIC OF IRELAND

Is there anybody here with any Irish in them? Are there any of the girls who would like a little more Irish in them?—Phil Lynott, off Thin Lizzy's *Live and Dangerous*

Ireland's traditional music heritage is stronger than that of any other western European country. Celtic music flourishes today and traditional music has an important influence on the island's rock output. As many American roots artists will attest, it was the Irish immigrants to America who brought the airs and tunes that formulated the high, lonesome sound of Appalachian old-timer music that's still apparent in many country and Americana recordings today.

Horslips began the first successful fusion of traditional and rock sounds in earnest and maintained popularity throughout the British Isles in the '70s. It was Thin Lizzy, however, who enjoyed greater commercial achievement with their reworking of "Whiskey in the Jar," a surprise hit in Britain in 1972. Since then, artists as diverse as Van Morrison, Enya, and the Hothouse Flowers (who, like Christy Moore and Paul Brady, are equally at ease using traditional or rock instruments) have mixed the two sounds. Folk and trad acts like the Chieftains and the Dubliners have recorded with rock artists such as Sinead O'Connor and the Pogues.

Prior to the late '70s, most Irish rock artists, like Thin Lizzy, Rory Gallagher, and the Boomtown Rats, had to move to London to pursue their careers. The immediate post-punk years saw improvements in the rock media, recording facilities, and general rock & roll attitudes. Out of this came U2, who have done as much for the country's GNP as Abba did for Sweden's and whose business interests and activities have reshaped the Dublin nightlife scene. The capital city dominates

Sinead O'Connor

Irish music, but other towns have made their mark, including the festival city of Galway, and Limerick, where the Cranberries originated.

Today, the country's music successes are eclectic and diverse, from the continually popular U2 through singer-songwriters like Sinead O'Connor and Mary Black, to more traditional acts like Enya and Altan. The nation has also showed it can compete in the lucrative spheres of musical productions (Riverdance), movie tie-ins (The Commitments) and manufactured boy bands (Boyzone).

The definition of what constitutes an Irish artist has also broadened, thanks to the government's very generous tax scheme for artists. Among those now resident and working in the country are Carole King, the ex-Lone Justice singer and Dylan fave Maria McKee, Donovan, Brendan Perry and Lisa Gerrard of Dead Can Dance, Shane Mac-Gowan of the Pogues, Marianne Faithfull, and Def Leppard's Joe Elliott.

Like that of the rest of Ireland, Dublin's music scene was, up until the late '70s, under the complete stranglehold of showbands—cheesy cover outfits usually attired in matching satinesque suits. They dominated the live circuit and took up the column inches; the studios were geared to their needs. Those local rock acts that showed promise, such as Thin Lizzy, had to leave for London to consolidate any first hints of success.

Things took a turn around 1976 when bands like the Radiators from Space and the Boomtown Rats started a new-wave scene centered around Moran's Hotel. In many ways this was a catalyst not only for the development in Dublin of a self-sufficient rock scene but also in the breaking down of the Catholic church's dominance of everyday life in Ireland, particularly with respect to sexual outlook. The Boomtown Rats' commercial success shifted A&R attention to the city in a big way, spurred on the formation of more and more new bands, and opened up a citywide live scene in places like the Baggot, McGonagle's, and the Project Arts Centre. As confidence in the city's rock community grew, a group of journalists and musicians founded *Hot Press,* the first national music magazine. Also in 1977, the pirate radio stations succeeded in breaking the monopoly of RTE, the staid national broadcasting service, and 2FM, the first national station devoted to rock, came on the air. Another vehicle of change was Windmill Lane Studios, opened to work with rock rather than trad, country and Irish, or showbands.

My Bloody Valentine

In this heady environment, four pupils at the Mount Temple School formed a band that would soon become U2. Unlike Thin Lizzy, they found an infrastructure in their home city that enabled them to complete the rock learning curve. It also meant that when they achieved their phenomenal international success, they could still be based in Dublin. At the same time, their continuing presence in Dublin boosted the music industry. More studios opened and venues were upgraded. As more and more bands appeared on the scene, most of them, like A House and An Emotional Fish, tried to ape U2's big stadium sound, and for a long while the Dublin scene was boring. Eventually, in the mid-'90s, the scene began to diversify, My Bloody Valentine's 1991 *Loveless* album having shown that Ireland could compete with the rest of the world in the alternative rock sphere. It opened the way for Whipping Boy and others to come through. The Dublin scene, once the preserve of rockers with a Celtic strand thrown in, is now more diverse than ever, with power-pop bands like Revelino and Bawl promising to break through alongside singer-songwriters like Eleanor McEvoy and Naimee Coleman.

Not only does Dublin dominate the Irish scene today, but it is also one of the most important rock industry centers in Europe. Its studios attract top artists from all over the world, more venues have opened up (even though techno is giving rock a real run for its money), and the city is now on most European and American touring bands' itineraries. For visitors interested in music, there's a *Rock 'N' Stroll* walking tour, a Music Hall of Fame due to open in early '98, a range of brilliant pubs, and an accessible and inexpensive club scene.

EATINGDRINKINGDANCINGSHOPPINGPLAYINGSLEEPING

Dublin's center is very compact and, for most, extremely walkable. The Liffey divides the north and south sides into the respective D1 and D2 postcodes. The *Event Guide* is a free fortnightly tabloid stuffed with listings available from all venues and good hangouts; before you go, check them out at http://www.dkm.ie/events on the net. *Hot Press* also has critical previews of all the major music shows. **DUBLIN TOURISM** (Suffolk St. at St. Andrews St., D2, tel. 01/605–7777) is more sussed-out than most city visitor offices. As well as giving good directions, they can book tickets for major rock concerts. They produce the handy *Rock 'N' Stroll* booklet, which details all 16 rock plaques in the *Rock 'N' Stroll* walking tour. Summertime sees the organized *Dublin Rock Trail* walks, which last around 90 minutes and cost £5, including a free copy of *Hot Press* and a Guinness in the great old International Bar. Contact *Hot Press* (tel. 01/670–8949) for current details.

THE ATTIC (above the White Horse Inn, 1 George's Quay, D2, tel. 01/679–3068) holds less than 100 people but hosted the Dublin debuts of Therapy? and Green Day, no less. For the most part, it promotes the more experimental local bands. **BAD BOB'S BACKSTAGE BAR** (35–37 East Essex St., Temple Bar, D2, tel. 01/677–5482) is a long-established party zone with country, Cajun, and R&B bands seven nights a week. The club holds up to 500. **BARNSTORMERS II** (141 Townshend St., D2, tel. 01/671–4955), in the docks area, is a small, rowdy bikers' bar that also has an early (7 AM) license for post-club stragglers. **BARRY FITZGERALD'S** (90 Marlborough St., D1, tel. 01/874–4082) is well known for its trad ballad sessions and lively crowd. The **DA CLUB** (3/5 Clarendon Market, D2, tel. 01/671–1130), a popular artsy venue with good sound quality, seems to be shifting more from cutting edge live bands to DJ nights. **EAMONN DORAN'S** (3a Crown Alley, Temple Bar, D2, tel. 01/679–9114), formerly the Rock Garden, has a downstairs room that holds 400 and concentrates on new bands, with few name acts passing through these days. They released a *Live at Eamonn Doran's* CD sampler recorded in '96 with mostly unknown local acts. The **GAIETY THEATRE** (South King St., D2, tel. 01/677–1717) occasionally has concerts, outside is a *Rock 'N' Stroll* plaque dedicated to leading singer-songwriter Christy Moore. The Georgian **HARCOURT HOTEL** (60 Harcourt St., D2, tel. 01/478–3677), where George Bernard Shaw once lived, has music seven nights a week. It's mostly high-quality traditional and country, but there are some dodgy cover bands in the early part of the week. The **INTERNATIONAL BAR** (23 Wicklow St., D2, tel. 01/677–9250) is a great, old-style bar at street level with a small room upstairs with comedy and singer-songwriters (Eleanor McEvoy made her name here) and a basement bar with a jukebox. Much was expected from the Dublin branch of the **MEAN FIDDLER** (26 Wexford St., D2, tel. 01/475–8555) when it opened with a Christy Moore gig in June 1995. The **OLYMPIA THEATRE** (*see below*) is one of the best places to see a band anywhere in the world, especially at its midnight shows. Many bands even play the Olympia in preference to the much larger **POINT DEPOT** (*see below*), the country's main indoor arena. **RED BOX** (Old Harcourt Street Train Station, Harcourt St., D2, tel. 01/478–0166), at the side of the more famous PoD club, opened in '96 and has succeeded in getting Pavement and other top alternative acts. The **SFX CENTRE** (*see below*) continues to serve as the shed for touring alternative bands to play. Revered for its long-running trad sessions, **SLATTERY'S** (*see below*) also books good local rock bands in the upstairs room. **TEMPLE BAR MUSIC CENTRE** (*see below*) opened in 1996 and has music most nights in its purpose-built gig hall. **WHELAN'S** (*see below*), with its diverse roster, is the pick of Dublin's smaller venues.

FIBBER MAGEE'S (O'Connell St. at Parnell St., D1, tel. 01/874–5253) offers an alternative and quite gothy rock disco over two floors with droves of punks, metalheads, and other cultists. Owned by Bono and the Edge, **THE KITCHEN** (below the Clarence Hotel, East Essex St., D2, tel. 01/677–6635) mixes all types of contemporary dance sounds in likeable subterranean environs. **LILLIE'S BORDELLO** (Adam Court, Grafton St., D2, tel. 01/679–9204) is famous for being where the movie stars and such come and play. Door staff are well trained to sniff out undesirables. **THE SYSTEM** (21 S. Anne St., D2, tel. 01/677–4402) and the **TEMPLE OF SOUND** (Ormond Hotel, 7–11 Ormond Quay Upper, D1, tel.

© Cathal Dawson

Therapy? at Red Box

01/872–1811) both have techno, house, and the latest sounds with fairly youthful crowds. Perhaps the most happening and alternative dance space of all is the **ORMOND MULTIMEDIA CENTRE** (*see below*). **THE POD** (Old Harcourt Street Train Station, Harcourt St., D2, tel. 01/470–0166), which stands for "Place of Dance" is one of the most popular and trendiest spots in town, attracting as many VIPs as the Kitchen and Lillie's. Also in the complex is the pre-club Chocolate Bar and the Red Box venue.

The **CLARENCE** (*see below*), owned by Bono and the Edge, is definitely the top place to stay. The other five-star option favored by many visiting bands is the **WESTBURY HOTEL** (off Grafton St., D2, tel. 01/679–1122), where Oasis spent a much-chronicled and debauched weekend in 1996. Rooms are around IR£170 a night. Most hotels around Temple Bar and Grafton Street are pricey; the **HARDING HOTEL** (Copper Alley, Fishamble St., D2, tel. 01/679–6500) is a clean budget option for around IR£45 a night.

CLADDAGH RECORDS (2 Cecilia St., Temple Bar, D2, tel. 01/677–8943) is a specialist store dealing in traditional and roots music. **COMET RECORDS** (5 Cope St., D2, tel. 01/671–8592) is a friendly little store with new and alternative releases. The **RECORD COLLECTOR** (basement, 30 Wicklow St., D2, tel. 01/679–1909) stocks a wide range of used goodies. There are various chains around, including the Irish-based **DOLPHIN** and **GOLDEN DISCS** outfits. Of the international chains, **TOWER** (6 Wicklow St., D2, tel. 01/671–3250) is the best stocked. **HMV** (65 Grafton St., D2, tel. 01/679–7817) is best for concert tickets. The **VIRGIN MEGASTORE** (14–18 Aston

Quay, D2, tel. 01/677–7361) has in-store performances by Irish bands.

Dublin's reputation as a great tourist city centers on its legendary pubs; the **INTERNATIONAL BAR** (*see above*) is as good a place as any to start. The "rock" restaurant in town is **TOSCA** (20 Suffolk St., D2, tel. 01/679–6744), owned by Norman Hewson, Bono's brother.

For contemporary art shows of all kinds, including some rock gigs, check out the listings for the worthy **PROJECT ARTS CENTRE** (*see below*). The nearby **IRISH FILM CENTRE** (6 Eustace St., Temple Bar, D2, tel. 01/679–3477) offers two screens showing art-house movies, organizes special events, and has a decent bar and café.

Courtesy of Dublin Tourism

Comet Records store

Temple Bar

This compact area of cobbled streets and smartened-up warehouses was in the 18th and 19th centuries occupied by artisans' workshops and brothels. By the 1970s it was starting to tumble down, and the authorities bought almost the entire area to build a massive bus depot. While waiting to finalize their plans, they rented out premises cheaply to artists. Soon the place had a bohemian feel, with lots of little studios and trendy retail stores. The new residents thought they had scored a major success when the government dropped plans to demolish the place, but, as some of the more cynical Dubliners would have it, Temple Bar was then designated as the city's official arts zone, and big money moved in. Swanky galleries and grant-aided arts centers were created, yuppie eating houses appeared, and even the tatty old boozers like the Norseman and the Oliver St. John Gogarly have been smartened up. Despite much of the late-'70s spirit having been squeezed out, it's still an exciting place to hang, with several decent live venues, some unusual places to eat, and a number of small, independent record stores. The **TEMPLE BAR BLUES FESTIVAL** is a growing event at the end of each July that in recent years has seen Otis Rush and Buddy Guy play. For information on this and anything about the corporate arts zone, contact **TEMPLE BAR INFORMATION CENTRE** (18 Eustace St., D2, tel. 01/671–5717).

Andrew Flyn

Rollerskate Skinny on Temple Bar

BAD ASS CAFÉ

Sinéad O'Connor used to be on the waitstaff here, and there's a *Rock 'N' Stroll* plaque outside to confirm it. Before she worked at the Bad Ass, O'Connor had already had some recording experience in 1982 when, as a 14-year-old, she co-wrote and sang on a single by In Tua Nua. By 1985, while she was serving dinners here, she was in Ton Ton Macoute, another Dublin rock outfit, and was working on some solo material. She soon picked up a contract with the Ensign label that led to the release of *The Lion and the Cobra* in 1987.

The bright, airy café is worth a visit for its good pizzas and livened-up diner food. Crown Alley—one of the first streets in Temple Bar to be developed—still has a sense of cool about it, with brightly painted record and clothing stores. *9 Crown Alley, Temple Bar, D2, tel. 01/671–2596.*

CLARENCE HOTEL

In the late '70s, when U2 was playing and hanging out around the Project Arts Centre (*see below*), Temple Bar's drinking joints were of a rather different character from what they are today. Backing onto East Essex Street, right across the way from the Project, was the faded old Clarence Hotel, built in the 1850s and popular with priests and nuns. It had an old oak-paneled bar where members of U2, the Virgin Prunes, and other punky types would drink with the clerics and other regulars.

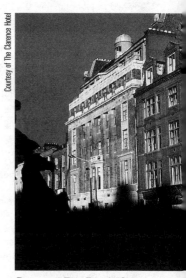

Courtesy of The Clarence Hotel

In 1992 Bono and The Edge decided to invest some of their royalties, and, along with a local businessman, bought the hotel. They ran it as it was for a while and opened the Kitchen nightclub in the basement, along with the punky Garage bar, which had a Trabant car in the center of the floor but has now been closed. Then in 1994 they shut the place down for 18 months, pumped in some IR£5 million, and reopened in June 1996 as the city's premier five-star hotel. Today the 50-room Clarence retains its old Dublin character and its oak-paneled walls but has a stylish contemporary

Bono and The Edge's Clarence Hotel 1996

feel, boasting all the facilities you need, such as 24-hour room service, a night chef, a residents' lounge with an open fire, a great restaurant, and a young staff who don't take their lead out of some corporate handbook. Rooms are from IR£165 per night including tax; the penthouse suite costs a cool IR£1,450. It's easily the best place to stay in Dublin, providing the credit card can stand it. *6–8 Wellington Quay, D2, tel. 01/670–9000 or 800/447–7462 in the U.S.*

PHIL LYNOTT PLAQUE AND VIDEO LOCATION

Thin Lizzy bassist and singer Phil Lynott has a *Rock 'N' Stroll* plaque dedicated to him in the covered alley of Merchants Arch, which leads from the quayside into an array of small specialist stores in the heart of Temple Bar. The archway looks out onto the famous humpbacked Ha'penny Bridge (a footbridge across the Liffey that dates from 1816), which was one of the most prominent landmarks that Lynott featured in the 1982 video for the "Old Town" single, off his second solo album. Considering this LP flopped, the site is not the most appropriate place to choose to commemorate such an important figure in Irish rock. *Riverside end of Merchant's Arch, which connects Aston Quay and Temple Bar.*

OLYMPIA THEATRE

Probably one of the nicest settings for a gig anywhere in Europe, this great, old 19th-century theater still has the intimate feel of an old-style music hall behind its rubescent wrought iron facade. For many years now it's hosted the extremely popular "Midnight at the Olympia" gigs on Friday and Saturday nights featuring everyone from country folk artists to loud, thrashing rockers. It also attracts artists who would easily outsell its

1,300 capacity: on February 11, 1993, all of U2 bar Adam Clayton played with Johnny Cash and Kris Kristofferson in a show taped for RTE television. Even Van Morrison played here in '96 in preference to bigger venues. The Olympia is also used for plays and musicals.

The *Rock 'N' Stroll* plaque outside is dedicated to ex-De Danann vocalist Mary Black, who grew up (along with her younger sister Frances, another signed recording artist) in the Liberties part of town, a mile or so down Dame Street in the shade of the Guinness brewery. *74 Dame St., D2, tel. 01/677–8962.*

PROJECT ARTS CENTRE

Perhaps the most worthy institution in the increasingly upscale Temple Bar area is this scruffy little complex that has been putting on cutting-edge stage plays and dance productions since the mid-'70s. At that time it was a more modern alternative to smelly Moran's on the northside, and its booking policy promoted the best new local rock bands, as well as getting in the best of the English new wave, such as the Distrac-

The Olympia Theatre, 1996

tions. U2 played a very early show here in May 1978 supporting the Gamblers. More important, U2 met their manager, Paul McGuinness, for the first time. He, impressed by what he saw, brought the band for some beers in the nearby Granary pub. McGuinness's new charges were back here several more times, including an appearance at the 24 hour Dark Space Festival in February 1979. Headlined by the Mekons (after PiL had pulled), the bill also featured the Virgin Prunes and a contingent of Belfast bands headed by Rudi, Protex, and Ruefrex, all of whom were on the cool Good Vibrations label. Another Good Vibes band at the fest was Zebra, billed as Ireland's first reggae band. They never quite managed to get an invite to record in Jamaica; their sole 12-inch single was a feature in the bargain bins for years.

Although rock gigs have been and always will be no more than an exciting sideline for this venue, it's always well worth looking to see what's coming up at the Project. There's also a bar, a café, and a gallery here. *39 E. Essex St., Temple Bar, D2, tel. 01/671–2321.*

TEMPLE BAR MUSIC CENTRE

Completed in 1996, this grant-aided center provides an impressive modern resource for the nation's music business. Housed in the TBMC is a venue with a capacity of 600 (or 340 seated) that has already hosted the likes of Goldie and Gene; the space also doubles as a television studio. It hadn't been opened long before controversy arose over a November '96 commemorative gig for the executed Nigerian dissident Ken Saro-Wiwa. Featuring over a dozen top Irish artists, it also served as a fund-raiser for African children's charities. However, Trocaire, one of the third-world agencies involved, disassociated itself from the event because it was headlined by a certain Sinead O'Connor. They were worried about her rants against one of their main supporters, the Catholic church. O'Connor's response was, "Do the children of Africa give a shit where the money comes from?" and the gig successfully went ahead.

Also in the center are Temple Lane Studios, comprising five different well-equipped rooms, a Sound Training Centre, and the MusicBase organization, which offers a range of free advice to those involved in the Irish music industry. There's also a small bar with lots of old pictures of Irish rock heroes, including Thin Lizzy and U2. *Curved St., D2, tel. 01/670–9202.*

Grafton Street

Although it's got posh department and chain stores, this pedestrian strip running between Trinity College and St. Stephen's Green has long been a popular meeting place for arty types and bohemians: James Joyce documents the area well, while Brendan Behan was known to have a drink or two in McDaid's and many of the other little pubs in the adjoining streets. Many Irish bands have spent hours discussing ideas over a coffee at the landmark Bewley's (*see below*) or the Coffee Inn (6 South Anne St., D2), which was a favorite place for Phil Lynott.

The street is dotted with buskers, ranging from chancey pavement artists to full-fledged acoustic bands. One group that made their name here was the Hothouse Flowers, who, when still known as the Incomparable Benzini Brothers, won the city's Street Entertainers of the Year competition in 1985. After playing along Grafton, the band would adjourn for a few pints from the proceeds at the Duke pub (9 Duke St., D2, tel. 01/679–9553), outside of which is a *Rock 'N' Stroll* plaque dedicated to them. After residencies at some clubs they secured a deal and had a huge 1988 hit with "Don't Go." Their raggle-taggle fusion of trad, blues rock, and soul has achieved world-wide success. Another more recent busker was a teenage Edmund Enright from the small County Offaly town of Birr. He busked after leaving school; after adapting the performance name of Mundy in 1996 at age 21, he was offered a major contract by Epic, who have high hopes that this singer-songwriter's Doors-y folk will find a world-wide audience. In 1994 Nanci Griffith did a track called "On Grafton Street" on which the U2 rhythm section played.

BAGGOT INN (BIG JACK'S BAGGOT INN)

Even though it was a bit behind Moran's (*see below*) in adapting to new bands, the Baggot forever has a leading place in Dublin rock lore. For much of the late '70s, rock enthusiasts could come here and see residents Skid Row—the band led by Brush Sheils, a player's player who had fired one Phil Lynott from its number years before. The atmosphere changed at the end of that decade as younger bands were also given the opportunity to play. U2 are associated with the place thanks to a summer '79 gig when they had managed to get top A&R people over from EMI. The record company reps left the show early, but the band did get some consolation when *Sounds* centered a major feature on new Irish bands around U2's energetic performance that night.

The hot ticket of the early '80s was the agit-rock supergroup, Moving Hearts, who really rocked this sweaty 200-capacity venue to its low-slung ceiling. The Moving Hearts fused rock with Irish traditional, jazz, and blues and included a hard political lyricism. They featured such legendary names as Christy Moore, Donal Lunny, Davey Spillane, and Declan Sinnott. There's a *Rock 'N' Stroll* plaque outside in honor of their wild, raucous gigs here.

The Baggot carried on mixing bands old and new right up to the mid-'90s, when it was eclipsed by Whelan's and sold to a consortium that included former Irish soccer team coach Jack Charlton. Cashing in on his fame, they changed the name to Big Jack's Baggot Inn and fitted it out as a sports bar (with some covers bands playing at weekends). The final night of the old-style Baggot was marked with a huge party attended by U2 and all the country's top rock movers and shakers. There are still some pictures of U2 and the like dotted around the place. *143 Lower Baggot St., D2, tel. 01/676–1430.*

BEWLEY'S ORIENTAL CAFÉ

Grafton Street's main landmark has been a regular meeting place for arty Dubliners for over a hundred years. This gorgeous Victorian café (still a likeable place even though they took out the old wooden pews over a decade ago in an attempt to go upmarket) has been a hangout for many bands. One such group was the Boomtown Rats. This was were the idea for their calling-card song, "Rat Trap," came about. At the end of the '70s some sectors of the Irish establishment branded the Rats' lead singer, Bob Geldof, an antichrist for his outbursts against the Catholic way, but by the mid-'80s he was rechristened "Saint Bob" for his role in Live Aid. There's a *Rock 'N' Stroll* plaque dedicated to Geldof and the band outside the café. U2 didn't hang here; they favored the McDonald's just down the street.

Bewley's still retains a good atmosphere, though leave the ground floor to the tourists and get a table in one of the nooks or crannies on the upper floors, along with the bohos and Trinity students, where you can linger over a coffee or plate of fries for hours. *78/79 Grafton St., D2, tel. 01/677—6761.*

CAPTAIN AMERICA'S

A doorway on Grafton Street leads up the stairs to Dublin's first rock & roll eatery, operative since 1971. Along the walls is a collection of

Hot Press *seller outside Bewley's, 1996*

rock odds and ends that they call a museum; here you'll find Larry Mullen's first drum kit, a guitar signed by all of U2, and another one bearing the autographs of R.E.M. The burger joint stays open to 1 AM every day and there are live bands on weekends. It's also got a *Rock 'N' Stroll* plaque outside to signify that this was where, in the early '70s, Argentina-born Chris De Burgh, still a Trinity College student, earned some money by playing acoustic sets for diners before he went on to treat the world to his cheese-enriched ballads. *44 Grafton St., D2, tel. 01/671—5266.*

DANDELION MARKET (CHICAGO PIZZA PIE FACTORY)

A *Rock 'N' Stroll* plaque dedicated to U2's five or six formative gigs at the long-gone Dandelion Market is on the wall of the Chicago Pizza Pie Factory. This restaurant stands on part of the site of the market, a fairly alt-culture place that sold clothes, records, and trinkets, where the band did a handful of gigs in spring 1979. These gigs, on busy Saturday afternoons in a part of the market that doubled as a parking lot, were designed so that the band could do all-ages shows. At these shows, which have gone down in the band's history as legendary, Bono developed many of his stage antics. *Adjacent to St. Stephen's Green Shopping Centre, St. Stephen's Green West, D2.*

DAVE FANNING PLAQUE

Affixed to the Baton Rouge restaurant is a *Rock 'N' Stroll* plaque dedicated to the popular-as-ever DJ and television presenter Dave Fanning. In many ways it's a broader tribute to all those involved in pirate radio because, up until 1977, Ireland's airwaves were the exclusive preserve of the (dull) state broadcasting body, Radio Telefis Eireann (RTE).

It was from one of the upper floors of this Georgian terrace house that the Big D station, one of the most dynamic pirates, broadcast new music. Fanning, with a strong Dublin brogue, was their most popular DJ. He got a job with 2FM upon its creation in 1977. He has since been a regular on radio and TV in both Ireland and Britain, building a reputation for playing demo tapes and spotting acts at formative times in their careers. *119 St. Stephen's Green West, D2.*

[HOT PRESS]

Nowadays it might seem only obvious that Ireland should have a rock & roll fortnightly paper, but back in the grim days of '77 it was a brave step to launch a magazine that put no censorship on music and topical affairs. Brothers Niall and Dermot Stokes, along with other university graduates, including the late Bill Graham (the writer who has gone down in Irish music legend as the person who introduced U2 to their long-time manager, Paul McGuinness), started the magazine in 1977 looking more toward the format of *Rolling Stone* than to the weekly British "inkies." From the start, *Hot Press* set out to cover rock & roll internationally, give Irish acts the exposure they needed, and promote good journalism that very often challenged the backwardness of the mainstream Irish society. Not surprisingly, it was able to cover the likes of U2, Sinead O'Connor, the Cranberries, and others long before the British papers had a clue to what was happening. Today, the magazine has a very respectable circulation of over 20,000 and has published books on U2 and Phil Lynott. It also produces the *Hot Press Yearbook* every January, a superbly accurate listing of all venues, studios, management companies, and all other music businesses in the country. *13 Trinity St., D2, tel. 01/679–5077; http://www.iol.ie/hotpress, e-mail: hotpress@iol.ie.*

MANSION HOUSE

R.E.M. attended an October 1994 function at the official residence of the Mayor of Dublin in this early-18th-century civic building set back from the street behind a cobbled forecourt. They were the guests of the city's first "green" mayor and environmental campaigner, John Gormley. Three years earlier they had endorsed his campaign for the city council, and in 1995 members of the band actually joined the Irish branch of the Green Party. *Dawson St., D2.*

MCGONAGLE'S (THE SYSTEM)

For much of the '70s and '80s this club just off Grafton was one of the most important gigs in the city for bands hoping to break into the big time. It was owned by Bill Fuller, a wheeler-dealer personality who owned property throughout the world, including the famous Fillmore West club in San Francisco. U2 had an affection for the place: Adam Clayton managed to book his band a support gig here in 1978, when U2 was still called the Hype. They were asked how much they wanted and naively demanded a £7 fee. Instead, they received the standard £25 support band fee. Within a year, U2 was drawing capacity crowds to events such as the hyped-up Jingle Ball in June 1979, when they decorated the joint with out-of-season Christmas trimmings.

In April 1981 Phil Lynott and his pal and promoter Smiley Bolger hit on the idea of staging an Alternative Eurovision Song Contest. Ireland had won the real contest the previous year and therefore was to host the competition in '81. The two events took place on the same night; Lynott did a totally messed-around version of the old standard "Mountains of Mourne"; a band did a spoof of Pink Floyd's "The Wall," with "Just Another Prick in the Dail" (a reference to the Irish parliament), while another contestant came up with a riposte to Johnny Logan's "What's Another Year?" (the winning Irish entry in the actual Eurovision contest—which features tacky pan-European schlock pop—the year before) with "I Just Don't Give a Fuck Anymore."

Something Happens recorded their *I Know Ray Harman* mini-LP live here in the late '80s. The place has since been renovated and renamed The System; it's a techno and house club with no live acts. *21a S. Anne St., D2, tel. 01/677—4402.*

O'DONOGHUE'S

This traditional city center pub was an extremely popular location in the '60s for bawdy folk bands. The most famous of them were the Dubliners, who formed in 1962 as the Ronnie Drew Band and played their first show in the back bar of O'Donoghue's. They soon changed their name, taking on the title of James Joyce's book about Dublin characters, and in 1967 had two Top 20 U.K. hits with "Seven Drunken Nights" and the great "Black Velvet Band." Their success in the Irish charts was much more sustained. Even though their lead singer, Luke Kelly, had died in 1984, they teamed up with the much-younger Anglo-Irish Pogues for a No. 8 U.K. hit in 1987 with "The Irish Rover." The pub attracts tourists for the trad music sessions, and there's a *Rock 'N' Stroll* plaque outside dedicated to the Dubliners. *15 Merrion Row, D2, tel. 01/660—7194.*

ST. PATRICK'S SECONDARY SCHOOL

Before he went to Mount Temple School and hooked up with the other future members of U2, Paul Hewson (a.k.a. Bono) attended this Protestant boys' school in the shade of the huge 12th-century St. Patrick's Cathedral, where he apparently rang the bells on Tuesdays. He didn't seem to like the place too much and left by mutual consent after he allegedly threw a dog turd at his Spanish teacher one lunchtime in the little park beside the cathedral.

St. Pat's is one of two great medieval cathedrals in the city. The other one, Christchurch, which gets a mention in U2's 1982 single, "A Celebration," is just 100 yards or so away, toward Temple Bar. *St. Patrick's Close, D8.*

[WHELAN'S]

A pub has been on this site since 1772. The music room to the side of the beautiful old dark bar was only renovated in 1989; until then it had been part of a warehouse. You can still see a flywheel that was used to shift goods between the balcony level and main floor. Reproductions of Michelangelo's work and the Book of Kells adorn the walls and ceiling; just past the entrance look for the "Stone Man," a lifesize woodchip statue propped up against the bar.

Even if the music were only so-so, Whelan's would still probably be a decent enough venue. What makes it really special is the eclectic booking policy—Whelan's not only covers most musical genres, it also has quality acts night after night, whether it's Americana (the Jayhawks, Guy Clark), worldbeat (S.E. Rogie, Awatinas), Irish folk and trad (Davey Spillane, Ronnie Drew), rock (the Amps' first Euro gig, the Bluetones), jazz and blues (Honeyboy Edwards) or up-and-coming Irish bands (Whipping Boy, Mundy, the Corrs, the Devlins, the Frames DC). *25 Wexford St., tel. 01/478—0766 or 01/478—2420.*

The Docks

Beginning more or less directly east of O'Connell Bridge, Dublin's grimy docks area has little but decayed warehouses, blighted inner-city projects...and a handful of key sights that no U2 fan would want to miss, especially Windmill Lane Studios. All of these are on the southern bank of the Liffey. Across the river is the Point Depot, the city's major arena.

DOCKERS BAR

Ever since U2 started recording at Windmill Lane Studios just 'round the corner from this basic little quayside bar, Bono and the rest of the band have popped in here regularly for beers. Even in the '90s, when they were household faces throughout the world, they still came in here, where few of the regulars ever batted an eyelid. *5 Sir John Rogerson Quay, D2, tel. 01/677–1692.*

OCTOBER COVER LOCATION

For their second album, U2 was photographed in this grim dockside area full of tatty sheds and industrial archaeology. The band also shot the video for "Gloria" in this locale in fall 1981. It's about a half-mile east from the original Windmill Lane studio. *Near junction of Hanover Quay and Grand Canal Quay.*

POINT DEPOT

Dublin's major arena lies just east of the city's main drag. Before it was renovated in the late 1980s, it was a railroad depot. When it was still a depot, U2 used the Point to film some of the interviews from *Rattle and Hum* as well as the footage of "Desire." Ireland's best-selling band also play the Point (which holds 7,500) when they want to perform in what is, for them, a small, hometown venue. On December 26, 27, 30, and 31, 1989, they played their first indoor shows in the city in some seven years, with B.B. King in support. The band was criticized for high ticket prices and for playing too small a venue for the number of fans who wanted to get in. In the past, the same people had complained when U2 played at big stadia around the city. The New Year's Eve show, when the band started playing at the stroke of midnight, was broadcast live on radio to a score of European countries. U2 encouraged fans to tape it as a bootleg, and ads in some music papers had a cut-out cassette inlay sleeve for that purpose.

All the biggest names play the Point. There have been more than a few unfortunate incidents in the '90s. In May 1995, Bob Dylan decided to invite a crowd of old pals onstage to play with him. One of them was Carole King (a member of the growing artistic tax exile community in Dublin). As she came on, Dylan gave her a big hug, but the show of affection was too strong; King lost her footing and fell eight feet off the stage into the photographers' pit, breaking an arm upon landing.

A much more serious incident took place the following May when, at a jam-packed Smashing Pumpkins gig, 17-year-old Bernadette O'Brien was crushed to death just after the band came on stage. Such was the confusion that D'Arcy and Billy Corgan (who came on at the end to say it was only a concert and not "worth dying for") tried hard to calm the moshers and crushers. They had to cancel their show in Belfast the following night. Subsequent enquiries showed that the Point management had not contravened major capacity or safety regulations, but there was much debate in the media about how to make concerts by ultrapopular bands safer. Just a few months later, the Fugees came to town and one of their number pissed many people off by allegedly trying to bodysurf the crowd during their show.

The Point was also the venue selected in 1996 for the 10th *Vibe for Philo* concert, held to commemorate the anniversary of Phil Lynott's death. Topping a great lineup that included Therapy? and Henry Rollins, the remaining members of Lizzy put on an emotional, power-packed performance.

As well as rock shows, the depot has hosted Luciano Pavarotti, the Riverdance show, major techno extravaganzas (including the wonderfully named Night in Front of the Big Speakers series), and the albatross that is the Eurovision Song Contest. Since Johnny Logan boosted national pride in 1980 by winning it for Ireland for only the second time, the little country has won it seven times in total up to 1997—more times than most people care to recall. Although all these victories might sound great for the national image, it also requires that every time Ireland wins, it has to host the following year's event. The millions that RTE television must spend on broadcasting the event cannot be recouped

Bryan Adams sells out at the Point

from advertising, meaning that new programming has to be cut. *East Link Bridge, North Wall, D1, tel. 01/836–6777 or 01/836–3633.*

[WINDMILL LANE STUDIO I]

Along with the founding of *Hot Press* magazine and the 2FM rock station in the late '70s, the opening of the Windmill Lane Studio was a key element in the rise of Irish rock & roll. Windmill wasn't just well equipped; it was run by people with an enthusiasm and sensibility for rock as opposed to trad acts or showbands. Not long after the studio opened, U2 made their first recordings here for CBS Ireland, doing their sessions at night, as it was cheaper. They also recorded their first four albums at Windmill Lane. The little L-shape street that the studio is on has become a shrine for U2 fans. On the once-quaint, 100-yard-long turning of the lane that runs parallel with the quay, fans from all over the planet have taken hundreds of cans of spray paint and transformed it into an other-worldly landscape. Italian fans in particular seem intent on getting their message to Bono by writing 12 feet up the wall. There are also a few dedications to other Irish bands, including Hothouse Flowers and Something Happens (who did their 1989 album *Been There, Seen That, Done That* here). In among all the graffiti (mostly a series of bad scrawls with little if any artistic merit) is a *Rock 'N' Stroll* plaque saluting U2's recording output. Many other bands have used the studio, including Def Leppard, who did their multiplatinum 1987 album, *Hysteria,* here (their singer and professional York-shireman Joe Elliott has lived as a tax exile in the city since the early '80s). The Water-boys, Elvis Costello, and Steve Winwood have also recorded major albums here.

U2 set up their own label—Mother Records—to encourage and promote new (mostly) Irish bands. This was based, until 1996, just around the corner at 32 Sir John Rogerson Quay, but operations have since been transferred to London. Meanwhile, the band retains a share in Windmill Lane Studios. These days the studio deals with video and soundtrack work, and U2 now record in a new high-tech studio about a mile farther east along the quay. *4 Windmill Lane, D2, tel. 01/671–7271.*

WINDMILL LANE STUDIO II

U2 outgrew the original Windmill Lane premises by the late '80s and now record in this purpose-built ultra high-tech facility. The new joint hasn't been entirely trouble-free how-

U2 graffiti at Windmill Lane Studio

ever. November 1996 saw a cyber first, when hackers took incomplete versions of "Discotheque" and "Wake Up Dead Man" and put them on the internet for thousands of fans to download. The tracks also appeared on bootleg discs retailing for £6 in the run-up to Christmas. The U2 label had to bring the release of the single forward in early '97. The incident came about after U2 had been showing off their technology-friendliness by installing a video camera in the studio and pasting footage of the rehearsals for the *Pop* album onto their Web site. *20 Ringsend Rd., D4, tel. 01/668–5567.*

City Center-Northside

Downtown Dublin is cut in two by the Liffey. The part to the north is the decidedly less touristed half. Despite the grand, broad thoroughfare of O'Connell Street and the presence of the city's two main theaters (the Abbey and the Gate), the northside is mainly the preserve of locals who do their shopping in the stores and markets that run off the main drag. At night it's a lot less lively than Grafton Street or Temple Bar, and some parts, particularly Gardiner Street, can be seedy and rife with petty crime. Nevertheless, the foundation of the *Hot Press* Irish Rock and Roll Hall of Fame draws a stream of music-lovers to the area, and venues such as Slattery's, the Ormond Multimedia Centre and the SFX (a mile north of Parnell Square) are worth seeking out.

BONAVOX HEARING AIDS

Around the time U2 was getting together, the aspiring vocalist Paul Hewson hung with other escapist and like-minded souls (including future members of the Virgin Prunes) who called themselves the Lypton Village. They all decided to give themselves alternate (some would say daft) names such as Day-Vid, Guggi, and Gavin Friday.

Bonavox Hearing Aids, 1997

One day when some of them were walking along O'Connell Street, they noticed a hearing aid shop called Bonavox and decided that the Latin phrase for good voice could be tweaked into an appropriate tag for Hewson, who would from then on be known as Bono Vox. There wasn't a store called The Edge; the Villagers thought that one up all by themselves.

U2 fans from all around the world come into the shop and ask for business cards and other mementoes. The staff take it all in stride and will tell you that if you want a real "bonavox," then listen to Placido Domingo. *13 N. Earl St., just off O'Connell St.*

GRESHAM HOTEL

The most famous traditional Irish band of all time, the six-piece Chieftains—fronted by Paddy Moloney and his Uilleann pipes—first came together in 1964 in this classy old hotel with its busy public bar. The Chieftains released their first album in 1964 (by 1997 the count had gone up to 22), and since then members have collaborated with top rock names including Don Henley, Jackson Browne, and Marianne Faithfull, as well as providing soundtracks and scores to numerous movies. Their biggest crossover success was in 1988 when they did *Irish Heartbeat*, a joint effort with their lifelong fan, Van Morrison. Rooms at the four-star Gresham are IR£85 to IR£115 per person per night. *23 Upper O'Connell St., D1, tel. 01/874-6881.*

HORSE AND TRAM PUB

John Lydon had a taste of old-school Irish justice when he was arrested for assault, refused bail, and spent a weekend in Mountjoy jail. It all started on the afternoon of Friday, September 26, 1980, when the ex-Pistol had flown in to see his brother Jimmy's band, the 4 BE 2's, play at Trinity College. He checked into his hotel and headed to the nearest bar, accompanied by another guy. According to Lydon, two burly barmen refused to serve him and ejected him onto the street. The altercation was spotted by an off-duty cop, who arrested Lydon while the other (still unnamed) drinker fled the scene. The court found him guilty of assault and sentenced him to three months, which was later reduced on appeal to a IR£100 fine. Lydon recalled his brief taste of jail in the title track of PiL's next album, *Flowers of Romance*. *3 Eden Quay, tel. 01/874-5316.*

HOT PRESS IRISH MUSIC HALL OF FAME

Although Dublin probably does more than any other city in Europe to promote its rock heritage, until now it has had no major focal point for visitors. Plans for a national music museum were announced in late 1996. The IR£3.5 million project presents music in Ireland from the roots of modern traditional music to the big names of the past three decades. The musicians' stories are told against a backdrop of what was happening at the time in Irish society and worldwide music trends. As well as memorabilia and interactive displays, the museum will have a live music space with gigs, workshops, talks, and performances by well-known Irish and touring artists. The music store will stock hard-to-come-by releases of lesser-known artists. *Tel. 01/679-5077. http://www.iol.ie/hotpress.*

MORAN'S (O'SHEA'S HOTEL)

This smelly basement club is legendary in Dublin rock. Smiley Bolger started promoting bands here in the early '70s. Most of them tried to ape the "California cool" sound. Both Bolger and the punters tired of this stuff pretty quickly, and he started booking newer, wilder bands, egged on by his mate Phil Lynott, who would often pop in to jam and keep an eye on what new sounds were emerging. Lynott was highly impressed by a 1976 gig by a local band called the Boomtown Rats, which featured an unkempt singer wearing a T-shirt proclaiming, "Geldof Is God." The best band of the period was the Radiators from Space (later simply the Radiators), which, like Geldof's ensemble, was not really punk but certainly way left-field for mid-'70s Dublin. They signed with Chiswick in 1977 but had no commercial success. Their members included Steven Rapid (a.k.a. Steve Averill), who designed many of U2's album covers, and guitarist Phil Chevron, who later joined the Pogues. Moran's has since changed its name to O'Shea's Hotel (one star!). The basement bar now hosts traditional "diddly-dee" music. *Gardiner and Talbot Sts., D1, tel. 01/836–5670.*

ORMOND MULTIMEDIA CENTRE

Although it has only been open since March '93, this labyrinthine former printing works has established itself as an innovative alternative venue in both rock and techno circles. Fugazi (Ian MacKaye is a particular fan of the place) and 7 Year Bitch have played here, as have Kerbdog, Joyrider, Backwater, and other good noisy Irish bands. Among the top-name DJs that have been here are Darren Emerson (of Underworld), Autechre, Robert Miles, and Carl Cox. When MTV Europe was looking for somewhere to film a special on Dublin nightlife, it correctly chose the Ormond in preference to the glitzier clubs and then incorrectly transformed it into a glitzy guest-listed affair for the night.

As well as the performance spaces, the Ormond houses offices used by record and theater companies, plus a gallery and exhibition space. The many rehearsal rooms are used by locals and big names like the Cranberries and Aimee Mann. To keep up its alternative image, there are skateboard ramps at the rear of the venue. *16–18 Lower Ormond Quay, D1, tel. 01/872–3500.*

ROTUNDA HOSPITAL

Bono was born here as Paul Hewson on May 10, 1960, in the first purpose-built maternity hospital in Europe, a stunning building on the north end of O'Connell Street that dates back to the 1740s. *Parnell Square West, D1.*

SFX CENTRE

The SFX, or, to give it its old name, the St. Francis Xavier Hall, is an unfancy space about a mile north of downtown toward the Drumcondra district. Despite being a bit out of the way, it retains a busy schedule as MCD, a major promotions firm, deems it the best place to put on cutting-edge bands just before they become massive. Hence, the SFX has rocked to the sounds of the likes of Primal Scream, Beck, and Korn in recent years. In 1996 Ash was given a surprise presentation of a platinum disc for Irish sales of the band's *1977* album midway through their set; singer Tim Wheeler immediately threw it into the crowd. Back in the early '80s, U2 played several shows here and also shot part of the video for "Pride (In the Name of Love)" here in 1984. *23 Upper Sherrard St., D1, tel. 01/874–5227.*

SAVOY CINEMA

U2 presented the world premiere of their *Rattle and Hum* movie at this big but unremarkable city center movie house on October 27, 1988. Tickets were £50 a head, with proceeds going to charities for the homeless. Rumors had been rife about the band's doing a live show outside the movie house, and just before the film was due to run, the band duly entertained the crowd of 5,000. They did an acoustic set (with Larry Mullen, Jr. on tambourine) that was repeated after the film show.

It fitted in neatly with the promise of a U2 show for the city's millennium celebrations—an ironic set of events, as the city is much older than that, but the marketing people actually claimed their city to be younger than it is so they could do some civic boosting. *19 O'Connell St., tel. 01/874–8487.*

SLATTERY'S

Even though this big old bar is on the less chichi north side of the river, it's a big stop for tourists and lovers of trad music ever since Paddy Slattery started folk sessions in the early '50s. At one point or another *every* major figure in Irish folk, blues, and trad circles

Ash at the SFX Centre, 1996

has played here. Christy Moore has performed countless times, and the man who replaced him in Planxty—Tyrone-born Paul Brady—has a *Rock 'N' Stroll* tour plaque honoring him outside. Up until the '80s, when fire regulations started to be applied to venues after the tragic Stardust Ballroom blaze, there were sessions on all four floors of the pub. Today, the trad sessions are held in the main bar. Such is the reputation of the place that any of the big names could walk in, order a beer, open an instrument case, and start jamming along.

Since 1992 rock gigs take place most nights of the week in the nicely faded upstairs room. Among those to get early gigs here are Whipping Boy and the Frames DC, while thanks to the connections of promoter Smiley Bolger, the likes of Gary Moore, Sinead O'Connor, and Shane MacGowan have come in and done a turn. *129 Capel St., D1, tel. 01/872–7971.*

South Dublin

BLACKROCK COLLEGE

This posh, rugby-playing school in the prized community of Blackrock, 3 miles southeast of the center, counts among its alumni Bob Geldof, the late *Hot Press* journalist Bill Graham, and radio presenter Dave Fanning. Geldof recalls his period at junior school here in his autobiography: "I was OK at school. Good results, the odd prize, but my main claim to fame was the fact that I knew the lyrics of every song Cliff Richard ever recorded...." In his teens, Geldof got back at the school's authoritarian priests by skidding a battered old Volkswagen round the playing fields. *Rock Rd., Blackrock, Co. Dublin.*

KILMAINHAM GAOL

U2 shot the bulk of their video for the 1982 single, "A Celebration"—a video noted for its bad haircuts and Bono in a terrible pair of red trousers—in this disturbing-looking gray hulk of a jail. Built in 1780, it has now been converted into a museum; tours show the courtyard where leaders of the 1916 Rising were executed by British officers. The jail is near the Guinness Brewery, some 2 miles west of Trinity College. *Inchicore Rd. at South Circular Rd., D8, tel. 01/453–5894.*

NATIONAL STADIUM

Although better known as a boxing venue, this old arena has been staging key rock gigs for years, and continues to do so occasionally. A 1966 Who gig was threatened by people purporting to be from the IRA who said that they'd blow the band up if they appeared on stage in Union Jack regalia, as was their style at the time. Instead, they wore tricolor jackets.

In February 1980 U2 played before a capacity 2,400 crowd that included some top dogs from Island records, who, in the dressing room immediately after the show, offered the band a contract. Nine years later B.B. King played here and, thanks to his inclusion in the *Rattle and Hum* movie, attracted a fair number of U2 fans to the gigs. They weren't disappointed, as Edge and Bono came onstage to muck about with some numbers at the end, including a version of "When Love Comes to Town." *South Circular Rd. near Leonard's Corner, D8, tel. 01/453–3371.*

ROYAL DUBLIN SOCIETY—SHOWGROUNDS

At these beautifully tended grounds, home to show jumping and agricultural shows, one of the most controversial Irish rock events in recent history was held on May 17, 1986. In the wake of the Live Aid shows, Bob Geldof and some other music industry movers in Ireland decided that they could prick the conscience of the Irish public and politicians by putting on a similar bash to highlight the country's dire unemployment problems. They got together a lineup of almost 30 acts, who played before a crowd of 30,000 while the show was also broadcast live on RTE television and radio for viewers and listeners to pledge donations. Some, including the Irish socialist journalist Eamonn McCann, wrote at length that pop stars shouldn't be doing the government's job for it. The Self Aid thing also led some to think that fundraising extravaganzas were getting out of hand, were giving the music industry a nice bit of credence, and didn't do those artists who appeared (especially those whose career had been on a downturn) any harm at all. On the other hand, most people involved argued that it gave the government a kick where it was needed, and the show itself was a success. Proceedings were started by veteran Skid Row man Brush Shiels. Others to play included the Boomtown Rats, Christy Moore, Chris de Burgh, Van Morrison, U2, and Rory Gallagher, with a Thin Lizzy reunion rounding things off.

Bono of U2 at the Royal Dublin Society showgrounds

U2 returned in August 1993 to end their Zooropa tour with two dates here; they were joined onstage for a bit by the model Naomi Campbell, who was dating Adam Clayton at the time. Other recent big performances have been by the Eagles and Bon Jovi. *Merrion Rd., Ballsbridge, D4, tel. 01/668–0866.*

ROYAL DUBLIN SOCIETY—SIMMONSCOURT PAVILION

Nirvana was to have played here on the night of April 8, 1994, when Kurt Cobain was found dead at his Seattle home. Tickets with a face value of IR£16.75 were being offered for over 10 times that amount on news of his death, and although the promoters had offered a full refund for tickets, many were never returned and have become highly collectible. *Merrion Rd., Ballsbridge, D4, tel. 01/668–0866.*

North Dublin

BONO BOYHOOD HOME

One of the two Irish-born members of U2, Bono (Paul Hewson) had an unconventional background. Unusual in '50s Dublin, his father was a Catholic and his mother a Protestant. The family moved into this lower middle-class development about 6 miles north of Dublin city center, when Paul, the younger of two sons, was just a few weeks old. At the time, it was on the frontier between town and country, but in 1967 the council built an overspill estate (low-income housing on the outskirts of the city), the seven ugly apartment towers that are Ballymun Flats. The flats themselves soon became a local byword for deprivation and addiction—"Running to Stand Still" off *The Joshua Tree* has Bono singing of seeing seven towers and only one way out, a reference to the drug problems endemic in the project and other parts of his home city. In Bono's teenage years a group of friends regularly hung out at the Hewson home, where Bono lived right up to the time U2 broke. One of the friends, Gavin Friday, came round one night to see if Bono was in. When there was no answer he left a note that read, "11 O'Clock Tick-Tock Gav Called," which Bono adopted into the title "11 O'Clock Tick-Tock," U2's third and one of their best-ever singles, which was produced by Martin Hannett. *10 Cedarwood Ave., Ballymun, D9.*

CROKE PARK

When U2 played before a sellout crowd of 55,000 at the home of the Gaelic Athletic Association in June 1985, the ecstatic homecoming welcome reflected the fans' sense that the band had conquered the world of rock & roll. On the support card were Squeeze, the Alarm, R.E.M., and In Tua Nua. The performance of "Sunday Bloody Sunday" had special significance that day, as it was one Sunday in 1920 in Croke Park that British troops shot 12 civilians, an incident (featured in the recent movie *Michael Collins*) from which the more recent shootings in Derry take their name. U2 returned on June 27 and 28, 1987, with Lou Reed as principal support both nights, plus others including Christy Moore, Hothouse Flowers, the Dubliners, and the Pogues. *Parc an Crochaigh, off Clonliffe Rd., D3, tel. 01/836–3222.*

Christy Moore at Croke Park

GINGERBREAD HOUSE

Prior to recording their debut album, *Boy,* U2 spent many a day hashing out ideas in the disused gate lodge of Balgriffin Cemetery, about 6 miles north of downtown Dublin. They referred to the little building as the Gingerbread House, and it's been on U2 fan itineraries ever since. Bono's mother, Iris Hewson, who died in 1974, is buried in the graveyard. *Balgriffin Cemetery, off Malahide Rd., Balgriffin.*

PHIL LYNOTT GRAVE

Phil Lynott, the leader of Thin Lizzy, died in Salisbury, England, in 1986 from a wild lifestyle. He's buried in Plot 13c of the St. Polan's section of the cemetery with a flat gravestone inscribed with the Gaelic, "Go dtuga Dia suaimhneas da anam" (May God give peace to his soul). Fans still come and leave mementoes at his graveside. *St. Fintan's Cemetery, Sutton, 7 mi northeast of Dublin.*

[MOUNT TEMPLE SCHOOL]

All four members of U2 came together in fall 1976 after Larry Mullen, Jr. put up note on a school bulletin board asking for guitarists. A music teacher suggested Dave Evans, and four others (including Hewson and Clayton) applied and had their first rehearsal at Larry's parents' house (*see below*). After they worked out their strongest formation, the five-piece band (then called Feedback and featuring Dave Evans's brother Dik) played their first gig in a school talent competition. They did Frampton's "Show Me the Way," a Bay City Rollers number (tongue-in-cheek of course), and a Beach Boys medley. After the show they changed their name to the Hype and did their second gig at St. Fintan's Church of Ireland Hall in Sutton.

Mount Temple School opened in 1972 as the first comprehensive, nondenominational, coed school in Dublin, more than a tad radical in those days. *Malahide Rd., D3, tel. 01/ 833–6984.*

LARRY MULLEN JR.'S HOUSE

Like the Hewson family, the Mullens lived in a lower-middle class area that was in the shadow of a nasty project, in this case, the Harmonstown Estate. Born on October 31, 1961, Larry is the only member of U2 with Catholic Irish parents. His father worked for the mail service and managed to get his percussion-loving teenage son a place in the Post-Office Band, a marching ensemble that played throughout Ireland at festivals and parades. Larry Jr., keen to put his rhythm skills to use in a rock band, put up a notice asking for guitarists at Mount Temple school, which was just a mile south of his home. In 1976 he organized the first get-together of what would become U2 at his house. His ad attracted five would-be guitarists: Adam Clayton, Dave and Dik Evans, Paul Hewson, and Neil McCormick, another Mount Temple student, who didn't stick around for many more sessions and who is now a rock journalist. The five would-be axe heroes crammed into the kitchen while Larry had to bang away on the drums in the back garden. Everyone wanted to land the role of lead guitarist, but Dave Evans earned himself the job with a rendition of Taste's "Blister on the Moon" that the others were in no position to match. The first jam led Hewson and Clayton to believe that their futures lay as vocalist and bassist respectively. Dik Evans played the first gig as a second guitarist and then moved on to the Virgin Prunes. The bunch decided to call the band Feedback after the noises that came out of Clayton's banged-up amplifier. *60 Rosemount Ave., Artane, D5.*

STARDUST BALLROOM

One of the most tragic incidents in Irish nightlife happened when this old dance hall burned down on St. Valentine's Night, 1981, killing 49 party-goers. Four years later, Christy Moore wrote, "They Never Came Home," which alleged that compensation had been slow in being paid out, but it was banned by the Dublin High Court and the best-selling *Ordinary Man* album had to be withdrawn and a new track inserted. A commemorative park now occupies the ground where the club stood. Although the Stardust mostly offered DJ'd music, it also had live shows, such as when a young U2 supported the Greedy Bastards—a kind of have-a-laugh supergroup featuring Phil Lynott, ex-Pistols Cook and Jones, and Gary Moore among its cast. *Artane, D5.*

Out from Dublin

Bray

A popular getaway for Dubliners who come for the sandy beach or walks along Bray Head, the resort of Bray, 10 miles south of Dublin, is a faded Victorian affair with a seafront dominated nowadays by cheap cafés, B&Bs and amusement arcades. For a time in the early '80s, Bono and his wife, Ali, lived in a converted Martello Tower (one of a series of defensive bunkers built along this stretch of coast during the Napoleonic wars), and Bono wrote "Promenade," off *The Unforgettable Fire*, about walking through the town.

Malahide

The swanky bedroom community of Malahide, 11 miles northeast of Dublin, with its little teahouses, historic castle, and affluent marina, was where two members of U2 spent their boyhood years. Adam Clayton (born March 13, 1960, in Chinnor, Oxfordshire) came here at an early age when his father took up a job as a pilot with Aer Lingus; the Claytons lived on Yellow Walls Road. Dave Evans's parents were Welsh, but he was born in Barking, Essex (August 8, 1961). Soon afterward, his father got a job in a Dublin electronics factory and the family (including another son, Dik, who was in the Virgin Prunes) moved into a house on St. Mary Park Road.

OTHER IRISH TOWNS

Though Dublin truly dominates the Irish rock map, the other main cities of Cork, Limerick, and particularly Galway, have something to offer rock & roll travelers. Although Ireland hasn't quite managed to come up with a hardy perennial festival like Reading or Glastonbury, most summers do see a major music festival. Some of the earliest such events were the big-drinking fests at the tiny County Clare spa village of Lisdoonvarna, at the start of the '80s, and the last-ever public performance of the Undertones, in Castlebar, County Mayo, in 1983. The longest-running event, the Feile (which scored a coup over the U.K. festivals by getting the Stone Roses for their only outdoor show in the British Isles in 1995) had to go indoors in 1996 with a series of gigs in the Point Depot, Dublin. Its future is in doubt, though there is usually no shortage of big one-day events in and around Dublin, particularly at the impressive Slane Castle site.

Cork

The Republic of Ireland's second city (population 175,000) is best known in rock circles for the cult '80s band Microdisney, whose songwriting partners, Cathal Coughlan and Sean O'Hagan, went on to, respectively, the '90s outfits Fatima Mansions and the High Llamas, both of which still pull in top critical reviews.

Frank and Walters

A couple of less substantial bands emerged at the start of the '90s. Named for two local street people, the Frank and Walters had some minor U.K. chart entries for their quirky pop. The Sultans (formerly the Sultans of Ping), when their fans at an early gig were told by the promotion staff to sit down, showed solidarity by playing sitting down with everyone butt-dancing. This was a trademark of their gigs for several years. A current Cork band that might go farther are the dark and moody Orange Fettishes.

Out in the hinterland, Donovan lives in an old rectory in Mallow, while his daughter Oriole Skye lives nearby with Shaun Ryder of Black Grape.

PAIRC UI CHAOIMH

U2's Zooropa tour, with Utah Saints in support, arrived here in 1993 to find that Frank Murphy of the Gaelic Athletic Association, owners of the stadium, had banned sales of special promotional "Achtung Baby" condoms. The U2 organization got their own back by giving them away, but during his MacPhisto routine on stage, Bono went into a rant about the social backwardness of people like Murphy and, as was the gimmick on that tour, he phoned Murphy's home to complain, but there was no reply: Murphy was actually there in the stadium "enjoying" the show. The gig was not a sellout, at around 1,000 short of the 40,000 capacity.

In 1996, the same year that they were being downsized in U.S. venues, Oasis broke attendance records in England and Scotland. When they played Cork that summer, their publicity machine hyped up the claim that, with tickets going at a rate of 150 a minute for their two shows, this was an Irish record. This sparked a minor war of boasting in the media, with the camp of squeaky-clean country 'n' Irish star Daniel O'Donnell claiming that he held the record, followed by the people promoting Garth Brooks's shows in Croke Park. In among the hot air was a humble claim from the promoters at a Radiohead gig at the Olympia in Dublin (capacity: about ⅓₀ of Pairc ui Chaoimh) that it was indeed they who sold out tickets faster than anyone else. *The Marina.*

Gweedore, Co. Donegal

A small northwestern town in the spectacularly wild Bloody Foreland region, Gweedore, in a strong Gaelic-speaking area, is revered for being home of three huge-selling acts. Often referred to as one of the traditional Irish supergroups, Clannad formed in 1971 and in the '80s had mainstream success with the theme for a TV program called "Harry's Game." It later collaborated with Mr. Bono. A onetime member of Clannad was classically trained Enya (a.k.a. Eithne ni Bhraonian), who has heaped up platinum discs for her brand of woozy New Age sounds. The third major act from Gweedore is Altan, who is to carry the trad standards set by Planxty and De Dannan into the next century.

Mark Begly

Clannad

Meanwhile, neighboring Kincasslagh is the hometown of every Irish granny's favorite boy, Daniel O'Donnell, the most successful artist in the dubious country 'n' Irish genre. Rory Gallagher was born in Ballyshannon, a likeable market town near the resort of Bundoran in the south of the county.

There might even be some of Kurt Cobain present in the county of Donegal after reports from 1994 that his wife, Courtney Love, came to this remote part of the country to seek out the "Cobain Nub"—one of several Neolithic tombs in the county—to spread some of the Nirvana singer's ashes.

Dunquinn, Co. Kerry

Cranberries singer Dolores O'Riordan, purportedly the richest woman in Ireland by a mile, chose this backwater village on the postcard-pretty Dingle Peninsula to build a palatial pad for herself and her spouse. When construction started on the slate-and-glass dream home high up the hill, some locals were said to be less than pleased.

Galway

The compact, studenty city of Galway ranks as the west's major music and arts center; after Dublin it is also the best city to visit in the country.

EATING **DRINKING** **DANCING** **SHOPPING** **PLAYING** **SLEEPING**

The annual **GALWAY ARTS FESTIVAL** (tel. 091/583800) takes place over 12 days in mid-July, and as well as drama and film, features some major rock and trad music shows.

One of the best pub venues in the country, the **ROISIN DUBH** (Dominick St., tel. 091/586540) takes its name from a mythical Irish female character (also a track off Thin Lizzy's *Black Rose (A Rock Legend)* album) and has a 24-track digital recording facility in house; Connemara native and hard-living blues-ish singer Mary Coughlan recorded her 1996 *Live in Galway* album here. A selection of other recent performers run the range from Arlo Guthrie and the late Townes van Zandt to Aslan and Alabama 3. **SALLY LONG'S** (Abbeygate St., tel. 091/565756) is a gothy, hard-rock boozer with some live bands on weekends. **GPO** (Eglington St., tel. 091/563073), a popular nightclub, has live acts from Grant Lee Buffalo to Us 3, plus all the top DJs, including LTJ Bukem and Jon Carter. Most of the busy pubs are found along Quay Street; the **QUAYS** (11 Quay St., tel. 091/568347) is a huge bar that also doubles as a clubbing and gigging space.

The adjacent resort town of Salthill is a seedier and more youthful area with several nightclubs, though the cops have recently done their best to close down the more cutting-edge ravey joints. The **WARWICK HOTEL** (tel. 091/521244) has hosted many big names over the decades in its old-style ballroom, which still has a revolving mirror ball. Recent gigs have included Jonathan Richman and Steve Earle. The largest venue in the area, also in Salthill, is in the shape of **LEISURELAND** (tel. 091/521455).

Limerick

Limerick (by Irish standards) is a big town that tends to be unpopular with everyone who lives outside it and has a reputation for a rowdy street life. It's best known as the home-town of the Cranberries, who began life as an all-male quartet in late 1989 under the dumb name of The Cranberry Saw Us. With Niall Quinn (then and now the drummer for the Hitchers) as vocalist, they did their first gig at the long-gone veggie hangout, the Flag Café.

After they cut a demo and played a few more local gigs, Quinn left. The remaining three auditioned for a replacement at Xeric (The Foundry, Edward St., tel. 061/410566), a rehearsal and studio space whose owner, Pearse Gilmore, was the band's first manager. They settled on Dolores O'Riordan, then a 19-year-old student at Lauren Hill School whose hairstyle and dress-sense were very different from her spiky-haired, leather-clad image of today. They played their first gig with her on vocals at the Cruise Hotel in 1990, supporting the local act They Do It with Mirrors, with an audience of

© Cathal Dawson

The Cranberries early on

about 50. By the time they headlined at the University of Limerick's Stables Club (tel. 061/333644), A&R scouts were out. By the end of 1991, when they headlined the Theatre Royal (Cecil St., tel. 061/414224), the major venue in the southwest, the Cranberries would not have that long to wait until they took America by storm with their 1993 debut album, *Everybody Else Is Doing It, So Why Can't We?*.

Other current Limerick bands include the still-thumbing Hitchers, the Driven, and pop slackers Fat Buck. It is also the birthplace of actor Richard Harris, who had a chart hit with "MacArthur Park" (the song that won American humor writer Dave Barry's contest in his weekly newspaper column for the worst song ever).

Slane, Co. Meath

The beautifully set Slane Castle, looking out onto a great natural amphitheater, is the home of the left-field Lord Henry Mountcharles, an Anglo-Irish aristocrat who hit upon the idea of raising funds to restore his massive pile by putting on huge rock concerts in the grounds.

One of the earliest such events was in 1981, with Thin Lizzy headlining above a wildly ambitious U2 outfit whose second album was due out a few weeks later. Each act tried hard to upstage the other and both hit on the idea of arriving at the castle by helicopter. The problem was that there was a major airshow in the area at the same time, and all the choppers were booked. The Thin Lizzy brigade proved more resourceful and managed to get a pilot to bring Lynott to Slane, much to the chagrin of the Bono camp. U2 became friendly with Mountcharles, and they were allowed to use his impressive home to work through ideas for *The Unforgettable Fire*; part of the video for "Pride" was also shot here. Other big name acts to play here in the '80s included Bob Dylan, Bruce Springsteen, the Rolling Stones, and David Bowie. R.E.M.'s show in 1995 holds the attendance record of 70,000. *29 mi north of Dublin.*

Tuam, Co. Galway

This small agribusiness town 25 miles north of Galway has become synonymous with the Saw Doctors, a cultish folky rock band who sell records by the truckload despite being universally frowned upon by critics, who see them as bogtrotter (shitkicker) rockers. The band misses no opportunity to sing about the local area, naming its 1992 album *All the Way from Tuam* and recording songs with titles like "Tuam Beat," "Green and Red of Mayo," and "N17" (the name of the main road between Galway and Sligo). The band, on their song, "Pied Piper," mentioned playing in Spiddal, a town 20 miles west of Galway, with the Waterboys, another rag-tag bunch who lived in that town for a while during the mid-'80s.

BIBLIOGRAPHY

Magazines

Hot Press, The Wire, TOP (Tower), New Musical Express, Melody Maker, Vox, Alternative Press, Rolling Stone, Whirlpool, CMJ New Music Monthly, Volume.

Web Sites

Thousands of band and venue sites on the web, particularly:

Knowhere Guide to The UK (http://www.state51.co.uk/state51/knowhere); Dotmusic (http://www.dotmusic.co.uk); Strangeways Guide To the UK Indie Scene (http://www.wam.umd.edu/~cure/strangeways.htm\); Rough Guide to Rock (http://roughguides.com); Addicted To Noise (http://www.addict.com).

Books

Azerrad, Michael. Come As You Are—The Story of Nirvana. New York: Doubleday. London: Virgin, 1993.

Bacon, David, and Maslov, Norman. The Beatles England. London: Columbus, 1982.

Bret, David. Morrissey Landscapes of the Mind. London: Robson, 1994.

Brown, Tony. Jimi Hendrix, A Visual Documentary—His Life, Loves, and Music. London: Omnibus Press, 1992.

Collis, John. Van Morrison: Inarticulate Speech of the Heart. London: Little, Brown and Company, 1996.

Davis, Stephen. Hammer of the Gods, The Led Zeppelin Saga. William Morrow: New York, 1984.

de la Parra, Pimm Jal: U2 Live: A Concert Documentary. London: Omnibus Press, 1994.

Denselow, Robin. When the Music's Over: The Story of Political Pop London: Faber & Faber.

Dunphy, Eamonn. Unforgettable Fire: The Story of U2. London: Viking, 1987.

Dickson, Dave. Biographize: The Def Leppard Story. London: Sidgwick & Jackson, 1995.

Eden, Kevin S. Wire: Everybody Loves a History. Wembley, Middlesex SAF, 1991.

Evans, Mike, and Jones, Ron. In the Footsteps of the Beatles. Liverpool: Merseyside County Council, 1981.

Forsyth, Ian. The Beatles Merseyside. Sussex: B. B. Publications, 1991.

Frame, Pete (compiler). The Harp Beat Rock Gazetteer of Great Britain: A Geographical Guide to Rock Music Past and Present. London: Banyan, 1989.

Geldof, Bob. Is That It? London: Penguin, 1986.

Gillan, Ian (with David Cohen). Child in Time. London: Smith Gryphon, 1993.

Gimarc, George. Punk Diary. New York: St. Martin's Press. London: Virgin, 1994.

Gray, George. Last Gang in Town, The Story and the Myth of the Clash. London: 4th Estate, 1995.

Gray, Marcus. London's Rock Landmarks. London: Omnibus Press, 1985.

Hardy, Phil, and Laing, Dave. *The Faber Companion to 20th Century Popular Music.* London: Faber & Faber, 1992.

Harry, Bill. *The Ultimate Beatles Encyclopedia.* London: Virgin, 1992.

Jones, Ron. *The Beatles Liverpool.* Merseyside: Ron Jones, 1991.

Juby, Kerry (editor). *In Other Words...David Bowie.* London: Omnibus Press, 1986.

Kendall, Paul. *Led Zeppelin—A Visual Documentary.* London: Omnibus Press, 1992.

Larkin, Colin (ed). *The Guiness Who's Who of Indie and New Wave. Music: 2nd Edition.* London: Guinness/Square One, 1995.

Lydon, John, with Keith and Kent Zimmerman. *Rotten: No Irish, No Blacks, No Dogs.* London: Hodder & Stoughton, 1993.

Lynott, Philomena with Jackie Hayden. *My Boy: The Phil Lynott Story.* Dublin: Hot Press, 1995. London: Virgin, 1996.

MacDonald, Bruno (editor). *Pink Floyd Through the Eyes of...The Band, Its Fans, Friends, and Foes.* London: Sidgwick & Jackson, 1996.

Macfarlane, Colin. *Tom Jones: The Boy from Nowhere.* London: WH Allen, 1988.

McGartland, Tony. *Buzzcocks: The Complete History.* London: Independent Music Press, 1995.

Marsh, Dave. *Before I Get Old, The Story of the Who.* London: Plexus, 1996.

Middles, Mick. *The Smiths, The Complete Story.* London: Omnibus Press, 1985.

Miles. *Pink Floyd, A Visual Documentary.* London: Omnibus Press, 1980.

Norman, Philip. *Shout! The True Story of the Beatles.* London: Hamish Hamilton, 1981.

Palmer, Myles. *Mark Knopfler: An Unauthorized Biography.* London: Sidgwick & Jackson, 1991.

Platt, John. *London's Rock Routes.* London: 4th Estate, 1985.

Putterford, Mark: *Phil Lynott: The Rocker.* Chessington, Surrey: Castle Communications, 1994.

Raphael, Amy. *Never Mind the Bollocks—Women Rewrite Rock.* London: Virago, 1995.

Rogan, Johnny. *Van Morrison: A Portrait of the Artist.* London: Elm Tree, 1984.

Rogan, Johnny. *Morrissey & Marr, The Severed Alliance.* London: Omnibus Press, 1989.

Savage, Jon. *England's Dreaming: Sex Pistols and Punk Rock.* London: Faber & Faber, 1991.

Schrouders, Piet, Lewisohn, Mark, and Smith, Adam. *The Beatles London.* London: Hamlyn, 1994.

Shutkever, Paula. *Manic Street Preachers: Design for Living.* London: Virgin, 1996.

Stokes, Niall. *Into the Heart: The Stories behind Every U2 Song.* London: Carlton/Omnibus Press, 1996.

Stokes, Niall (editor). *Hot Press Yearbook 1997.* Dublin: Hot Press, 1997.

Strong, M. C. *The Great Rock Discography.* Edinburgh: Canongate Press, 1994.

Tobler, John. *This Day in Rock.* New York: Carroll & Graf. London: Carlton, 1993.

Tremlett, George. *The David Bowie Story.* London: Futura, 1974.

Twomey, Chris. *XTC The Definitive Biography.* London: Omnibus Press, 1992.

Welch, Chris. *Hendrix, A Biography.* London: Omnibus Press, 1982.

Index

SOUND ADVICE

www.fodors.com/

Fodor's

ROCK & ROLL TRAVELER USA

THE ULTIMATE GUIDE TO JUKE JOINTS,
STREET CORNERS, WHISKEY BARS AND HOTEL
ROOMS WHERE MUSIC HISTORY WAS MADE

BY TIM PERRY & ED GLINERT

AVAILABLE AT BOOKSTORES, OR CALL
1-800-533-6478.

Fodor's An adventure on every page™